BORDERLAND RELIGION
The Emergence of an English-Canadian Identity, 1792–1852

Since colonization, Canadians and Americans have viewed religious matters differently. While this is not surprising given contemporary Canadians' reluctance to embrace US-style social conservatism, the roots of the phenomenon are seldom examined. J.I. Little seeks to correct this oversight with *Borderland Religion*.

Focusing on the settlement period of the Eastern Townships region of Quebec, Little addresses the role played by religion in forging a distinctive national identity for English Canadians. While radical evangelical churches and sects developed in the hill country of New England, they failed to gain a strong foothold in the neighbouring Eastern Townships despite the majority of the population there being of American origin. Rather, the British-based Church of England and Wesleyan Methodist Society became much the largest denominations in this border region.

Borderland Religion is effectively a borderlands study in reverse. Rather than examining the dynamics of contact between two distinct cultures in a common geographical space, or middle ground, it explores how a common culture became differentiated on either side of an international boundary line. In the process, it also illuminates the woefully neglected history of Protestantism in Quebec.

J.I. LITTLE is a professor in the Department of History at Simon Fraser University.

BORDERLAND RELIGION

The Emergence
of an English-Canadian
Identity, 1792–1852

J.I. Little

UNIVERSITY OF TORONTO PRESS
Toronto Buffalo London

© University of Toronto Press Incorporated 2004
Toronto Buffalo London

Printed in Canada

ISBN 0-8020-8916-X (cloth)
ISBN 0-8020-8671-3 (paper)

Printed on acid-free paper

National Library of Canada Cataloguing in Publication

Little, J.I. (John Irvine), 1947–
  Borderland religion : the emergence of an English-Canadian
identity, 1792–1852 / J.I. Little.

Includes bibliographical references and index.
ISBN 0-8020-8916-X (bound)   ISBN 0-8020-8671-3 (pbk.)

1. Protestant churches – Québec (Province) – Eastern
Townships – History – 19th century.   2. Canadians, English-speaking –
Québec (Province) – Eastern Townships – History – 19th century.
3. Protestant churches – Missions – Québec (Province) – Eastern
Townships – History – 19th century.   4. Eastern Townships (Québec) –
Church history – 19th century.   5. Eastern Townships (Québec) –
History – 19th century.   I. Title.

FC2943.5.L535 2004   280'.4'097146   C2004-901126-X

University of Toronto Press acknowledges the financial assistance to its
publishing program of the Canada Council for the Arts and the Ontario
Arts Council.

University of Toronto Press acknowledges the financial support for its
publishing activities of the Government of Canada through the Book
Publishing Industry Development Program (BPIDP).

This book has been published with the help of a grant from the Canadian
Federation for the Humanities and Social Sciences, through the Aid to
Scholarly Publications Programme, using funds provided by the Social
Sciences and Humanities Research Council of Canada.

Contents

TABLES   vii

PREFACE   ix

Part I: Introduction

1 Protestant Identity in the Eastern Townships   3

2 The Pioneer Era   25

Part II: Postwar American Initiatives

3 The Congregationalists   55

4 The Baptists   90

5 The Smaller Sects   109

6 The Millerites   128

Part III: Postwar British Responses: The Wesleyan Methodists

7 Laying the Foundations   149

8 Revivals, Reversals, and Shifting Strategies   177

Part IV: Postwar British Responses: The Anglicans

9 Building a Colonial Church   227

10 Messianism and Popular Response   252

Conclusion 279

STATISTICAL APPENDIX 287
NOTES 295
BIBLIOGRAPHY 351
INDEX 373

Illustrations follow page 176

Tables

1.1 Denominational Affiliation in Relation to Place of Birth, Eaton Township, 1852   19
1.2 Denominational Affiliation in Relation to Place of Birth, Melbourne Township, 1852   20
1.3 Mean Number of Acres Held and Improved by Farmers of Each Denomination, Eaton and Melbourne, 1852   23
3.1 Data for Eastern Townships Congregational Churches, 1836   87
3.2 Data for Eastern Townships Congregational Churches, 1839   88
3.3 Data for Eastern Townships Congregational Churches, 1842   89
8.1 Female and Male Sunday School Students, Eastern Townships Wesleyan Circuits, 1843–52   210
A.1 Protestant Denominations in the Eastern Townships and Upper Canada, 1852   287
A.2 Agricultural Variables Related to Religious Affiliation of Farmers in 11 Townships of Lower Canada, 1831   288
A.3 Agricultural Variables Related to Religious Affiliation of Farmers in the Townships of Inverness, Ireland, Leeds, and Halifax, 1831   289
A.4 Agricultural Variables Related to Religious Affiliation of Farmers in the Townships of Stanbridge, Shefford, Brome, and St. Armand, 1831   290
A.5 Wesleyan Methodists in Eastern Townships Circuits, 1818–52   291
A.6 Apportionment of Wesleyan Missionary Grant, Eastern Townships Circuits, 1835–48   292
A.7 Wesleyan Missionary Monies Subscribed, Eastern Townships Circuits, 1835–50   292
A.8 Wesleyan Methodist Data, Eastern Townships Circuits and Canada District, 1842–8   293

Preface

It has become a truism that Canadian identity is essentially local and regional in nature, with geographic isolation generating what Northrup Frye referred to as a 'garrison mentality,' and Cole Harris termed an 'island archipelago.'[1] But English Canadians from coast to coast arguably share more common values with each other than they do with the Americans who live a few miles to the south of their communities. For example, while there is obviously a broad spectrum of religious belief and practice on either side of the border even among Protestants, the Canadian orientation has tended to be less radical and fundamentalist than that of the Americans. Rather than exploring the roots and ramifications of this distinction, however, historians in Canada have, in George Rawlyk's words, demonstrated 'an embarrassing reluctance to try to understand the religious mind – to try to drill deep into the individual or collective Canadian religious experience.' Rawlyk's essay, written in 1988, added that 'It is both noteworthy and puzzling that popular religion – the religion of ordinary folk – religion from the bottom up if you will – has been largely neglected by Canadian historians.' Pointing out that 'for decades, scores of leading American historians, sociologists and theologians have been probing the links between popular Christianity and the evolving society of the United States,'[2] Rawlyk proceeded to describe several dramatic revivals in Upper Canada. In doing so, however, he was missing what is probably the main reason popular religious beliefs and behaviour have been much more neglected by Canadian historians than by their American counterparts, namely that radical sectarianism played (and continues to play) a considerably less important role in this country than it did south of the border.[3] But that fact in itself is reason enough for those interested in understanding the development of an English-Canadian identity to pay more attention to what was, after all, a fundamentally important institution and force in people's daily lives. The stereotypical view has been that English-Canadian society played the secular materialist counterpart to a profoundly spiritual and conservative French-Canadian society. But, while popular religious culture has been undergoing revisionist exploration in Quebec,[4] historians of religion in English Canada have for the most part continued to focus on the ideas of the elite and the development of religious institutions.

As a result, few studies of English Canada have integrated religion into the dynamic of community development, focusing instead on the economy and the state as agents of social change, at least prior to the rise of the social gospel movement and Catholic corporatism in the late nineteenth and early twentieth centuries.[5] My own study on institutional reform in the Eastern Townships during the pivotal decade of the 1840s examined muncipal government, the court system, and the public schools system in order to learn how the population responded to, and influenced, the establishment of a modern interventionist state.[6] Religion was largely ignored in that volume for want of time and space, though I was well aware that it played a crucial role in defining popular political culture. During the early 1830s, for example, the Protestant churches introduced the temperance movement, which eventually led to the demand for increased state regulation of liquor production and sale.[7] And, before the introduction of elected municipal and schools councils in 1841, the various religious denominations represented virtually the only institutions of local self-governance. The result was the inculcation of a voluntarist ethos which, while welcoming state support for roads and schools, responded negatively to the imposition of compulsory taxes during the early 1840s, and insisted successfully that they be collected and managed at the local community level. Once the government had yielded to localism, municipal and school reform was accepted more readily in most of the English-speaking communities of the Eastern Townships than in the rural French-speaking parishes elsewhere in the province. The habitants' resistance was fuelled by their financial obligations to the seigneurs, as well as by their resentment of the control exercised by village notables over the tax-assessing fabriques or church councils.[8]

While the voluntarist ethos, a hallmark of evangelical religion,[9] helps to explain the insistence in the Eastern Townships on a high degree of local control, the general eagerness to accept state funds may have been conditioned by the years of substantial financial support from

British-based missionary societies. Outside funds obviously had strings attached, and the institutionalization of religion in the Eastern Townships – as with that of the school and local governance systems – is largely a story of the dynamic tension between localism, on the one hand, and pressures to conform to externally dictated norms and regulations, on the other. To emphasize only one of these impulses would be to misconstrue the social and cultural development of this or any other region.

While the 1840s marked a crucial transition in the process of economic development and state formation, the religious culture of the Eastern Townships, as with the rest of British North America, was undergoing a more gradual process of evolution. For that reason, this history of Protestantism on the northern frontier of New England settlement begins with the arrival of the first colonists after the American Revolution. The first section provides a brief overview of the geography and sociology of religious identity in the Eastern Townships, as well as examining the pioneer era when settlement had, to a considerable extent, outpaced the establishment of churches. The second section examines more closely the various religious institutions that the Yankee settlers brought with them, as well as those that followed later from New England. The next two sections trace the development of the two largest denominations in the region, the Wesleyan Methodists and the Anglicans. They explore how the majority of a largely American-origin population which bordered the New England states, and had relatively little contact with the rest of British North America, came to be affiliated with British religious denominations. They also attempt to determine how strong that affiliation was, and they speculate on what its ramifications were as far as cultural identity was concerned. In the process, this study will challenge much of the dogma that exists concerning religious history in British North America, including the (admittedly fading) assumption that the Anglican Church was defeated by the frontier environment. Because the Presbyterian Church focused almost exclusively on the Scots settlers, who remained a much smaller ratio of the population than in Upper Canada, it does not conform to the theme of British missionization on an American settlement frontier, and will not be included in this volume.

In a sense, this is a borderlands study in reverse, for, rather than examining the dynamics of contact between distinct cultures, it will explore how a common culture became differentiated on either side of an international boundary line. The Northeastern Borderlands Project based at the University of Maine defines a borderland as 'a region jointly shared by two nations that houses people with common social characteristics in spite of the political boundary between them.'[10] The Eastern Townships and northern New England obviously conform to that definition, but this is not a true borderlands study insofar as it does not include northern Vermont and New Hampshire. There are, however, a number of excellent studies of post-Revolutionary and early nineteenth-century religion in northern New England, and these will be referred to for comparative purposes. Furthermore, the Eastern Townships was, itself, a contested terrain between colonial domains, which is the definition of borderlands used in a recent overview by Adelman and Aron.[11] The contest was played out in terms of religious affiliation and identity, with conservative British missionary societies dedicated to the conversion of settlers from a radical dissenting tradition. Because they succeeded to a considerable degree, the forty-ninth parallel became more than an arbitrary line across the landscape. Perhaps, then, 'borderline' study would be a more appropriate term.[12]

The Eastern Townships had not been unexploited wilderness during the French regime. The St Lawrence Valley Abenakis, who crossed this territory to raid northern New England outposts, had established seasonal hunting camps there. The region was, however, virtually empty of habitation when the governor of Lower Canada invited American settlers to take up land claims there in 1792. These settlers would soon run into obstacles from government officials in Quebec, then come to resent the imposition of a powerful British administrative elite in Sherbrooke.[13] That resentment, fuelled by slow economic and population growth due to the lack of viable transportation links to external markets, would reach a climax in the 1830s. The Eastern Townships would, however, draw back from supporting the Patriotes as the rebellions approached, partly out of fear of French-Canadian nationalism, but also because New England's radical religious culture had failed to take deep root there. During the 1840s, voters tended to support the party in power in the hope of attracting government subsidies for road and railway construction. They were motivated by economic self-interest, not loyalty to Great Britain, but the fact remains that British-funded Anglican and Wesleyan Methodist missionaries had served as much more effective agents of colonializing hegemony than had the government-appointed officials of the pre-rebellion era.

From this perspective, the Eastern Townships was a middle ground in which the republican and non-conformist culture of the American settlers was confronted by the conservative religious institutions supported by the British colonial authority.[14] In the process, the British missionaries would make concessions to deeply entrenched Puritan beliefs as well as to the revivalist practices that were developing south of the border, but they remained answerable to the conservative church hierarchy and London-based missionary societies to whom they submitted regular reports. While a small number of Wesleyan and Anglican missionaries did become apostates, and most of them did continue to complain about the fickleness and indifference of their congregations, the Eastern Townships ultimately developed a much more conservative religious culture than that found across the border in the northern New England hill country. As Buckner has argued in his critique of the northeastern borderlands approach, during the nineteenth century the British North American colonies – as part of 'the most dynamic empire in the world' – were becoming progressively more British.[15]

The main goal of this study is to examine popular religious culture, but that would be impossible without having a clearer picture of how the various churches evolved, which is one reason why it adheres to a denominational framework. Another reason is the challenge of finding historical sources for a region whose English-speaking Protestant population has largely been dispersed across North America. While some fascinating diaries and collections of personal correspondence can be found in various archives,[16] the historian must largely rely on church records which obviously have an institutional bias. Furthermore, because most of the Protestant churches in the Eastern Townships have long since closed their doors to regular services, much of the local record, apart from parish registers and a few legal documents, has disappeared. We are largely left, therefore, with the correspondence of the various missionary societies that were active in the region. Fortunately, the letters and reports of the Congregational, Wesleyan Methodist, and Anglican missionaries are a rich source of information on local religious conditions and behaviour. While they form the backbone of this study, I have also relied upon a wide variety of other documents, including census enumerations, church newspapers, scattered local church records, spiritual diaries, personal letters, and local histories.

A word on terminology. While this study applies a dualistic framework to some extent – examining the generally more radical American religious denominations and the generally more conservative British ones in distinct sections – it avoids the value-laden 'church-sect' dichotomy applied most rigorously in Canada by the historical sociologist S.D. Clark. The Methodists identified themselves as a society rather than a church, but the word 'church' will be used in most cases, with 'sect' applied sparingly and only to the more extreme and marginal religious movements.

This book has been a long time in the making, in part because its research took me down some intriguing byways. Some of the results have been previously published, though only the sections on Ammi Parker and the Millerites are largely reprinted here with the kind permission of *Histoire sociale / Social History* and Brill Press, respectively. There is also some overlapping material in my articles on Methodism in Stanstead County (*Studies in Religion / Sciences Religieuses* [2003]) and Anglicanism in the Eastern Townships prior to 1831 (*Histoire sociale / Social History*, forthcoming). My research was made possible by a grant from the Social Sciences and Humanities Research Council of Canada, and much of the writing took place during a study leave funded by Simon Fraser University, for both of which I am very greatful.

For providing such a supportive research environment, and for their invariably friendly and prompt assistance, I am deeply indebted to a number of archivists and their assistants. Particularly helpful during my annual visits to Lennoxville were Sylvie Coté and Daniel Bromby of the Eastern Townships Research Centre which holds the region's United Church and Presbyterian records, and Jim Sweeney of the Anglican Church's Quebec Diocesan Archives, which is also located at Bishop's University. My thanks, as well, to Richard Virr of the Montreal Diocesan Archives; Susan Rice, who was then volunteer archivist for the United Church records held by the Archives Nationales du Québec à Montréal; Peter Kandalaft, who provided access to the St Peter's Anglican archives in Sherbrooke; and Patricia Kennedy who, as always, was my indispensable guide to the material in the National Archives of Canada. I am also grateful to the archivists and librarians who granted access to the United Church records at Toronto's Victoria University, the Baptist records at McMaster University, and the Freewill Baptist records and minute books at the Archives Nationales du Québec à Sherbrooke and the University of Vermont. David Arthur kindly provided information and access to the Jenks Memorial Collection of Adventual Materials at Aurora University; Marion Phelps made available the rich archives of the Brome County Historical Society; the Stanstead Historical Society granted access to the Merry diary and some local church records; Esther and Don Healey gave me much valuable information on a number of old churches in the

Richmond-Melbourne area; Richard Moysey allowed me to research his George Slack collection, and Phyliss and Terry Skeats responded to my questions concerning the region's Universalists.

Expert research assistance was provided by Joy Frith, Michelle Hallam, and Matthew Barlow. I also wish to thank Richard Vaudry, Marie-Ève Harbec, Bill Westfall, and the two official manuscript assessors for their very kind and helpful advice. In addition, John Craig, Derryl MacLean, Hugh Johnston, Michael Kenny, and other colleagues at Simon Fraser University lent support by responding to my questions and listening to my ideas. My ever-skilful copy editor, Diane Mew, once again relegated a lot of the details to the cutting-room floor, where they doubtless belong, while Len Husband, Frances Mundy, and the other staff at the University of Toronto Press were unfailingly courteous and helpful. Most of the writing was done on Hornby Island, a spiritual frontier in its own right, where the friendly and creative atmosphere greatly eased my labours. Finally, my love and thanks, as always, to Andrea, Mark, and Brett, who have put up with the absences and distractions involved with producing another book while the family was growing up. This volume is dedicated to my MA and PhD thesis supervisors, Phil Buckner and Jacques Monet, who, many years ago now, first raised my awareness of the complex interplay between British imperialism and cultural identity in Canada.

Part I
Introduction

1

Protestant Identity in the Eastern Townships

In 1842 the touring Congregational minister Henry Wilkes reported that five years earlier there had been only one place of worship in the St Francis Valley village of Melbourne, but now 'from a spot standing on which you cannot count fifty houses, you can see five Churches.' To the west, in the small village of Granby, there were two Congregational churches nearing completion, one for the American settlers and one for the British, as well as a Catholic church. An Episcopalian church was about to be erected, and 'Probably also a Methodist Chapel will in due time be built. If so there will be nearly as many places of worship as houses.'[1] One can still see a number of small white clapboard churches of various Protestant denominations in the villages and at rural crossroads of Quebec's picturesque Eastern Townships, though most of them have been closed for years. The same fate is now meeting the larger stone and brick buildings of the urban centres as the last of the region's church-going English-speaking population dies off, but they remain the most visibly striking reminders of what was once a dynamic and eclectic mix of Protestant communities.

First officially opened to settlement in 1792, the region bordered by the Richelieu, St Lawrence, and Chaudière Valley seigneuries to the west, north, and east, and by the Vermont–New Hampshire border to the south, was originally peopled by Americans from southern New England.[2] British immigrants disembarking at Quebec generally preferred to move on to Upper Canada rather than settle in a hilly region cut off from easy access to markets by the lack of a navigable artery to the St Lawrence. Beginning in the late 1820s, however, the imperial government's anxiety to dilute the American character of the region led to considerable British settlement in the St Francis Valley and northeast-

ern townships. French-Canadian expansion from the south-shore seigneuries into the neighbouring townships was discouraged by the long line of swamps at the base of the Appalachian plateau, and by the absentee proprietorship that retarded development of this freehold territory. But land shortages in the seigneuries began to push French-speaking families into the northern townships in the later 1830s, and, encouraged by the Catholic Church and provincial government, the trickle became a flood by the later 1840s.

The total population of only 28,509 in 1827 grew quickly to 37,040 in 1831, and 63,068 in 1844, when it was still 76 per cent English-speaking. Eleven per cent of the English-speaking inhabitants had been born in Ireland, 6 per cent in England and Wales, and 5 per cent in Scotland. Reflecting the deflection of the Americans' interest to their own mid-West after the Erie Canal was completed in 1825, only 18 per cent of the region's Anglophone population was American-born in 1844. But most of the remaining 36 per cent of the Anglophones who were Canadian-born would have been of American origin. Eight years later, in 1852, the English-speaking ratio of the Eastern Townships population had already declined markedly to 64 per cent, with the British-born proportion remaining unchanged at 22 per cent, and the Canadian-born proportion increasing 3 per cent in line with a decline of the American-born of 3 per cent. Upper Canada was much more British in composition, with 35 per cent of its inhabitants having been born in the British Isles as of 1852.

By the close of our study period, there were 58,203 English-speaking inhabitants of the Eastern Townships, according to the *Census Reports*. Overwhelmingly Protestant, largely of American origin, and economically and culturally cut off from the rest of the province (though that situation was changing with the recent completion of the St Lawrence and Atlantic Railway), they remained closely tied to the people of the neighbouring states. While the Protestant denominations of the Eastern Townships have been largely ignored by Canadian church historians, including those purporting to write national histories,[3] they provide a fascinating case study in the cultural development of what was effectively an American settlement frontier within a British colony. The same tensions certainly existed in the other colonies – indeed they are a characteristic of Canadian national identity – but not to the same degree as in the Eastern Townships.

Largely due to a deliberate policy of religious acculturation on the part of the imperial authorities, the Church of England and the British-based Wesleyan Methodist Church were the two largest Protestant denominations in the Eastern Townships in 1831 and again in 1852 (see table A.1 in the appendix). Twenty-nine per cent of the Protestants were Anglicans at mid-century, while 26 per cent were Methodists.[4] The third-largest Protestant church in the Eastern Townships, the Presbyterians, were only 10 per cent of the non-Catholic population, and almost exclusively of Scottish origin. Six per cent of the population claimed no religious affiliation (a ratio that was under-reported), leaving less than one-third of the Protestants to a variety of American-based churches. Of these, the Congregationalists and Baptists (12 per cent) were beginning to forge ties with British missionary societies.

Westfall has observed that 'Protestantism not only shaped how people saw God, it also shaped the culture through which the society interpreted the world.'[5] Certainly, religion was a significant force in the attempt to create a British identity in the Eastern Townships, but the process was not a steadily progressive one, and denominational affiliation was far from being a straightforward concept. The Anglicans and Wesleyan Methodists of the Eastern Townships remained much more independent than their clergymen would have liked, but, at the same time, the Protestant culture of this region differed markedly from that of the neighbouring American states where it was intimately linked with a democratic political ethos. In short, a new cultural identity was being forged in the Eastern Townships, as elsewhere in British North America, one that was a synthesis of radical American and conservative British values.

The Nature of Religious Identity in the Eastern Townships

Commenting on the large number of religious denominations in his area, the Reverend Edward Cleveland of Richmond wrote in 1856: 'It might be inferred that the people are very quarrelsome or very devotional.' In his opinion, however, 'they are not distinguished in either way,' the wide diversity simply reflecting their various origins.[6] Cleveland was only partly right in terms of the reasons that explained religious affiliation. The Scots settlers were nearly all Presbyterians or Congregationalists, and most of the English and Irish were Anglicans or Methodists. But those of American origin, including the Canadian-born, were to be found in a wide variety of denominations, and a large ratio were Anglicans or Wesleyan Methodists despite the fact that these churches were foreign to the New England Puritan heritage. Not only were there relatively few Congregationalists or Baptists in the Eastern Townships, but the radical sectarian movements that swept much of northern New England and western New York (known by historians as 'the burned-over country') largely bypassed the region, at least until the brief upsurge of Millerism in the early 1840s.

American historians have been nearly unanimous in attributing the northeastern region's radical revivalist tradition to the nature of the mass migration from southeastern and coastal New England, beginning in the 1770s. Marini reflects the consensus when he argues that the hill country attracted people who were pro-revival New Lights, products of the Great Awakening of 1736–45 who, unlike the Old Light Puritan Congregationalists, endorsed 'itinerancy and experiential standards for membership and ministerial calling, and attacked union of church and state.'[7] According to Roth, the New Lights accommodated their Calvinism with the conviction that 'God saved sinners only through dramatic conversion experiences of the sort that occurred during revivals and insisted that people show visible signs of spiritual rebirth before they could receive holy communion and be full church members.'[8] Calvinism and its religious culture were further challenged, Marini states, when a combination of frontier experience and revolution produced a massive religious revival that swept across the hill country from 1778 to 1782.[9] Radical sectarian movements such as the Universalists and Freewill Baptists emerged and developed systematic plans of church order, theology, and worship just as the Eastern Townships was being opened to American settlement in the 1790s. The Second Great Awakening of 1798–1808 subsequently introduced Methodism to rural New England, as well as giving birth to new sects such as the Christian Connection.[10] Roth claims that the settlers of the northeastern frontier of the United States 'dedicated themselves with extraordinary fervor to making it the most perfect society on earth,' so that by the 1830s 'the region had achieved the highest levels of active church membership and of enrolment in reform societies in the world.' Vermont, in particular, would become 'the symbolic fount of the young nation's truculent egalitarianism, militant faith, and crusading idealism.'[11]

Similarly, Ludlum states that the religious revivalists found a particularly fertile field in the north-central and northeastern plateau of Vermont, which 'spilled over into the Province of Lower Canada where New Englanders had settled, and these subjects of the Crown often emulated their republican kin across the border.'[12] On his official tour through the Eastern Townships in 1829 the Anglican archdeacon, George J. Mountain, complained that 'mushroom-like lecturers thrown out upon the spot deal always in high excitement & address themselves to the natural love of the marvelous.' He claimed that one person had recently been persuaded 'that his faith would enable him to cross' the St Francis River, while another 'undertook to fast for 40 days, & was brought back out of the woods about half-starved.'[13]

But such acts of religious zeal were rarely mentioned in the missionary reports, and the fact remains that none of the aforementioned sects gained a firm foothold in this northern extension of the New England settlement frontier. The Christian Brethren and Protestant (or Reformed) Methodists did briefly have a number adherents in the border townships, but there is no record of a Shaker or Mormon society in the region during our study period. Furthermore, the Universalists remained a rather shadowy presence, at least until the 1830s, and the Freewill Baptist initiative was quite localized and unstable. In contrast to the rest of British North America, even the American Methodist Episcopal effort was minimal in the Eastern Townships. And that effort would be interrupted by the War of 1812, which caused the American missionary societies to view the region for years afterward as hostile foreign territory. While the Millerite movement, which predicted that the Apocalypse would take place in 1843 or 1844, did make a dramatic impact on the border townships of Lower Canada, it failed to weaken the regional dominance of the Anglican and Methodist churches.

There were certainly a few powerful revivals in the Eastern Townships associated with the Wesleyan Methodist missionaries during the 1820s and mid-1830s, but the region remained a sharp contrast to neighbouring Vermont where the period from 1816 to the economic panic of 1837 saw an almost continual state of spiritual excitement.[14] In 1839 James Reid of St Armand East described a more pragmatic local approach to religion:

> Wherever a village commences – and a village always starts up wherever there is a stream to carry a grist and sawmill, a Church or meetinghouse will soon be agitating, not for promoting the glory of God, but to give an impetus to the rising village ... When all is finished, or rather in a condition to be used, a few women and children, only a small sprinkling of men, will attend public worship, but the bulk of those who contributed to build will never darken the door.[15]

The weakness in the Eastern Townships of the radical revivalist societies, which constituted about one-third of the New England hill country by

1815, was obviously not due to any deep-seated attachment to Calvinism. While the Regular Baptist and Congregational churches divided two-thirds of the New England hill country equally between them in 1815,[16] as of 1831 less than 12 per cent of the Eastern Townships Protestants identified themselves as Baptists (including Freewill Baptists), or Congregationalists/Presbyterians. Yet, not only was this region settled largely by people from the same areas at roughly the same time as those who migrated to the northern New England frontier, but the physical environment and economic conditions were quite similar on either side of the border, though the New England hill country was going into decline while the Eastern Townships was still being settled.[17]

That the religious culture of the Eastern Townships should contrast so sharply with that of the neighbouring New England territory tends to contradict the assumptions of American and Canadian historians, influenced by Frederick Jackson Turner, that the settlement frontier itself produced political radicalism and anarchy. While religious dissent may have flourished on the American frontier, the social atomization process stressed by Marini, Barkun, and others would not in itself have led to radical revivalism.[18] As Kenny stresses in his biography of Elias Smith, this development was essentially the product of a dynamic democratic tradition.[19] That tradition simply failed to take deep root in the Eastern Townships, where the town meeting system did not enjoy official sanction and where there were no local taxes to rebel against.[20] Independent-minded Yankees settled in the Eastern Townships partly to escape those taxes, and perhaps also to escape the system of publicly funded religious establishments that still existed everywhere but Rhode Island and Vermont after 1807.[21] Pioneer society in the Eastern Townships would, by necessity, be characterized by the voluntarism associated with the frontier, as settlers joined forces to build roads, schools, and chapels, but there was no political outlet except for petitions and informal representatives because the region remained effectively disenfranchised until divided into several constituencies in 1829. While the majority proceeded to vote for the pro-reform Patriote party, their minority status in the largely French-speaking colony left them powerless to follow the Vermont and Maine traditions of mobilizing effectively against the absentee proprietors who retarded the development of their region. The people of the Eastern Townships began to desert the radical reform movement in the later 1830s, largely due to the threat of French-Canadian nationalism and the demise of the local British oligarchy along with the rise of responsible government and an entrepreneurial elite whose chief political goal was to attract government investment in railways. Less obviously, but of undeniable significance, the growing majority of those born in the region, rather than in New England, had been more exposed to the conservative British religious influence than to the radical American one.

The unsettling effect of the rebellions of 1837-8 (which were followed by several years of cross-border raids), the crop failures of the early 1840s, emigration westward, and the controversy surrounding the introduction of tax-assessing municipal councils and school commissions, all served to make this a difficult period of transition in which not everyone could see bright hopes for the future. One can only speculate as to what impact the demise of the voluntarist approach to building and sustaining schools and roads may have had on the social cohesiveness of local communities, but the ongoing circulation of protest petitions to promote greater decentralization of state authority – a campaign which was generally successful – must have given the people of the Townships a strong sense of their own political purpose. This heightened political consciousness would culminate in the eruption of the annexation movement in 1849-50, which was essentially an outburst of political protest rather than the expression of a deeply felt desire to join the United States. While the Protestant communities of the Eastern Townships were not marked by the radical religious and political culture of the neighbouring New England region, then, they did continue to be characterized by a considerable degree of local independence.

Aside from the contrasting political situations, a more direct reason why two distinct religious cultures developed on either side of the international border was the fact that the evangelical churches of New England failed to make major commitments to the Eastern Townships simply because the region lay outside their country and they had their own expanding frontier to serve. The British branches of the Congregationalist, Baptist, and Presbyterian churches also remained rather disinterested, presumably because their concerns as Calvinists were largely confined to serving their own members who were much more numerous in the other British North American colonies. The Anglican and Wesleyan Methodist churches, on the other hand, felt it their duty to convert the 'undisciplined' republican settlers of this Canadian borderland to a more conservative religious and political culture. The British imperial agencies were well aware that the inculcation of conservative religious values could have a major impact on political ideology.

As a result of their missionary efforts, the Anglicans and Methodists soon became the two largest denominations in the region, with the former consistently outnumbering the latter though the gap was narrowing by mid-century. But the success of the Anglican and Wesleyan Methodist campaigns should not be exaggerated. The clergy of both churches complained frequently about the fickleness of adherents who continued to resist denominational control over their lives. Many who claimed to be members of the Church of England when the census enumerators called appear to have rarely attended church services, and the Wesleyans were losing members to more radical Methodist organizations during the 1840s.

In addition, the upsurge of the initially non-sectarian Millerites reflected the potential for a revivalistic American movement that took the trouble to proselytize heavily in the region. Because the American Millerite preachers withdrew to larger urban centres as the 'end days' approached, however, their influence peaked earlier in the Eastern Townships than in the United States. By 1852 only 2.5 per cent of the Townships Protestants belonged to the Second Adventist church, which was the institutional successor to Millerism. Also, the 'great disappointment' that followed the failure of the Apocalypse to take place in 1843 or 1844 did not cause disillusioned Canadian followers to follow the example of American counterparts by joining radical antinomian movements. Instead, it appears to have resulted in a widespread decline in religious fervour until mid-century, when the pendulum began to swing back.

After an episcopal visit to the Eastern Townships in 1861, George Mountain wrote:

> Wherever there is a predominance or a considerable infusion of settlers who are American or of American descent there is a great proportion of the population who ... are unconnected with any religious organization whatever, and who remain unbaptized, and, in a vast number of instances, totally regardless of the duty of attending public worship. And in what *does* appear in the shape of Religion, there is frequently to be witnessed a frothy torrent of extravagant fanaticism ... as well as a multiform exhibition of doctrinal error, (such as is propagated by the Universalists, the Adventists, the seventh-day Baptists, etc.) serving, altogether, to bewilder the minds of the people and to make many stand aloof from Religion.[22]

The fact remains, however, that the political culture of the Eastern Townships was not nearly as conducive to radical sectarianism as was that of the neighbouring states.

The Protestant profile of the Eastern Townships more closely resembles that of Upper Canada, with almost identical ratios of Anglicans, Methodists, and Baptists in 1852, though the *Census Reports* fail to reveal that the Freewill Baptists were more numerous than the Regular or Calvinist Baptists in the Eastern Townships. Also, the larger percentage of Scottish immigrants to Upper Canada resulted in a much higher ratio of Presbyterians – 26 per cent, as compared with only 10 percent in the Eastern Townships. Finally, Congregationalism, Universalism, and Second Adventism were more popular in the latter region (see appendix, table A.1), reflecting the fact that its ratio of American-born settlers was nearly twice as high as that of Upper Canada. Furthermore, we must distinguish between declared adherence to one of the mainstream denominations and unquestioning deference to the dictates of the clergy and the rules of the church. Before exploring this point further in the following histories of each of those denominations, we will examine their geographic and social profiles.

The Geography of Protestant Denominationalism

The first Lower Canadian census to include data on religious affiliation was taken in 1831, and the published schedules included only six denominations: Church of England, Methodist, Baptist, Congregationalist, Church of Scotland, and Roman Catholic. As a result, the second largest category in the Eastern Townships was 'all other denominations' with 4,624 people (12.1 per cent of the population). Many of these were probably Universalists, for, aside from a small number of Quakers, no other denominations have a significant number of adherents listed in the much more comprehensive *Census Reports* for 1851–2. But a considerable number could also have been Freewill Baptists; some enumerators did not include them in the Baptist category in 1852, so the same was doubtless true of 1831. The Roman Catholics would soon become the largest church in the region as a result of Irish and French-Canadian immigration, but, at 4,242 in 1831, they were still well behind the 7,823 Anglicans. These denominations were followed by the 3,364 Methodists, 1,912 Baptists, 1,099 Congregationalists and Presbyterians, and 923 members of the Church of Scotland.

There are a number of ways one could categorize these data. The standard approach is to minimize the Church of England's strength by noting that, with only 23.1 per cent of the Protestant population, it was far outnumbered by the evangelical churches. A recent history of the

Eastern Townships stresses, for example, 'la forte influence des confessions de type évangélique comme les méthodistes ou les baptistes, alors que des Églises plus traditionnelles, enracinées aux îles britanniques, comme l'Église anglicane ou l'Église presbytérienne, tentent modestement de prend pied dans la région.'[23] But one could stress, instead, that in this largely American-settled region the Anglicans were nearly all converts from other denominations, and that the British-backed Church of England, Wesleyan Methodist Society, and Church of Scotland represented 35.7 per cent of the Protestants. Or one could refer to the enfeebled Calvinists (Congregationalists, Presbyterians, and Regular Baptists), who were no more than 12 per cent of the Protestant population (the more evangelical Freewill Baptists were not separated in the census from the Regular Baptists), while the Arminians (Anglicans and Methodists) were one-third.[24] Furthermore, most of those in the 'other' category were obviously also non-Calvinists. Finally, and most dramatically, one would have to observe that the largest category of all was the 37.2 per cent of the total population who declared no creed whatsoever, thereby revealing how limited the 1831 census is as a tool for studying religion in this era of fluid and uncertain denominational identity.

Kesteman has suggested that many of those enumerated simply refused to divulge such personal information as their religious affiliation, referring to an article in the *Stanstead Journal* of 22 January 1852 to support his hypothesis.[25] However, this article is a reprint from the *Montreal Transcript*, it makes no allusion to attitudes in the Eastern Townships, and nearly everyone did declare a religious affiliation in 1852. It seems rather unlikely that religious identity would be guarded more carefully than acreage improved, livestock owned, and other information that could potentially be used for taxation purposes. The difficulty in interpretation is compounded by the fact that the 1831 manuscript census schedules did not actually have a category for those claiming no religious creed. It was simply constructed in the published *Census Reports* by subtracting those recorded with a religious affiliation from the total population, so some cases were undoubtedly the result of the failure of the enumerator to fill in the appropriate space. This category was more than a statistical fiction, however, for reports from Anglican clergymen in 1827 indicated that there were 5,739 people in Lower Canada and over 6,000 in Upper Canada who were not affiliated with any religious denomination.[26]

The more remote mountainous areas in the Eastern Townships often had no resident clergy, so it seems clear that many of their settlers simply did not have a church to belong to. In mountainous Bolton, Sutton, Potton, Brome, and Stukely – all lying to the west of Lake Memphremagog – nearly three-quarters of the 5,982 inhabitants apparently failed to declare any religious affiliation. But a different explanation must be found for the large numbers of non-affiliated people in the three more populous and accessible townships of Stanstead, Hatley, and Barnston. In Stanstead, 3,688 of the 4,226 inhabitants (87.3 per cent) were recorded with no religious membership despite the fact that this was the most prosperous and populous township in the region and the focus of one of the earliest missionary endeavours. The success of the Methodist religious revivals of 1824 through to 1829 make it unlikely that there were a great many deists or non-Christians in this township, though small numbers were reported throughout the region at mid-century. But the first church building in Stanstead was a large union chapel erected in 1816, so many members may have simply considered themselves to be unaffiliated Protestants. The local Methodist missionary, James Booth, reported in 1831 that the amalgamation of 'free will Baptists, Calvinists, Episcopalians, etc' was 'denominated the Methodist Society,' which suggests a certain lack of clarity about religious affiliation.[27] In neighbouring Hatley and Barnston, however, the ratios of the unaffiliated were also very high in 1831, even though there was no union chapel in either of these two townships. Most settlers presumably attended the services of whatever itinerant preacher happened to pass through. Given that the whole emphasis of the New Light 'stir' was against formal confessions or creeds, it is not surprising that people would resist identification with a particular denomination. This hypothesis is supported by Archdeacon Mountain's statement in 1819 that the people of Hatley 'were yet to be moulded to anything approaching to order, uniformity, or settled habits of any kind in religion.' They were, indeed, 'unattached for the most part' to any denomination, 'and in the habit of attending whatever simple preachers might come their way.'[28]

While less than 25 per cent of the residents of the United States claimed any religious affiliation at mid-century,[29] denominationalism made great strides in the Eastern Townships during the 1830s and 1840s. Those who declared no religious affiliation shrank from 13,432 in 1831 to only 2,900 in 1852. Even those who belonged to the union church in Griffin's Corner of Stanstead Township, which was completed in 1842, had distinct denominational identities, with use of the church being divided between the Freewill Baptists, Universalists, and Wesleyan Methodists according to the amount of money members of each society had invested in the building's construction. The constitution of the Griffin's Corner church ensured that each denomination elected its own trustee, and this arrangement persisted until the church finally closed its doors in the late 1920s. The minute book does reveal a certain degree of denominational fluidity, however, for the Freewill Baptists dropped from first to second place between 1844 and 1845, the Universalists moved from second to first, and the Wesleyan Methodists dropped behind the newly arrived Protestant Methodists to fourth place.[30]

Rather than being restricted to placing a check mark beneath a limited selection of denominations, as in 1831, census enumerators in 1852 spelled out each person's affiliation, or non-affiliation in the case of free-thinkers. The greatest concentration of those listed with no creed were in Brome (967), Farnham (678), Stanbridge (491), Shefford (220), Dunham (101), and St Armand West (92). But interpretation is still somewhat problematic in the case of Dunham, where the enumerator wrote that the people in this category had 'no church' which would not necessarily mean that they were not Christians. On the other hand, a close examination of religion columns for Eaton and Compton suggests that there were more free-thinkers in the region than indicated by the printed census. In Eaton forty-nine people in eleven farm households simply were identified as 'nothing' under the religion category, and one wag reported himself and his family to be Epicureans. In contrast to the peasants of early modern Europe, ordinary farmers in the Eastern Townships clearly did not lack the conceptual means to sustain unbelief.[31] But the Eaton enumerator resisted reporting this fact, for all forty-nine people in question were listed under the column, 'other creeds not classed.' The same policy was followed in neighbouring Compton where the manuscript census reveals that there were 127 free-thinkers, but the published census again reports none.[32]

While the non-Catholic population increased by little more than a third (by 18,693) between 1831 and 1852, the Methodists quadrupled in numbers (by 10,181), the Anglicans nearly doubled (by 7,286), the Congregationalists and Presbyterians (not including the Church of Scotland) increased eight-fold (by 7,638), and the Baptists by slightly less than half (by 869). In 1852 there were also 3,321 Universalists, a denomination not included in the 1831 census, and 1,362 members of the recently established Second Adventist Church. Despite the addition of a considerable number of new denominations to the census categories, those who belonged to 'other creeds' increased from 3,380 to 4,624, but this was less than 9 per cent of the region's Protestant population. The affiliation of most of these individuals cannot be identified because nearly two-thirds were in Stanstead County, whose manuscript census records have unfortunately disappeared. Given that no Baptists were reported for the county, however, and that Stanstead had an active Freewill Baptist circuit, it is very likely that most of the 2,921 individuals listed in 'other creeds' belonged to this denomination. An examination of other townships revealed that some enumerators placed the Freewill Baptists in the 'other creeds' category of the published census. Finally, given the number of free-thinkers we found in the Compton and Eaton manuscript census who were not listed in the 'no creed' category, it is clear that a proportion of the individuals recorded as belonging to unlisted denominations actually had no religious affiliation.

Though to a lesser extent than twenty years earlier, when much of the population was still concentrated along the southwestern border, denominations tended to remain clustered in certain townships in 1852. Thus, while Church of England members had been reported in forty townships in 1831, just three townships (Dunham, St Armand, and Stanbridge) accounted for over half that membership. By 1852, Anglicans were to be found in fifty-five townships, with ten of them now accounting for half the membership. Over half the Methodists had also been concentrated in the southwestern townships of St Armand, Stanbridge, Dunham, and Sutton in 1831, but their subsequent expansion was more limited to the townships bordering Vermont where the American-based Protestant Methodists had made incursions during the late 1830s. In the region as a whole, in 1852, the 5,206 Other Methodists outnumbered both the 4,897 Wesleyans and the 3,442 New Connection Methodists whose society had taken over for the Protestant Methodists. Most of those identified as Other Methodists in the published census had simply been recorded as 'Methodists' in the manuscript census schedules. We can only surmise that many people attended the services of whichever Methodist preacher happened to be in their neighbourhood. If denominational identity had become more distinct since 1831, the finer gradations within the Methodist Church seem to have remained somewhat fuzzy.

For the Baptists, on the other hand, theology was sharply divided between Calvinism and 'free will.' Yet, as noted above, the printed census again failed to distinguish between the two churches in 1852, presumably because there were few Freewill Baptists in Upper Canada. In the Eastern Townships, the Freewill Baptists appear to have outnumbered their Calvinist counterparts. While many of the enumerators, including the one for district one of Sutton Township, did not distinguish between the two groups of Baptists, in district two of the same township we find sixty-three Freewill Baptists and thirteen Regular Baptists. The Freewill Baptists were included in the 'other creeds' category of the printed census, thereby resulting in a significant understatement of the number of Baptists in the township (as we have argued was the case in Stanstead County). In Dunham Township, where only seventy Baptists were recorded in the printed census, there are seventy-nine Regular Baptists and thirty-six Freewill Baptists listed in the manuscript schedules. In Eaton, the manuscript census reveals that the Regular Baptists outnumbered their Freewill counterparts by two to one in 1852, but, in neighbouring Compton, the Freewill Baptists outnumbered the others (some of whom identified themselves as Christian Baptists) by eight to one. While there were considerably more Baptists in the region than the *Census Reports* of 1852 would lead us to believe, we shall see that substantial growth of both branches had been hampered by a lack of missionaries, and by the impact of the Millerite movement which closed a number of local churches.

As settlers who brought their religious identity with them, the Congregationalists and Presbyterians (Presbytrians outside the Church of Scotland were categorized with the Congregationalists in the 1831 census), were more widely distributed than the Anglicans and Methodists in 1831, despite their much smaller numbers. With only 1,099 adherents, as compared with 7,823 Anglicans and 3,364 Methodists, the Congregationalists and Presbyterians outside the Church of Scotland were to be found in thirty-one townships. There were significant numbers in the St Francis Valley township of Shipton (54), where the first permanent Congregationalist missionary settled, and in the northern township of Inverness (89) where a group of Gaelic-speaking Congregationalists had recently arrived from the Isle of Arran. But most of the region's Scottish settlers were Presbyterians, and by 1852 Presbyterians outnumbered the Congregationalists by 5,527 to 3,362, though many still had no ministers. While there had been 923 members of the Church of Scotland in the region in 1831, the Free Church secession of 1843 had reduced its numbers to only 152.

Representing the most extreme rebellion against the Calvinism of the Congregationalists and Presbyterians were the Universalists, who were not included as a distinct category in the 1831 census even though they were a major denomination in New England. In 1852, the 3,319 Universalists in the Eastern Townships outnumbered the Baptists, and were almost as numerous as the Congregationalists. With over half their membership in Shipton, Barnston, Hatley, Ascot, and Compton, the Universalists tended to be concentrated in areas of early American settlement which were not centres of consistent Methodist proselytism. Sharing a similar theology to the Universalists, there were also 261 Unitarians in the region, nearly all of whom were in Stanstead Township.

Whereas the Universalists preached universal salvation, the followers of William Miller believed that only they would be saved on Judgment Day. In 1852 there were 1,362 people in the Eastern Townships who were members of the church that arose from the ashes of this movement. These Second Adventists were to be found in the Vermont-border townships of Stanstead and Barnston, as well as farther north in Shefford, Melbourne, and Shipton where their three preachers had located. We shall also see that a denomination locally known as the Christian Brethren, which appears to have been the American-based Christian Connection, had some followers in the border townships during the 1830s, though it failed to take root in the region. Finally, the long-established Quaker settlements had also failed to grow by mid-century, numbering only 129 members in Farnham and fourteen in Bolton, with thirteen others scattered in neighbouring townships.

When we examine each church in more detail, it will become clear that this geographical pattern of denominationalism was largely a reflection of missionary effort. British immigrants, nevertheless, tended to cling more strongly than the Americans to their original religious identities, in part because of their more isolated locations, but also because missionaries of their denominations were more available by the time many Irish, Scots, and English settled in the region. Table 1.1 reveals that in long-settled Eaton Township nearly all the English-born household heads were Anglicans or Methodists, but a considerable number of American-born and Canadian-born (most of whom were of American origin) also belonged to the Church of England. The Canadians and American-born who claimed to be Anglicans even outnumbered their counterparts in each of the Congregational, Baptist, and Universalist Churches. Table 1.2 reveals that in more recently settled Melbourne Township, the Church of England was much more heavily dominated by the English and Irish, while the Scots were almost all members of one of the Presbyterian denominations. As in Eaton, the American-born and Canadian-born were more evenly dispersed among the various denominations, reflecting a rather independent attitude towards their choice of religious affiliation.

TABLE 1.1
Denominational affiliation in relation to place of birth, Eaton Township, 1852

	Canada	US	England	Ireland	Scotland
Anglican	31	16	16	4	–
Methodist	8	2	5	2	–
Congregationalist	24	18	1	2	1
Regular Baptist	24	17	–	–	1
Freewill Baptist	5	12	2	–	–
Church of Scotland	–	–	–	–	1
Universalist	14	10	1	1	–
Adventist	–	1	–	–	–
Free Thinkers	7	6	–	–	–
Roman Catholic	15	1	–	7	–
Total	128	83	25	16	3

Source: Manuscript Census for Canada East, 1851–2.

One might expect this religious pluralism to have undermined the sense of community, but community ties, in turn, weakened the sense of sectarian exclusiveness. Unfortunately, because the manuscript census reports prior to 1852 do not provide enough information to make linkages possible, we cannot examine the fluidity of household denominational identity for our study period, but the Wesleyan Methodist and Anglican missionary reports repeatedly complained about shifting allegiances and the non-conformity of their membership. Many would simply attend the church that provided a clergyman demanding the least financial sacrifice on their part, even if he happened to be a Tory Englishman. Winning their true allegiance would be another matter, but the Anglican clergy's hopes were largely pinned on the younger generation, for they realized that custom was a powerful force.

The Sociology of Denominational Identity

While certain assumptions are generally made about the socio-economic ranking of the various religious denominations in Canada, very little research has been done on the subject, especially for early nineteenth-century rural communities. What work has been published generally

TABLE 1.2
Denominational affiliation in relation to place of birth, Melbourne Township, 1852

	Canada	US	England	Ireland	Scotland
Anglican	7	6	25	40	1
Methodist	8	10	5	11	1
Congregationalist	6	6	2	–	–
Regular Baptist	4	7	–	–	3
Freewill Baptist	–	–	–	–	–
Presbyterian	3	1	–	11	21
Free Church of Scotland	–	–	–	1	10
Universalist	10	2	–	1	–
Adventist	14	11	3	–	–
Free Thinkers	1	1	–	–	–
Roman Catholic	10	–	–	50	–
Total	63	44	35	113	36

Source: Manuscript Census for Canada East, 1851–2.

compares Catholics with all Protestants as a group.[33] Our computer-assisted analysis of eleven townships[34] in the manuscript census of 1831 suggests, contrary to the accepted wisdom, that there was not a great deal of variation in economic well-being between the various Protestant denominations. None of them was exceptionally far above or below the mean of 141.9 occupied acres, 36.4 improved acres, 8.2 cattle, 1.5 horses, 10.9 sheep, 5.4 hogs, 21.5 bushels of wheat, 21.8 bushels of oats, and 186.1 bushels of potatoes (see appendix, table A.2). The small degree of variation around these means reflects the fact that farming was still more focused on economic self-sufficiency than on the market,[35] though the Catholic farmers were an anomaly with less than one-third the improved acreage of the study group as a whole, much less livestock, and lower crop production. Not only were they more recent arrivals to the region, but the French Canadians and particularly the Irish Catholics had generally arrived with fewer economic resources, though the famine immigration had yet to begin.

While the most significant finding for the Protestant denominations may be their rough socio-economic equality, the differences that did exist are of some interest. Conforming to Weber's theory that evangelicals were more involved with 'this-worldly asceticism' and a methodical regulation of life than were Anglicans or Catholics,[36] the Baptists clearly were the most affluent group in 1831, while the 459 Anglican households occupying at least ten acres were only marginally higher than the overall mean in every economic variable examined. The 115 Baptists had slightly smaller farms than the Anglicans but considerably more livestock and larger harvests of the three main crops. But, the fact that the Baptists also had slightly larger households, with 6.4 members as compared with 6.0 for the Anglicans, and had improved considerably more land (49.0 acres versus 38.7 acres), suggests that their main advantage lay in having been longer established in the region. There were large numbers of Anglicans among the recently arrived British settlers in the northern part of the region, and they had much lower improved acreages than the regional norm (see appendix, table A.3). In the longer-settled area of St Armand, Stanbridge, Brome, and Shefford, the differences between the Anglicans and Baptists were small, with almost the same amount of land cleared and livestock owned (see appendix, table A.4). The 184 Methodist farmers, members of the second-largest Protestant denomination in the Eastern Townships, were even closer to the norm for the study area as a whole, trailing the Anglicans only very slightly in almost every variable.

Reflecting the deeply ingrained Scots' appetite for large land holdings, the average farm sizes of the eighty members of the Church of Scotland were significantly higher than those of the other groups (mixed households excepted), but their improved acreages were smaller than for all but the Catholics, again due to their relatively recent arrival in the region. The Church of Scotland settlers did harvest more wheat and potatoes than the norm, but they had far fewer cattle and sheep, and very few horses. The small Presbyterian/Congregationalist cohort of fifty-five farmers was a combination of long-established Americans and recent British immigrants whose economic variables were generally somewhat below the mean. A glance at tables A.3 and A.4 reveals the importance of geographic location and therefore duration of settlement as far as those variables are concerned. The twenty-nine Presbyterian and Congregationalist farmers who lived in the older southwestern area had improved an average of 44.8 acres, and owned 28.2 head of livestock, while the twenty-two in the Megantic County townships to the north had on average only 15.7 improved acres and 7.7 cattle, horses, sheep, and pigs.

Most of the forty-eight farmers who belonged to unrecorded denominations were clearly Universalists and Freewill Baptists, and their economic variables were generally only very slightly lower than the norm despite their somewhat smaller farms (104.3 acres versus the norm of 141.9 acres). As for the 149 households that claimed no denominational affiliation, they had larger farms (122.5 acres) than the foregoing group, but their other economic variables were somewhat below the norm, though certainly not enough to suggest that they were a marginal group. In fact, all but one of such households in the townships studied here were in Shefford and Brome, where their economic variables were very close to those townships' averages.[37]

Finally, the 119 farm households of mixed denominational composition had much the largest farms (208.7 acres) and improved acreages (59.6), on average, as well as much the highest crop production (370.9 bushels of wheat, oats, and potatoes) and livestock ownership (37.6 head), including nearly three horses per farm. While their household size of 8.1 was larger than the norm of 6.2 – meaning they had more mouths to feed – the greater wealth of the farmers in this cohort is reflected in their much higher tendency to employ farm servants (0.6 versus the norm of 0.1 per household). Indeed, the very presence of such outsiders, and not denominational plurality within the family (which the 1852 manuscript census reveals was still quite uncommon),[38] would explain why many of these households were categorized as of mixed denominational composition. Unfortunately, because we cannot determine the religious affiliation of the household head with complete certainty from the 1831 manuscript census, this cohort is of little value for our analysis.

Darroch and Soltow suggest that the passing of the pioneer phase and increasing institutionalization of the Protestant churches was accompanied by greater social and economic homogeneity. As noted above, there were obviously sharp distinctions between pioneer farms and those that had been established for a considerable period of time. One might, nevertheless, expect that increased integration into the market and population pressure on the land would lead to greater socioeconomic stratification within a community. Darroch and Soltow do find that while there was a relative parity among Ontario's various religious denominations in terms of farm ownership in 1871, there were 'significant' differences in the property sizes, varying from a high of eighty-five acres for the Baptists to a low of seventy-one acres for the Catholics, with the average Anglican property being only seventy-two acres. They argue that 'these figures could have represented considerable differences in investments and in margins of potential production.'[39]

TABLE 1.3
Mean number of acres held and improved by farmers of each denomination, Eaton and Melbourne, 1852 (no. of cases in parentheses)

	Eaton[a]		Melbourne	
	Held	Improved	Held	Improved
Anglican	164.9 (33)	90.8	110.5 (57)	49.5
Methodist	121.4 (7)	41.3	76.9 (23)	43.1
Regular Baptist	119.6 (36)	49.1	89.4 (9)	42.8
Freewill Baptist	141.1 (18)	56.2	–	–
Congregationalist	176.4 (25)	72.6	83.3 (14)	43.1
Presbyterian	–	–	131.5 (23)	48.7
Free Church	–	–	84.1 (8)	44.0
Universalist	165.8 (19)	74.8	84.0 (9)	43.3
Adventist	100.0 (1)	25.0	92.4 (17)	46.2
Free Thinker	157.5 (8)	70.6	49.0 (1)	44.0
Roman Catholic	95.8 (16)	32.1	90.6 (25)	32.1

[a] Part of the Eaton agricultural schedule is missing.
Source: Manuscript Census for Canada East, 1851–2.

Our analysis of acreages both occupied and improved in Eaton and Melbourne townships in 1852, though based on small sample sizes, does reveal somewhat contrasting situations among various denominations (see table 1.3). In Eaton the differences in acres improved are more striking than those for acres occupied, but the Anglicans, Congregationalists, and Universalists were clearly in the top range in both respects, while the Baptists and Methodists were significantly lower. Denominational variations in land occupied and improved were much less apparent in the more recently settled township of Melbourne where the British outnumbered those born in the United States and Canada. Here, only the Presbyterians stood out in terms of farm size (with a mean of 131.5 acres), confirming the Scottish characteristic noted above, though the poorer Free Church families were clearly an exception. (The high proportion of female servants belonging to the Free Church suggests that their families were dispossessed Highlanders fleeing the potato famine). There was an even more remarkable uniformity among Melbourne's various denominations in terms of land improved, with only the Catholics (most of whom were Irish-born) again falling well below the range of 42.8 to 49.5 acres.

In short, the fact that land variables were greater in longer-settled Eaton than in Melbourne suggests that length of settlement led to greater economic stratification,[40] a stratification that lay, to a limited extent, along denominational lines. Finally, the Eaton example contradicts Weberian assumptions about a distinctively evangelical work ethic, for the three more economically favoured groups – the Anglicans, Congregationalists, and Universalists – were from widely disparate theological traditions, none of which were strongly evangelical. The causal factors were more likely reversed, with the more successful farmers in Eaton being attracted to churches that had a less stringent interpretation of the doctrine of salvation. It is, nevertheless, clear that adherence to the Church of England was not largely confined to the most affluent sectors of society, as widely assumed.[41] Anglicans were also more widely distributed throughout the region than were other denominations, though their decline in their old southwestern stronghold during the 1830s and 1840s, as well as the emergence of Protestant Methodism and Millerism at the expense of Wesleyan Methodism, indicates that the British missionaries had faced a formidable challenge on this northern frontier of American settlement. But Millerism was largely a spent force by mid-century, and the Protestant Methodist Society had been replaced by the English-based Methodist New Connection which would, in turn, be relatively short-lived in the region. The Eastern Townships had not only been drawn into the political and economic web of Montreal, Upper Canada, and Great Britain, but their religious web as well.

2

The Pioneer Era

The pioneer era of Eastern Townships history, with its slow population growth and hesitant institutional development, persisted until at least 1815. During these years of religious revivalism in New England, the Lower Canadian borderland was included in the circuits of various American Calvinist and evangelical churches, with the result that settlers saw circuit preachers only on an occasional basis. Even these visits were largely interrupted by the War of 1812, leaving the Eastern Townships largely dependent on unordained local preachers. The situation would not change much after hostilities had ended, thereby leaving an opening for the Church of England's Society for the Propagation of the Gospel (SPG), which had already sponsored two missionaries in the earliest-settled southwestern corner of the region. One of these men, Charles Stewart, would lay the foundations for a rapidly expanding Anglican Church in the postwar era.

Joseph Badger

While church records and missionary reports provide valuable information on the religious beliefs and behaviour of those with a denominational affiliation, what about those who fell outside these parameters in the early nineteenth century? How can we gain insights into the minds of this large category of individuals? Personal letters and diaries are obvious sources, but rare ones for the pioneering era in particular. The best correspondence collections for the Eastern Townships are those of the township leaders at the turn of the nineteenth century, but their letters are largely preoccupied with acquiring land titles and other business matters. More useful, as far as religion is concerned, are spiritual diaries and memoirs, though they obviously portray the beliefs and behaviour of a particularly dedicated few. Only one diary has been uncovered for an Eastern Townships layman during the pre-1815 era, and that was revised and published as a biography many years later because the individual in question became an important religious figure in the United States. Still, the story of Joseph Badger, who became editor of the Christian Connection's popular *Christian Palladium* in New York, does shed light on this turbulent era of colonization and war.[1] During these years, the advancing northern frontier of American population expansion was outstripping the ability of the various religious denominations to provide more than irregular and infrequent religious services.

Joseph Badger's grandfather was a patriot general during the American Revolution, and his father, Peaslee, later became a major in Gilmanton, New Hampshire. In order to provide for his maturing sons, Peaslee Badger sold his farm for the considerable sum of $4,000 to $5,000 in 1801, and moved to 'the fertile woodland region of Lower Canada, which at that time was regarded as the best part of the world (*Memoir*, 24). Peaslee Badger was a well-read deist, at a time when religious scepticism flourished in Vermont, but opportunities for his son to receive a formal education were quite limited. Joseph Badger's biographer, E.G. Hubbard, claims that his life disproved the assumption that intellectual greatness could be produced only by exposure to 'college routine, and the aids of walls of books and of titled professors.' Nature was also a good teacher: 'We like it that a prophet should, in early life, hail from the woodland world, and that the vastness and tranquility of landscapes should rise in his public discourse; that his words and manners should savor, not of dry scholastic pretension and mannerism, but of songsters' voices, of colossal trees, wild rose and rushing brooks.' Badger's spiritual journal contains the standard accounts of early flirtation with salvation, as when he became seriously ill in 1807, or when he was moved by itinerant Baptist preachers. After the Episcopal Methodists had effectively replaced the Baptists in his home area, Badger remembered that local preacher David Blanchard's sermon 'was the first that ever brought tears from my eyes' (32–5). He also recalled that there were frequent visits from the American missionaries, but, interestingly enough, 'I do not remember that their preaching had much effect on my own mind or that of any other person.'

Badger was forced to take on a heavy load of work and responsibility at an early age, as his older brothers became established elsewhere and his father suffered serious financial losses, as well as breaking a leg which later had to be amputated. However, Badger claims that 'I was quite wild and had several bad habits' (33–4). These included dancing and reading novels on the Sabbath with his best friend, whom he would cease to associate with after his conversion. In 1811, at the age of nineteen, Badger was converted under the influence of Methodist meetings that he initially attended only because there were no other spiritual guides in his area. A close friend had admonished, 'you know it is a disgrace to go among those foolish and ignorant Methodists,' and Badger was initially a rather hesitant participant in their services: 'I derived much benefit and instruction from the conversation of the saints, and though I asked their prayers, I neither united with them in prayer, nor kneeled according to their custom.' But he did identify with their testimonials of spiritual struggle, and he eventually announced his own determination to 'seek my happiness in religion' (46–9).

Badger consequently lost his inhibitions about socializing with an 'inferior' class: 'I felt a vital union with all the saints without any respect to name, age, or color. I loved them and could say, they are my people. Some who were poor and ignorant, whom I had formerly despised, I was able to embrace as my best friends.' Badger's 'oppressive gloom' turned to joy, but he was still concerned that he had not experienced the dramatic conversion described by others (50–1). Finding the local Methodists unable or unwilling to discuss the theological issues that interested him, Badger flirted for a brief time with Universalism, but he decided that it lacked the Methodists' 'sacred enthusiasm of religious love.' He continued in fellowship with the Methodists, but held back from joining their church because he regarded its discipline as being too formal 'and in many respects unlike the Scriptures.' He was apparently also concerned about sectarianism, wondering why 'the saints cannot all be one' (52–3).

By the fall of 1812, Badger had become convinced of the need for full–immersion baptism, and, after attending a Freewill Baptist meeting in Hatley, he asked Elder Avery Moulton to preach in Compton.[2] Here, once the service was over, Badger announced his desire to be baptized, and, having chosen the Coaticook River, the congregation walked 'two and two, in large procession, the distance of half a mile, singing the praises of God as we advanced.' With his approving but still sceptical father sitting on a horse 'a few rods above me, in the water, so as to have a fair prospect,' Badger was baptized while 'Some praised, others wept, and a sweet peace and calmness filled my soul' (56–7). Badger's inclination towards preaching was strengthened by the fact that Baptist missionaries were being deported for refusing to take the oath of allegiance. As 'a citizen of the country' who 'knew the manners and customs of the people,' he 'could easily take a position from which the same persecuting powers could not drive me' (67). His journey with Elder Moulton up the St Francis River to Westbury Township strengthened his resolve to become a missionary. In spite of his lack of education and training, Badger reasoned: 'As swimming is learned by swimming, and agriculture is acquired by active pursuit, it struck me that fidelity in the new work would secure the only effectual skill in conducting it' (69–70).

Since Badger 'felt commissioned from God's throne,' he 'saw no necessity of applying to men for license or liberty to preach,' but the local Methodist minister 'gave me a letter stating that my moral and Christian character was good, and that the religious community believed me to be called to preach the Gospel.' From his new home in Ascot, where he attended school, Badger decided in the early winter of 1812 to embark on a sixty-mile preaching tour down the St Francis River in the company of another neophyte preacher, Zenas Adams. They 'met large assemblies, who had convened to hear what the boys could say,' but after spending several days in Shipton, they were arrested by the local magistrate, Elmer Cushing, 'as it was a time of war between two nations, and we were strangers' (74–5).[3] Badger presented 'the British tyrant' with his certificate of allegiance, and, upon being told that 'you'd better be at home than to be strolling about the country,' he boldly replied: 'I thank you, sir, I shall attend to what employment I think best, and shall visit what part of the country I please' (75–6). Adams had to be more circumspect because he had no certificate to prove that he had taken the oath, though the fact that he was accompanied by Major Badger's son clearly mollified Cushing's initial suspicions. Badger and Adams went their separate ways the following year when the latter decided to join the Methodists. To the independent-minded Badger's argument that they should not be 'confined to sect or party, but preach a free salvation to all who would hear us,' Adams replied that 'he thought it best to preach upon an established circuit, where he should be sure of a living and where he should have homes to receive him.' Adams returned to the United States, and Badger, 'more from duty than inclination, remained among enemies in Lower Canada, to stem the torrent of opposition alone' (77).

In the spring of 1813, Badger moved to Shipton where he wrote, 'my greatest pain was to see the inroads made by the enemy into our little church whilst I was absent' (91). But, in his words, 'a reformation immediately began among the youth, and the spirits of the aged pilgrims revived like the golden life of a second summer.' This was not a revival of the poorer people alone, for Badger lived with a militia captain, and he was invited to Kingsey by a colonel who was one of the principal men in the township and a close acquaintance of his father. Here, where the 'inhabitants were said to be remarkably hardened and wicked,' he enjoyed much the same success as in Shipton. Whereas he and his tired horse had not been offered any refreshment on their first arrival, several weeks later 'I could not pass a house where I was not urged to go in' (79–81).

The Baptist and Methodist missionaries appear to have cooperated with each other, for both Moulton and Gilson spoke at an August meeting in Shipton, where it was decided to hold a general three-day meeting in Ascot in early October. The local magistrates, suspicious of the preachers' constant movement from place to place, and angered at the population's resistance to bearing arms, had been sending spies to these meetings to determine whether or not they promoted sedition. When the impertinent young Badger was accosted by an officer for not praying for the king, he replied: 'You are mistaken, sir, I do pray for the king ... I pray that he may become converted, and be a child of God.' To the officer's declaration that he should pray for the king's arms, Badger responded: 'I do, sir, pray for his arms, that his swords may be beaten into ploughshares and his spears into pruning-hooks' (81–2).

Such answers were hardly calculated to placate the local authorities, and when the Ascot meeting was held in October 1813, it was learned that six leading lay members and three preachers, including Badger were to be arrested as enemies of the crown. Badger ensured that there would be no disturbance on the part of the congregation by going quietly with the others to the nearby tavern where the trial was to take place. That evening, however, Badger held a prayer meeting in one of the tavern's rooms, inviting the three justices of the peace, Jesse Pennoyer, Gilbert Hyatt, and Moses Nichols, to attend.[4] The next morning, after hostile witnesses had testified that the accused had 'opposed our brethren in bearing arms' and spoken 'diminutively of the British King,' they were bound over to appear before the court at Trois-Rivières. When the nine men were given only half an hour to post bail, they refused to do so on principle, though a number of those in attendance offered to serve as guarantors. At this point, the authorities' plans began to miscarry: 'sympathy became contagious, and the spectators, who had thus far been watchfully silent, began to damn the squires, two of whom were observed to stagger, having taken too much whiskey to retain a respectable command of their persons.' Badger's biography claims that 'Esquire P.' was found drunk in a ditch the following morning, and that the suit was dismissed on the advice of a local militia captain (*Memoir*, 83–5).

During the winter of 1813–14, according to Badger's memoirs, 'party rage seemed to die away, and persecution greatly subsided.' The energetic young man began to feel restless; in the spring he decided to recuperate his failing health and broaden his horizons by travelling to New England, 'around which my feelings of friendship and reverence warmly clustered.' Badger continued in his resolve to be 'a missionary to men, and not from men, looking on high for the mission, and to the just and careful operations of His providence for all necessary support' (86–8). In New England, he would preach free, universal salvation, and remain independent of any church, though he would win the support of the Freewill Baptists (102–3).

Despite the interruption that the war had caused to the Methodist and Baptist circuits, then, there appear to have been a number of local preachers either affiliated with those churches, or independent, as in Joseph Badger's case. Rather than causing a decline in religious enthusiasm, the war may have increased it in this essentially neutral zone, just as the Revolutionary War had done in Henry Alline's Nova Scotia.[5] Joseph Badger's zeal and independence were, in fact, reminiscent of Alline, who was a precursor of the Freewill Baptists, and he was clearly a very effective preacher. According to Hubbard, 'there was a charm in his voice, and a rich command of plain, apt, and elegant language in his speaking, that, all in all, I never saw equalled by any other man ... There was music in his discourse' (*Memoir*, 135). But Badger apparently never claimed to have the mystical visions experienced by Alline, and his loosely-defined theology did not challenge the region's few denominational preachers in this essentially post-Calvinist era when the Anglican Church was still only a marginal presence. As we shall see, it would be left to Isaac Bullard to play that role briefly in 1816.

In the meantime, the American preachers were not welcomed back with open arms once the peace was signed; when Joseph Badger returned for a visit to the Eastern Townships in 1815, he was arrested for having entered the United States in time of war. This time he was less compliant than he had been in 1813, largely because he was to be transported to the Trois-Rivières court in a canoe manned by 'savages.' Once they reached Drummondville, Badger insisted on meeting the commanding officer who ordered his immediate release (127–32). Badger then returned to New England, where he became a prominent (and moderating) figure in the radical new Christian Connection. He would not be the last native of the Eastern Townships to find a more promising field of operations as a revivalist preacher south of the border. Written for an American audience, Badger's biography doubtless takes certain liberties with his journal by dramatizing his confrontations with British military authority. It does illustrate, however, how American in its cultural outlook much of the Eastern Townships still was in 1815, nearly a quarter century after it had been opened to settlement. And, unlike Upper Canada, there would be relatively few British settlers to change that outlook in the era following the Napoleonic Wars, leaving the task largely to the British missionaries.

The Congregationalists

Congregationalism held that authority lay essentially with the local worshipping community bound together and to God by a covenant of belief. Members believed that at their monthly meetings they were guided by the Holy Spirit to a consensus in the transaction of their business. Not only did Congregationalism go into a steep decline in New England after the American Revolution, but its polity was not well suited to expansion into new settlement areas. As a result, a Plan of Union was signed with the Presbyterians in 1801 whereby the latter would be responsible for organizing new congregations outside New England.[6] This would explain why the Congregationalists and Presbyterians are lumped together in the 1831 census of Lower Canada, but they failed to gain a strong foothold in the Eastern Townships despite the fact that most of the early settlers were of this background.

The first recorded attempt to establish a Congregational church in the Eastern Townships was in 1796, shortly after the first settlers from Massachusetts and New Hampshire arrived in Stanstead Township. That year, ten adults and ten children gathered in a log barn to hear the visiting preacher, John Taplin. They continued to meet in the barn, usually without a minister, until James Hobart of Berlin, Vermont, visited his sister in the settlement in 1804, he agreed to preach there as often as he could spare time from his own parish, which was almost one hundred miles away. Stanstead was also served on an irregular basis by the Congregational minister from neighbouring Derby, Vermont, with the War of 1812 apparently not presenting a problem, but no church would be formally organized until 1816.[7] The only Congregational church to be established in the Eastern Townships prior to the war was founded in Eaton Township at some point in 1810–12, and in 1814 a Presbyterian from New Hampshire named Jonathan Taylor was promised $200 a year to serve as its minister. But the Church of England won in the end because in 1819 Taylor transferred his allegiance, and that of most of his flock, upon being offered an annual salary of £200 ($800) by the Society for the Propagation of the Gospel (SPG).[8]

The Congregational Church's remarkably weak presence in the Eastern Townships was largely due to its poor missionary effort. Despite the arrangement with the Presbyterians, it was not even able to keep pace with population expansion within the United States. As early as 1780 there were reportedly sixty 'destitute' parishes in Vermont, sixty in New Hampshire, and eighty in Massachusetts and Maine, most of them in new settlement and rural areas, representing over one-third of all New England Congregational parishes. Marini explains that the 'political revolution of 1776 weakened the government structures upon which the Congregational establishment depended.' Between 1763 and 1820, church organization in Vermont typically lagged behind the legal recognition of towns by more than fifteen years.[9] Furthermore, even if the families who moved north of the forty-ninth parallel had been anxious to reconstitute the old restrictive Puritan commonwealths, the scattered settlement pattern would have made it difficult to do so.

The Baptists

The Baptist Church had been the major beneficiary of religious dissent generated by the first Great Awakening of 1736–45, and it continued to develop rapidly in the post-Revolutionary period. Baptists practised baptism by immersion of believers only, and, like the Congregationalists, they stressed the independence of local congregations from any form of centralized control. The Canadian Baptists' historian, E.R. Fitch, attributes the church's weakness in the Eastern Townships to its pro-revolutionary stance, but he is wrong in assuming that the region was largely settled by Loyalists.[10] It is clear from early missionary accounts that many Baptists did move into the Eastern Townships, therefore denominational migration patterns do not explain why they became so heavily outnumbered by Methodists and Anglicans. The main reason, as with the Congregationalists, was clearly that these British churches sustained a more effective missionary effort.

Not all the Baptists supported the Revolution, for the first resident Baptist preacher in the Eastern Townships was the Loyalist settler, William Marsh. In 1796, shortly after he was ordained by a council from the churches in Fairfax and Cambridge, Vermont, Marsh and many of the Baptist congregation at Caldwell's Manor on the western side of Lake Champlain decided to leave the seigneurial zone. They moved east to mountainous Sutton Township, from which base Marsh preached for a number of years in the surrounding townships, supporting his family by farming during the summer and making shoes during the winter.[11] Around 1806, Marsh and his family moved again to the more prosperous township of Hatley where in 1799 nine male and four female Baptists had begun to hold meetings in their houses on the shores of Lake Memphremagog, between Georgeville and the Outlet (Magog). Marsh moved back to the 'destitute' community in Sutton around 1809–10, when a Hatley resident named Harvey Clark began to 'improve his gift' for preaching.[12] A missionary who attended Clark's ordination reported that 'The assembly was large and respectable, for so new a place, and during the exercises people were very solemn. On the whole, the prospect here appears quite flattering.'[13] There were seventy-five members of the Regular Baptist Church in Hatley by 1817, served largely by Elder Clark.[14]

By 1812 Marsh had moved once more, this time to Stanbridge from where the Methodist missionary was deported by the military due to the tale told against him by the local Baptists.[15] Marsh also preached in Brome and Dunham until 1825 when he followed some Townships Baptists to Whitby, Upper Canada. Marsh had been a vital link between congregations for a denomination whose evangelical efforts were hampered by a spirit of independence which discouraged organization beyond the local level. There was also a sharp rift between 'strict' and 'open' communionists, with the former believing that only those who had been baptized should share in the Lord's Supper, and the latter accepting all professing Christians. Marsh was torn about baptism itself. During his early days, he was inclined to baptize anyone who gave evidence of piety, but he later rather reluctantly restricted the ritual to those who wished to join the church.[16]

One other name that emerges in the prewar period is Jedediah Hibbard, a pro-Revolutionary soldier, land surveyor, and Baptist preacher who in 1791, at the age of fifty-one, was sent by the Woodstock Association on a missionary tour to northern Vermont and Caldwell's Manor. In 1797 Hibbard settled at Abbott's Corner in St Armand, where he became the pastor of the Baptist church organized in 1800.[17] Two years later, the congregation built a square-shaped meeting house, with a door on each side as well as at the front; seats for warming on either side of the stove; and a space for the singers to stand at the east side of the pulpit. After each hymn, they would return to their family pews.[18] Rather than being an enclosed sanctuary, then, this building promoted movement both in and out, as well as internally. By 1820, 241 members had joined the St Armand church, at least 139 of whom were women.[19]

Baptists were also among the earliest settlers of Barnston Township, but their church services were largely conducted by deacons until around 1809, when Elder Roswell Smith moved from Windsor, Vermont, and organized a local church. But the church would be short-lived, for visiting missionaries reported two years later that illness had prevented Smith from regular preaching. As a result, the Barnston church would collapse after Smith's departure in 1817.[20]

As resident preachers, Marsh, Hibbard, and Smith worked largely alone, for Ivison and Rosser state that in 1806 Barnabas Perkins of Hanover, New Hampshire, became the first known Baptist missionary to visit the Eastern Townships in seven years. Perkins spent approximately three weeks in the eastern part of the region, and reported having to travel over a dreadful road through a dreary wilderness, but he stated that the people received him 'with much affection.' Two years later, in 1808, the American missionary again 'laboured in the northerly parts of New Hampshire, Vermont, and Lower Canada,'[21] but he was not able to complete his full term of service due to poor health, and there is no information on this visit to the Townships. The Eastern Townships churches belonged to the Richmond (later Fairfield) Association in Vermont, and other American missionaries toured the region between 1807 and 1811, but the brevity of their reports suggests that their impact was quite limited.[22] The War of 1812 interfered with the arrangement, such as it was,[23] and the Massachusetts Baptist Missionary Society also ceased activity in the region at this time, forcing local congregations to become more reliant on their own resources.

Aside from the lack of external support, the 'Regular' or 'Calvinist' Baptist Church suffered from competition from its anti-Calvinist offshoot, the Freewill Baptist Church, which outgrew it in popularity in the northeastern states after the Revolution.[24] The Freewill stronghold was in Maine and central New Hampshire, though the sect was also very popular in the northern counties of Vermont. In New England as a whole, there were over 150 Freewill Baptist congregations by 1815.[25] Their first recorded activity in the Eastern Townships was in 1800 when, according to a history published sixty-two years later, the people of Hatley found themselves with no one to officiate at the township's first burial. Prayers were consequently offered by a pious Freewill Baptist layman from New Hampshire named Christopher Flanders. Flanders returned permanently the next year, when a prayer meeting was established and some settlers were converted. The next step was the invitation for a Freewill Baptist missionary to visit though, curiously enough, this seems to have been the result of meetings organized in 1802 by the Congregationalist Avery Moulton, and a Methodist minister from New Hampshire. Shortly afterward, the Reverend Joseph Boody of Strafford, Vermont and a newly-ordained 'evangelist' named Robinson Smith crossed the border into Canada, where, according to a nineteenth-century Baptist historian, 'great were the displays of Divine power that attended their labors, especially in Stanstead and Hatley, where many were converted and churches were organized, the first in the province.'[26]

The same historian, I.D. Stewart, claims that Avery Moulton became a Freewill Baptist minister in 1803. After a fire destroyed his house and the $40 he had saved to pay for his land, 'he went from settlement to settlement, sometimes guided only by spotted trees, successfully preaching the unsearchable riches of Christ.'[27] By 1806 Moulton was living in Stanstead, where a log meeting house was constructed, with one window on each of three sides, a stone back, and a stick chimney. According to local historian Hubbard, the efforts of Moulton and Robinson Smith, who settled in Hatley around 1809, resulted in another revival among the Stanstead and Hatley Freewill Baptists in 1811–12.[28] This revival also reached Compton,[29] where Joseph Badger later remembered that Moulton's 'voice to me was like thunder. For several days after, it seemed as though I could hear the sound of it.' Badger was equally impressed by the sermon of a visiting Baptist named Benjamin Putnam, a young man who 'looked very pale, and much worn out ... I thought this discourse more glorious than anything I had ever heard. I thought him the happiest young man I ever saw.'[30] But Badger's memoirs leave the impression that the Methodists dominated the township, and the Church Record of the Compton Freewill Baptists states that 'nothing very spetial occured' there for a decade after the 1811 revival.[31] As with the Regular Baptists, the War of 1812 had clearly cut short the development of this radical New England sect in the Eastern Townships.

The Episcopal Methodists

The founder of Methodism, John Wesley, taught that each person had been granted sufficient grace to be able to achieve sinlessness. This doctrine struck a chord with a population in the process of achieving political independence, and in New York Methodism became a separate entity with its own superintendent or bishop in 1784. The Methodist missionary campaign began later in New England, which was already well served by the Congregationalists, than it did in other regions of the United States. Only in 1790 were the first seven Methodist missionaries appointed to New England, but the Methodists had one big advantage over their rivals; Methodist conversion was accompanied by a sense of elation and confident optimism that was missing from the Calvinist experience. By 1804 there were 2,529 Methodist members in Vermont, which had become the largest district in the New England Conference.[32] In the Eastern Townships, however, Methodism suffered the same handicap as the other American-based denominations – a critical shortage of preachers.

One of the first missionaries to visit the Eastern Townships was the eccentric young Lorenzo Dow, known as Crazy Dow, whom Semple identifies as 'The first important evangelist for Methodism,' and a representative of 'the transition from the old-style itinerating preacher to the nineteenth-century specialist in mass evangelism.'[33] Butler, on the other hand, states that Dow's claim that he could 'locate lost and stolen objects, raise the Devil, and perhaps cure disease' was characteristic of early American Methodist syncretism. In the minds of many, the label of 'crazy' confirmed rather than denied his religious calling.[34] In 1799 Dow became the first itinerant preacher on the Essex, Vermont, circuit which extended 'some twenty or thirty miles into Canada.' He was sent the first year into the Eastern Townships to establish a new circuit in the Missisquoi Bay area which had originally been settled by Palatine Loyalists from New York, many of whom had been converted by Wesley before leaving England.[35] Dow described his experience as follows:

> borrowing a horse, I went to break up fallow ground, and proceeded to Dunham, towards Mumphrey Magog [Memphremagog] Lake, and held meetings in different parts of the town. Some were angry, and spake evil of the way, and some were serious and tender, and desired to hear again. The people of this part of the world, were the offscouring of the earth, some having ran [*sic*] hither for debt, others to avoid persecution for crimes, and a third character had come to accumulate money. They were like sheep

without a shepherd, having only two ministers, one of whom believed one principle and preached another.[36]

The twenty-two-year-old Dow claimed to have met considerable success in the Townships – 'the Wilderness did bud and blossom as the rose' – but he was anxious for a sea voyage to Ireland to restore his health. Discouraged from doing so by other preachers who said there was a great chance of a revival in New England, he went without permission even though he was still on probation as a minister. Dow's independence was not unusual among the pioneer preachers in the region, though it was certainly frowned upon by the early Methodist historians. In the words of George Playter, who wrote a history of Canadian Methodism in 1862, Dow 'loved to do good, but his way of doing it was like the course of the comets, which come and go, and no one knows when they will come again.'[37]

Though Playter states that Dow was the first regular Methodist missionary to Lower Canada,' he is not even mentioned in Carroll's history of Methodism in Canada, published in 1867. According to Carroll, the first Methodist preacher to visit the Eastern Townships was Peter Vannest at Missisquoi around 1800–1.[38] In 1802 Bishop Asbury wrote that 'We have sent three choice men as missionaries into Lower Canada,' and the following year the New York Conference (created in 1800) sent four others to replace them.[39] The Stanstead and Dunham circuits were created in 1804 and 1806, respectively.[40] They remained connected directly with districts in the United States rather than the newly established Lower Canada district of the New York Conference, even though their 415 souls represented a sizable proportion of the 2,375 Methodists on Canadian soil.[41] Dunham was attached to the Ashgrove district (and later the Champlain district) of the New York Conference, while Stanstead was linked with the Vermont district of the New England Conference.[42] Neither circuit had a preacher with full ministerial powers as of 1809, but membership had increased to 319 in Dunham and 129 in Stanstead. In addition, the St Francis River circuit, established by Robert Hibbard of New York, had 116 members in 1809.[43]

The membership continued to grow steadily in the Dunham and Stanstead circuits, and, according to Carroll, Deacon David Kilborn of Stanstead was by 1810 'esteemed as one of the most faithful and powerful preachers of the denomination.'[44] Joseph Badger's memoirs recall that, in his home township of Compton, Joseph Dennet and David Blanchard succeeded in converting 'many of the old and the young.' Only

Dennett is officially listed as serving the circuit, so Blanchard was presumably a local preacher. Itinerant preachers apparently continued to live in the United States rather than within their assigned territories, for a posting for two missionaries was known as a four-weeks circuit.[45]

The men selected for the Stanstead circuit in 1812 did not cross the border due to the war, but the Dunham appointees served Stanstead as well as their own circuit for a time.[46] These two new preachers were both neophytes, having recently been received on trial, and their circuit was almost entirely in Lower Canada. In 1813 John T. Addoms, known as 'Crazy Addoms' because of his demonstrative style, petitioned the governor asking to be admitted into Lower Canada, and he continued to work throughout the year without disturbance. Addoms' colleague, William Ross, was not so fortunate. Carroll describes how in Stanbridge, where there was a large number of strict Calvinist Baptists under the ministry of William Marsh, Ross challenged their rather curious belief that a Christian who had fallen from grace could not die until he or she was restored. His argument was that 'In that case, sin is a sure preservative of life; and if you would provide me with an army of five thousand *backslidden Christians*, and they could be *kept from praying*, I could conquer the world; for no bullet could touch them as long as they could be kept from prayer.' The following day, several of the Baptists informed the commanding officer that Ross had publicly declared that with five thousand troops he could easily conquer Canada. When Ross was ordered to take the oath of allegiance or immediately return to the United States, he chose the latter alternative. One of his successors reported that many of the settlers had done likewise, leaving small clearings of ten to fifteen acres grown over with weeds and bushes, which 'gave to the country a very desolate appearance.'[47]

Some of those who remained behind resorted to inventive measures in order to avail themselves of religious services. According to a Methodist missionary, one strategy to accommodate those who had been 'cut off from their accustomed public means of grace' involved holding a quarterly meeting in a large building which had been erected across the Lower Canada–Vermont border to facilitate the active smuggling trade. The Canadians and Americans remained on their respective sides of the line, 'yet they passed very closely on both sides, and never was there a heartier hand-shaking than on that occasion – nominal belligerents, but real, heartfelt friends and brethern.'[48]

But the war did have a significant impact on Methodism in the Eastern Townships. Ross was not replaced on the Dunham circuit throughout that period, Stanstead remained vacant, and the preachers appointed to the St Francis circuit failed to appear.[49] Even Addoms did not return in 1814, and the membership of the Dunham circuit had already declined from 335 in 1811 to 245 in 1812, and 230 in 1813.[50] No returns were submitted for the Stanstead circuit between 1811, when there 238 members, and 1815, when it had only fifty members, but Joseph Badger's memoir refers to a well-respected Methodist minister named John Gilson being in the area during the war. At one Ascot meeting attended by Badger in January 1813, 'Mr. Gilson, and a colored man by the name of Dunbar, who was both a godly man and a faithful preacher, were our principal speakers.'[51] There is no evidence of Methodist preachers advocating subversion during the war, and the New York Conference had already warned them to avoid state politics in 1810, but they were naturally distrusted as members of a society which taught that when a government stepped outside the limits delegated by God, citizens had a duty to challenge it.[52] Furthermore, these Methodist preachers were Americans, and the democratic principles and emotional appeal of their style of religion appeared to threaten the conservative desire for authority and order. The result, as we shall see, would be a a rather one-sided struggle between the British and American branches of Methodism in the postwar era.[53]

The Universalists

The Universalists, like the Freewill Baptists, were an anti-Calvinist product of revolutionary New England, but they went much further than the other evangelical movements by rejecting the concept of eternal damnation. The position arrived at by the Welsh revivalist James Relly, and carried to America by John Murray, was that Christ's death on the cross had effectively restored the union between God and man that had been destroyed by sin. Elhanan Winchester later developed a theory of Universalism which involved personal responsibility for sin and the need for purifying retribution, and Hosea Ballou added a unitarian strain that would come to define American Universalism. It claimed that the atoning work of Jesus was not meant to substitute for humanity's sinfulness, but to serve as a moral example.[54] Despite these moves away from universal salvation, the clergy of the other denominations refused to recognize Universalists as Christians. To the Anglican and Wesleyan Methodist missionaries they were the most subversive of the New England religious societies in the Eastern Townships.

The first New England General Convention convened by Elhanan Winchester in 1794 appointed Universalist missionaries to preach in upper New England for a year, and assumed the authority to ordain candidates for the ministry. The convention continued to meet annually thereafter, and from 1800 onward it made formal arrangements for ordination councils and received written reports from constituent churches. It also undertook to arbitrate disputes between ministers and congregations, but no provisions were made for coercive discipline, and each local body continued to possess full powers of self-government. In Marini's words, 'The Winchester Profession of Faith did little more than legitimate the anarchy of Universalist practice and formalize ad hoc institutions that had existed for a decade.'[55] After 1815, however, the challenges posed by geographical expansion and theological disputes caused the Universalists gradually to take on the characteristics of a mainstream denomination with a bureaucracy, ministerial authority, and restrictions on their basic creed of gospel liberty.

The hill country Universalists were strongest in the upper Connecticut Valley, which was an important migration route into the Eastern Townships. The Northern Association, established in 1804, embraced most of Vermont, part of New Hampshire and eastern New York, and, theoretically, the border communities in Lower Canada, though most of them were too small and scattered to 'fellowship' with the American societies.[56] The memoirs of Joseph Badger claim that an old Universalist by the name of Huntington was the first preacher of any denomination in the Compton area, but also recall that, after a summer's efforts, 'I do not remember to have seen anything like reform among the people.'[57] The farmer and teacher, Christopher Huntington was indeed an old man when he moved to Compton in 1804, having been born in Connecticut in 1734. He is credited as the first person to preach Universalism in Canada. In 1811 Badger also briefly attended the services of a Universalist named Farewell,[58] but there would be no concerted missionary effort in the region until the early 1830s.

The Quakers

The Quakers, or Society of Friends, represented a much weaker threat to the mainstream churches than did the Universalists. They were not active prosleytizers, and they set themselves apart from society by virtue of their pacifism, adherence to a 'moral economy,' and what they termed 'plain' dress and speech. The latter phrase refered to their practice of using 'thee,' 'thou,' and 'thy' for the second-person singular. Quakerism, which originated in seventeeth-century England, followed George Fox's teaching that the ultimate criterion of truth was not the Bible but an 'inner light' through which Christ reveals himself to the heart. While the Quakers were generally not loyalist in sympathy during the American Revolution, their pacifism made them victims of persecution even after the war was over. As a result, an interconnected migration trickled into the Eastern Townships from Vermont, southern New Hampshire, and northern Massachusetts.

The first Quaker settler in the region was the loyalist Nicholas Austin, leader of a group of associates who acquired Bolton Township in 1797. But Austin had been disowned for marrying outside the faith and most of his associates were not Quakers; they probably did not establish a meeting after settling on the mountainous western shore of Lake Memphremagog.[59] The main influx of Quaker settlers went, instead, to the flat land of East Farnham Township on the western periphery of the Eastern Townships, where they purchased land from private owners. The first Quaker family to arrive was that of Gideon Bull from Danby, Vermont, in 1800 or 1801, though he appears never to have been a member of the Society himself, and other Quaker families did not follow until 1814.[60]

The Anglicans

Anglicanism covered a wide religious spectrum, from high churchmanship to latitudinarianism to evangelicalism, but its basic values included episcopal succession with freedom from the papacy, a limited monarchy with freedom from the 'mob rule' commonly associated with republican government, and the profession of a 'rational religion' which rejected 'enthusiasm' on the one hand and 'superstition' on the other. To the Anglicans of Upper Canada, Grant argues, these were the values that 'were held to qualify England to an unusual degree as a Christian nation.'[61] Certainly, they were the values that the SPG missionaries attempted to instill in the Eastern Townships, but the degree to which they were shared by most of the church's American-born adherents is another matter. The financial support of the London-based missionary society did, however, enable the Church of England to establish a stable presence in the Eastern Townships, and to gradually expand its influence from the more densely-settled southwestern corner of the region.

In 1799 the Reverend John Doty of William Henry (Sorel) wrote to the SPG that he had twice visited St Armand – 'a new and flourishing settlement' of 1,200 to 1,500 souls – where the people were planning to build a church, and had expressed a willness to pay £30 annually to support a missionary. The seigneur,[62] Thomas Dunn of Quebec, offered two hundred acres as a glebe, and others were to provide sufficient land for two churches with burial grounds. The aim was to build one church in St Armand and another in neighbouring Dunham Township, with the incumbent's house located between them. With the colonial administration contributing £100 annually, and the SPG an additional £50 a year, the Oxford-educated Robert Quircke Short was attracted from Kingston where he had been practising medecine. Two years later, in 1801, Short was moved to Trois-Rivières in order to make room for James Marmaduke Tunstall, son-in-law of the wealthy proprietor of the upper Richelieu seigneuries, General Gabriel Christie. Tunstall was apparently being removed from his military chaplaincy in Montreal because he had been abusing his wife. The controversial cleric resigned in 1802, and no successor was found until Charles Caleb Cotton arrived two years later.[63]

The eldest son of an impecunious schoolmaster, Cotton received his degree from Oxford in 1797, and emigrated to the United States soon afterward. His plan was to remunerate his struggling family for its financial sacrifice, but this he never managed to do. After teaching school in Charleston, South Carolina, the peripatetic Cotton served as a clergyman in the states of New York, New Jersey, and Pennsylvania. He soon became dissatisfied with an income that, in his words, 'is frequently uncertain & ill paid and depends entirely on the ability and disposition of the people.'[64] In 1804, the prospect of an SPG subsidy lured him to Quebec where he was elevated to priest's orders and assigned to St Armand and Dunham. Reporting Cotton's appointment, the SPG journal stated that 'He appears to be peculiarly suited to the situation, having great simplicity, becoming gravity of manners, good ability, and much facility in communicating his thoughts, and from his residence in America, sufficient familiarity with the manners prevalent among their new settlers, which are so apt to give an Englishman disgust.'[65]

Cotton informed his sister in England that the settlers were actually not native Americans, but German loyalists and immigrants from the Hudson Valley. While this was hardly the wild frontier that he would depict in his reports to the Bishop of Quebec, isolation from Montreal and proximity to the border made law enforcement very difficult. Unfortunately, Cotton's inflexibility and lack of religious ardour made him a poor choice for any new settlement. To his sister, Cotton confided again in December 1804 that he was 'obliged to submit to a thousand inconveniences which I have not before experienced,' and he would likely return to one of his former American positions in the summer.[66] On the positive side, Cotton's background as a teacher was reflected in his genuine concern for the youths of his parish. He lamented that 'a surprising apathy with respect to the morals of the rising generation obtains almost everywhere,' and encouraged the local schoolmaster to assign Bible readings to his students. Cotton himself attempted to catechize and lecture to the children after his Sunday services, but this soon fell through, he reported, due to the general laxity of morals that prevailed and the 'poisonous influence of infidelity.'[67]

Cotton began complaining to Bishop Mountain about his new appointment as early as February 1805. Despite his 'utmost endeavours,' he had failed 'to unite the hearts of the people to remove their scruples, satisfy their doubts and inspire them with an affection and zeal for the support of our Church establishment.' The fault was not his, Cotton insisted, for he strongly suspected 'a settled & regulated plan of secret opposition to the benevolent views of Gov.t in supporting the Mission at this place.' The churchwardens had only been able to raise a subscription of £12 for his annual support, and no room had been set aside for divine service. Cotton also complained that the local people commonly went to the magistrate to be married because this alternative was less costly. In April he informed the bishop that 'My hopes of being useful here have been very much damped by a residence of six months and when to this circumstance is added a thousand privations which every Minister must bear with in this wild country, your Lordship will easily conceive my situation to be not the most comfortable in the world.'[68] The following month Cotton reported that church attendance had increased despite the indescribable condition of the roads, but the subscription had almost entirely failed. Only £2.9s had been collected, and Cotton complained that 'with my present stipend only to depend on I have been obliged to forego many comforts which the habits of a person decently brought up have rendered necessaries.' Finally, he had baptized a number of infants but only one adult since arriving in St Armand, suggesting that little progress was being made in converting the majority who were Methodists and Baptists.[69]

Cotton refused to assume any responsibility for his lack of progress, claiming that 'the people are well satisfied with their Minister and as desirous that he should remain with them as they are unwilling to requite his humble services.' Rather, he blamed Methodism for thinning his flock, and causing 'some among us to act a wavering part, and wander from the Church to the meeting, and vice versa. The temperate and sober form of Episcopal worship is often unfavourably received by those whose minds have been heated by the vehemence and rant of the Conventicle.' Cotton concluded that 'with my present stipend only to depend on I have been obliged to forego many comforts which the habits of a person decently brought up have rendered necessaries.' He requested the bishop 'to change my present station for another that promises more comfort and equal usefulness.'[70]

The main reason for Cotton's discontentment was actually boredom, for he wrote to his sister in 1807:

> The people in general seem to have but little regard for a Gentleman & a person of education, they have hardly any conversation except about farming affairs, which is a standing dish with them from Jany. to December. They discover no wish for information, & no curiosity to hear anything but about the crops, the weather & a passing word or two of the latest news. – You can judge, Sister, what a burthen conversation must be, instead of a satisfaction, under these circumstances, & how impossible it is for me to derive much pleasure from this source.[71]

Cotton painted a similar picture for another sibling:

> The people here live very much to themselves and visit but very little ... As they provide everything within themselves, a very little money suffices them. To a person who has resided in England their mode of living appears very parsimonious & uncomfortable. – The tea we drink here is not at all better than good bohea in England, often not so good, & they make it much weaker than at home. As I cannot endure the strong taste of maple sugar in it, & do not think it prudent under present circumstances (see what a saving brother you have got) to go to the expense of loaf sugar, I abstain from using any.[72]

Nor were wine, beer, or cider readily available, forcing Cotton to drink only water. But he did allow himself the indulgence of smoking, writing to his father that 'a pipe of Virginia is my constant friend & solace, and I cannot perceive that it hurts me at all, for I guard against too free expectoration.' Cotton had also saved enough money by boarding with a family to travel to Long Island in the summer of 1806, and to engage in land speculation, purchasing two two-hundred-acre lots in Sutton Township for $350. Soon afterward, he convinced the bishop to divide his charge in two, with him taking responsibility for Dunham Township.[73]

Cotton informed his father that he had chosen this less-developed township over St Armand because he could not afford land near the place of worship in Philipsburg, and he had grown tired of boarding out in small houses with large families. The endeavour would be costly – Cotton estimated $650 for one hundred improved acres with barn, plus $120 to $140 per year for servants, not to mention the cost of 'furniture, provisions, stock utensils,' and so on. But he had concluded that 'there is no such thing as living with any comfort in these woods without undertaking the culture of a little land.' Cotton had also, despite his more prudent father's attempt to dissuade him, and despite his inability to sell his two uncleared lots in Sutton, decided to pay $200 more to the New York proprietor of a patent for distilling liquor. In return, Cotton was to have the exclusive rights to the patent in England, and he declared rather cavalierly: 'if it fails it will involve me in debt for some years to come, if it succeeds I shall have it in my power to render your situation as to worldly affairs much more comfortable.'[74]

The patent speculation was, indeed, a failure,[75] and by 1810 the ever restless clergyman had decided that his property was too isolated for his clerical duties because he had to travel four miles on one Sunday and ten miles on the other, presumably to hold services in schools because there would be no Anglican church in Dunham until 1821. These were considerable distances for one who, according to a local historian, was 'as devoid of equestrian skill as he was then unequaled through the whole country for pedestrian ability.'[76] Nor had Bishop Mountain been pleased with Cotton's location, chastising him for settling in that part of Dunham where he would have 'the smallest possible beneficial influence,' since he was in the corner closest to the St Armand incumbent. Mountain added: 'We have not received our ministry chiefly for the purposes of our own comfort, or enjoyment, but for the propagation of the Gospel, & the salvation of souls.'[77]

Cotton had, consequently, purchased on credit a farm with a dilapidated house close to where a temporary place of worship was supposed to be built. While he had employed as servants a married couple with six children, he continued to complain of loneliness to his sisters, writing that 'I have no one, ... to unbosom my thoughts to, since I am separated from our dear family, & what an irksome state this is to remain in so long, one can hardly conceive without the experience of it.' He was anxious to marry, noting that 'any idea of fortune' or 'finished education' was out of the question in this country, 'But yet, some education, a pleasing behaviour, and the useful qualifications of good housewifery are to be found *among* us.'[78] Three years later, in 1814, Cotton finally did marry Drusilla Pettes, the much younger daughter of an invalided loyalist.[79] Without describing his new wife, or her family, Cotton explained to his eldest sister that 'with my comparative inexperience of the deceitfulness of the World, & the want of a faithful Counsellor to consult in all my plans, since my first residence in this Township, I have extended much money to but little advantage which had I been a married man, might (much of it at least) have been avoided.'[80]

Cotton's sisters and brothers had been hoping that he would return permanently to England, but he explained that the rising cost of living there would necessitate a salary of £200 to £250 'to enable me to support the expense of Housekeeping with any tolerable comfort, & with a decent regard to my situation in life.' Not only was there a superabundance of young men wishing to enter into Holy Orders, but an English rector could count on only £100 a year. The much-travelled Cotton would spend the remainder of his long life in Dunham, not returning to England even for a visit. As a rather stereotypical example of the worldly Anglican cleric, Cotton is a good example of why historians have generally assumed that the Church of England was ill-suited to the frontier environment. But Cotton's letters reveal that he did become reconciled to his borderland parish once he began to raise a family, and even though his professional attention was largely confined to that parish, it is worth noting that Dunham long boasted the highest ratio of self-proclaimed Anglicans in the Eastern Townships.

The Church of England, nevertheless, owed much of its early success in the region to an appointee of a very different background and character. While Cotton's parents had faced persistent financial and status anxiety, Charles James Stewart belonged to one of Scotland's oldest and most prestigious families. Furthermore, in contrast to the self-centred Cotton, Stewart's career as a missionary in the Eastern Townships was marked by religious zeal, generosity of spirit and purse, and uncomplaining asceticism. While studying at Oxford's Corpus Christi College, Stewart had been strongly influenced by the evangelical and anti-slavery teachings of William Wilberforce, a friend of his older sister.[81] Stewart was ordained to the priesthood at the age of twenty-four in 1799. His health was delicate, and Bishop John Henshaw of Rhode Island described him at the age of thirty-six as having a robust but slightly bent frame, 'with small, but keen grey eyes, a Roman nose, more pointed and hooked than ordinary; a mouth partially opened, with irregular and projecting teeth, never fully covered by the lips; hair of a bluish cast ... in thick, bushy locks, profusely covering the shoulders, and lightly sprinkled with powder, giving the appearance of a large grey wig. His limbs were badly formed, his carriage extremely awkward, the expression of his countenance void of intelligence, and the *tout ensemble* most ungainly and forbidding.'[82] Stewart's successor in Frelighsburg, James Reid, complained that Henshaw 'has endeavoured to make the memory of a good man supremely ridiculous.' But Henshaw had concluded his vivid description with the moral lesson that, just as 'we sometimes find the best specimens of humanity in the thatched cottage, or other mean abode, so that unsightly form was tenanted by a soul of noble principles and lofty aspirings.'[83] Despite his reputation for humility, however, Stewart had certainly not been born into a thatched cottage, and he was fully aware of the advantages his privileged birth had given him in influencing the powerful.

After eight years of service in a comfortable English parish, Stewart was inclined towards service in India, but his bishop recommended him to Bishop Mountain, who was then in England and looking for someone to replace Cotton in St Armand. The young Scottish aristocrat jumped at the opportunity to minister in what was still an isolated outpost of American settlement.[84] King George III had warned Mountain that Stewart was suspected of Methodism, but when he arrived in Quebec in the fall of 1807 the bishop's sister, Mary Mountain, wrote that he 'has charmed us all, and indeed even those who were prejudiced against him ... With no advantages of person and address, with real disadvantages of voice and manner in the pulpit, before he left Quebec he gained general respect, and certainly *did* make converts of those who were disposed at first to call the real goodness of his design in question.'[85]

After considerable difficulty in finding someone to rent him a room in the initially hostile village of Frelighsburg, which he chose to locate in because Cotton was still in nearby Philipsburg, Stewart began church services in the local school. He wrote to his mother that the country 'scarcely furnishes the necessaries of life,' and later recalled that 'we had to get whatever we wanted from Montreal, as there were no stores in the country, and the northern parts of Vermont were as yet unsettled.'[86] Stewart assured his mother, however, that 'the people are worse in appearance, or rather manner, than in reality, or principle. They are very free and rude, but less profligate than in our country. They have all sorts of notions and sects in religion, rather than being less religious, or more unchristian than our people: far from it. I find sincere Christians of all denominations; and no wonder they are divided, where they have no teachers except Methodists and Baptists, and they very ignorant.' Stewart added that the people were willing to be instructed by him, and concluded, 'In short, they suit my object – of being useful to them and the Church of Christ ... I was never so much engaged in the exercises of religion as I have been since I came to St. Armand, and I never was happier.'[87]

Judging from a lengthy sermon on love that he delivered in 1815, Stewart did not tend to dwell on sin and retribution.[88] His positive outlook and his tolerant attitude towards the Yankee settlers, combined with the many acts of charity that his personal wealth made possible, quickly produced results. In his first report to the SPG in April 1808, Stewart reported that 'there are many Methodists and Baptists who have Meetings in this Neighbourhood, and it is but fair to say they are not illiberal towards me.' The church services were 'wonderfully well attended,' and the inhabitants had contributed toward the building of 'a suitable Church on a very good situation' donated by the Freligh brothers.[89] Stewart did not mention that he had paid the Frelighs £52.10s for two adjoining acres, or that half the £680 cost for the construction of Holy Trinity (which was to be the first Anglican church in the diocese of Quebec, aside from the cathedral) had been covered by himself.[90]

The conversion process had begun quickly, for Stewart's first report stated that he had baptized three adults – all were parents with several children – as well as twenty-six infants. At the Lord's Supper on Christmas Day 1808 there had been only nine communicants, but at Easter there were twenty-three. The following August, when Bishop Mountain confirmed sixty people, he wrote that 'in no part of the world, perhaps, has the power of Religion more decidedly & more rapidly manifested itself than here. Mr S., without any sort of cant, & without the least appearance of enthusiasm, has more zeal, & more persevering activity, than it has ever before been my good fortune to witness; & it has pleased God to prosper his endeavours in an extraordinary manner.' After the confirmation service, Mountain preached to a congregation of about six hundred, reporting that the psalmody was the best he had ever heard:

> The Singers, without any distinction of rank, (tho' the greater part of them were of the better class) assemble in the middle aisle, men & women; many

of them, especially the latter, young; but no children. They sing, in three parts, not with that vulgar twang, & discordant bawling which are too common at home, but with a soft & a chasten'd tone & manner; & with a perfectness of tune, & a sweetness of voice, that were really surprising ... I can not express to you the effect that this truly devotional music had upon my mind, any otherwise than by saying, that if you had been with me, I am sure you would have wept outright.[91]

Stewart obviously felt that singing was crucial to the religious service, for he had hired a choir master and had a selection of psalms printed in Montreal at his own expense.

The SPG report for 1810 claimed that satisfactory progress had also been made in Philipsburg, which Stewart had been serving since Cotton's move to Dunham in the spring of 1808. St Paul's was opened the following year at the considerable cost of £800, and, once again, nearly half the amount was contributed by Stewart.[92] Stewart's diary from this period reveals that, in addition to serving the two churches in St Armand, he was frequently on the move, preaching, baptizing, and so on, not only throughout the southern townships but also into Vermont.[93] He obtained a special licence to perform these services in Sheldon, Vermont, after the government ended unregulated cross-border traffic in September 1812. With the outbreak of hostilities, a number of families moved to the safer location of St Johns, where there was a military post, and others returned to the United States. As a result, the number of Easter communicants declined (to fifty-one) for the first time in 1813, though Stewart also blamed a prevailing sickness.[94] The following October an American surprise attack on Philipsburg resulted in one member of the militia being killed, eight wounded, and ninety taken prisoner. Stewart took an active role in lobbying for their release, stressing that the Indian corn and potatoes had not yet been harvested and 'many of their famil^s are suffering materially in consequence of their absence.' Ever the optimist, Stewart also hoped that these 'visita^{ns} of the Lord will not be unprofitable to us.'[95]

The prisoners were finally exchanged the following January, and no further conflict took place in the region because the British were content to allow the American Colonel Clark and his men to move back and forth across the border without resistance. Despite these incursions, Bishop Mountain visited the border area in March 1814 when he confirmed seventy people in the two St Armand churches, and twenty in Dunham.[96] The loyalty of most of the local American-born settlers during the war confirmed Stewart's warm feelings towards them. In a pamphlet first published in 1815 to encourage the government to develop the region, he stated that it 'must and will be settled chiefly by persons emigrating from the United States.' Stewart added that 'In many respects they make the best settlers in a new country; and the most certain way of making them, and all men, good subjects, is, taking care to promote the welfare and prosperity of the country they live in. This is chiefly to be done by making laws and regulations calculated to maintain industry, morality, and religion among the inhabitants.'[97]

A recent study claims that most of Stewart's efforts went towards constituting a regional elite,[98] but the detailed advice he sent to the young minister appointed to replace him while he travelled to England in 1815 illustrates his careful attention to pastoral work:

> Old Mr. Strike has been negligent, but I sh^d hope he will improve, & be fit if duly exhorted. Young Mrs. Wehr sh^d be counselled to be watchful and diligent, also Jo Smith & R ... Duncan has drawn back, but perhaps is recoverable. Mrs Varney, I told you, is not acceptable, at present. Miss Su Stewart, you will remember, sh^d be examined. Exhort Dr May, Mrs Moul & Mrs Yates, Humphreys – his Wife & her Sister to exercise private Devotions, etc. The following Young People particularly attend to – Vanderwaters, all Rosses & Aitkens' Family – Wehr's & Jov^h Rychard's Daughters – Fittermores – Millers – Russells – & my Godchildren – as far as you can.[99]

Conclusion

Given the limited scope of the Anglican mission in the Eastern Townships prior to the War of 1812, particularly in comparison with that of the Episcopal Methodists, one might assume that much of the radical New England religious culture had been transferred to the region. Many of the Palatine loyalists from New York may have fallen under the influence of the Anglican Church, but Joseph Badger's memoirs paint a sharply contrasting picture for the settlers east of Lake Memphremagog, even during the War of 1812. The situation was very much in flux, however, and, as Canadian historians have stressed, the war would mark a turning point, with American preachers being stopped at the border during the hostilities, and patronage as well as immigration and land policy promoting British imperial ties after peace had been attained. Colonial authorities did not prevent the expansion of American-based churches and sects in the Eastern Townships during the postwar era, but the new political context helps to explain why, rather than expending their limited resources in a British colony, they chose to focus on the demands of their own country's rapidly expanding western frontier. The result would be a religious vacuum that conservative British-based societies would hasten to exploit.

Part II
Postwar American Initiatives

3

The Congregationalists

Alhough most of the pioneer settlers were undoubtedly Congregationalists prior to leaving New England, there was no settled Congregational minister in the Eastern Townships during the pioneer prewar era. As late as 1831, Lower Canada's first official census report recorded that there were only 1,099 Congregationalists and Presbyterians (outside the Church of Scotland) in the region, or 3.2 per cent of the total Protestant population. The American missionary societies had not paid much attention to the region, and only in 1833 did the American Home Missionary Society (AHMS) begin to show an interest. That year, society president R.S. Storrs described for prospective Congregational missionaries what had originally attracted New England settlers to the Eastern Townships :

> Besides the fertility and cheapness of the soil, producing larger crops of grass, oats, wheat, etc., etc., than are produced on an equal extent of surface in New England, there is an entire exemption from taxation, except for the repair of roads; and judging from the character of most of the roads, this tax cannot be a heavy one. The large roads are constructed by the government, and paid for by funds brought from Europe. Schools and Academies are supported liberally by the same foreign munificence, more than $100,000 per annum having been expended for two or three years past, in the instruction of youth; and an established ministry is maintained by the same strong arm, giving an opportunity for the weekly worship of the sanctuary to all who value it, as conducted by an Episcopal ministry, with too little efficiency perhaps, and with no expense.

Despite the advantages enjoyed by the Church of England, however,

Storrs argued that there was ample opportunity for a more American and more independent ministry, stating that

> it is to be remembered that the clergy are, almost without exception, foreigners; that they are not chosen by their congregations, but appointed by superior authority; that they are chiefly supported by government, and not at all by the contributions of the people; that such responsibilities are not felt by them, nor by their congregations, as to create that mutual confidence, and reciprocal action, on which the usefulness of the pastoral relation essentially depends.[1]

From within the Eastern Townships, later the same year the Reverend Ammi Parker of Shipton was quoted by Storrs to the effect that '50,000 souls, descended from "freedom's pious fathers, who first landed on Plymouth's rock," and, planted within 280 miles of that consecrated spot,' should not be 'overlooked in the distribution of the means of grace, and left to die unpitied and uncared for by their more favored brethren.' Parker asked further why members of the New England church 'have compassion on the Indians of the west and the south, and have no compassion [on] us? Are our souls less precious? Are our minds less capable of culture?' He noted that from his village of Danville 'I can look to the east and the west, the north and the south, and not find a Congregational, or Presbyterian, or Baptist (except one Freewill), or Methodist minister, so near as fifty miles. Not one Congregational Church or minister so near as sixty-five miles. One High Church Episcopalian preaches within ten miles of me, half the time, and there is but one more so near as fifty miles.'[2]

Storrs added a note of urgency to the plea by claiming that, because the government-supported 'foreign' Church of England clergy would never win the hearts and minds of the American settlers, the region had become a moral wasteland. It propagated sects such as the 'Mormonites' and the 'Pilgrims,' who had set out on a pilgrimage 'toward some imaginary elysium in the West.' Storrs had his geography wrong as far as the former sect is concerned, for there is no record of a Mormon society in the Eastern Townships, and, while the Pilgrims were the one radical sect to originate in the region, they did not remain there long, as we shall see. Storrs next referred to counterfeiting, claiming that nearly all the bogus currency circulating in the United States was produced in the Eastern Townships, with paper notes coming from St Armand and coins from Barnston:

Here (until quite lately), the men employed in such works of darkness have walked forth in open day unmolested. Hundreds of subordinate agents gain their subsistence by aiding and abetting the villainy which they have not themselves ingenuity enough to practice, and the moral sense of the great mass of the community is so blunted, that speculations of this sort are regarded as no more criminal than the speculations of the merchant or the mechanic, in their regular course of business. Yet thousands and tens of thousands of our industrious citizens have been defrauded of their honest gains, by these knavish practices, and will continue to be defrauded, till the whole system of iniquity shall be broken up, by the simple energy of the Gospel.[3]

A third reason, according to Storrs, for sending Congregational missionaries into the Eastern Townships was to challenge the influence of Catholicism in the region. He stated that the priests did not proselytize among the settlers from New England, knowing that 'it is in vain to attempt to reduce them to a servile dependence,' but 'a corrupting influence is insensibly extended over them, which reaches their principles, affects their regard to the Bible, and allures them to infidelity; and yet more remotely touches the character of their children, and seduces them early into an habitual contempt of all religion.'[4]

Finally, in 1835, the AHMS did begin to support Lower Canadian missionaries through the Canada Education and Home Missionary Society (CEHMS), which had been founded in 1827 by the pastor of Montreal's American Presbyterian Church.[5] The CEHMS had, to this point, played only a small role in the Eastern Townships, helping to fund ministers in Shipton and Granby. Churches would also be established in Stanstead, Melbourne and Durham, Eaton, Compton, Sherbrooke, Potton, Philipsburg, Brome, and Inverness prior to mid-century, but the Congregationalists would remain a small minority of the region's Protestant population. Despite the willingness of most of the clergy to adapt to local circumstances, and their active role in promoting Sunday schools and temperance societies, the Congregational Church tended to have the worst of both worlds; it lacked both the radical revivalist tradition of the other American denominations, and the solid base of external support enjoyed by the Anglicans and Wesleyan Methodists. Furthermore, the highly decentralized organizational structure and strong lay tradition led to debilitating factionalism between the American and British adherents, who came from somewhat different church traditions. The Congregational churches were also damaged by the rebellions of

1837–8 which caused many American members to return to the United States. To explore these themes in more detail, the following chapter will focus on three of the principal congregations: Stanstead on the Vermont border, Shipton in the lower St Francis Valley, and Granby on the western border of the region.

Stanstead

While the village of Stanstead had been served on an irregular basis by Congregational ministers from across the border prior to 1816, it was only in that year that a covenant was drafted by a council of several American ministers meeting in Stanstead and signed by twelve men and nine women. These individuals thereby became charter members of the first Congregational church in Lower Canada. Late in 1817 a call was accepted by Thaddeus Osgood, a widely travelled itinerant evangelist of uncertain denominational affiliation who had established non-sectarian Sunday schools in Quebec and Kingston. Osgood was invited to preach in the village's large new union meeting house. As the only resident minister in the community, he served people of all the local denominations, as well as establishing the second Sunday school in the colony.[6]

Osgood was in many respects an ideal choice to serve a union church, since his first loyalty was to an evangelical united front and its many agencies of social and religious reform. According to Bishop Mountain, the Stanstead preacher had applied to him for ordination as an Anglican minister around 1810, but had been rejected as an untrustworthy and 'ignorant' man, 'unable to spell his own language correctly.'[7] Osgood was not sufficiently Calvinist to satisfy Stanstead's hard-liners, so in 1818 a council of American ministers was called to test his theological thinking. The union church, which seated fifteen hundred, was filled to overflowing and prolonged cheers reportedly followed the finding that Osgood was orthodox in his views, but this did not prevent several members from leaving to worship in the Derby, Vermont, church. As a result, Osgood soon resigned to continue a career as a well-known, if controversial, promoter of the social institutions which would ultimately replace revivalism as the primary vehicle for evangelicalism in North America.[8]

After Osgood's departure, the union church chose an Anglican minister, who was followed by two successive Wesleyan Methodists. When it became evident that another Methodist would be appointed in 1827, the Congregationalists finally withdrew to hold their own meetings in a schoolhouse. The following year, they began to build a small brick church, with a tower and bell, and sent out a call for a minister. Ammi Parker, who had recently graduated from the Congregational Theological Seminary of Vermont, happened to be visiting the grave of his father in nearby St Alban's, Vermont. Here he heard of a deputation's recent visit to recruit a minister for Stanstead, and decided to pay a visit despite his apparent trepidation about entering British territory, even fifteen years after the war had ended. Parker 'found the deacons, and the school house where they held services, to be less than two miles from Vermont, and in sight of her hills, and so felt myself safe.'[9]

Another clergyman had already answered the call, though he had yet to arrive, and Parker was invited to remain for a week in order to attend the gathering of seven Sabbath schools in the union church. He later described how approximately three hundred people arrived in carts and lumber wagons, as well as riding bareback and on foot. While encouraged by their numbers, Parker was obviously unimpressed by the meeting, for the only detail that he later recorded concerned 'an unpremeditated dog-fight' which was 'not particularly instructive to those outside, or inside,' and which 'provoked some queer remarks from the newly arrived Englishman who was at that moment the speaker.' The young preacher nevertheless agreed to remain an additional three months, for he was favourably disposed towards the two deacons and the Massachusetts-born majority of the congregation who 'were not the refuse cast off from churches there.'[10]

Parker eventually made way for the Scottish-born Joseph Gibb, who had written several volumes on contemporary theological questions but had proven to be too liberal for the majority of his Scottish congregation. While Gibb attracted large congregations in Stanstead, his dour personality and refusal to preach hell-fire apparently alienated some people. The resulting strain is said to have contributed to his early death in 1833. His supporters, some of whom had followed him from Scotland, then withdrew from the Stanstead church, probably attending services held by James Robertson, who had been a friend of Gibb's in Scotland and who now served the nearby church in Derby. As a result, there were too few families to support another Congregational minister in Stanstead.[11]

The Hampshire Central Association of Massachusetts sent ministers to supply Stanstead from time to time, and the AHMS subsidized the American Presbyterian, Austin Osgood Hubbard, in 1834. A rift now developed between Hubbard's supporters and those of another clergyman who had been on the scene before Hubbard's arrival, and who was more favourably disposed to religious revivalism. Hubbard subsequently sought out a more compatible congregation in Melbourne, leaving Stanstead without a minister after the AHMS refused financial support for his rival.[12]

Finally, in the spring of 1836, the Hampshire Central Association agreed to fund Lewis Sabin, said to be 'a young man of fine talent,' for one year.[13] Sabin reported in September of the same year that there were seventy church members, with one hundred to one hundred and fifty regularly attending Sabbath services. He admitted that there were more Methodists than Congregationalists in his church, but argued that most of the people were still indifferent to religion: 'multitudes have learned from the [sy]stem of Universalism to whisper – 'peace, peace' – to the troubled conscience & others have declined to infidelity.' Sabin felt that the most promising development was the establishment of six Sabbath schools with over two hundred scholars, many of whose parents did not attend meeting themselves.[14] When Sabin's term ended in June 1837, he decided to leave Stanstead despite the majority's wish to retain him. He claimed that 'there are very strong prejudices against this church which will very much hinder a minister's usefulness,' and added that 'they are directed against some of the principal & most valuable members of the church.' Sabin failed to explain what he meant by this statement, but Stanstead was sharply divided politically in this pre-rebellion era, and three of the most influential tories in the community – Benjamin Pomroy, William Ritchie, and Dr Moses French Colby – were members of the Congregational Church. Sabin stated that he had preached 190 times during the year, and travelled eighteen hundred miles, but had added only five members to the church. He concluded that his talents were not suited to Stanstead because he was not sufficiently 'ready in extemporaneous speaking,' and he was too inexperienced to have 'hundreds of sermons prepared, like Br. Chapin.' Finally, Sabin, who was married, had not expected the cost of living to be so high. While the AHMS had promised $600, his final salary was only $400, to which the people would be able to add very little.[15]

Some stability was finally achieved with Sabin's successor, R.V. Hall, who was a native of Stanstead. Hall reported in December 1837, after the outbreak of the rebellion, that he had set aside a day of fasting and prayer, for 'Truly it is time for Christians to humble themselves & cry unto the Lord to have mercy upon our blood-stained country.' The congregation of about 150 was finally 'in a harmonious state,' though there had been 'none of the special outpouring of the Holy Spirit upon us since I arrived here.' By the following month, in January 1838, Hall was able to report that meetings were 'becoming serious & solemn and I have greate [*sic*] hope that the Lord is about to pour out his Spirit.' But attention was soon distracted by the military threat to Stanstead. Hall made his own political sympathies clear when he reported that approximately 150 active rebel sympathizers had fled the country 'for their country's good.' He added that the Americans would probably provide 'as much sympathy for them as though they were poor Polanders just escaped from Siberian slavery.'[16]

As of July 1838, Hall detected no 'very apparent seriousness on the minds of the people,' though the five Sabbath schools were well attended. But one of the major problems faced by the church was the ongoing departure of so many of its prominent members, including Silas Dickerson, whose reform newspaper had been put out of business, and J.S. Walton, who had left to publish a conservative newspaper in Sherbrooke. In December, Hall reported that the meeting house was taken over as a barracks, with the pulpit being used for whiskey bottles and the sacred desk converted into a card table. While the officers had put an end to the gambling, 'it is still like a cage of unclean birds.' No weekday meetings could be held, and the house was not fit for worship on the Sabbath. Hall had also been preaching on the Vermont side of the border, thereby attracting many to the Stanstead meetings, but he now lamented that 'all the People at the Line are strongly prejudiced against the Tory party, & will probably not very soon attend meeting again in Canada.' Approximately one hundred people from the Eastern Townships had gone to Derby, 'and they enlist a great deal of sympathy for the '*poor Patriots*' by their falsehoods.'[17]

Hall was not entirely discouraged by the political situation, however, for he claimed in January 1839 that the wounding of Captain Kilborn by a hidden assailant the previous November had resulted in a tremendous change in the Eastern Townships: 'Almost all classes who desire the civil, moral, & religious welfare of this county have rallied around the standard of their country & girded on their armour, with a determination to defend their property, their wives and their children from a hoard [*sic*] of robers [*sic*] who fear not God nor regard the rights of man.' The ladies had formed a sewing circle of forty members to help in 'the great & glorious work of 'enlightening & christianizing the world''; Hall's wife was leading 'an interesting Bible class of 10 or 12 young ladies'; the five Sabbath schools were well sustained; and, even though more than forty

Congregationalists (including eighteen full members) had left, the congregation was larger than ever. Hall concluded, however, that the large garrison had impeded religious progress, and there had still 'been nothing like a "*Revival of Religion*" with us the past year.'[18]

Two months later, in March 1839, Hall reported that there were 72 churchmen, 52 of whom were in communion. Since the congregation was said to be about 150, with an average of 100 attending Sabbath, a considerable number of them were presumably not Congregationalists. During the following months, influential members continued to move away, and Hall lamented in October that it would be many years before the church recovered 'from the pernicious effects of the late unhappy commotions.' The congregation nevertheless continued to grow, there was a good Sabbath school, and the ladies' sewing circle remained in a prosperous state. Finally, in March 1841, Hall was able to report that many neighbourhoods had been 'blessed with an interesting revival of religion,' though the village of Stanstead 'has not been so signally blessed as some other parts of the town.'[19]

Hall was more dissatisfied with his remuneration, complaining that the congregation had been unable to make up for the $50 reduction in the AHMS grant to maintain his salary at $500 a year. In order to help them, he had taken 'a considerable part of my salary in such things as they could best spare from the farm or the shop.' Not only was the cost of living higher in Stanstead than in Montreal, but because of his location on the border he received a good many calls from American ministers on their way to visit friends in the Eastern Townships, or simply to report

> that *they have seen Canada* ... They look upon me as a missionary in a *foreign* land, and they think I must be as glad to see people from the *United States* as an American missionary would be if he were in the middle of *Affrica*. Some of them I am glad to see, others are really tedious, some of them ask a hundred questions about the *Despotism*, the *Heathenism* & the *Romanism* of Canada, and I want to say that it does not grieve me much when they give me an affectionate farewell saying 'we shall *probably never meet together again in this world.*'[20]

The Stanstead church had barely recovered from the rebellions when it was hit by another crisis, the arrival of millenarian Millerite preachers from south of the border. Hall reported that in May 1842 the Millerites held a local meeting 'which continued about three weeks and was attended by thousands, more than 20 ministers took part in the meeting and nearly all of them proclaimed to their hearers that the world is to be burned up in 1843. During this meeting all other meetings except ours was suspended.' Hall did not attend himself, and did what he could to discourage his congregation from doing so. While only two Congregational members had joined the movement, a number of supporters now refused to contribute to Hall's support, 'for say they a minister cannot believe the Bible and not be convinced that the world is to be destroyed in the Spring of 1843.' Despite the excitement, Hall felt that a reaction was already taking place 'and I hope after a while this wild fire will be quenched without any serious injury to the cause of truth.'[21]

But matters turned dramatically for the worse the following fall, for Hall reported in November 1842 that some of the township's most respectable families had converted to Millerism, though most of the converts had been Methodists. Several Congregational families (but only three church members), had joined them, 'but how soon others may leave us I know not. I have witnessed such astonishing scenes during a few weeks past that I am prepared for almost any thing.'[22] In January 1843 Hall reported that eleven people had joined the Congregational church during the previous year, but 'the Millerite excitement still prevails to a very alarming state.' The AHMS had withdrawn its support from Canada in 1842,[23] and the finances of Stanstead's Congregational church remained in very shaky condition. Hall had been paid only $60, not in cash but in cabinet work and produce. Even the Ladies' Sewing Society had been inactive because Mrs Ritchie (the treasurer) had moved to Sherbrooke, and Hall's wife (the president) had been confined to her bed for eight months.[24]

Hall's report of April 1843 was still more alarmist concerning the Millerites, whom he said had been holding meetings every day and night. Without giving Millerism any credit for the heightened religious zeal in the community, Hall added that 'a number of our congregation have been awakened by the Holy Spirit.' Within the previous nine months, sixteen people had joined the church, and there had been revivals, especially among the young, in the villages of Stanstead Plain and Derby Line. Clearly contributing to the general sense of religious hysteria was the erysipelas epidemic that had persevered in the area for months. Hall's April report added: 'During the past year there has been more sickness in this town than was ever known since the country was settled. Many of our most enterprising inhabitants have been suddenly removed by death.' Hall had preached forty funeral sermons during the previous year, and 'been called almost daily to visit the sick or dying.'[25]

The following month Stanstead's church committee wrote that Millerism remained 'the blast and the mildew to all this part of the country,' and that Hall's strong stand against it had 'offended some, who have withdrawn from him their aid and left our congregation.' Only two members had resigned, however, and prospects were encouraging: 'A number of our congregation have been led from darkness to light.'[26] Stanstead's Congregational church was clearly recovering by December 1844 when Hall wrote that the meetings were very well attended, more than usual interest was shown in the Sabbath school, and there was more harmony among the people than at any point since he had arrived.[27] The reports end here, but by mid-century the Stanstead Congregationalists remained a rather small minority even in this border township where their missions in the region had first begun. The 1852 *Census Reports* list 380 Congregationalists, the second largest number in the region, but outnumbered by the township's 1,955 Methodists, 459 Catholics, and 424 Second Adventists (successors to the Millerite movement), and only slightly ahead of the 363 Universalists and Unitarians, and 356 Anglicans.

Shipton

Upon leaving Stanstead to Joseph Gibb in 1828, Ammi Parker's explorations farther afield revealed 'the nakedness of the land, in reference to the stated ordinances and Institutions of religion.' He therefore decided that his calling lay north of the American border, though 'I knew of no friend in all New England who would approve my choice of such a Field, nor any Society ready to give me any appointment in such territory.' Parker's sense of providential mission was reinforced after he had ridden the two hundred miles back to Burlington, only to learn from the secretary of the Vermont Domestic Missionary Society that a newly formed missionary society in Montreal (the CEHMS) was asking that missionaries be sent to a little-known section of the country where there resided a considerable New England population. Because Parker had been 'upon the very ground,' he was the man they needed. After being ordained as an evangelist at the quarterly meeting of the Addison Association, Parker presented his credentials in Montreal to the officers of the CEHMS. He received the first commission issued by that society, and was given free rein to choose a specific field of operations.[28]

Parker initially decided upon the Lake Memphremagog area, which included the communities of Georgeville, Brown's Hill, and the Outlet

(Magog), but competition from Baptist and Methodist preachers soon caused him to retreat to the outermost frontier of New England settlement, the village of Danville in Shipton Township. Joseph Badger had preached there briefly during the War of 1812, and there had once been a Methodist society in the settlement which had collapsed with the withdrawal of the Methodist Episcopal ministry from the region in 1821. Congregational ministers were generally not interested in competing for converts from other denominations, and Parker clearly felt that his services would be most useful in a community deprived of any religious institutions. He also later claimed that by establishing himself on the outer edge of American settlement he had hoped to attract more New England Congregationalists northward to take land in the intervening townships.[29]

Parker painted a bleak picture of the state of religion upon his arrival in Shipton. The Sabbath was devoted to 'excursions for fishing, gaming & caballing,' every family included members 'who habitually profaned the name of Jehovah,' and 'the few who professed religion slept with the world or like the Ishmaelites had "their hands ags't every man & every man's hands ags't them".' Parker's first sermons attracted large crowds, though 'there were few praying ones among them.'[30] By 1829, however, Parker could report to the CEHMS that 'already Society wears a very different aspect from what it wore when I commenced here. If there has been no revival of *religion* I hope there has been a revival of *morals*.' Each Sunday 250 or more gathered to worship, and there were over one hundred in the Sabbath school, many of them older than fifteen. Parker's wife, Eveline, later wrote that the Sabbath school embraced all but the elderly, and that it had never been closed, even in winter.[31]

Despite Parker's optimistic reports, the Lower Canadian census for 1831 records only fifty-four Congregationalists in Shipton Township, a full two years after his arrival. Clearly feeling that a more dramatic initiative was needed before attempting the formal establishment of a church, the tall, slow-spoken preacher organized a four-day outdoor prayer meeting with the assistance of Stanstead's Wesleyan Methodist preacher, John Hick, and a Congregational clergyman from Irasburg, Vermont, named O.T. Curtis.[32] They were joined by four or five 'lay brethren' from various other localities. As a result, the long-awaited religious revival finally took place, but it would prove to be a somewhat problematic event in Parker's rather conservative mind.

The second Great Awakening that followed the War of Independence had, in turn, spawned a puritan counter-reformation which adhered to the Calvinist orthodoxy that revivals were solely the work of God 'who would bestow his saving grace only as he himself willed upon a totally undeserving people.' Parker was a product of that tradition, but, during the late 1820s, Charles Finney of western New York developed his so-called new measures of revival preaching. His strategy included protracted meetings that were announced and prepared for in advance in order to build up the community's anticipation, an 'anxious bench' in front of the congregation to isolate the half-willing so that they could be made the object of direct concern during the preaching, and an 'inquiry room' where they could be met with privately between the services.[33] Finney's theology challenged Calvinism by arguing that the unconverted were responsible for resisting saving grace, and a process which had taken several months to two or three years to complete was now experienced 'as an abrupt, cataclysmic, and deeply transforming event.' The emphasis was no longer on private devotion and individual consultation with the pastor, but on 'prayer, exhortation, song and confession' to meld the entire congregation into 'a fervent community of feeling.'[34]

The Danville revival, as described forty years later by Eveline Parker, clearly took on many of these dramatic characteristics. Because it rained the first day, the meeting opened in the log school house, which could seat one hundred. At the end of the day's exhortations, meetings of prayer and enquiry were held in the evening. With the second day opening bright and sunny, the congregation moved to the nearby maple grove in which seats and a platform had been built. According to Mrs Parker, the sermons of the Methodist Reverend Hick, who did most of the preaching during the first two days, 'were plain and pungent, destroying the sinner's hope and refuge, only as he rested on Christ for his hope and Salvation.' Though the British Wesleyans had rejected the use of camp meetings, Hick had succeeded in launching a successful revival in Stanstead. The Congregational Reverend Curtis had a different style, for he was 'persuasive and earnest,' though apparently no less effective. Finally, two deacons went from house to house, 'confirming the words of the preacher and entreating the parents and children to become reconciled to God.' The week culminated with the Sabbath when as many as one thousand met 'in this wilderness' which had been made 'to bud and blossom as the rose.'[35]

Ammi Parker was obviously less comfortable than his wife was with this 'socially engineered' process, which would come into disrepute among Congregationalists when the University of Vermont condemned the flamboyant Jedidiah Burchard's revivals of 1835–6.³⁶ Even though Parker claimed to be convinced that the 'spirit of God moved upon the hearts of the people,' he later wrote that he had been concerned that too many people had been 'merely awaken^d & excit.^{d} without much knowl.^{g} of truth – or of steady Chr.^{n} purpose, or example.' They would 'need to consider & pray & learn before they c.^{d} safely assume the responsibility of taking lead in such an association as a Ch.^{n} Church.' Parker's reservations about quick conversions prevented him from establishing a church in 1831, and he appears never again to have sponsored a religious revival.

Finally in 1832 the cautious Parker decided that the time was ripe to establish a church.³⁷ The first meeting was attended, in Parker's words, by only three 'feeble & faint-hearted' men. But there was also present a 'Mother in Israel' who asked 'Couldn't we have a *female* church? Don't you think the Lord would approve of it, if the men were not willing to come? For one I have been starving without the Gospel ordinances, till gray hairs are upon me, and if the Lord will grant me such a privilege, I desire to sit down at his table, at least once before I die.' This speech proved to be the turning point, for the decision was then made to proceed with the formal organization. Sessions were repeatedly held until twelve men and twenty-three women were 'approved and accepted' as charter members by those who would later join the church 'according to Cong.'l Church usage.' Parker proceeded to baptize seven persons by immersion and two by sprinkling, for he regarded either model to be valid, declaring them to be members of 'a *Church of Christ* duly constituted.'³⁸ The following year, in March 1833, Parker reported that the 'political & irreligious excitements' of the era were not disturbing his congregation, which was 'gaining ground gradually.' A few months later, however, the local church committee reported to the CEHMS that 'few of the independant [sic] Farmers are pious; & [a] universalist Preacher, (like Rubshukah of old) has been in this place a portion of of [sic] the time, for 2 years past, Opposition to the preaching of Mr Parker has been waged with some violence by the more irreligious & a numb[er] who were among the most liberal at first, now find an excuse for doing nothing.'³⁹

Parker himself later admitted that his church remained in a somewhat languid state, but the temperance movement would soon renew local religious enthusiasm. Parker claimed in one of his sermons that an 'intemperate man reclaimed seems almost a Saint & there is great probability if men can be induced to repent & reform *that* sin that they will renounce all *others*.'⁴⁰ The Danville minister's message was clearly heard, for he recorded in 1834 that 'Intemperance appears to have received the stamp of reprobation in our community. Buildings are raised and farm work prosecuted, without the monster's aid, except as a few of the more worthless perpetuate the curse upon themselves.' Parker estimated that the amount of ardent spirits consumed in the parish had declined by four-fifths during the previous year.⁴¹

As a result of the emergence of societies such as the American Bible Society (1816), American Sunday School Union (1824), American Home Missionary Society (1826), American Temperance Society (1826), and American Anti-Slavery Society (1833), the spiritual energy generated by the religious revivals was channelled towards the establishment of a moral order.⁴² But one would be mistaken to associate this process with secularization, for Parker's temperance ardour revealed him to be a product of the Congregational Church's 'Age of Benevolence' during which social reforms and evangelization were promoted as harbingers of the millennium, that is (in contrast to the premillennialism of the Millerites), the thousand years of peace and plenty prior to Christ's return and the end of the world. The temperance cause clearly benefited Parker's religious mission, for the church committee reported in 1834 that it 'has served, more than any one thing else, to do away prejudice from the minds of unreasonable men against him who is set over us in the L^d.'⁴³ But his strongest support, according to Parker, came from the women's prayer meetings which were more fully attended than those of the men. Parker's strong temperance stance may largely explain why women continued to dominate the Danville church in terms of numbers, for they still outnumbered the male full members by sixty-eight to twenty-six in 1850.⁴⁴ Parker's reports to the CEHMS during the early 1840s also reveal that there was a Ladies' Home Missionary Society in Danville, and that women were more successful than men in teaching Sunday school.

Meanwhile, because Parker had been forced to act as his own bishop (to use his words) when he established the local church in 1832, he was formally installed by three Congregational missionaries and a deacon two years later. One of them described how 'the most perfect order and regularity of deportment' prevailed among the large congregation, which met 'on the bare, outspread earth' beneath 'the broad canopy of heaven, and the stately forest.'⁴⁵ Parker's formal installation may have been stimulated by the fact that the provincial government had recently removed the civil disabilities of the dissenting churches. He would be the first minister from a non-established church in the district to take advantage of the new legislation by applying for the credentials which would allow him to register baptisms, marriages and burials.[46] Parker later recalled that, after reading his certificates, Judge John Fletcher of Sherbrooke 'threw them back with a contemptuous sneer,' stating that they should be printed on parchment rather than on common paper, and that he had no proof that the signatures were not forgeries. When the young clergyman submitted a four-page affidavit testifying to the authenticity of the signatures, Fletcher announced that the new legislation simply permitted dissenting ministers to record the acts in question, not actually to perform them. Parker reportedly replied that such prerogatives came from a higher source than civil government, but he was forced to find two influential Congregationalists in Sherbrooke who would provide security for £200 each. Finally, after further interrogation and another ten days' delay, Fletcher provided Parker with the authorization he had applied for. Such arbitrary and officious behaviour was typical of the English-born judge, who single-handedly did much to alienate the local population from the colonial administration.[47]

During the thirty-four years which followed his accreditation, Parker performed 393 marriages, 446 burials, and 431 baptisms. The low ratio of baptisms to marriages during an era of high birth rates is striking, and to some extent it probably reflects the exodus of newly-wed couples. But it also resulted from the American Congregational practice of distinguishing between 'church' and 'society,' that is, between covenanting and non-covenanting members. While the Puritans' 'Half-Way Covenant' permitted the children of full church members to be baptized, those of non-covenanting members would presumably not have qualified. The Canadian churches which followed the British Congregational tradition apparently never adopted the division between covenanting and non-covenanting members, and Eddy claims that it soon ceased to be more than a nominal distinction even within the American-founded churches of the Eastern Townships. But table 3.1 reveals that the Congregational Church in Lower Canada separated church members from the congregation as a whole, and Eddy admits that this distinction was not formally abolished in the Stanstead parish until 1912.[48] In congregations of mixed American-British composition, as we shall see, baptisms became a major bone of contention.

United as his congregation was, Parker was never able to rely entirely on the financial support of his rather small flock. Parker's contract continued to be renewed annually (at least in the early years) by a committee which declared simply that he would be paid the amount noted beside each of the attached names.[49] Considerable pressure must have been exerted on each church member to subscribe a fixed amount because the congregation had pledged at the start to pay Parker $200 a year, plus 'all that is in our power to collect & obtain' as a supplement for his family's support. The pledge was soon raised to £100 ($400) a year, which was the sum that the AHMS considered necessary for a minister to support a family, but the Danville congregation appears never to have delivered the full amount.[50] The agreement signed in August 1832 by a committee of five lists twenty-eight names (one was later crossed out), all male, with promised contributions ranging from $1.00 to $10.00, and totalling only $132.50. However, the deficit was met in part by the CEHMS, which arranged for Parker to spend one-quarter of his time serving as its agent in return for a £25 annual grant to supplement his income. Two years later, in 1834, the Ladies' Sewing Circle of Montreal's American Presbyterian Church became Parker's chief source of outside support.[51] A contract signed in 1837 also reveals that Parker was granted $150 that year from the AHMS on condition that he receive no subsidy from any other such organization. This contract was renewed the following year,[52] and the CEHMS records indicate that Danville remained dependent on outside support until at least the mid-1840s. The closest the growing congregation was able to come to the agreed-upon salary during these early years was in 1839, when fifty individuals agreed to payments totaling $227.50.[53]

The initial contracts had stated that two-thirds of the payments would be in produce of the country and one-third in cash, but Parker later claimed that his early payments were almost entirely in 'truck', with the cash being barely sufficient to pay his postage.[54] An examination of Parker's accounts reveals that he was exaggerating to some extent, but that most families did deliver their payments in kind.[55] Thus the 110 entries in 1830 produced $45.48 in cash and the rest in goods or labour, not all of which was given a monetary value. The most common commodity was wheat, with eighteen deliveries throughout the year totalling twenty and a half bushels. Other food items included potatoes, corn, rye, buckwheat, apples, cheese, butter, pork, beef, lamb, mutton, veal, maple sugar, vinegar, cabbages, and turnips. Six deliveries of oats were recorded in a variety of ways – bushels, bundles, and cash value – while the four hay deliveries were recorded as loads, cash value, and 'enough to keep my horse about 11 weeks.' Another payment, valued at $7.00, was simply listed as being in grain, keeping a cow, and hay. The remaining miscellaneous items included wool, tallow, soap, one dozen candles, 24 'skns' sewing silk, an unspecified quantity of fulled cloth, one pair of shoes and slippers, one pair of socks, two tumblers, four tin milk pans, 55 bricks, and 95 pine boards. This wide variety of goods presents a striking contrast to the seigneurial parishes, where tithes were paid to the curé only in grain, though in the Catholic parishes of the Eastern Townships there was commonly a supplement of hay, potatoes, and maple sugar.

The fact that these goods were delivered to Parker on a regular basis throughout the year, suggests that most were consumed by his family rather than being sold for cash. With twenty-five entries for July, this was much the most popular month for payments, but September – when Parker could rely on his own small harvest – was the only month in which none were forthcoming. Thereafter, each family appears to have delivered produce or other items as they could spare them or as the minister needed them. Two men paid with their labour or by exchanging services, such as providing Parker with a cutter to go to Montreal.

The degree to which Parker's daily material life was tied to that of his parishioners is remarkable, and much the same pattern can be discerned for the last full year of his account book, 1847. The number of entries had declined to fifty-two, cash payments totalled only $27.50, and contribution in food items had declined, but labour had become a more important mode of payment than in 1830, perhaps because Parker had his own land to work by this time. This farm was doubtless necessary to feed his growing family, which by 1851 had reached seven children aged five to twenty, plus his mother-in-law and a young servant. Parker wrote somewhat bitterly in 1850 that his yearly income was less than $30 per family member, and that he had never purchased 'a coat for my back from any property or money contributed by the people for my salary.'[56] Though he fails to mention it in any of his writings, however, Parker was clearly involved in more than a small subsistence agricultural endeavour. In 1852, thirty-eight of his 480 acres were in crop, thirty acres in pasture, and two acres in garden and orchard. Indeed, the Danville minister's farm was operated on a larger scale than those of nearly all his neighbours, for the average holding in Shipton Township was 109 acres, with thirty-seven acres under improvement. Only twenty-one of 397 farms were larger than two hundred acres.[57]

Despite the ongoing poverty of the Danville congregation, its church passed quickly through the primitive pioneer stage. A sizable chapel, measuring forty-two feet by fifty feet, was completed in 1837 with the assistance of $400 'from benevolent friends abroad.'[58] Visiting the area in 1843, the Anglican Bishop of Quebec wrote in his journal: 'I passed through the good-looking village of Danville, having a respectable Congregational meeting-house, with a steeple, and some houses indicating the possession of substantial comforts.'[59] A local resident, F.P. Cleveland, later recalled the high-backed pews, the 'fair library of books for those days,' and 'the gallery over the front vestibule which was occupied by the choir.' The 1830s and 1840s had brought the emergence of music as a major component of evangelical devotion in New England,[60] and Cleveland's most vivid recollection was of the choir, which he himself belonged to. It initially consisted of four sopranos, two altos, three tenors, and five base voices. In 1848 the tuning fork was replaced by a cello, to which was soon added a small reed instrument of about four octaves: 'The Keys were upright ivory pegs, the bellows was worked with rocking motion by the forearms.'[61] In this respect, the Congregationalists contrasted sharply with their more dour Scots Presbyterian brethren, many of whom continued to view the organ as the devil's instrument.

Cleveland's description speaks to the well-established nature of the Danville congregation, but Parker himself must have had little time for such cultural pursuits. His 1834 report to the Montreal Ladies' Sewing Society provides a good description of his weekly routine in the early years. He preached twice on Sundays, '& when weather & health would admit attended a third service in the evening.' Each week he rode from two to eight miles to 'attend' lectures, and on Saturday evening he led a Bible class and prayer meeting. During the week previous to the Communion service, held on the last Sunday of the year, Parker had attended a temperance meeting, a church meeting and 'Preparatory Lecture,' a funeral, and a Bible class, as well as preparing for a meeting in Vermont on behalf of the CEHMS. En route to this event the following week, he preached in several 'destitute places' where people pleaded for regular religious services.[62] During his many absences from Danville, Parker was replaced by a young teacher who had studied for the ministry.[63]

Parker's arrangement with the Montreal missionary society was initially to travel to New England in order to raise funds and interest American clerics in serving Canadian churches. During his first five-week tour through Vermont in February and March 1833, he collected $130.22 and interviewed a number of ministers, but failed to exact commitments from any of them.[64] Prior to his second two-month tour, the following year, Parker asked for more specific instructions: 'Tell me how much you want I should beg for *money*, whether I shall spend much time ... with any ministers in order to get them ousted from their present stations, etc. ... & pray much for success for I feel as tho. you had chosen a poor thing for an agent, & fear that the Tour may not tell upon the interests of Zion as we *wish*.' The society secretary's only response was to leave 'almost everything to your discretion.'[65]

Parker was able to find two or three prospective candidates,[66] but both he and the missionary societies were very selective about the type of men they wanted. The secretary of the Massachusetts Society, R.S. Storrs (who had sent a lengthy plea for the Eastern Townships mission to the AHMS in 1833), wrote in January 1834: 'It will be utterly in vain to send men to Canada who will not go from house to house, from village to village, from town to town, and from county to county 'if by *any* means they may save *some*'.'[67] The following June, Storrs added that several ministers had expressed their willingness to serve in the Townships, but they were not the 'right' men: 'You know full well that it is not *every* man who does good in N. Eng. that will do good in C. And we must find *young* men – men of spirit, zeal, and devotedness, who will readily identify themselves with the people – none others can become permanent Pastors.' The rub, according to the Massachusetts spokesman, was that these young men would not go to Canada without their fathers' permission, and this would never be granted until more was learned of the country. The Townships settlers would, therefore, have to await the results of temporary missions which would make their region better known. Adopting Storrs' strategy, the AHMS did send two missionaries into the Eastern Townships in 1834, but without substantial short-term results.[68]

Enticed by the prospect of a $500 annual salary, Parker somewhat reluctantly agreed to become the CEHMS's travelling and corresponding agent on a more permanent basis in 1835, but he refused to give up his Danville post, and he insisted on limiting his absences from home to two or three months per year.[69] The CEHMS soon offered the position of full-time agent to the more accommodating W.F. Curry, though the board did ask Parker to attend the state ministerial meetings of both Vermont and New Hampshire in another attempt to recruit support.[70] Despite his approaches in private to a score of the Vermont ministers, Parker claimed that he found their watchword to be 'Fortify at home.'[71] As for New Hampshire, after labouring 'publicly & from house to house,' Parker did manage to elicit a promise from the secretary of the state missionary society to send and sustain one recruit in Lower Canada. New Hampshire's annual report for that year stated:

There are few of us who have not some relative, some former acquaintance, or neighbor now living in Canada. Yet it has not been generally known, until of late, that there is a protestant population in Lower Canada of 50,000, and but two ministers of our own denomination ... Now we are among the nearest neighbours to these our destitute brethren and sisters. Of whom have they a stronger and more reasonable claim![72]

Parker then broke off communications with the CEHMS for a couple of years, until he was asked in 1837 to keep an eye on the students from the Andover Theological Seminary whom Curry had begun to recruit as temporary workers in the Townships.[73] Parker congratulated Curry on his success in finding recruits, but he was less than sanguine about future prospects: 'I am not sure what the results of these things will be. The turmoils that exist, the itch for removal, the jealousy existing, & the prejudice ags.[t] our sort of religion & hatred of all religion & the covetousness & ignorance & dwarfishness of Christians in Canada hardly looks like making a successful onset upon the man of Sin in this province.'[74] The depressed state of mind reflected in Parker's letter stemmed in part from the onset of a prolonged period of debilitating illness. In August 1837 the Danville minister reported that during the previous six months he had been suffering from a 'spinal affection accompanied with nervous debility, loss of appetite & prostration of strength.' It is more than likely that the discouraging circumstances Parker himself faced during this era of economic and political crisis contributed to his illness. He had reported in July that the state of affairs in his parish was unchanged: 'most of our church is in depressed circumstances & caring & laboring to get bread for their families. Some of them have lived for some days in succession without Bread, Meat, or Potatoes.' Parker added that there was no actual physical suffering, and that the approaching harvest would soon bring relief, 'But while the mind is occupied intensely about bread or any thing else. The things of the K.[m] of God are crowded out.'[75]

Parker was contemplating spending half his time in another parish in order to make ends meet, but, with his physician's warning that further mental effort would lead to paralysis, he was instead forced to arrange with the AHMS in November 1837 for an assistant to take over most of his duties in Danville.[76] Despite their minister's forced inactivity, a Danville church committee reported a year later that it had found 'the voice of the people to be allmost [sic] unanimous' in wishing him to remain with them.[77]

Parker recuperated slowly thereafter, and, in April 1840, he reported that he had been 'performing the usual routine of pastoral labor as I had strength to do.'[78] By this time, Parker had once again begun visiting other churches in the Eastern Townships on behalf of the CEHMS. In 1841 the Montreal society offered him $150 a year to visit all the Congregational churches in the province in order to collect the Home Mission funds (subtracting his expenses) and ascertain their 'pecuniary capabilities.' His report was to include an account of all the property in each church and in its congregation, the amount of religious instruction, the state of the Sabbath schools and Bible classes, the degree of circulation of religious publications, and the religious state of the people in general. Finally, Parker was to 'make it a point to bring out their energies both in the support of gospel ordinances and in active benevolence.'[79] Thus began the Danville minister's travels to Inverness, Durham, Melbourne, Sherbooke, Eaton and other Congregational centres within the region for approximately six weeks each year. Parker had already helped to organize churches in Eaton Township and Sherbrooke in 1835, and another in Melbourne and Durham in 1837. His experiences on these often hazardous journeys would make up the bulk of his second major unpublished manuscript, 'Memories of Life in Canada', written in 1875.[80]

Parker was also the most diligent attendant of the meetings held by the St Francis Association of Ministers, and the one generally chosen to act as agent on its behalf. In 1837, for example, he was appointed to attend the annual conventions of the New Hampshire General Association and its Vermont counterpart. Following the American tradition of establishing ministerial associations rather than ad hoc councils, as in England, the five Congregational ministers of the Eastern Townships had organized the St Francis Association of Congregational and Presbyterian Ministers in 1836. By taking this step, they assumed the power to examine, and to issue licences to, those who were called to preach by local communities within the district. They also became a disciplinary body, for article twelve declared that 'Every member of this Association shall be answerable to the body as the proper board of trial in case of unchristian walk or heresy; and the rule of discipline shall be that pointed out in the 18th chapter of Matthew.'[81]

Association meetings were held several times a year (semi-annually by 1842) at the homes of the various members, with one of them preaching the public sermon and each of the others presenting a paper in closed session on a previously chosen topic. The topics chosen included the best means of promoting spirituality among ministers, the measures to be used in protracted meetings, and 'Ought women to be allowed to speak in public religious meetings.' Reflecting the distinctively ecumenical approach of the Congregationalists, Ammi Parker spoke at one meeting 'on the spirit we should exhibit and course we should pursue concerning other denominations immediately among us.'[82] Concerning the disposal of the clergy reserve revenues, the association upheld the voluntarist principle of church support in 1841.

The aim of the St Francis Association was clearly to provide the local ministers with a social, spiritual, and intellectual forum, as well as to act as a regulating and lobbying body. It attempted to launch a provincial association of evangelical ministers belonging to various denominations in 1838, but a meeting attended by delegates from Montreal and New Hampshire decided that 'it is *not expedient* at present to call such a convention.'[83] Pressures for a separate denominational identity were evidently stronger outside the Eastern Townships than within it. Other local attempts were made to form non-sectarian associations, but the only concrete result appears to have been the district temperance society launched in 1841. With several congregations bitterly divided between the quite distinctive American and British traditions, the forces of division were still stronger than the forces of unity even within the Congregational Church.

In addition to attending various association meetings in New England, Parker was selected by his colleagues in 1840 as the most suitable person to visit the member churches of the Eastern Townships and prepare a report on the same. Despite his many absences, Parker's role in his local community went beyond providing religious services for his own congregation. The 1840s brought major reforms to the provincial school system, with state aid tied to the taxes raised by locally elected school commissions, and Parker later recalled that because he was the only person in the community capable of conducting a business meeting, he acted as chairman of the Shipton school commission until about 1860. He also served as an official school visitor, going to every school in the township twice a year, and he was instrumental in raising the funds to build the village's first academy in 1854. Finally, Parker had initiated the local temperance movement, and he was one of Danville's two representatives at the region's first temperance convention held in Sherbrooke in 1846.[84]

The Danville minister had clearly adopted the evangelical ethic of 'usefulness,'[85] and it is striking that someone of his energy and influence would spend virtually his whole career in a rather remote rural community. Parker had often considered moving to a wealthier place, writing as early as 1833 that he was aware that 'this people need faithful & constant preaching,' and that the establishment of his church had exerted an influence on people elsewhere in the region, stimulating a desire for their own churches. But the calls were so pressing from other places 'that at times I have thought I ought to quit this for a more extensive field.'[86] But given the aggressive tactics of the Church of England and the more evangelical churches throughout the Eastern Townships, perhaps it is not surprising that the rather cautious and conservative Parker would remain where he had managed to establish a secure foothold within the community. By doing so, he perpetuated his church's tradition that the minister's tie was first and foremost to his congregation.

Despite his outside activities – motivated to a considerable extent by financial necessity – Parker's ministry represented the continuity of an era when pastors were tightly integrated into the social structure of the communities within which they were more or less permanently settled. (As we shall see, the same was true of a number of other Congregational and Anglican clergy in the region.) The fact that only a minority in Shipton belonged to Parker's denomination, which was outnumbered at mid-century by Catholics, Anglicans, Universalists, Methodists, and Presbyterians (in that order), was mitigated by his ecumenical outlook, and by the fact that he was the only cleric in the village of Danville for over thirty years of his career. Parker's primary role may have been to serve one small remnant of a religious denomination which had been eclipsed in the United States and English-speaking British North America by the rise of a more individualistic ethos, but by training and temperament he was inclined to interpret his community rather broadly.

Granby and Shefford

Adopting the Articles of Faith and Covenant observed by their Vermont counterparts, Granby's Congregational Church was founded in 1830, two years before Ammi Parker had organized the one in Danville. In Granby's founding congregation were only seven men and four women, and a year later the Lower Canadian *Census Reports* recorded only twenty-nine Congregationalists and Presbyterians in the township. Their first two ministers appointed by the CEHMS each left within a year and, unlike most of the other Congregational churches in the region, there would be a regular turnover of incumbents in Granby.[87] A major factor in that turnover was the internal division between the British and American factions of the church, though this friction was also common in other congregations.

The English-born John Gleed, who arrived in January 1833, would remain longer, though he failed to win the support of the American population, and particularly the elite in the village of Granby. Gleed's first detailed report to the CEHMS stated that he preached regularly in about half a dozen settlements, including the village of Waterloo in Shefford Township, that attendance was invariably good, except in inclement weather, and that he had established three Sunday schools. But he blamed his predecessor for 'the treatment I have been receiving during the last three months from a few of the Yankee people, – I mean Yankee members of the church.' In March 1833, a petition with forty-six signatures asked the CEHMS to send them an American clergyman.[88]

Gleed admitted several months later that it might seem strange that he remained in Granby 'after the unhappy things that have rent the Society asunder,' but he claimed that he had strong support in South Ridge, Four Corners, Red School, and Shefford, as well as all the 'pious and steady' members in the town. He complained, on the other hand, that he had been unable to acquire any local grain for two months before the harvest, and the bad weather in the fall had left him and his family of ten with nothing to eat but potatoes and salt.[89] Gleed obviously had opponents in Shefford as well, for a meeting in that township resolved unanimously in October 1833 that he 'be not considered our missionary.' However, he submitted a petition in December signed by ten men from England, fourteen from Scotland, nineteen from Ireland, and seventy-two Americans asking for the usual annual grant. Gleed claimed that only a small party was attempting to injure him, but they consisted of the town's elite, and the January 1834 minutes in Granby's church book record that he was to be no longer recognized as the minister.[90]

But Gleed was still in Granby in September 1834 when he emphasized to the CEHMS 'the vexatious trials & difficulties' that missionaries in the Townships 'have to encounter from the *mixed* state of our societies & the various & opposite opinions & customs peculiar to so many different nations of people ... A minister must be independent & yet sociable & kind to do much good among such a population of people. And moreover to form & raise Churches he must labour on the same spot for years.' Gleed's main point was that the ministers should be assured of a fixed annual salary, with the CEHMS prepared to make up for the congregation's shortfalls. He claimed that the local subscriptions were actually of little value because 'some are never paid, others are paid in things of but little service, & most in an irregular & untimely way, to say not of the trouble & unpleasantness the minister has to collect it.'[91] Finally, the lack of financial support from the CEHMS forced Gleed to resign in April 1835. He charged that 'I must now believe that my being an old Country minister, in connexion with the party spirit here, excludes me from your bounty.' The debt-ridden clergyman claimed that during the previous winter 'my family has been often half-starved & some of my dear children half naked,' and 'my foes (I mean your friends in the village) exult over me & my trials so far as they know them.' Still, he had decided to remain in the area as a farmer. If this failed, he would cross the line to the United States.[92]

The negligence of the CEHMS to pay Gleed did not mean that it wished him to resign, however, and it appointed J. Johnston to investigate whether he should be given further support. Johnston reported in May 1835 that he had talked to men not mixed up in party spirit, and that, while they were favourably disposed to Gleed in some respects, on the whole 'it was their firm belief that he could be no longer generally useful to them.' Gleed's meetings were reasonably well attended in isolated locations, but little or no progress had been made since his arrival. Johnston therefore suggested assigning him to a mostly British area and providing him with $50 to move.[93] Gleed was not happy with the report. He insisted that the opposition to him was based on the fact that he was 'an old Country minister & opposed most decidedly to the modern new fangled method of making converts.' He, too, 'could make plenty of converts were I dishonest enough to rouse the fears of a set of ignorant people, ... then get them into the church, & so send them to God's ... with a lie in their right hand. Of this way of making converts I have seen enough.' Gleed charged that of the six men opposed to him, one made no profession of faith, one was an excommunicated deacon, and one was an antinomian; the other three had no influence in the town. He concluded by stating that he wished to have nothing 'more to do with a society that can so grossly violate its own fundamental rule & trifle so easily with its solemn pledges.' The last word came from the secretary of the CEHMS, who denied that national distinctions had anything to do with the society's actions, and claimed that half the ministers it supported were of British origin.[94]

Gleed remained in Granby, presumably without CEHMS support, and in May 1836 a report by a Charles Sherman finally explained the crux of the conflict between him and his American parishioners. Sherman wrote that Gleed had little influence because he was 'an *Englishman*, & receives members without any form of Covenant, & under slight examinations as to piety. He also baptizes the children of *all* that apply, whether christians or not.' Sherman may have been exaggerating, but we have seen that the English Congregational practice differed from that of the Americans insofar as it did not distinguish between full members and adherents. Sherman added that 'Their present discouraging prospect is inclining several of the most influential part of the society to remove where they can enjoy better religious privileges.'[95]

Two months later, H.B. Chapin, one of the young men sent on a short-term basis to the region by the Hampshire Central Association,[96] submitted an equally discouraging report from Granby. He echoed the observations of the other missionaries in areas of mixed British and American settlement: 'The diversity of national character – of religious sentiments above all the seated difference of the impressions & associations of childhood influencing still many of the old & grey headed render it a chilling process to reach the heart & produce conviction of sin.'[97] Chapin later elaborated that his territory included Catholics, Episcopalians, Methodists, Independents, Presbyterians, Scotch Relief, Universalists, Congregationalists, New Light or Christian Brethren, nothingarians, and anythingarians: 'Among such hearers subject to national & sectarian jealousies your Missionary once in two weeks comes in for his turn at the desk of a School House, for their [*sic*] is not a sanctuary whh belongs to our order, nor a chh ... within fifty miles of me – Any body, No Body & every Body can preach that comes along – hearers will flock in. The consequence is religious opinions are floating & unfixed.'[98]

In his July report, Chapin added that he had organized a church council to re-establish the church in Granby, and that conditions were now more promising in Waterloo, though a permanent appointee was required if they were not to 'sink back to their former state of discouragement.' If the pious families left, 'all ground of rational hope of saving these rising villages from the inroads of sin & error' would be lost. Chapin added that 'I say not this to the disparagement of the Weslyans [*sic*] – an itinerant ministry no matter what order will not meet the circumstances of this people.' He concluded that 'a crisis [meaning a religious awakening]' is forming in the Eastern Townships – among the villages & back settlements and 'the religious influence whh forms it may control the faith & future of the people for generations to come.'[99] In August, with his three-month term coming to an end, the loquacious Chapin again wrote that there were signs 'of special presence of God among this people,' leaving him 'exceedingly distressed to know what to do.' If his efforts were followed up, there would very likely be 'a revival of Religion,' and he felt it 'unkind to leave them without a Teacher of their faith to weep in vain.' On the other hand, Chapin felt he could not accept a permanent appointment because he was attached to his home and '*love* my people.' There was also the expense of the move to consider, the age of his father, and the health of his wife, not to mention 'the *rigor* of a Canadian winter,' and the fact that there were six vacancies within ten miles of his congregation in the United States. He would be willing to stay in Canada an additional six months, 'but how then shall I dispose of my wife – *put her in a nunnery*?' Chapin had clearly been moved by the response to his farewell service, where communion was offered for the first time in three years, but he concluded that 'Granby is a prodigious hard place' where 'Some of these *Scotch members* are the *stubbornest* oaks that ever grew on *Mount* Zion, ... stern *&* stiff as the Covenanters – all iron & care not for the file.'[100]

The CEHMS secretary, W.F. Curry, was highly impressed by Chapin. He wrote to an officer in the AHMS that Chapin 'is more popular amongst all classes than any other man who has been or who probably could be sent on to the ground.' The people were aware of 'all his peculiarities and seem to love him the more because as they say he appears to know nothing else but to preach.' Curry felt that it 'will be a new era in our operations if he can be had,' and offered Chapin $550 a year, which was $100 more than any other Congregational minister was receiving.[101] The young clergyman succumbed to these pressures, though he assured Curry that he was returning to Granby and Shefford out of duty rather than 'wish or inclination,' and asked him to write to his congregation explaining why he was needed in Canada.[102]

Chapin submitted an anecdotal journal in August 1837 in which he claimed that of eighty-five families he had visited in the back settlements, only forty-nine had Bibles. Some had only one of the testaments while others had hour Bibles – that is, fragments, given them as a farewell blessing when leaving their mother land. In sharp contrast to his predecessor, John Gleed, Chapin also declared that the congregation needed to be more aware of the necessity for revivals and of the qualifications of membership. Two months later, in October 1837, Chapin reported that by-laws had been passed by the Granby and Shefford churches stating that all persons must be examined prior to admission, as well as giving a 'pledge of entire abstinence from all intoxicating drinks except for medicinal purposes.' There were now forty members in Granby and twenty-three in Shefford.[103]

The enthusiastic Chapin's detailed report for the late fall of 1837 recounts a continuing increase in membership numbers. He opened a Sabbath school in Waterloo, where the exclusively Anglican one had failed, and reported that nearly $1,200 was subscribed for chapels in Waterloo and Granby. But all was interrupted by the outbreak of the Rebellion in November. At the peak of local excitement, Chapin went to a tavern 'crowded with men & implements of war & husbandry,' and asked 'all who believed in an overruling providence & deemed it a duty to seek divine direction in this day of alarm to accompany me to our house of worship.' A number followed him, but Chapin reflected, 'Alas how little did they think they were guilty of a more unreasonable Rebellion than the one they were called out to suppress.' By December, Chapin was lamenting, 'What a change has come upon us – am fearful this distracted state of the Country may prove the means of breaking us up.' Saturday militia musters were accompanied by drinking; on one occasion the volunteers were forced to break the Sabbath by going to Frost Village to receive their arms; and one of the prominent members had opened a tavern stand. But Chapin's main concern was that people's minds were on temporal affairs and news rather than contemplation and prayer.[104]

By the spring of 1838 Chapin was expressing concern that strenuous efforts were being made to wrest the village of Granby 'from our influence.' Resorting to another of his colourful metaphors, Chapin declared that 'our chh at the village is a *speckled* bird – she may have some feathers, but I hope will not be driven into the wilderness.' He advised the CEHMS to appoint a missionary 'who can convert Scotchmen. I cannot do it,' and added that 'Diversity of religious opinions is not so much to be lamented as national prejudice.' Chapin expressed some prejudice of his own, however, when he complained that liquor was killing the enterprise of the country, except for the American inhabitants – 'they are wide awake & will grow & flourish in spite of all the contrary influences whh naturally retard their improvement. But deliver me from the pride of the Englishmen, the stubbornness of the Scotch, & from the religious & national prejudice of them all.'[105]

Chapin remained somewhat pessimistic in July 1838 when he reported that during the previous year five members had been added in

Granby and eight in Shefford, but added that 'prejudices against all American influence is strong & with many families in G. remains unbroken.' Chapin's journal continued: 'How long it may be my duty to continue here is *uncertain*. Many of the Americans wish to leave the Province, but cannot dispose of their property. We have no meeting house, *no distinct society of our own*, nor can we have until we have a suitable house.'[106] Two months later, Chapin again reported that some of the church's strongest supporters were anxious to sell and leave because of the political climate: 'I scarcely know of an American near me from his heart does not wish he was well out of the Country.' He recommended that a British Congregational missionary be sent to Granby, adding that 'The more I think of the points of difference between us, & the nearer we come in contact, the more I am compelled to believe that sooner or later the New England Congregationalists must view themselves as a different denomination.'[107]

Chapin and the other Congregational ministers of the Eastern Townships had attended a meeting to establish the Congregational Union of Lower Canada in August 1838, but he refused to join because he felt that 'the system of faith & practice of the Independents differs enough from the Congregationalism of New England to make them *another* denomination. The systems when compared & acted upon in the same community will never harmonize – besides their Missionaries in Canada do not respect the rights & localities of the American Missionaries as they do those of their own order.' Chapin also claimed that his experience in Granby had taught him that 'It is a very easy thing to excite the prejudices of old Countrymen against an American who preaches against their prevailing sins,' which evidently included consuming alcohol.[108]

Chapin was particularly resentful of the incursion by Abbotsford's Presbyterian minister, Richard Miles, who by December 1838 was announcing his attention to open a second church in Granby, which became known as the Scotch Church. The CEHMS refused to take a stand on the case, but Chapin confided to his journal that Miles 'is altogether mistaken does he suppose that the chh whh was planted by American Missionaries & saved from ruin *thro* their instrumentality will after my departure conform to his views.' The American clergyman was more specific in a later entry: 'If Mr M introduces the peculiarities of his system, a chh without articles of faith & Baptizes the infant children of unbelieving parents in G[ranby,] I can very readily anticipate the consequences.'[109] Chapin was clearly torn between his belief that there was a fundamental difference between the Scottish and American churches, and the traditional Congregational position that denominational divisions were counter-productive. He insisted that he had not been 'a controvertist,' but had 'endeavored to let the ... word of God work its own way to the understandings of men. Tho we are a distinct chh & society we worship in harmony with others.' The Congregationalist clergyman even held a joint prayer meeting with the local Anglican minister, and concluded that it is 'rather discouraging if not ludicrous to see three ministers at different times preaching in the same house, to the same audience each laboring to gain a society for himself.'[110]

By January 1839 Chapin felt able to report that some progress had been made during his tenure. Clearly a non-Calvinist himself, he wrote that 'perversion of some of the doctrines of our faith common in some neighbourhoods has been in a measure done away & candid intelligent men will no longer pretend that we *know* whether infants are doomed are not.' But Chapin was certainly not optimistic as far as the future was concerned, reporting that 'a great change has taken place in my society at Waterloo, not as to attendance on my ministry for the house is full as ever, but in the *feelings* & *circumstances* of my people in relation to the affairs of the Province. Real estate is sadly depreciated – Many would rejoice to sell even at a great sacrifice ... Enterprise is at an end, plans cannot be formed for the future, & he that sows knows not who will reap – few indeed of my chh & society feel at home, & those on whom I depended the most are making arrangements to sell & remove the *first opportunity*.'[111]

Chapin's American flock was apparently less concerned about the political uncertainty caused by the Rebellions than it was by the repression which followed. A number of local residents had been tried at a court martial in Frost Village in late December 1838 due to the discovery of an apparent conspiracy involving at least one member of Chapin's congregation. Colonel Head was lenient, however, for Chapin later recorded that 'the affair was disposed of far better than our fears.' The Scottish settlers were clearly much less ambivalent than the local Americans about the Rebellion's outcome, for Chapin wrote that 'It is very different at Granby, especially the South Ridge – here the people feel at home & are contented, united & happy. The *Sab.* School has *prospered*, the chh increased, society improved & advancing.' He could not resist stating, however, that the Scots 'occasionally have their nightly dances & bottles.'[112]

In May 1839 Chapin wrote that he would soon be leaving for an appointment in Maine, and that the church at Waterloo 'is breaking up, its members on whom I depended for support leaving the Province. The political disturbances have fallen on my society here with a heavy hand, & connected with our unbelief & unfaithfulness, ruined & dispersed us.'[113] To the extent that Congregationalism had a future in Shefford and Granby, it lay with the British branch of the church, but the remaining Americans would find this hard to accept. In November, a Granby committee asked for an American replacement for Chapin on the grounds that those who attended Miles' meetings 'have no articles of belief, and as they do not approve of our articles, we do not deem it our duty to unite with them.'[114] Granby and Shefford did receive yet another American the following spring, when the student, Nathaniel B. Fox, received $150 from the AHMS. Fox reported that the Granby Congregationalists had subscribed $1,400 towards building a meeting house, but he complained that, while there was no prayer meeting, a successful dancing school was in operation. At South Ridge, however, where the largest part of the membership lived, eight or ten women met weekly in their determination 'to wrestle with God till they prevail.' A year later, in 1840, Fox reported a 'general declension of religious emotion,' but the house of worship had been erected, and he had been promoting temperance among the youth with the result that nearly forty had signed the teetotal pledge.[115]

Fox's main concern, for the time being was financial. Although the AHMS had increased his grant to £50, and the Granby congregation promised another £50,[116] the failure of the hay crop meant that cattle had become almost worthless. Fox claimed that his family was not forgotten whenever crops were gathered or cattle killed, but he felt it was ungenerous of whoever had complained to the CEHMS that his employment as a teacher for nine weeks was taking too much of his time. With no school open in the township, he had taken in seventeen students in order to supply his family's urgent needs. He had been £50 in debt before leaving New England and had paid £75 for necessities in Canada, but had no chair, workstand, washstand, dressing table, bureau, chest, sofa, carpet or rug. His clothing was worn out, he owned only one pair of homespun pants, his horse and wagon had not been paid for, and he did not have a sleigh, saddle or bridle. Fox's students apparently paid only for their board, based on his wife's hard labour, for he stated that he asked nothing for his teaching. He also claimed that his students had begun to think and reason, but he was discouraged. About half the five hundred school-age children within his charge were illiterate, and the youths were 'a listless lawless – gaping – gazing race. I do them apparently no good. Yet the woods are full of them ... They come to meeting sometimes & they sometimes stay at home or go hunting.' Clearly feeling discouraged, Fox closed his April 1841 report with the words 'May you never know ... the inconvenience of living & preaching among a coarse wild people of the woods.'[117]

A year later, Fox noted that the remnant of the once-flourishing Shefford church was now absorbed into Granby, and he preached in Waterloo only once a month during a week-day evening. He recommended withholding the missionary grant until the people organized a society for his support, chose a committee responsible for the punctual payment of his salary, and pledged to pay in regular quarterly instalments with a reasonable proportion in cash.[118] These conditions had been met by October 1842, after a summer revival was launched by Fox's ministry to a young woman on her death bed. As a result, forty members were added to the Congregational church, while others joined the Methodists. Fox's work with the youths had clearly paid off, for twenty-one of the new members were young unmarried persons, and only fifteen were heads of families. The membership, which had previously included only one unmarried person, had thus been doubled. One tavern was now operated on temperance principles, and a great temperance festival had been held in June 'in a beautiful orchard upon the tavern keepers premises.' The revival had ended with Fox's need to go to his wife's sick bed for six weeks in the United States, but another was begun by the Methodists during the following winter, adding approximately ten more members to the Congregational church.[119]

When Fox made plans to leave Granby in February 1844, the people took immediate steps to liquidate his heavy debt and signed a subscription paper for his support.[120] Fox did leave that year in any case, being replaced by David Gibb, a graduate of Dartmouth and Andover. Gibb remained until his death in 1848, the same year that the Scottish Presbyterians re-entered the fold. In January 1849, the arrival of Henry Lancashire, a graduate of the Montreal Theological College, finally marked the end of the American ministry in Granby.[121] According to the 1852 *Census Reports*, there were 489 Congregationalists in Granby, more than in any other township in the region, but they were only slightly more numerous than either the Anglicans or the Methodists. In Shefford, there were a mere fifty-nine Congregationalists and seventy-two Presbyterians. The years of internal factionalism between the British and American adherents had clearly taken their toll.

TABLE 3.1
Data for Eastern Townships Congregational churches, 1836

Place	Grant	In congregation	Members	Added previous year	In Sabbath school	In temperance societies
Shipton	$150	250	58	3	80	150
Melbourne	$200	100	32	32	50	80
Sherb./Len.	$200	200	35	–	–	–
Compton	$300	60	0	–	0	400
S. Eaton	–	(no min.)	26–30	7–10	–	–
Stanstead	$150	130	70	2	200	–
Potton	$ 80	–	–	–	–	–
Missis. Bay	$250	100	12	2	75	500
Granby	–	200	35	1	60	90
Shefford	–	250	24	8	30	270
Total	$1330	1290	294	57	495	1490

Source: CEHMS, 1836 Report of Congregations in Lower Canada

Conclusion

One might have expected the Congregational Church to be quite successful in the Eastern Townships. Unlike the Methodists, it was aware (in the words of its mouthpiece) that 'very little permanent good would be done by adopting an itinerating course of missionary labour.'[122] Long-serving clergymen such as Ammi Parker provided a valuable measure of local stability, their latitudinarian approach was well-suited to a region of mixed religious origins, and their social reform program was in the mainstream of the new social and economic era. As tables 3.1 to 3.3 demonstrate, the Congregational ministers in the Eastern Townships were heavily involved in the temperance movement, as well as in promoting Sunday schools. In 1851 the St Francis Ministerial Association discussed how to unite the ministers of different denominations, as well as lay delegates, 'for promoting the general interests of society,' referring specifically to Sabbath observance, the temperance movement, Sabbath schools, and the Bible cause.[123]

Perhaps this zeal for reform represented, in part, an attempt to tran-

TABLE 3.2
Data for Eastern Townships Congregational churches, 1839

Place	Temperance pledges	In Sabbath schools	Volumes	In Bible class
Granby	–	–	–	–
Potton	200	70	–	–
Stanstead	60	200	–	35
Melbourne	100	–	–	–
Danville	160	50	–	–
Compton	–	100	–	–
Sherbrooke	–	–	20	–
Eaton	200	70	80	–
Totals	720	490	100	35

Source: *Report of the American Home Missionary Society*, 1839

scend their internal differences, particularly between the American and British traditions. The contrast in those traditions was made strikingly visible in two church buildings that survive to the present day. While Eaton Corner's wooden structure (built in 1841) conforms to the classical New England meeting-house design (despite its steeple), Melbourne's brick church (built in the late 1830s) is an early example of English neo-Gothic design, with its arched windows, steep roof, and sharp spire (see illustrations 1 and 2). The American influence, given a strong boost when the AHMS finally launched its Canadian missionary initiative in 1835, was dealt a serious blow by the Rebellions only two years later. By 1840 the American society was considering abandonment of the Canadian field. One of its officers, Milton Badger, referred to the economic hard times, 'the prejudices incident to the civil commotions there,' the collisions with Britain's Colonial Missionary Society, and the AHMS commitments in the western States. But the officers of the British society informed him that they lacked the means to take over all the Canadian missions, and promised to instruct their missionaries to avoid conflict with their American counterparts. The AHMS therefore extended its assistance on a reduced basis for five more years on the grounds that there were many Americans living in the Eastern Townships.[124]

The Colonial Missionary Society finally took over after January 1845,

TABLE 3.3
Data for Eastern Townships Congregational churches, 1842

Place	Temperance pledges	In Sabbath schools	Volumes	In Bible class
Melbourne	200	40	45	24
Granby	700	–	–	–
Stanstead	–	95	120	–
Danville	350	90	100	–
Eaton	400	55	200	–
Totals	1650	280	465	24

Source: *Report of the American Home Missionary Society*, 1842

when the Lower Canadian Congregationalists withdrew from the CEHMS to establish the Congregational Missionary Society.[125] How active this society was in the Eastern Townships is impossible to say, since its papers have apparently not survived, but Congregationalism clearly went into decline with the withdrawal of American support. Some of the churches probably also felt the effects of the general spiritual exhaustion which followed the Millerite excitement of the mid-1840s. None of them appear to have been directly affected by the movement, but in 1846 the St Francis Ministerial Association passed a motion declaring 'that in view of our mournful state' the ministers would spend an hour each evening, from 8:00 to 9:00, praying that God would 'revive his work in the hearts of the ministers & members of the chs. particularly in the bounds of the St Francis Ass.'n.' Each minister was also to do what he could 'to interest every member of the ch. in the same.' Six months later, the still demoralized association moved that 'No revivals of religion having been enjoyed & our members diminishing some by death, some by removals & some by apostacy, it was felt that there was need of special prayer to God that he wd pour upon us his Holy Spirit.'[126] As of 1852 there were only 3,364 Congregationalists in the Eastern Townships, a mere 6.4 per cent of the region's Protestant population. Not only had this quintessentially New England denomination failed to take strong root in the Eastern Townships, thereby leaving a vacuum for the Anglican and Wesleyan Methodist missionaries to fill, but it had fallen under British influence itself by the mid-1840s. The result could hardly avoid being a distinctly Canadian hybrid or synthesis.

4

The Baptists

The somewhat sporadic development of the Baptists in the Eastern Townships was curtailed by the War of 1812, and, by 1831, they still numbered only 1,912, or 5.6 per cent of the region's Protestant population. This percentage would fail to increase during the following two decades, and the reasons remained much the same as they had been in the pre-1815 pioneer era. The Baptist churches in the Townships continued for a number of years to be linked to American societies, such as the Danville, Vermont, Calvinist Baptist Convention, which by 1824 included Potton, Eaton, Hatley, and Stanstead.[1] Rather than being centralized ecclesiastical organizations, however, these were associations of autonomous churches with no legislative powers.[2] Pitman argues that Baptist church polity was well suited to spreading the gospel in sparsely settled areas, since it gave a great deal of independence to local churches. Each church could adapt itself to the particular religious needs of its community, it did not have to rely on aid from any central body, and it could choose one of its own members as a preacher regardless of his lack of education or other qualifications. As Pitman admits, however, local church freedom could also be a source of weakness. Churches perished from lack of outside financial assistance, or when the local preachers who had organized them moved elsewhere.[3]

The result was that the fortunes of the Baptist Church in the Eastern Townships tended to vary widely, depending upon the congregation in question, but the overall growth was limited. F.A. Cox and J. Hoby, two British Baptist missionaries who passed through the region around 1835, reported 'fifteen to twenty calvinistic baptist churches, almost destitute ... of settled pastors.'[4] Cox and Hoby were referring to the Regular or Calvinist churches, not their Freewill counterparts. Unfortunately,

Lower Canada's official census reports of 1831 and 1852 fail to distinguish between the two branches, but, as we saw in chapter one, examination of the manuscript schedules for some townships suggests that the radical revivalist Freewill Baptists were more numerous than their Regular counterparts in the region. But the Freewill Baptist churches were particularly prone to local factionalism, and we shall see that they would be gravely compromised by the emergence of Millerism in the early 1840s.

Regular Baptists

The region's first Baptist church, that in Sutton, disappears from view with the onset of the War of 1812 until it is noted as a member of the Danville, Vermont, Baptist Convention in 1842. Three years later, Sutton's Baptists, Wesleyan Methodists, and New Connection Methodists commenced building a church together, but a local historian reports that 'due to a lack of harmony as well as of finances, it was not completed until 1861,' when the Adventists also participated.[5] The *Census Reports* state that there were 116 Baptists in Sutton Township in 1852, though many of them were clearly Freewill Baptists, for we have seen that the enumerator for district one of the township did not distinguish between the two Baptist denominations.

In contrast to Sutton, the St Armand Baptist church appears to have remained active after the War of 1812. Its pastor was William Galusha, of whom the local Anglican curate, James Reid, reported in 1816 that 'He is a Calvinist, but very illiterate, and of no consideration, except among themselves.' Galusha was still the minister in 1829, yet Reid wrote that year that 'Sometimes they have a Preacher, but by far the greater part of the time they have none; so they are either all zeal when they have a Preacher, or sunk into carelessness when he is gone: but whatever be their condition, the Church can expect no accession from them. They are bigoted in their zeal; they are bigoted in their indifference.'[6] In 1833 the St Armand Baptists found themselves divided between the supporters of Galusha and those of the Vermont-born Homer Smith, who had been ordained to replace him three years earlier. The division was longstanding, but harmony was eventually restored with outside assistance.[7]

In 1838 a missionary from the Vermont Baptist State Convention held a series of meetings in St Armand which resulted in a powerful revival. Most of those 'converted' are said to have joined the Baptists, but the list of members shows no addition since 1835. In 1839, there were reportedly forty-nine members, but no minister.[8] Finally in 1841 another church was erected to replace the one that had been torn down in the early 1830s. Built of brick, it boasted a gallery for the choir, as well as round-topped windows in a region where most American-based denominations remained content with square ones.[9] The Eastern Townships had remained outside the Ottawa Baptist Association when it was founded in 1836, but St Armand's minister was British by 1841, and, two years later, the church broke its formal ties with New England by joining the Montreal Association. This move did little to increase its strength, however, for only nineteen new members were added between 1841 and 1851, by which time they were approximately sixty in number. The nearby farming community of Stanbridge Ridge, where a Baptist society had been established in 1809, also had an English minister by 1843. The small stone chapel it had built the preceeding year conformed to the classical New England style, with a full gallery across the back and no tower or spire. But the coloured glass panes were a rather anomalous feature. They set the building apart as a sacred space during an era when lack of bright artificial lighting meant that large clear windows were favoured by Protestant denominations whose worship priorities focused on reading and preaching the Word of God (see illustration 3).[10]

While Hatley's Regular Baptist Church survived the War of 1812 intact, it went into decline thereafter. The local Anglican minister reported in 1823 that the Baptists were 'at present in a very torpid state.' His report for 1827 recorded 126 Baptists in the township, but only twelve Calvinist Baptists.[11] The church depended largely on the services of its elder, Harvey Clark, but he left around 1830. While Clark continued to make occasional visits during the following years,[12] the 1852 *Census Reports* list no Baptists in Hatley.

The Baptist church in nearby Barnston, which collapsed when its elder departed in 1817, was reorganized in 1832 upon the principles of the Danville, Vermont, Calvinist Baptist Convention.[13] The following years were active ones in Barnston, for thirteen people were baptized in 1834, thirty in 1835, and thirty in 1837, when a church was constructed under the supervision of Elder John Ide, who was a carpenter and joiner by trade.[14] The last surviving charter member, Susan Crooker (known as Grandma Parker) recalled in 1898 that 'Some with their own teams and sledges went to Barnston Mountain and secured some fine granite for the foundation; others went to the woods and hewed out a frame from the finest pine.' Still there was a deficit which eight of the leading men met by taxing themselves according to the municipal assessment role drawn up in the 1840s. This was a significant step, given the resistance to the province's introduction of compulsory school taxes on the part of local elites in the border townships, and in Barnston in particular. In her memoir, Susan Crooker proudly added that 'The women came to the rescue and taxed themselves $3 each,' selling butter at 8¢ a pound to raise the money.[15] There were eighty-eight members in 1839, the largest number in the region, but a sharp decline in baptisms followed during the ensuing decade. The cause was apparently the impact of Millerism, for fifty-four members of the Baptist church were dismissed without letters between 1837 and 1845.[16]

A Baptist church was also organized in Eaton, where seven women and six men joined forces for that purpose in 1822. The membership reached twenty-five the following year, but expansion was slow thereafter. By 1833, when Edward Mitchell from the Isle of Martinique via Vermont was installed as pastor, only thirty-three non-founders had been baptized and nine added 'by letter.'[17] To stimulate growth, the members held a two-week 'protracted meeting' in a shed two years later, with the result, according to a local historian, that 'The Holy Spirit was present in mighty power, and many souls were hopefully converted.' The meeting voted 'that hereafter we invite to the communion of the Lord's Table those persons who have been immersed or buried with Christ in baptism and are members of some one of the orthodox Churches,'[18] which was effectively a close-communion stand for it excluded all those not baptized by immersion.

Mitchell was not replaced when he moved to Georgeville in 1837, but during the winter of 1839–40 another protracted meeting was held in the old shed, at which sixteen believers were baptized by a Vermont elder. When two Canadian missionaries visited the township the following summer, they reported approximately sixty members, most of whom were very poor. The only occasions in which Baptist services were held in Eaton were when a clergyman travelled forty to sixty miles to administer the Lord's Supper every two months.[19] Eaton finally gained another minister when the Scottish-born Archibald Gillies was ordained in 1842, though only nineteen Baptists are recorded in the 1852 census.[20]

Edward Mitchell became the first resident Baptist minister in Georgeville when he arrived in 1837, but it appears that he had already become a supporter of Vermont's William Miller, who would cause a major religious upheaval due to his prediction that the Apocalypse would take place in 1843 or 1844. The Reverend Titus Merriman claimed that 'A very healthy and extended revival of religion' sprang from Miller's labours in the Georgeville area, providing Mitchell with many young candidates for baptism.[21] There were seventy-nine members by 1839, and thirty were added after Miller's visit in July 1840.[22] But the long-term result was that the Georgeville Baptist church ceased to meet after 27 June 1844, presumably because most of its members were awaiting the Apocalypse. Hubbard claims that many of the founding Baptist families eventually joined the Freewill Baptists or Methodists,[23] and no one claimed to be a Baptist to the census enumerator in 1852.

In nearby Potton, where the aforementioned Merriman became the Baptist minister in 1845, Baptist meetings had apparently been held since the arrival of the first settlers. A society of twelve was established there in 1817 as a branch of the church in Troy, Vermont, and the Potton Baptists finally became formerly organized twenty years later. A church was constructed in 1845, but, once again, no one claimed to be a Baptist at the time of the 1852 enumeration.[24] Much the same story was repeated in Barford where a pastor was installed in 1838 with financial support from the Vermont Baptist Convention. There were thirty-five members in 1839, and a revival added more two years later, but numbers remained below forty thereafter, and the 1852 census lists no Baptists.[25]

Not all the Baptists were Americans. A number of Scots Baptists settled in the vicinity of Beebe Plain (Stanstead Township) during the 1830s, but they attended the nearby church in Derby, Vermont. They established a church on the Canadian side of the border in 1851, only to reunite with Derby several years later.[26] Finally, the 1831 census records sixty Baptists in the British-settled townships of Leeds and Inverness, some hundred miles to the north, a number which grew to 131 in the 1852 census, but the church would never gain a strong foothold in this area.[27]

The Regular or Calvinist Baptists, then, remained a small and struggling minority of the Eastern Townships Protestants at the middle of the nineteenth century. There had been a brief flurry of activity in 1837 when the Baptist Canadian Missionary Society was formed, but British missionaries Topping and Bosworth reported after their tour of 1840 that 'loose ideas as regards religion are prevalent' in the Eastern Townships, where 'universalism and unitarianism find many advocates.' The great need was for more ministers, as there were only four in the region serving 472 members in nine scattered stations, and the Vermont Convention could not provide much support.[28] Of the four ministers in question, a report in 1841 stated that two had to labour to procure a livelihood, one was very poor with no horse and therefore could not travel, and only one (presumably Mitchell, who was black) was quite well off and educated.[29] Most of the Townships churches joined the British-supported Ottawa/Montreal Baptist Association between 1842 and 1845, but Millerism effectively ended whatever progress was being made before the required reinforcements were received from the short-lived Canada Baptist College.[30] In short, while the people of the Eastern Townships were strongly predisposed towards local control over their churches, the decentralized polity of the Baptist denomination was susceptible to schism, and its Calvinism precluded a sustained missionary effort.

Freewill Baptists

Reflecting developments in the adjacent New England states after the Revolution, the Freewill Baptists were more successful in the Eastern Townships, at least for a time, than were their Calvinist counterparts, though they did not receive more external support. Unlike the Regular Baptists, the Freewill Baptists were able to establish two regional associations by 1843, but they would be severely damaged shortly thereafter by the rise of Millerism, a movement which appealed to the same radically-oriented constituency. And, while the broader associational framework provided by the Quarterly Meeting added a certain measure of stability to the Freewill Baptist society in the Eastern Townships, the surviving minutes of the Compton Monthly Meeting reveal how unstable this revivalist sect could be.

While the War of 1812 served to cut the Freewill Baptists' tenuous links with New England,[31] the Compton Church Record reports that in 1821 or 1822 'the Lord again begun a good work and carried it on till some more were hopefully converted to the Lord and added to those imbodied.' Dudley Spafford was ordained 'and called a help or an overseer,' and a new covenant was written. In terms of Benjamin Randall's 1792 covenant, which established the basic guidelines of the Freewill Baptist Church, Spafford was probably a ruling elder, a position aimed at maintaining loyalty and monitoring covenant obligations rather than preaching and administering ordinances. The Compton adherents now called themselves a church, but they were yet to be formally organized.[32]

Another 'reformation' of several months duration took place in the northern part of Compton two or three years later, in 1824 or 1825, and another covenant was drafted with new names added to it, but still 'without the voise of the church.' As a result, according to the Record Book, 'from this time till Sept. 1828 all was confusion' and 'the Brothering was as it were scattered like sheep with out a shepherd.' Then, with Elder Avery Moulton of Stanstead in attendance, and Elder Nathaniel Perry of Cabot, Maine, representing the Yearly Meeting (which dealt with general matters of policy and theology), yet another covenant was signed by twenty-seven men and twenty-one women. This short document was completely silent on doctrinal matters, emphasizing instead the fellowship of the church members, or what the sect's most prominent founder, Benjamin Randall, called 'gospel union.' As with the first agreement drafted by Randall in 1792, they swore 'to watch over each other in the bonds of Christian fellowship,' and 'to maintain our Christian fellowship by a close walk with God and a familiar Correspondence with each other believing that in so doing the Lord will more abundantly bless us.'[33]

According to the system established by Randall, churches met weekly for worship and monthly for discipline and conference. The monthly meetings, attended by the entire congregation, were the fundamental unit of Freewill polity. Governed by itinerant teaching elders or local ruling elders, these meetings heard each member's account of his or her performance of covenant obligations during the preceding month. Members were expected to admit all failures in belief or practice, and could be challenged for unconfessed transgressions. The elder would then 'labour' publicly with the offender, offering exhortation and moral advice. Marini states that 'When all members had testified to the 'satisfaction' of the covenant, the congregation was considered in gospel union, sanctified and empowered by the Holy Spirit to continue its "travel" toward Christian perfection.'[34] This church's survival and expansion clearly depended upon a high degree of commitment and cooperation on the part of its membership, and these features would not always be evident in Compton or its neighbouring townships.

As part of their reorganization, the Compton Freewill Baptists voted in 1828 to join the recently established Quarterly Meeting at Stanstead. The Yearly Meeting had originally been a final court of appeal from the Quarterly Meetings, but rapid expansion ended this provision in 1803, with the result that the Quarterly Meetings increasingly became the administrative centres of the connection. The Freewill Baptist Church had taken root in Stanstead as the result of a revival that had spread from neighbouring Barnston in 1823, when the Wheelock, Vermont Quarterly Meeting – which included most of the Lower Canadian Freewill Baptist churches – held a session there.[35] In 1828 the Stanstead Quarterly Meeting replaced the Wheelock Meeting north of the border, thereby providing the Freewill Baptists of the Eastern Townships with the coordinating mechanism and mutual support that the region's Regular Baptists lacked.

At the inaugural ceremony of the Stanstead Quarterly Meeting, 'a large concourse of people' heard the unordained American preacher, Martha Spalding, deliver a discourse. This was one of the few recorded times that a woman would speak publicly in the Eastern Townships of this era, but, according to Billington, Spalding was largely responsible for building up a circuit of eight churches in the Stanstead district.[36] Her speech was followed by the ordination sermon of an elder from Sutton, Vermont, and the 'laying on of hands' by three American Presbytery elders. The session then licensed Avery Moulton's son, Abial, 'to preach the Gospel.'[37]

Despite the levelling nature of the Freewill Baptist Church's doctrine, a considerable amount of power was concentrated in the hands of the elders, who attended the conference held the day before the proceedings of the quarterly meeting were opened to the other members. No specific duties or powers were outlined for this plenary session, but it was clearly where the meeting's important business took place, including examination of the men presented by local churches for ordination. The minutes for the general meeting the following day were confined to the reports from each church. Non-members were soon allowed to attend the elders' conference and pose any question 'that shall not interfear with the business of the Conference.'[38] In June 1833 steps were taken to regularize (and democratize) procedures to a greater extent by declaring that the conference should include the local church officers and delegates, rather than simply the elders. Preachers could attend the conference, but might be asked not to vote. The recommendations of this body were to be taken to the quarterly meeting of the following day, at which any church member could vote.

There were definite limits to the influence of the elders, for they failed in their attempt to create a cohesive and stable organization by declaring at the second quarterly meeting that church building and governance would be supported by an assessment of half a cent on the dollar, to be paid in produce but with a discount for cash. This initiative was a more centralized enactment of Randall's provision for each Monthly Meeting (local congregation) to collect funds based upon the tax assessment and real property of each member. The elders' attempt to do away with voluntarism may seem paradoxical for a church that placed such stress on individual freedom, but most of the other denominations in the region had the luxury of outside financial support from their missionary societies. The elders of the Stanstead Quarterly Meeting were, nevertheless, forced to abandon their attempts to introduce standard assessments if only because local government and municipal assessment were not introduced to Lower Canada until 1840.

Delegates from each Monthly Meeting did, at least, report the status of their membership to the Quarterly Meeting, though these reports would prove to be rather laconic. In June 1829, for example, the churches in Stanstead, Head of the Bay (Fitch Bay), Durham, and East Hatley were simply recorded as 'steadfast.' In West Hatley, the brethren were 'in good standing and the work of the Lord still progressing'; Barnston reported 'a rise in the minds of the Brethren, Monthly meeting kept up, and a seeming good prospect'; and Stanstead South was said to be 'Specially favored of the Lord and in a flourishing state.' Of the 179 members reported (East Hatley was omitted), the range was between 59 in Barnston and 7 in Durham.[39]

Membership in the existing churches did not increase greatly in the coming months and years, but it was agreed to admit Compton and Westbury Townships and Newport, Vermont (with only nine members) later in 1829. At the September meeting of that year, West Hatley reported 'a considerable revival in the Bolton part,' only to be followed by 'rather a declention' in January 1830. At the following meeting, Georgeville reported 'some trials,' having dismissed three of its twelve members. It issued a 'request for help,' as did the Head of the Bay, and, in January 1831, the Stanstead Quarterly Meeting itself asked the New Hampshire Yearly Meeting for assistance.

While the Regular Baptist Church eventually became more British, the more numerous Freewill Baptists remained loosely tied to American associations. Strongly localist in nature, these churches continued to grow in an unsynchronized roller-coaster fashion during the early 1830s, with no uniform ups and downs among the various congregations. The Compton minutes offer the most intimate glimpse of developments at the local level. After a small summer revival in 1831, Compton expanded to include members in Ascot, where William Jones was ordained as a second deacon. A second regular Monthly Meeting was to be held at his residence. Perhaps due to Jones's influence, more effort was now made to institutionalize the local church, for in February 1832 a committee of five men was appointed 'to adopt some measure for the support of the Gospel and to examine the Church record.'[40] Fifty-seven members were reported to the Stanstead Quarterly Meeting in June, but no attempt was made to erect a church building. Members continued to meet in various local schoolhouses as well as in Jones's home.

Jones's influence on the Compton congregation was shortlived, for his township of Ascot was established as a distinct Monthly Meeting with twelve members in November 1832. Presumably to re-ignite flagging interest within Compton, a committee of six was struck in December 'to visit the absent members.' Its January 1833 report 'Found fellowship good axept betwene Sister Hews and Sister Cummins,' and a committee of three was appointed to visit the two families in order to 'strive by the help of the Lord for Reconciliation.' According to the 'gospel rule' established by Randall, if the select committee of males or females named by the aggrieved parties should prove unable to bring about a reconciliation, the case would be reported in detail to the congregation which would attempt to restore the union. If either party refused to be subject to the public discipline, they were 'cut off from communion, fellowship, and membership.'[41] Recent research by Lynne Marks reveals that a principal preoccupation of the locally enforced church discipline in Upper Canada's Baptist Church, and to a lesser extent its Presbyterian Church, was to restore community harmony that had been disrupted by gossip and mutual recrimination. This tendency, according to Roth, increased with the rise of the temperance and sabbatarian movements. Roth has also found that such moral policing attempts were increasingly challenged in early nineteenth century Vermont's Connecticut Valley.[42] In the Compton case, the committee reported that there was no hope for reconciliation because Sister Cummins 'did not show a Christian spirit and requested a dismission from the church.' She was therefore expelled, but her husband's request for dismissal as well was not granted because 'he was in good fellowship with Bretherin.'

By May 1833, the Compton Church had grown to approximately forty-five men and thirty-nine women (judging from the Christian names). Enthusiasm remained low, however, for the July minutes reported 'a tolerable good seasen, no business done,' followed in September by 'rather a Low time, no business done.' October's monthly meeting 'Found the Fellowship good amog the presant brethering except Brother S. Killam am Brother R. Miller did not Fellowship with Sister Eunice Killam.' Again a committee was appointed 'to visit absent members.' No record was kept for the next three years 'In consequence of the neglectfull and scattering situation of the Church.'

There continued to be little uniformity in the waxing and waning of religious enthusiasm in the local churches, which may explain why, in

September 1833, it was decided 'to promote an itinerancy' within the area of the Stanstead Quarterly Meeting by establishing a society with a president, vice-president, secretary, and two treasurers. This society would pay three travelling preachers $100 a year 'in such property as shall answer their domestic use,' with all local societies except Bolton (which had not submitted a report) to have an equal share of their services. Local churches would form themselves into auxiliary societies, and a contribution rate was set for each of them, ranging from $45.75 for Stanstead no. 1 (Stanstead Township now had four churches) to $12.00 for Ascot, though not all the churches were listed. Once again, the effort to create even a modestly bureaucratic structure failed to get far off the ground. In January 1834, Stanstead no. 1's $50 was the only contribution listed for the itinerant ministry. The committee on itinerancy reported that it could make no arrangement due to 'want of proper means,' though it did appoint two preachers to fill the role of one itinerant for the coming year.

The member churches were no more forthcoming at the following meetings, but, a year later, Elder Harvey of Barnston reported receiving $55.40 from different sources, and labouring 205 days, while Elder Moulton worked 183 days for $51.73, and Elder Cross reported 100 days for only $13.70. Despite the efforts of the three itinerants, many of the churches were reported as being in a 'low state' in June 1834, though membership had increased by forty-nine over the year to reach 385. In Matters had not changed much by June 1835, except in Stanstead no. 1, which was 'experiencing refreshments from the presence of the Lord,' and Stanstead no. 2 where 'a good reformation' was said to have taken place. These two churches alone had 153 members.

An ecumenical spirit was clearly running through the evangelical churches at this time, for two Congregational ministers, Ammi Parker and Samuel Talbert, were given seats at the September 1834 conference. In September 1835 a New Connection Methodist named Amos Tylor was invited to preach 'among us as the Lord may direct,' and to attach himself to one of the local churches. Tylor was 'called to the ministry' in Hatley a year later,[43] a move which the Quarterly Meeting would later have cause to regret. There were limits to their tolerance for other denominations, however, for when Ascot asked in January 1836 whether it could dismiss a member to the Universalists, the answer was no.

While campaigning for the right of their church to perform marriages, the elders entertained some rather surprising questions and provided some surprising answers related to the state of matrimony. Thus, the Westbury church asked in September 1831 'whether a woman living with a man who has another wife shall be a member of the Church.' The question was referred to the next meeting, which in turn referred the local church to the New Testament. In January 1836 an elder asked if the conference would 'approbate' a married man or woman who had been remarried by a magistrate in the United States, or members 'marrying with infidels and licentious persons.' To the first question the answer was simply no, but to the second it was that the church should advise the members in question 'to desist from such a connection,' which was effectively condoning dissolution of the marriage.

Nor was it always easy to enforce the basic rules of the church, for the September 1836 meeting was informed that a Barnston deacon had administered the laying on of hands. When the Compton church met again the same month, after a hiatus of three years, it was still subject to a division between two members due to the fact that one of them believed 'in the universal Restoration of all.' A committee was also appointed by the Quarterly Meeting to investigate the qualifications necessary for taking communion.

Tentative attempts were nevertheless being made to become a more integral part of a larger institutional structure. The meeting of January 1836 tied the Stanstead Quarterly Meeting to the rising temperance movement by condemning 'the constant use of ardent spirits ... so as to be frequently disguised by it,' as well as the manufacturing or vending of the same. In June 1838 a resolution was passed supporting the American-published *Morning Star*'s stand on slavery, popery, temperance, foreign missions, Sabbath schools, and so on.[44] Finally, in September 1839 the Quarterly Meeting also voted to support 'all literary institutions by which knowledge of the Holy Scriptures is opened,' especially those about to be established under the direction of the Freewill Baptist Church in Vermont.

Such efforts would obviously require a reasonably stable financial base, and one more attempt was made to establish one when the January 1836 Quarterly Meeting voted to impose half a percent on all possessions to support preaching. But this attempt to break down localism was poorly timed because crops were failing and the economy heading into a recession. The assessment motion was rescinded the following September when it was decided to appoint someone from each church to determine what their fellow members would do for the cause. The answer was apparently very little, for the itinerant ministry came to an end, and the local churches had to be appealed to for funds to send one delegate to the Yearly Meeting.

The more immediate concern, however, was the declining membership. The larger churches of East Hatley and Stanstead no. 1 continued to grow in 1835 and 1836, but economic conditions had a negative impact elsewhere. In January 1837 the Durham meeting reported 'the cause of religion languishing in consequence of the continual tide of emigration to the West.' The following June, it reported that thirty-six members had taken this path, and Eaton's report simply stated 'This church mostly gone to the West.' A committee was appointed to visit the delinquent churches in January 1838, and in September it reported that the two Eaton churches had become one, Westbury had only three or four members, and there were 'some trials' in the new Coaticook church, though Stanstead no. 5 was 'somewhat awakened.' Those committee members who were supposed to visit the other churches failed to submit a report. Clearly, the Freewill Baptists were being undermined by more than emigration, for the lack of institutional support kept them reliant on a level of local enthusiasm that was impossible to sustain without periodic declines and divisions, particularly in an era of political turmoil such as that of the Rebellions.

An admittedly self-serving report submitted in 1838 by Hatley's Wesleyan Methodist preacher, John Rain, provides a revealing glimpse into the tactics used by the Freewill Baptists to attract and hold followers. Rain complained that they had greeted his arrival by informing the people that the Wesleyans would baptize only by sprinkling. When it was pointed out that his predecessor had recently baptized twenty or thirty adults by immersion in one day, the Baptists had responded that only they had the spiritual right to administer this sacrament 'because Jesus Christ was baptized by John the Baptist and they were the linial descendants of that great preacher of righteousness.' Finally, the Baptist preachers reportedly claimed that the Wesleyan missionaries were all Free Masons 'and that the Discipline of Wesleyan Methodism was administered upon the principles of freemasonry,' and also that they were Tories 'and as such inimical to the interests of the Country.'[45]

After years of decline, 1840 brought a general renewal of religious enthusiasm in the Eastern Townships, and membership of the Stanstead Quarterly Meeting increased from 540 in June to 695 in September. New churches were established at Massawippi, Dudswell, and Bury, and the membership reached 870 by June 1841. Attempts were also made to impose some surprisingly basic rules. In June 1841 it was resolved that baptism by immersion was an indispensable prerogative for membership in the church, and that ministers should not 'baptize persons who are unwilling to unite with any Christian Church.' To save embarrassment, it was moved that the former resolution not be sent to the *Morning Star* for publication, but Stanstead no. 1 proceeded to receive a member without immersion. This step the September meeting considered to be 'not a sin but a deviation from F.W. Baptist principles,' and asked the Stanstead church not to repeat the practice. The social reform initiative was also continued, for another resolution was passed condemning slavery, and in June 1842 a meeting was called to amend the constitution 'so that the church may be built on temperance principles.'

In Compton, where the monthly meetings had been infrequent in 1838 and 1839, the church members expressed a desire in February 1840 to 'renew there covenant with God, and be more faithfull in the discharge of there duty.' There were now thirty-three men, outnumbered for the first time by the forty-five women. The new covenant began much like the earlier ones by pledging 'to exercise a mutual care as members one of another to promote the growth of the whole body in Christian knowledge, holiness and comfort to the end that we may stand completed in all the will of God.' But it was also a longer document which stressed attendance at regular public worship, prayer meetings, and monthly conferences, as well as contributions proportionate 'to our several abilities and circumstances for the suppoart of a faithfull ministry of the gospel among us.' Committees were eventually established to determine how much each person should contribute.

Reflecting the preponderant number of women in the church, as well as the rising general interest in childhood and social reform, the covenant also stated that 'we will not omit closet and Family religion at home nor allow our selves in the too common neglect of the great duty of training up our children and those under our care with a view to the service of Christ and the enjoyment of heaven.' In addition, adherents were to support missions, Sabbath schools, and temperance societies. Indeed, those who signed the covenant agreed not to 'drink ardent spirits our selves, nor allow them to be drank in our Families nor furnish them for persons in our employ unless in either case they are cautiously used as a medicine where no substitute [exists].' The initiative begun several years earlier by the Stanstead Quarterly Meeting had, therefore, penetrated to the local level.

More members were added during the following meetings in Compton, at one of which 'a number of young converts' appeared for the first time. In June 1841 two Compton churches were reported by the Quarterly Meeting, with sixty-one members in the first and thirty-nine in the second. Puritanical zeal also increased during the following months, for in September a clause was added to the covenant stating that it was the members' duty to 'shun the ball rooms, card playing, circus ride, horse racing and all other places of carnal recreation.' Three months later, predictably enough, it was found that a number of members had transgressed the church rules. As attendance at the Monthly Meeting declined, complaints were entered against a woman 'for attending balls and neglecting religious worship,' and against three men 'for using ardent spirits for a Drink.' The minutes then became less frequent until they skip nearly four years to August 1846, though the two churches did continue to submit dispirited reports to the Stanstead Quarterly Meeting. Membership fell from 105 in June 1843 to sixty-five two years later.

The Freewill Baptist membership had also passed its peak in the Eastern Townships as a whole by June 1843, when it declined to 616. For unspecified reasons, however, the churches in the County of Sherbrooke withdrew that month to establish the St Francis Quarterly Meeting, leaving the Stanstead Meeting confined to the County of Stanstead. The St Francis constitution, subsequently adopted by Stanstead, provided for a minimum of one delegate from each church, with those having 25 members allowed to send 2, and those with 75 permitted 3.[46] The St Francis Quarterly Meeting began with ten churches, but in June 1844 there were only 283 members in the eight that remained. From the earliest meetings, the situation was recorded as unfavourable in four or five of these Monthly Meetings. For example, there was dissension in Melbourne from the start because the preacher, Howard Lothrop, refused to state that he believed in the church discipline and organization. He asked to be dismissed, but proceeded to publish critical articles in the *Morning Star*, having failed to return his credentials.[47]

The Sherbrooke churches had established their own Quarterly Meeting at a particularly inopportune time due to the invasion of Millerite preachers from across the border. Even though William Miller himself was a firm Calvinist Baptist, the dramatic message of his movement was attractive to many members of the more radical evangelical sects.[48] The Millerites' strategy was to preach their doctrine from within the existing churches, but internal dissension became more heated after the Apocalypse failed to take place as predicted, causing many members to leave or be expelled. Those who remained committed to the premillenarian cause established their own Adventist churches. Thus, a large minority left Dudswell's Monthly Meeting in 1845, and, in September of that year, only one church submitted a favourable report to the St Francis Quarterly Meeting. In an attempt to hold on to its remaining adherents, this meeting passed a resolution stating that 'we Believe in the Speedy Coming of our Saviour & have Fellowship with those who preach it without Date.' The final resolution of the St Francis Quarterly Meeting in June 1846 was to dissolve itself back into the Stanstead Quarterly Meeting, which had begun supporting reunion a year earlier.

It appears that popular disillusionment with religion in general had set in with the Millerites' 'great disappointment,' just as the editor of the *Register* had predicted.[49] The Stanstead Quarterly Meeting had resolved in September 1843 'that we approbate the preaching of the 2nd Advent without stating the time.' But the meeting of June 1844 drew a firmer line: 'Resolved that we do not approbate the preaching of the doctrine of annihilation.' But neither tactic was successful, for only a small number of churches submitted reports, and only occasionally from late 1843 to 1846.[50]

It appears that two churches in the Stanstead Quarterly Meeting were taken over by the Millerites, for in June 1845 the West Hatley church was dropped 'Agreeable to their wish,' and in February 1846 the Creek Church (formerly Stanstead no. 3) was 'reported out of order.' In addition, Norman Stevens, who had first been licensed to preach to the Coaticook church in September 1837, was expelled in September 1844. Two years later he was asked to surrender his credentials, 'as he has left the Q.M. in disorder occasioned by the Miller excitement.'

But the region's Freewill Baptist churches appeared to be making a slight recovery in late 1846. The September meeting reported 'some revival' in Barnston, and the Creek Church was re-established in February 1847, when Massawippi also reported 'some revival,' and Compton no. 1 claimed 'encouraging prospects.' Only four churches reported membership numbers in June 1847, but six delegates were chosen for the Vermont Yearly Meeting, and by September the Quarterly Meeting was emboldened to recommend that churches 'be more strict in discipline.' The impact of Millerism had not ended, however, for it also chastised Elder William Warner of Eaton – one of the original preachers in the Stanstead Quarterly Meeting – for his long absence, unsupported accusations against certain members of the conference, 'and his Course in Attending Meetings Casting his influence with Modern Comouters in preference to uniting His influence with us in Building up the Cause of God.' The group referred to was clearly the Adventists, who had been instructed to 'come out' of Babylon, now identified as the other Protestant denominations as well as the Roman Catholic Church. Warner was expelled by the June 1847 meeting for supporting another sect 'who are using their influence Against us.' A year later, the Eaton Monthly Meeting was still said to be undergoing 'trials on the Account of Comeoutism,' and it disappeared from the records for more than two years.

The Stanstead Quarterly Meeting clearly continued to include a significant component with Adventist tendencies, for visiting delegates from Wheelock asked to withdraw from the June 1847 meeting when a Mr Litch began to lecture, stating that because they had 'some conscientious scruples' concerning him. The person in question was obviously the prominent American Adventist, Josiah Litch, who visited the region several times.[51] The Wheelock delegates proceeded to complain to the Yearly Meeting which asked Stanstead in December 1848 to 'make some acknowledgement' of its transgression. This, it initially refused to do, thereby revealing that the local churches were not alone in their resistance to higher authority.

And local resistance did persist, for in September 1849 Dudswell was reported to be 'out of *order.*' The problem appears to have revolved around the appointment of a particular individual as preacher, which led to secession by a group that was, nevertheless, then admitted to the Quarterly Meeting as a sister church. Other churches were simply dissolved for unspecified reasons, as in the case of Barnston and Ascot in March 1850. Three months later, the committee that had visited the Head of the Bay reported that there was no use attempting to revive the church unless a minister settled among them. Only Compton (now down to one church), East Hatley, Stanstead no. 1, and Coaticook (Barnston-Barford) had significant membership numbers, with the Quarterly Meeting as a whole reporting only 290 adherents.

A concerted effort had been made in Compton the previous January to re-establish what had clearly been a moribund church. Committees had been appointed to nominate a deacon, to take up a subscription to employ preachers, to 'receive members into the Church,' and to visit members of the Ascot church. In April a committee had been appointed 'to visit delinquent members on Sleeper Hill and in the Carr neighborhood,' and more members were added then and during the following meetings. Membership in the Compton church reached eighty-four by June 1851 but, as in the past, internal dissension had already begun to emerge.

Amos Tyler, who had converted from the New Connection Methodists in 1835, had apparently launched a funding campaign without the permission of the local church, which had its own committee for the purpose. He subsequently accused Moses Folsom, who had been elected preacher for the year, of being a liar. In July 1851 a resolution was passed asking Tyler and one of the other two men charged with him to promise that, 'if the Church will overlook their past errors, they will strive to live with and for the Church in future, and avoid speaking or pursuing any course that is likely to savour bad feelings and that they will strive to love and build each other up in their most holy faith and labor for the good of souls.' When the two men refused to comply, the three members of the Quarterly Meeting Council were empowered to make a binding decision on the matter. In August, they reported that there was no proof that Tyler had been ill-intentioned in launching the subscription, and his action should not, therefore, be considered 'a breach of Christian fellowship.' But they did ask him to apologize for accusing the pastor of falsehood. The stubborn Tyler still wanted time to consider, and in October a committee was appointed to visit him in an attempt 'to regain him to the fellowship of the Church,' as well as warn him that he must submit by the next meeting. This Tyler refused to do, and the March 1852 session finally expelled him from the church. Twenty-two others subsequently left the church in sympathy with Tyler. In May 1852 the Monthly Meeting responded by voting that these individuals 'be reported as having gone out from us because they were not from us.' What local jealousies were behind the rift is not clear, but, in an attempt to prevent such schisms in the future, a resolution had been passed that all complaints and requests should be introduced to the church through its officers.[52]

The Freewill Baptists were supposed to live in – but not of – the world, centring their community 'around procedures that required doctrinal, moral, and spiritual union.'[53] But judging from the reluctance of the Compton members to submit to criticism, and the surprisingly small number of discipline cases recorded in the minutes of the Stanstead Quarterly Meeting and the Compton Monthly Meeting, this loosely-structured and non-hierarchical denomination was in a weak position to enforce church discipline. The Tyler case clearly also reflected a weakening sense of loyalty to the Freewill Baptist Church in the post-Millerite era when dissension continued to plague the rest of the Quarterly Meeting as well. In September 1850 the East Hatley church – which remained the largest in the district – took steps to revive itself by examining its members 'with a view to a renewal of their Fellowship and covenant with each other as church members.' But only a minority did so, and the June 1851 meeting reported considerable division in East Hatley because of this initiative. It was subsequently dropped in September when the church stated that it was 'praying for better days.' The Creek Church of Stanstead Township was expelled at the same meeting because many of the members were 'not worthy to bear the name.' Conditions had not improved by March 1852, when the Stanstead Quarterly Meeting decided to correspond with the parent Home Missionary Society in order to 'lay before them our circumstances and anxieties.' The women had established a successful branch of the Female Missionary Society, but otherwise the Freewill Baptists of the Eastern Townships had failed to recover from the Millerite incursion.

Conclusion

Assessing the strength of the the Freewill Baptist Church presents a challenge as it does not appear as a distinct denominational category in the census reports, and the manuscript schedules of many enumerators therefore simply include its adherents with the Regular Baptist Church. But the evangelical branch does appear to have been the more popular one in the Eastern Townships, which should not be surprising given its strength in neighbouring Vermont.[54] Even the lack of support from a missionary society was a less serious handicap than it would have been for most other denominations, given that three levels of office – the preaching elder, the ruling elder, and the deacon – could perform the ordinances. Nor was the Freewill Baptist Church plagued by the doctrinal disputes which divided their Calvinist counterparts between the American and British traditions. And if Millerism was largely a reaction against the formalization of the evangelical pietistic denominations, as Rowe argues,[55] the Freewill Baptists should have been relatively immune to its appeal. Despite efforts to strengthen the role of the Quarterly Meeting by introducing tax assessments, and by making the covenants reflect the American-inspired shift towards social reform, the Freewill Baptists remained intensely localized. It was this characteristic that left this denomination vulnerable to instability and schism, as well as the appeal of the well-organized Millerites. While obviously not all Freewill Baptists were attracted to the Adventist Church, which established only a small number of congregations in the region, the Millerite movement did stir up a level of debate and dissension that fragmented most of the local congregations.

5

The Smaller Sects

The Pilgrims

In 1816, the year that June snows destroyed crops in many areas of the world, including Lower Canada, there was a widespread religious revival.[1] It may not be coincidental, then, that this was the year that witnessed the appearance of the one radical religious movement ever to originate in the Eastern Townships, a sect generally known as the Pilgrims. The independent preacher Joseph Badger recorded in his journal that when he returned to the Eastern Townships from New England in 1816 he found that the 'Christians' in Ascot, whom he had lived among when he first left his parental home, had become a cult. According to Badger, they had adopted 'the spirit of self-righteousness' by recognizing one of their members as 'Apostle and Prophet,' whose 'authority was equal to anything in the Holy Scripture.' Badger's rather remarkable description continued:

> *He* had revelations concerning all the business to be done by his followers; also his pretended illumination extended to marriages and to the intercourse of the sexes, and when his *ipse dixit* was given on these points, immorality was unblushingly practiced. Pretending to have personal interviews with angels he had six followers, who, at his command, would fall upon their knees, lie prostrate upon the floor, or walk in a pretended labour for souls. Sometimes he kept them walking for several days and nights without eating or sleeping, when they would frequently faint and fall upon the floor. They often screamed, howled, and barked, making various strange noises, and bending themselves up into many shapes. They most tenaciously held that they were the only true church on earth, and that no per-

son out of their pale was capable of giving them the least instruction. Like all the fanatics I ever saw, they evinced great hatred and spite when opposed, and sometimes they were full of the spirit of mocking.[2]

After eighteen hours of debate with his old friends, Badger was unable to shake their heretical beliefs.

According to another contemporary account, this one by the early Vermont historian Zadoch Thompson, the leader of the group, named Isaac Bullard, had experienced 'a long confinement by sickness' before he 'assumed the character of a prophet.' He 'wore a leathern girdle and rough garments to deceive, and with a few adherents known as the Pilgrims entered the north part of the State' in 1817. Later proceeding southward, Bullard had only eight followers when he reached Woodstock, Vermont where he succeeded in converting approximately forty people, including a local Christian Connection preacher. Thompson claimed that 'they were frequently seen, even the adult females, rolling in the dirt of the highway, and presenting a spectacle as indecent and loathsome as can well be imagined.' Described as a red-bearded giant, Bullard controlled all their property as well as 'their most intimate domestic relations, marrying and unmarrying, rewarding and punishing, according to his sovereign pleasure.'[3] Bullard's doctrine called for a life of repentance, poverty, and rigorous self-denial, with penances that increased in harshness with the degree of 'perfection' that had been attained. The newly converted might be required to stand for as long as four days without sleeping, but fasting was the prinicipal mode of penance.[4]

Having exhausted their means of subsistence in Woodstock, the Pilgrims migrated across the Green Mountains to Bennington County where they won some converts before proceeding westward on foot in two groups to the Ohio River in the spring of 1818. By this time, according to Thompson, they had grown to two or three hundred. En route, the Pilgrims attracted considerable attention from the press, whose uniformly hostile and sensationalist descriptions suggest that the sect or cult served as a convenient foil for the promoters of American economic and social progress. When Bullard and his followers were barred from entering Cincinnati because of their 'affliction by the smallpox, and of their extreme filthiness,' thousands of citizens jammed the roads to witness the 'seat of filth.'[5]

Believing that the Land of Canaan was to be found in the trans-Mississippi West, the Pilgrims next took a boat to the old Spanish garrison town of New Madrid, Missouri, which had been devastated by an earthquake in 1811. Here, in Thompson's words, 'Many died by sickness produced by hardship and deprivation, and others abandoned the company to avoid the same catastrophe.' After still more mishaps, Bullard's band was reduced to his wife, another woman, and two children by 1819.[6] Clearly seen as an anomaly even in the radical climate of the burned-over country, it is rather ironic that a British colony should have produced what one historian (writing before the emergence of the apocalyptic cults of recent history) has identified as 'the most bizarre and primitive sect in American religious history.' But the most notable feature of Bullard's Pilgrims, as far as understanding religious culture in the Eastern Townships is concerned, is that they remained in the region only a short period of time.[7]

The Quakers

In a sense, the tightly knit Quakers, or Society of Friends, lie outside this study's underlying theme of a competitive struggle between the American and British denominations, as well as between radical revivalism and religious conservatism. While Quakerism conformed to the religion of experience as opposed to the religion of order, the Friends' isolationism and small numbers meant that they represented little threat to British hegemony in the Eastern Townships. While the region's Quakers were not immune from the powerful evangelistic impulse of the early nineteenth century, their proselytizing efforts were confined to quixotic adventures among the First Nations of the American West. As previously noted, the Eastern Townships Quakers were largely concentrated in East Farnham Township, where the majority arrived in the 1820s. There were never more than one to two hundred members at the peak of the Farnham Meeting, which was the only Quaker community in Lower Canada. The fact that the Farnham Meeting survived for nearly a century (which was much longer than its counterparts in Vermont), attests less to its dynamism than to its persistent isolation in an increasingly French-speaking Catholic environment.[8]

One reason for the failure of the Society of Friends to grow was the strict discipline imposed on its members. Each local congregation, known as the Meeting for Worship, held twice-weekly religious services, as well as a monthly Preparative Meeting in which were read 'Queries' concerning adherence to Quaker practice as outlined in the *Discipline*. The responses were recorded by a clerk as the 'sense of the meeting,' and at least two representatives reported this 'minute' to the Monthly Business Meeting, which dealt with the recognition of ministers, complaints concerning non-compliance with the *Discipline*, applications for membership or marriage, and so on.[9]

In 1821 fourteen applicants from Farnham obtained from the Ferrisburg, Vermont, Monthly Meeting one year's permission to hold Meetings for Worship on Sundays and Thursdays. A year later, after a committee from Ferrisburg had visited Farnham, the community was allowed to hold an 'indulged' Preparative Meeting. The first meeting house was built in 1823, and in 1826 Farnham was recognized as a Preparative Meeting under the authority of Ferrisburg. Two members of the Farnham Meeting were supposed to attend each Monthly Meeting in Ferrisburg, some eighty miles away, where they would present the minutes of their meetings, various requests (often for money), and obtain instructions as well as solutions to minor problems. The Monthly Meeting held all property in the Preparative Meetings, and had the power to receive or reject new members as well as to disown members for infractions of the *Discipline*. This arrangement represented a remarkable degree of external control for a society that officially rejected all forms of priesthood and hierarchy.[10]

In addition, internal control was assured by a number of elders, who held office for life, and whose duty it was to advise and counsel the ministers.[11] Although Quakers believed that the universal accessibility of the Inner Light precluded the need for an ordained clergy, in practice the silence during the Meetings of Worship was interrupted at frequent intervals by those recorded as ministers. At the Farnham Sunday meeting, members would sit in silence for approximately an hour, listening for the 'Divine Voice' to speak to their souls. Theoretically, anyone might have a vocal message for the meeting, becoming for the moment the mouthpiece of the spirit, but in Farnham, according to Zielinski, 'really inspired testimonies were rare.' Instead, the period of silence was generally followed by an hour's sermon from one of the ministers.[12] A local member claimed in 1908 that at one time there had been seven recorded ministers in East Farnham. Their duties were confined to preaching, since the Quakers did not have baptism or communion, and couples married themselves before witnesses (with the permission of the Monthly Meeting).[13]

In keeping with the evangelicalism of the era, a spontaneous and unorganized itinerant ministry also developed, though the man or woman called by God to perform a religious service required authorization to do so by a 'minute' from the appropriate meeting. According to Dorland, these missionaries were 'the makers and leaders of Quakerism' during the eighteenth and early nineteenth centuries.[14] As early as 1823, Samuel Knowles of East Farnham joined Joseph Hoag of Ferrisburg to make the longest trip on the record of either Meeting. They travelled 7,600 miles in twenty-one months, visiting New York, Upper Canada, Ohio, Virginia, North Carolina, Tennessee, Indiana, and Illinois, though it is not clear if Knowles was present for the entire journey.[15]

Perhaps to compensate for the community's insularity, the missionary impulse remained alive among the East Farnham Quakers during the 1830s. At some point during that decade, a married woman named Sarah Knowles left on a preaching tour, apparently never returning. Then in 1839 David and Drusilla Knowles 'felt a concern' to preach to the American Indians, about whom they knew very little. Though David was lame, and the Committee on Indian Affairs attempted to dissuade them when the couple reached New York, they crossed the Allegheny Mountains in a January snow storm, reached Independence, Missouri, in August 1840, and spent ten months in Indiana and Michigan, finally arriving home in July 1841. They had enjoyed no success with the Natives, but had travelled some five thousand miles with the same horse and buggy while the Farnham Meeting took care of their farm and children. David left again in 1847, travelling to Upper Canada, Michigan, Wisconsin, Indiana, and Ohio.[16]

Such 'religious visits' could impose significant hardship on a Meeting, for it was expected to take care of the 'temporal concerns' of the minister, who was usually a farmer and head of a family. In 1830 the Farham Meeting established an evaluation role for the purposes of supporting itself on a proportional basis. The fact that the Quakers thereby became the only religious society in the Eastern Townships to succeed in imposing a tax on its membership, at least during the first half of the century, clearly attests to the power wielded by their elders.[17] Funds must have been limited, however, for the first meeting house was not replaced for three years after it burned down in 1831. Like other chapels in the region, it had two doors – one for men and one for women – and a gallery, though access to this was restricted to the ministers and elders. A more unique feature was the two rocking chairs in front of the gallery reserved for two local men, one of whom had an infirmity.[18]

By 1826 the East Farnham Quakers had organized committees for the care of schools, the poor, the meeting house, missions to the Indians, investigating the morals of certain members, and so on. Only two years later, however, the Farnham Meeting was briefly closed without warning by the Ferrisburg Monthly Meeting. Edward Hicks was leading a Quietist reaction in New England against the society's evangelistic trend, thereby splitting it into Hicksite and the paradoxically named Orthodox factions. Because the Farnham Meeting remained Orthodox while the Ferrisburg Meeting was briefly controlled by the Hicksites, the latter closed the former for a short period.[19] This imposition of external authority on Farnham was a rather ironic development, given Hicks's rejection of the society's increasingly denominational pattern of organization, but it represents another example of how religious culture in the Eastern Townships was less radical than that to the immediate south.

Owing to the political disabilities imposed on Quakers in Britain, as a result of their insistence upon 'affirming' their loyalty to the crown rather than taking an oath, they tended to dissociate themselves from public affairs. The British government allowed the affirmation option in 1833, but this legislation was initially not recognized when the Farnham Quakers were asked to take the oath during the Rebellions of 1837–8. Fortunately for them, the influential John Joseph Gurney of England happened to be visiting the community in the fall of 1838, and he was personally acquainted with Lord Durham. Gurney encouraged the Farnham Quakers to submit a petition testifying to their loyalty, and he provided those who carried the address to Quebec with letters of introduction. Durham then issued a statement confirming that the British Parliament's act of 1833 had established the right of affirmation in British North America.[20] Independence from the Americans followed naturally, and finally, in 1842 (after twenty-two years of existence) the Farnham Meeting became a regular Monthly Meeting independent from Ferrisburg.

While the external political threat had been dealt with satisfactorily, the social and economic influence of the outside world would not be so easy to resist. As their religion dictated, the East Farnham Quakers avoided mercantile pursuits as worldly distractions, and most of the businesses in the village of Allen's Corner (later East Farnham) were owned by a non-member. In 1843 one member was informed that he had 'extended his business beyond his ability to manage and had entirely neglected his family and temporal concerns by absenting himself from them for a long time.' A committee appointed to investigate the charge finally reported four years later that the man in question had 'manifested a more satisfactory disposition of mind than before' and had acknowledged the error of his ways, asking the Friends 'to pass it by and continue me as a member.' This apology was accepted by the Meeting.[21]

But commerce was not the only bone of contention. In 1843 another member was accused of having 'departed from plainness of dress and address' (the standard formula that introduced all charges), and having 'embraced and advocated by print and otherwise principles differing from those of our Society.' After eight months and two reports, the investigating committee disowned the individual in question.[22] Religious dissension was also affecting the Society as a whole, for it was split a second time in 1845 when the Wilburites left the evangelical Orthodox branch because of Joseph Gurney's opposition to John Wilbur when the former visited the United States in 1837. The Farnham Meeting was not affected at first, and it reached its peak of influence in 1850 when the Ferrisburg Quarterly Meeting began to meet there once a year. According to the *Census Reports* for 1852, however, there were only 129 Quakers in Farnham, with an additional twenty-eight scattered among eight other townships. When the Gurney-Wilbur controversy finally did reach East Farnham in 1853, the Gurneite victory was at a very heavy cost of disownments, resignations, and general dissatisfaction.[23] Growing numbers were also being disowned for marrying outside the Society, or simply leaving the Meeting, so that its survival until past the turn of the century must be attributed to the religious tenacity of a very small number of people.

The Universalists

Paradoxically, while Universalism emerges from the mainstream missionary correspondence as an even greater bogeyman than atheism, it was not included as a distinct category in the 1831 census, making it impossible to estimate how pervasive its presence was during the early nineteenth century. What is clear, however, is that the Universalists who did migrate to the Eastern Townships were largely left to their own devices by the New England parent societies until the early 1830s. Aside from the fact that this region was assumed to be hostile foreign territory, the Universalist movement lacked the organizational structure to coordinate an effective missionary campaign. With no acknowledged single leader, the Universalists remained institutionally diffuse, embracing a polity of anarchy in which local church observation of the ordinances remained optional, and every person was free to pursue the truth as he or she saw fit.[24] From the early period of settlement, however, travelling evangelists did carry the Universalist message into the New England hill country and the Eastern Townships. They expounded scriptures to small informal gatherings, which might then convert themselves into informal house-churches for worship and mutual support. These churches, in turn, mobilized their own leaders and resources for small-scale local proselytizing.

Missionary reports from competing denominations suggest that, despite the lack of outside support or internal organization, Universalism was quite pervasive in the southern townships. In 1822, for example, the Welseyan Methodist missionary Henry Pope reported from Melbourne that 'There are in these parts many professed *Universalists* who afford but little ground to expect[?] their ever being reclaimed from their delusion[?] as they seldom attend the preaching or any other religious service.'[25] In 1829 the Church of England suffered from an embarrassing blow when Bishop Stewart of Quebec learned, to his horror, that Sherbrooke's Anglican minister was maintaining 'that all punishment for sin was confined to this life, and that the prophecies of Scripture predicting the day of Judgment referred entirely to the destruction of Jerusalem.'[26] The son of a cleric attached to Pembroke College, Oxford, the thirty-two-year-old Clement Fall LeFevre claimed to have served as chaplain to the British embassy in Paris.[27] He later described his conversion experience in terms similar to those of a mystic: 'There was in it a transport, an ecstasy, a bliss which is beautifully described in Scripture as imparting to the soul, "a joy unspeakable and full of glory" ... If it did not impart to me another sense, it quickened and enlivened those which I already possessed. I thought that the sun looked brighter; the music of the birds sounded more melodious; the fruits of the earth tasted sweeter; the flowers smelt more fragrant; and the very air of heaven felt more balmy.'[28]

The Anglican minister in neighbouring Lennoxville, Adam Hood Burwell, reported that LeFevre had been reading Balfour's *Second Inquiry*, which had come into his hands by accident. According to Burwell, the book claimed that there were no evil spirits, no future punishment, no other day of judgment than the downfall of Jerusalem, no Trinity, and the ministry 'is all fraud & imposition ... I candidly confess it came nigh making me an Atheist.' LeFevre had expounded upon these positions from Burwell's Lennoxville pulpit in late May 1829. When asked to recant, 'he spoke in much assurance of the sudden & rapid spread of these infidel opinions, & prophecied from it a *glorious era of the*

Church!' He also apparently complained 'that he must expect so much severity from mere opinions,' when so much leniency was displayed toward the grossly immoral conduct of other Anglican clerics.[29]

Burwell was concerned that LeFevre would attempt to arouse popular sympathy on the basis of his dismissal: 'the poor deluded rabble are already counting upon the *good* he will do in opposing the Church. His self sacrifice is magnified as a glorious proof of the *truth* of his cause, & the crown of martyrdom seems already suspended over his head.' Burwell added that Le Fevre had been 'accommodating himself to the pecularities of the Americans, for they are all charmed with his insinuating manner. Absolam has been kissing the people.' Furthermore, LeFevre's partisans had been bold and active in proselytizing, and he had sent 'for more copies of those pestilent books' as well as a Universalist translation of the Bible. Should LeFevre decide to remain as a Universalist preacher, Burwell asked for permission to 'neutralize ... the moral poison of these "damnable heresies" in print.'[30]

Bishop Stewart ensured that LeFevre would leave for the United States as quickly and quietly as possible by paying him the inflated sum of £1,000 for his house. LeFevre had, however, obviously left a strong impression on the community, for a farewell address published in Stanstead's *British Colonist* stated that, despite differences of opinion about LeFevre's

> change in religious sentiments, ... we believe there cannot be one found, who would not feel inclined to applaud the high honor and integrity of principal and conscience which have inclined you to relinquish an independent support under a powerful patronage, rather than sacrifice or withold those doctrines or opinions which you conceive to be true, and which you felt it an imperious duty, by reason of your attachment to justice, and your desire for the attachment and dissemination of knowledge, to promulgate.[31]

A number of LeFevre's former parishioners subsequently joined the Universalists.[32] By 1834 there were three preachers and five societies reported in the Eastern Townships, the only ones that existed in the Canadas.[33] The impetus for this sudden growth may have come from the establishment in 1833 of the Vermont State Convention, which included Lower Canada, though such conventions concerned themselves largely with moral reform and Sunday schools. But this emphasis was a large part of Universalism's appeal in New York's Burned-Over

District, where, according to Cross, it 'acquired recruits in increasing numbers through the thirties, as people became satiated with protracted meetings and revivals.'[34] Whether or not the same was true of the Eastern Townships, this region was obviously affected by the growth in Universalism's popularity south of the border.

The Townships societies were served mostly by American itinerant preachers who generally stayed only a few days at a time in any one place. C.S. Lebourveau recalled in later years that the services of American preachers travelling through from Stanstead on foot were confined to houses and barns, 'as they were not to be tolerated in any of the churches, for their owners would as soon burn them as let such heretics, as they were then called, inside them.'[35] One American preacher who did settle in the region for a time was James Ward, a former Calvinist from New York who arrived in Stanstead in 1831.[36] He was one of the fourteen clergymen present at the founding of the Vermont Convention in 1833, and the Congregational minister for Ascot, A.S. Ware, reported the following year that 'Mr Ward is spreading universalism through this region with considerable activity & some success.'[37] Ward returned to Vermont in 1836, but he continued to visit the Townships into the 1840s.[38] In addition, a local history claims that Eli Ballou began to serve Knowlton and surrounding communities in 1831, but he remained only a year, and there was no more preaching in the area until 1835. The only societies identified for 1835 are Stanstead, Shipton, Ascot, Compton, and Brome, but, the following, year Jacob L. Watson was ordained in Shefford.[39]

The clergy of the other denominations were far from pleased with this somewhat limited and belated Universalist impulse. A local resident reported to the *Universalist Magazine* in 1833 that the Universalists' sermons 'have set the country on fire,' causing other clergy to use 'all their power to put down "*infidels*" and their ministers.' The following year, a Stukely correspondent wrote that 'Our limitarian brethern are very much opposed to Universalism. There is no slander too bad for them.'[40] These reports were not exaggerated. In 1833, when the Universalists of Ascot petitioned the government for the right to hold a marriage register, the prominent Montreal merchant George Moffat pronounced in the Legislative Council that he opposed 'granting privileges to loosely formed congregations – to sects that had no visible existence.' Bishop George Mountain was less restrained: 'He hoped that a Legislature which prevented by law the slandering of the name of an individual would still protect from blasphemy the name of God,' and declared that

'Privileges ought to be limited to Christians only.' The Anglican newspaper of the diocese went still further when it declared that 'Arians, Unitarians, Universalists, or other questioners of some part of the creed, should be refused naturalization, the right to circulate literature, the ownership of land, or even the possession of a cemetery in which to bury the dead.'[41]

Despite the limited scope of their missionary campaign, the Universalists appear to have been feared by the Anglican clergy for the possible contaminating effect of their message. Charles Cotton of Dunham complained in 1835 that 'The Universalists have been attempting by occasional meetings, to spread the influence of their pernicious and unscriptural views of the Gospel, among our people, but thanks be to God, their efforts have hitherto met with but little success.'[42] The Universalists took on a more threatening image with the outbreak of the Rebellions, when Cotton claimed that they included 'the chief abettors of disloyalty and sedition' in the region. It is clearly no accident that Universalist clergymen such as James Ward of Stanstead and Joseph Baker of Waterloo returned to the United States at this time.[43] In 1839, Cotton reported that one benefit of the military presence was that it had stopped 'the influence of Universalist itinerant Teachers, who had heretofore been busily engaged in endeavouring, by the dissemination of heretical doctrines, to undermine, if possible the foundations, or at least, to lessen the influence of sound Church principles, in the minds of our people.'[44]

The clergy of the other denominations were not much more tolerant. In 1836 the Wesleyan Methodist missionary for the Shefford circuit, Thomas Turner, reported that for the previous several years Brome Township had been served only by Unitarians and Universalists whose preaching 'only tends to the increase of ungodliness and immorality among them.' And in 1837 the Methodist New Connection missionary, John Addyman, declared that in some parts of Bolton 'the people are very wicked; and many of them are abandoned to universalism, which is awful prevalent in different parts of Lower Canada.'[45]

Butler observes that 'Among a people simultaneously sweeping away the encrustations of the past and forging new constitutions to bring new states and a nation into being, an emphasis on simple, universal religious principles held considerable appeal.'[46] That appeal was obviously transferred to the Eastern Townships to some degree, but the political and ideological context was quite different in post-revolutionary British North America. Despite the belated missionary impulse and the rapid growth of Universalism in Vermont during the 1830s and 1840s, the Province of Canada's 1852 census reveals that there were only 3,319 Universalists (6.3 per cent of the Protestant population) distributed over thirty-five townships in the Eastern Townships. The region's only enduring centres of Universalism were the town of Waterloo and Ascot Township's Huntingville, where a handsome meeting house of neo-classical design was dedicated in 1845 (see illustration 4), and where Caleb P. Mallory focused his activities for nearly forty years.[47]

The Christian Brethren

In January 1832 Charles Cotton reported that in the townships of Brome and Farnham

> a new sect has arrived, not known here before, stiling themselves, 'Christian Brethren.' With a view, as is reasonably supposed of acquiring a larger share of influence and popularity, they profess to be in true fellowship with all Christian people, yet they disclaim every other mode of baptism excepting that by total immersion, and it has been for some time suspected, and lately ascertained, that their belief is antitrinitarian, and that they also believe in the doctrine of annihilation.[48]

Cotton was not far off the mark. The sect in question appears to have been the Christians founded in 1801 by a group of laymen in Lyndon, Vermont, and associated chiefly with the premillenarian, Elias Smith, who later became a Universalist.[49] Like the Unitarians, they preached the absolute independence of each church, disclaimed creeds, and believed in the unity of God. But, like the Baptists, they also emphasized regeneration by conversion, adult immersion, and a literal reading of the Bible.[50] The appeal of this sect on a settlement frontier is not hard to understand, for it incorporated some of the cathartic elements missing from Universalism, but Cotton claimed that 'Since their absurd and unscriptural doctrines have been discovered, those who were entirely attached to this new sect have become very lukewarm in the cause, and they are now, as a separate (and for a time flourishing) sect, fast going into decay.'[51]

The Christian Brethren did not disappear from the region at this point, however, for four years later, in 1836, Thomas Turner reported a small group of adherents in Stukely Township. He claimed that 'They are in their religious opinions Semi-Arians as to the person of Christ, and Unitarians in regard to the doctrine of the Trinity.' The Stukely group had left the Methodist Society a few years earlier, and 'On account of the specious name by which they call themselves and as they generally conceal their real sentiments on the doctrines named above, and as they hold some sentiments in common with ourselves, they are rather a dangerous people among our members.' Turner added that their preacher had recently left, however, and they had 'for some time past been much on the decline.'[52]

But the sect emerges in the historical record once again in 1840, when Shefford's Wesleyan missionary, John Tomkins, reported that the Christian Brethren 'afford a liberty to the people in religious matters which we think incompatible with the constitution of the Christian Church, and by these plausible pretenses carried off from our societies considerable numbers.' The disapproving Tomkins noted that each member had an equal right in the church's governance, 'and may speak or exhort in all their publick assemblies.' He also stated that it was 'customary among them, for the Preacher when he has done to desire any one present to address the people, who may be disposed to use his liberty. And even sometimes the Preacher in the midst of his discourse has to sit down while a brother or a sister communicates what, as they say, has been revealed to them. Visionary as these notions may appear to you, they are considered by many in the country among the essentials of a Christian liberty.' Once again, however, it was claimed that their societies had dissolved. According to Tomkins, one of their preachers had informed him that he would use his influence to have them rejoin the Methodists.[53]

Under the guidance of Joseph Badger, the Compton Township native who edited the sect's *Christian Palladium* in the later 1830s, the Christian Connection had moved towards formalism, developing regional conferences similar to those of the Methodists. This development may explain why Turner felt there was some similarity between his denomination and the Christians. But Badger's successor in 1839, Joseph Marsh, became a Millerite supporter, which could in turn explain the apparent disappearance of the Christians in the Eastern Townships by the early 1840s.[54] The 1852 *Census Reports* list only two 'Christians' in the entire region. The Christian Brethrens' radical ideology obviously had some appeal in the Eastern Townships, but not enough to sustain expansion without the outside assistance that the sect was apparently in no position to offer.

The Protestant Methodists and New Connection Methodists

James Reid, the Anglican minister for St Armand, reported in 1831 that the Methodists had begun to introduce camp meetings, known as 'Four Days' meetings, to the area:

> Several preachers are engaged during the four days, and great assemblies of people attend. The discourses and exercises are all calculated to work on the passions. For instance, at the close of the day, it is very common for the preacher to conclude thus, viz. 'All you that are now determined to serve God, you will please stand up, and you that are determined to continue in the service of the devil, keep your seats.'

Reid claimed that 'Five such Meetings were held last summer within twelve or fifteen miles of this place. Two of them within the limits of the Province, and three in the neighbour parts of the state of Vermont.' Reid was clearly referring to an incursion by the radical Protestant Methodists, also known as the Reformed Methodists, for the minutes of the Wesleyan Methodists' Dunham quarterly meeting noted in July 1831 that two of the local preachers had deserted to that sect; a third followed a year later.[55]

Reid's colleague, Christopher Jackson of Hatley, submitted a similar report, claiming that in June 1831 a four days' meeting had been held in Stanstead, 'at which five or six ministers of various persuasions attended, some of whom were from the U. States. Service was commenced early in the morning by one of the preachers, who, on his service being finished, resigned his place to another, etc till night, while Prayer Meetings were held in the tents around by those not engaged in preaching.' Another such meeting had been held in Compton in July 'which diminished my congregation about one third, for five or six weeks.' Finally, a third four days' meeting was held in Hatley in September, 'which produced little effect at the time,' but which now had resulted in the establishment of prayer meetings.[56]

Jackson did not mention the Protestant Methodists in particular, but there can be little doubt but that they were the main force behind this initiative. The society had been founded by Vermonters seventeen years earlier, in 1814, but did not formally split from the Methodist Episcopal Church until 1830 when it claimed approximately three thousand adherents. The Protestant Methodists rejected the episcopacy as being contrary to Scripture (replacing the bishop with a president elected each year), looked forward to the imminent second coming of Jesus, and practised faith healing. Some of them migrated north to Canada when their communal experiment in Bennington County collapsed.[57]

In 1832, a year after the Protestant Methodists were first referred to by Reid and Jackson, William Squire of Stanstead's Wesleyan circuit reported that two of his classes of about thirty members had defected to them.[58] By 1837 they had about six mission stations in the region. The particular appeal of the Protestant Methodist connection, as far as one Wesleyan defector was concerned, was its democratic polity. Recalling the withdrawal of the Methodist Episcopal preachers from the region in 1821, Bolton's Alexander Thompson (who was a local preacher) reportedly stated that 'we were turned over to another body, without our advice or consent, which was the first time we saw the impropriety of the clergy having all the power in their own hands.'[59] However, the Champlain District – which sponsored the Protestant Methodist work in the Eastern Townships – was torn by the slavery controversy, with the result that the Canadian mission received no financial support from it after 1835. Also concerned that their preachers could not legally perform marriages, the Canadian circuits voted in 1837 to sever their American ties and draw up their own constitution.[60]

These circuits were in no position to support preachers, however, so they subsequently made advances to England's New Connection Methodist Conference, which in 1836 had sent John Addyman to investigate establishing missions in the Canadas. Under the leadership of Alexander Kilham, the New Connection adherents had broken from the British Wesleyans in 1797 because they objected to their ongoing subservience to the Church of England. They also departed from Wesleyan practice by instituting equal lay representation in their courts and giving local societies a significant role in receiving and expelling members, electing local officers, and calling candidates to the itinerancy. Given their similarities, the Wesleyan Thomas Turner felt that the region's Protestant Methodists would gladly accept New Connection missionaries.[61]

Turner nevertheless reported that Addyman was 'very much disappointed to find the most important places in the Townships so generally supplied with a Methodist ministry.' This statement was confirmed by Addyman himself, though he also referred to the work of the Congregationalists and Baptists, and added that there remained a need for missions in Brome, part of Bolton, and the northern parts of Potton and Sutton. Addyman reported of this mountainous borderland that 'generally speaking, the cleared settlements are only like specks, scattered through immeasurable extent of forest, and though the people are not by any means so ignorant as I imagined, they are *awfully* wicked.'[62] Turner expressed doubt that there was a plan to compete directly with the Wesleyan Conference; nevertheless, he sent his own assistant to preach in East Bolton on a regular basis in 1838 before the struggling Methodist Protestant Church (which had over one hundred members) could be succeeded by the New Connection.[63]

Even as radical an American initiative in the region as that of the Protestant Methodists was therefore being absorbed by a British organization, though not without some local resistance. The diary of Ralph Merry, who lived at the Outlet on the eastern border of Bolton Township, reveals that, as of 1839, the local Protestant Methodists had refused to join the New Connection. Instead, on 13 June 1839, the rather grandly named first conference of the Protestant Methodists of Lower Canada was held in a local schoolhouse. The four delegates, who included Merry, agreed to adopt the American Protestant Methodist discipline of 1834, except that leaders' meetings would be blended with quarterly conferences, there would be no weekly collections by class leaders, and they would not refuse 'coulered brethren the privilege of voting. [W]e give the liberty to black as well as white to give their sufferages.' The dissident Methodists of the area thereby declared their independence from both British and American control, but they had already begun to fall under the influence of New York's William Miller, for they declared that their next general conference was to be held in seven years, 'if the world shall stand.'[64]

It would not be until 1844 that Bolton's Protestant Methodists agreed to join the New Connection. In the meantime, the Dunham circuit's Wesleyan missionary, John Brownell, reported two years earlier that 'four Local Preachers & Exhorters have left us and joined the Kilhamites (New Connection) and are with their Head – Mr H.O. Crofts of Montreal – doing their utmost to tear our Society in pieces, and in this work, as was the case at home, circulate all manner of untruths against me personally and against our system. We shall lose I believe from 20 to 25 members – many of them disaffected to the Government and everything British.'[65] The very fact that this British-based sect could simply absorb the Protestant Methodists meant that they were not suitably loyal to the crown, in Brownell's view. In February 1842 the New Connection leader, H.O. Crofts, claimed that the work in Dunham was 'going on gloriously' with 'the conversion of sinners in almost every meeting on the Circuit,' and one hundred members recorded as of the last quarterly meeting.[66]

The 593 members of the region's five Methodist Protestant circuits – Bolton, Barnston, Potton, Stanstead North, and Stanstead South – finally followed the Dunham dissidents into the New Connection in 1843, the year that Vermont's Protestant Methodists were absorbed into that state's newly established Wesleyan Methodist Church.[67] The New Connection had by this time transformed itself into the Canadian Wesleyan Methodist New Connection Church through union with Upper Canada's Canadian Wesleyan Methodists (Ryanites) in 1841. In November 1843 Crofts reported 'a glorious revival' in Stukely, which was 'notorious' for Universalists. With the help of special religious services, 'the Lord honoured his servants by the conversion of many of those characters who had made a jest of damnation.'[68]

The previous spring, however, the Wesleyan Reverend Brownell had reported that the New Connection threat had been replaced by a more serious one from the Millerites.[69] The New Connection appears to have been particularly vulnerable, presumably in part because the local Protestant Methodists had been influenced by Miller from the start, as we have seen. In addition, New Connection preachers, like their Wesleyan counterparts, were beginning to place less emphasis on protracted meetings and more on nurturing religion among the children and youths through Sunday schools and the promotion of family worship.[70] Its radical constituency may thereby have been alienated. Whatever the reasons, in early 1845 the preacher for the Bolton and Potton circuit reported that, while fifteen new members had been added to the New Connection Society, 'I am very sorry to say that four of our numbers have embraced the great error that all the churches are Babylon, and have declared their independence.' Crofts preached against this doctrine to a full house at Potton Lake in March, arguing that 'though these features all applied to Popery, they could not by any possibility apply to the Evangelical Churches of this Province.' But nowhere on this circuit, or in Barnston or Stanstead, was he able to take up a collection.[71]

In December 1845 the new appointee to Stanstead, F. Haynes, reported that he had been led to believe that there were eight local societies on the circuit, but he had found none. He added rather needlessly that 'our prospects for the future are not very encouraging.'[72] The church's Colonial Missions Committee was never able to send the required number of missionaries or adequate subsidies to the region. From the quarterly provincial grant of £203.10.2 in January 1846, for example, the six Eastern Townships circuits received total sums ranging from £4.3.4 to £6.5.0.[73]

In 1846 the report from Bolton and Potton's fall quarterly meeting bravely declared that, notwithstanding 'the wild vagaries of some, who think it a sin to belong to a Christian church, still the power of vital godliness is posessed [sic] by many who hold fast their profession, and are determined to walk in the good old way.'[74] By 1848, however, the Canadian missions had declined by nearly nine hundred members over the previous five years, clearly because of the Millerite movement.[75] Adventism continued to attract defectors as late as 1851, for the founding minister of the Sutton New Connection Church, Paul Vining West, joined the local Christian Adventist Church that year.[76]

The *Census Reports* nevertheless record that the Eastern Townships still had 3,442 New Connection adherents in 1851, or 6.5 percent of the Protestant population. Most of them were in Stanstead County, with 1,077 reported in Potton, 790 in Bolton, and 577 in Stanstead Township. The census somewhat surprisingly indicates that the New Connection outnumbered the Wesleyans even in the latters' stronghold of Stanstead Township, but also that it in turn was outnumbered by that township's 934 'Other Methodists.' The manuscript census schedules for Stanstead County are unfortunately missing, but those for neighbouring townships reveal that most of the 'Other Methodists' were in fact people who were simply recorded as Methodists. One can probably assume, therefore, that the majority of them attended Wesleyan services, even if they resisted full identification with this society. Without sustained outside support, the local New Connection movement continued to decline, and, in 1855, the 528 members of the Eastern District, which included the Eastern Townships, were simply dropped by the church. This decision was reversed the following year, but the Eastern Townships circuits were only re-added one at a time from then until 1871.[77]

Conclusion

The Pilgrims, Quakers, Universalists, Christian Brethern, and Protestant / New Connection Methodists were all radical movements, though some were much more evangelical than others. The fact that none of them found particularly fertile ground in the Eastern Townships speaks not simply to the small degree of outside support, since these sects did not depend on a trained ministry or build expensive churches, but also to the political climate of the region, particularly after the Rebellions. Important as well was the impact made by the Millerite invasion during the 1840s. Small Quaker and Universalist communities survived in the

Eastern Townships until the relatively recent past, but the Christian Brethren in particular were, like the Freewill Baptists, simply overwhelmed by Millerism. In New England the failure of the predicted Apocalypse to take place fostered even more radical antinomian and perfectionst sects, but in the Eastern Townships it represented a sharp blow to sectarianism. A small Adventist movement would persist, but the Vermont-born Shakers and Mormons failed to take root north of the border, and the Christian Brethren simply withered away while the New Connection Methodists went into a slow but steady decline.

6
The Millerites

Writing in 1908, Miss M.A. Titemore remembered that, as a child of twelve living in the Lower Canadian border community of St Armand East, she had been somewhat uneasy on the day of 13 April 1843, 'but my mother, being a very sensible woman, quietly went about her household duties, which had a tendency to alleviate our fears.'[1] What the Titemore family had been at least slightly worried about was William Miller's prediction that the Apocalypse would take place on that day, for many people in the borderland region had been thoroughly convinced by his interpretation of the Scriptures. What came to be known as Millerism was a manifestation of apocalyptic millenarianism, or what Barkun refers to as 'the belief that the world is about to experience an overturning, in which all that is imperfect or corrupt will vanish and in its place will stand a new order of things, where human beings will live without sin, evil or suffering.'[2] In America, the traditional premillennial belief that Christ's second coming would predate the thousand years of peace and harmony had been undermined in the 1740s by Jonathan Edwards's teaching that humanity must prepare for the Millennium by converting to Christianity and stamping out sin. According to this postmillennial view, the second advent would occur only at the end of the ensuing thousand years of peace. But premillennialism was revived by the political cataclysm associated with the French Revolution, especially after Napoleon's temporary dethroning of the Pope in 1798 had given Bible scholars a fixed point in the prophetic chronology of Revelation and Daniel.[3]

While postmillennialism remained the dominant outlook in the United States and British North America in the 1830s and 1840s, premillennialism made a dramatic appearance in the northeastern states and the Eastern Townships with the rise of the Millerite movement.[4] Millerism has been studied intensively by a number of American historians, yet they have all ignored the fact that its leaders did not hesitate to proselytize north of the border in what was, after all, an American-settled region.[5] Millerism was introduced early to the border townships, but it developed its own dynamic. It reached a fever pitch in early 1843, but that fever burned itself out quickly, for little was heard of the movement in 1844 when American apocalypticism was reaching its peak. Adventism did survive in the Eastern Townships, but only on a marginal basis.

Millenarian prophecy was not unknown in the Eastern Townships even before the rise of Millerism. In 1823, when aberrations in the climate were causing widespread hardships throughout northeastern North America, the Anglican minister of Hatley asked Bishop Mountain if Winchester's *Lectures on the Prophecies delivered in the Borough of Southwark in 1788-90* had been criticized by anyone. The Reverend Johnson explained that Winchester was a 'Universal Restorationer, & Interprets the Prophecies in a Literal sense,' and 'I find that the Lectures are very industriously consulted in my cure.'[6] Several months later, Stanstead's *British Colonist* reported that a local man had claimed to have been told by God that the Millennium would take place seven years from the previous October. God had also declared that all Christian denominations were corrupt, that they constituted the New Testament Babylon, and that two thirds of the people would be destroyed.[7] The later 1830s brought more crop failures, as well as the political turmoil caused by the Rebellions of 1837-8. Perhaps it is not surprising, then, that Millerism found a receptive audience in the Eastern Townships. Because it remained a non-sectarian movement prior to 1843, converting from within existing denominations, it is impossible to know how many people were involved. But the movement did make a major impact on the region's evangelical denominations, manifesting itself not so much as a large exodus from them as in a general revival within them, followed by a sharp decline in religious enthusiasm which some churches never recovered from.[8]

William Miller, who had once been a deist, was a Baptist farmer from Low Hampton near the New York–Vermont border. His careful study of the Bible in search of a rational verification of his restored faith led him to conclude in 1818 that the world would come to an end by 1843. The calculating of such chronologies was not unusual at the time, though few were as precise as Miller, and he hesitated to preach his beliefs until the Great Revival of 1831. Two years later, he was licensed as a Baptist minister, attracting large audiences from the start, though Cross notes that he was 'not an inspired prophet but a solid, sober, sincere student, driven only by the irresistible conclusions of patient research.'[9] With his health failing, Miller might have remained a relatively unknown country preacher had not the energetic young Joshua V. Himes of Boston effectively taken over management of the movement in 1839. Himes was a Christian Connection minister who became editor of the leading Millerite newspaper, *Signs of the Times* (later the *Advent Herald*), and shifted the focus to mass audiences in the larger urban centres.

Miller had begun proselytizing in letters to his sister and brother-in-law at the Outlet of Lake Memphremagog (Magog) as early as 1825, and in 1831 he sent them a graphic description of his prophecy of what would take place at some point during the next twelve years:

> the dead saints or bodies will rise, those children of God who are alive then, will be changed, and caught up to meet the Lord in the air, where they will be married to him. The world and all the wicked will be burnt up (not annihilated) and then Christ will descend and reign personally with his Saints; and at the end of the 1000 years the wicked will be raised, judged and sent to everlasting punishment. (This is the second death).[10]

Four years later, in 1835, Miller visited the Townships for three weeks, preaching twenty-four sermons in Bolton, Hatley, Georgeville, the Outlet, and Stanstead Plain, as well as neighbouring Derby, Vermont. Ralph Merry of the Outlet, who became a convert, recorded in his diary that the result was 'a reformation' in several local villages. Miller was clearly making a considerable impression, for two Baptist clergymen from the region were among those who signed a certificate supporting his views after hearing him preach in Lansingburgh, New York, in 1836. Miller returned to the Eastern Townships a second time in 1838, preaching twelve sermons in the Outlet area, but his most successful visit was in 1840, when he reported that twenty people 'were under serious conviction.' In Georgeville, the Baptist preacher was a supporter, and thirty people joined the Baptist church after Miller preached to large congregations for eight days.[11] Despite his preoccupation with the coming Apocalypse, Miller was not entirely indifferent to temporal affairs. As a constable and justice of the peace, he deprecated the ongoing attempts in this post-Rebellion era to foment war through border raids in the Potton Township area west of Lake Memphremagog, arguing that the American government should arrest the 'villains' or 'they will soon commit crimes with impunity on either side of the line.'[12] Nor was Miller without a sense of humour, for his letter to his son continued: 'I think the French people where I came, are all Harrisonians for they all live in "*Log cabins,*" but they lack one thing, "*hard cider*".'[13]

But the Canadian audience for Miller's message was still rather limited, and the growing popularity of the movement in the United States would prevent him from returning to the Eastern Townships for several years. In July 1841 the Millerite *Signs of the Times* announced its first Canadian agent in Stanstead, but the movement would not make a major impact on the region until Josiah Litch, a former Methodist Episcopal minister from Rhode Island, led a prolonged revival in 1842. Litch, who was Millerism's leading theologian and its third most important personality,[14] began lecturing in Stanstead's Union church on 31 May. According to the local Congregational minister, more than twenty preachers took part in the meeting.[15] Litch subsequently reported that half the people could not get into the large building on the following Sabbath, when over nine hundred horses were counted around it. With popular excitement building, Litch decided to prolong the Stanstead meeting by another week, and to hold a camp meeting in Hatley Township beginning on 21 June. Not only were camp meetings a relative novelty in the Eastern Townships, but this was the first one ever held by the Millerites anywhere.[16]

Litch reported that the 'waves on waves of people' who attended the Hatley camp meeting exceeded his expectations. Within a short time $100 was subscribed for the free distribution of publications concerning the second advent. Fifty to sixty people were converted on the second day, and by June 26 the crowd was estimated at 2,300, though one observer noted that not everyone present could 'unite in advocating second advent doctrine, as there propagated.' Litch moved on to the Outlet, where sixty to seventy were added to the movement, then began lecturing at a second camp meeting in Bolton Township on 29 June. Despite the isolated location and inclement weather, Litch claimed that thousands attended and that another two or three hundred were converted. They were evidently a mixed group, for Litch wrote that they included 'old and grey headed Universalists, stout hearted infidels, bold blasphemers, drunkards, the giddy and vain youth, and the thoughtful child of many prayers.' He concluded that 'In no community, probably, has the doctrine of the Second Advent at hand taken a stronger hold than in Canada.'[17]

Nor had Litch been the only Millerite to preach in the Eastern Townships during the summer of 1842. In August, Edwin Adrion reported to Miller from Fairfield, Vermont that he had recently returned from a preaching tour in Canada where 'more than 100 were converted in les than 12 dayes.' The following month, he wrote to Miller from Stanbridge Mills, claiming that 'I have devoted all my time to the work of sounding the midnight cry. I have laboured 4 months in trying to make the people understand that the Lord was comming in 1843. Praise the Lord it has not been in vaine, more then one thousand of the Church have got there eyes open, and I have witnessed within that 4 months over five hundred conversions to God as the result of my labours.'[18]

Given that Stanbridge did not become a Millerite stronghold, this report was probably exaggerated, but another camp meeting was held in Eaton in September, and Litch was followed in the fall of 1842 by H.B. Skinner who spent six months in Canada, the first two months travelling with Luther Caldwell. The Congregationalist Reverend R.V. Hall of Stanstead reported alarmingly in November that 'Scores of individuals have recently embraced this wild delusion and several of our most wealthy and respectable families fell in with it, and they are so carried away with it that they have given up all business and they are waiting the Coming of Our Lord. They expect he will soon come in the clouds of heaven and they (*and they only*) will soon be caught up to meet the the [*sic*] Lord in the air.' The Millerites had taken over the old meetinghouse, 'and are intending to hold religious exercises there day & night so long as the world shall stand. Their congregations are large and are daily increasing.' According to Hall, most of the converts in Stanstead were Methodists, about half of whom had 'embraced this wild fanaticism.'[19]

The local Methodist minister, Robert Cooney, corroborated the latter statement, and later added that 'The opinion that the world will end this year is producing strange effects; and with a great many "*Wesleyan Methodists,*" so called, the authority of the "The Bible" is completely superseded by visions, dreams, and revelations; and to interpret which would be a task of great difficulty to the most erudite soothsayers.'[20] In November 1842, the Stanstead customs officer wrote to his wife that some of the Millerites 'are actually maniacs, and more will soon be if not checked.' The following month, the *Montreal Transcript* claimed, based on rumours, that a man in neighbouring Barnston had become insane because of Millerism, and that another in Stanstead had tried to murder his family. Finally, in January 1843 Hall, too, claimed that several Millerites had become insane.[21]

These rumours were never substantiated with names, but *Signs of the Times* did claim in January that the excitement in Canada 'is very great, and a subject of almost universal discourse, both among foes and friends. The Protestant Methodists, as also the Freewill Baptists, both of the clergy and laity, very generally believe and teach the doctrine. The French Catholics are also expecting the coming of the Savior near, to a very great extent; three *Jesuit Priests*, missionaries from France, held some time last spring a series of meetings at Point Le Mule, and publicly advocated the sentiment.' Himes added that there was 'little or no difficulty in getting access to the people; the chapels of the different denominations are thrown open, and the Advent brethren are made welcome.'[22] The Protestant Methodists and Freewill Baptists were not the only denominations in the Eastern Townships whose clergy were attracted to Millerism, for the Wesleyan Methodist Richard Hutchinson would become the leading force behind the movement in the region, as well as playing a prominent role in introducing it to Great Britain.[23]

Skinner reported in May 1843 that hundreds were converted, but the Millerites had met strong opposition from the Montreal press in particular. To fight fire with fire, and to reach as wide an audience as possible while avoiding customs duties on American newspapers, Skinner and Caldwell decided to launch a Millerite mouthpiece in Canada. Himes appealed for funds, and by the end of January 1843 Skinner was publishing the *Faithful Watchman* in Sherbrooke.[24] It quickly grew to 140 subscribers, and the remainder of the thousand copies were distributed at no cost each week. One American supporter wrote that 'It will cause men's hearts to fail them for fear, as amid the deep snows, and piercing winds of a those cold regions, its voice is heard in deep-toned thunders, crying "Behold the Bridegroom cometh".' But the *Faithful Watchman* soon perished in the cold Canadian climate due to lack of funds.[25] In the summer of 1843 the *Watchman*'s place was taken by the *Voice of Elijah*, edited by Richard Hutchinson at his own expense (though he asked for donations) first in Montreal, then in Sherbrooke, and finally in Toronto. Within a few months, twelve thousand copies were distributed in the British North American colonies and Great Britain, until the *Voice* was silenced in the fall of 1844.[26]

As the anticipated time for Christ's second advent drew nearer, the pressure for a precise prediction grew more intense. Referring to the Jewish calendar year, Miller declared that it would occur at some time during the twelve months following 21 March 1843, but various groups of his followers searched the Bible for their own dates. Some of those in the Eastern Townships eagerly chose 14 February 1843, thereby anticipating the anniversary of the abolition of papal government by one day. While the movement's leaders had published a list of regulations to keep their camp meetings orderly,[27] the *Montreal Transcript* reported that in the townships of Stanstead and Hatley people had rolled on the floor with the 'struggles,' exhibiting convulsions and kicking and screaming fits. The editor added that these occurrences were 'looked upon as sure evidences of the immediate presence of the divinity, and were of great efficacy previous to the 14th instants, in converting the unbelievers to the faith.'[28] The Anglican bishop, George J. Mountain, painted much the same picture in his report to the Society for the Propagation of the Gospel, though he claimed that 'the struggles' were 'understood to be an act of devotion in behalf of some unconverted individual, who is immediately sent for, if not present, that he may witness the process designed for his benefit. Females are thus prompted to exhibit themselves, and I was credibly assured, that at Hatley two young girls were thus in *the struggles*, the objects of their intercession being two of the troopers quartered in the village.' In visiting Frost Village in February, Mountain recorded in his journal that he had warned the young people against the dangers of Millerism, 'which have in a manner flooded this part of the country, and produced, in many instances, conspicuous mischief. The pillar of the cause in this neighbourhood is a tinsmith of Waterloo Village, formerly a soldier in the British army, and now enjoying a pension. Another great preacher of the same doctrine in the township is a man who eighteen months ago, ran off with a neighbour's wife.'[29]

The failure of Christ to appear had left the Millerites open to such ridicule, which encouraged them to put their faith in another date, 14 April, the day of the Passover (which was the date recalled by Miss Titemore of St Armand East). A month earlier, an observer from Montreal wrote that 'The townships are mad with Millerism to an extent beyond all credibility.'[30] In April the Congregationalist Reverend Hall reported from Stanstead that during the previous winter the Millerites had held meetings every day and every night:

And they have literally sounded the *mid-night cry* and so loud had it been that it has often awoke us from our midnight slumbers. Their cry is '*Behold the Bridegroom cometh, go ye out to meet him.*' Many have been alarmed and overcome by their ferocious zeal and have fallen in with them. They have visions & dreams. They pretend to heal the sick, and they say that all who have faith will never see death.

Hall added that once the date when they were to be taken up into the skies had passed, 'they will be in a pitiable condition. Many of them will be without food and without homes having already disposed of all they possessed.' The local Methodist minister, Robert Cooney, had preached several sermons against the prophecy in vain: 'A single vision of some old woman like the witch of Endor would have more weight with them than all the sermons in the world.'[31]

Judging from Cooney's memoirs, his sermons against Millerism must have been emotional ones:

> We have heard of the extravagances of the fifth monarchy men – of the absurd opinions and vicious practices of the followers of James Naylor. We have heard of the wild and dangerous tenets of various sects in Germany, and in other places, and we are old enough to remember the monstrous delusion palmed upon the English public by Johanna Southcote; and our opinion is, that in absurdity, grossness, and impiety, *Millerism* was equal to any of them. I have witnessed scenes myself that would disgrace dancing Dervishes, and make Harlequins blush with shame. Kicking, jumping, pounding each other; shrieking, and so forth, were among their common rites and ceremonies. They evinced their renunciation of the world, and attested the truth of their creed by selling every thing at the highest price. Their charity consisted in getting for themselves all they could; and their meekness and gentleness were forcibly displayed in the manner in which they abused and denounced all who differed from them. Ministers were 'dumb dogs that would not bark;' 'lying prophets;' 'wolves in sheep's clothing;' 'Hirelings, Robbers,' etc.[32]

Cooney was referring to the fact that during the summer of 1843 the Millerite leaders began to advise their followers to withdraw from any churches that did not accept the imminent advent of the Lord.

The report submitted by John Tomkins of the Wesleyan Compton circuit in April 1843 was similar in tone to those from Stanstead. He claimed that the Millerite meetings

> have been of the most disorderly character, several persons in a most stentorious manner would be praying or speaking at a time; others would be on the floor struggling in a sort of hysterical fit, which they call the power of God, and that they were struggling for sinners. They have neglected all kinds of business, thinking it unnecessary to work, as they had property enough to last them till April, when the world was to end. It is true that some of the more prudent have not gone to this extremely excessive folly.

Others, however, claimed to have spiritual powers to 'tell what is the state of the heart,' and, still others, that it had been revealed to them that the world would end on the fourteenth of the month at 1:00 a.m.: 'then, they said, the arch-Angels trumpet would sound, the saviour appear in the air, take up his saints, burn up the world and all the wicked.' Tomkins concluded, 'I am prepared to say, from the influence of Millerism, the depression in every department of business, and the exceedingly low prices for agricultural produce, our Circuits and missionary receipts will be considerably diminished.'[33]

Writing from Melbourne on 18 April the Wesleyan missionary Edmund Botterell stated that 'Many of my neighbours expected the end of the world on Friday last. My family were awoke at the dead hour of night by one of the fanatics to come to judgement. I have seen two of them in a positively insane state. Some are neglecting their business. I fear we shall lose on this circuit scarcely fewer than Forty members.'[34] George Stacey of Ascot, also observed that 14 April 'passed in the usual way, and with it I trust will pass this most impious doctrine. It is lamentable to witness with what avidity this pernicious theory of Mr. Miller's, its leader, has been caught up by the thousands. To such a pitch has it been carried on in these Townships, that hundreds of families have plunged themselves into difficulties, sold up everything, and are now in such a state that it will scarcely be possible to extricate them from their predicament.[35]

These commentators were hardly impartial observers, and there is a formulaic quality to many of their statements that suggests they were gleaned from a somewhat hysterical press. Millerite theology was essentially orthodox, even conservative, aside from the precision of its adventist prediction, and many of the widely circulated stories about the fanatical behaviour and insanity of its followers have been debunked as fiction.[36] The lack of evidence about local indigence despite the general economic downturn suggests that few families failed to plant or harvest crops, closed their businesses, or gave away their property. The Baptist Lewis Hibbard later treated the matter rather lightly when he recalled that, as young boys in St Armand, he and his brother 'failed to fill the wood-box and cut turnips for the calves' on the day before 14 April 1843, 'as the coming end of the world made it unnecessary.'[37]

But the apocalyptic nature of the Millerite message and its dissemination by the means of mass meetings were highly conducive to public hysteria. The Millerite preacher H.B. Skinner admitted in March 1843 that the Stanstead faithful 'may have been a little too enthusiastic' in some of their meetings, and his May report described a situation that had moved beyond the control of the movement's leadership: 'The excesses to which we allude, consisted in a virtual, though not intended, abandonment of the word of God, and a trusting to special revelations of the Holy Ghost, through the medium of dreams, visions, etc. an excess, which developed itself in the greatest extravagances in their external modes of worship.' The lesson to be learned, according to Skinner, was that 'The Spirit and the word always agree; and when there is discrepancy between the teaching of the word, and that claimed as special revelation of the spirit, we may look for an error; for an error there surely *must be*.' Ultimately, however, Skinner played down the 'extravagances,' claiming that they had been 'indulged by but very few; a mere fractional part of the advent believers in Canada,' and the 'sincerity' of those involved 'was never doubted, or their piety questioned.'[38]

Anticipation built again toward 21 March 1844, the final day in the Jewish calendar year during which, according to Miller, Christ would return. When this prediction also failed, new leaders in the movement pointed to 22 October the Jewish Day of Atonement. Rowe refers to the psychology of 'cognitive dissonance' to explain the tendency of apocalyptic groups to intensify their belief in a specific date marking the end of the world as each predicted deadline passes without the event occurring.[39] But Fortin provides no evidence for his statement that enthusiasm in the Eastern Townships became still greater than it had been prior to April 1843, and my research revealed no detailed observations about Millerism by the hostile local clergy or other observers in 1844. The only possible reference uncovered was the claim by the Anglican Reverend C.B. Fleming in March that a man in the village of Melbourne 'last Sunday night, had the audacity to represent himself to his delighted followers as the Saviour.'[40] Finally, the Wesleyan Methodist parish registers for the St Armand and Dunham circuits reveal a dramatic increase in the number of baptisms (particularly of adults) from thirty-one in 1839, to 115 in 1840, and 231 in 1842, before declining slightly to 212 in 1843, then precipitously to eighty-two in 1844, eighteen in 1846, and eight in 1848.[41]

Aside from illustrating that Millerism simply intensified a religious revival that had already begun in the border townships in 1840, these numbers support the negative evidence that the peak of the Millerite phenomenon passed a year earlier in the Eastern Townships than in the northeastern United States. This hypothesis is further supported by several letters that appeared in Boston's *Advent Herald*, which had succeeded *Signs of the Times* in February 1844. In April, for example, J. Merry of Stanstead wrote that 'There are *a few* here who are looking for God to come ... We have no thoughts of giving up our faith, or turning back.' And, only a few weeks before the long anticipated October date, Leonard Kimball wrote on his way through Rock Island that there had been a major spiritual decline all through the region since the revivals of 1842, with many who had accepted the Millerite message having subsequently abandoned their faith. The travelling preacher, I.H. Shipman, repeated much the same message for Hatley: 'The brethren there are rather low; as they have never taken a decided stand against the sects, they of course sink with them.'[42]

Rather than continuing to expand, the Millerites began to meet with violent opposition. Richard Hutchinson reported that on December 29 the mayor and the captain of militia of Frost Village had used an armed force to drive him and his congregation out of the schoolhouse. On the following evening about thirty guns were fired close to the window of the private house where they were meeting. The situation became even more tense two weeks later in West Shefford where Hutchinson and Luther Caldwell were denied permission to lecture in the schoolhouse for fear of mob violence. Hutchinson reported that when the large congregation then went to a private house, 'a mob of about 40 men came. Some rushed into the house with deadly weapons. Others threw stones, clubs, etc. through the windows. Three windows were entirely smashed in. Some of the brethren were cut in the head, and some received blows.' The mob apparently wished to tar and feather Hutchinson, but did not succeed.[43]

Such persecution only reinforced the diehard Millerites' desire to separate from the other denominations.[44] In an attempt to rally the faithful, a Second Advent Conference was held at Hutchinson's headquarters in Waterloo from 9–12 January 1845. It attracted a sizable audience of three hundred people who were apparently unanimous in wishing to quit their churches in order to found a new one. The local Anglican minister reported that Millerism had 'shaken *the sects* to the foundation and pretty generally fused them into one mass which has now settled down into "Adventism." It had comparatively little success among the members of our Church – two or three only embraced it, and one has since returned.'[45] The Waterloo conference was followed by others elsewhere in the region, but the main impetus to establish a denominational identity came with the visit in February of Joshua Himes, whose *Advent Herald* played a more crucial unifying role than ever upon the demise of Hutchinson's *Voice of Elijah.* Himes's two-week tour, accompanied by Hutchinson, took him to Stanstead, Hatley, Melbourne, Shefford, the Outlet, Bolton Centre, and Odelltown, preaching two or three times a day at each place. Himes subsequently reported that the cause in Canada East was strong, 'and its friends are numerous; much more so than we had anticipated.'[46]

Several months later, in April 1845, the old Millerite leadership held a major conference in Albany, New York, with the aim of combating what they perceived to be the pernicious errors that had arisen since the disappointment of the previous October. In order to formalize the Advent faith and practice, the meeting adopted a statement of ten beliefs, and established the organizational principles of a distinct church. These included a congregational system of church government similar to that of the Baptists, and the ordination of new ministers, who could only be men, even though women had previously been permitted to preach. Instead of camp meetings, which were difficult to control, they would hold smaller conferences as a method of reaching new areas. Due to illness, Hutchinson did not attend this conference but he accepted its principles and committed himself to regular tours of the Adventist congregations in the Eastern Townships in order to ensure that they did not stray from the path.[47]

While Hutchinson was spreading the message in England during the summer of 1846, Shipman submitted a cautiously optimistic report on the various Adventist churches in the region, echoing Himes's earlier statement when he reported that 'the state of things in Canada is much better than I had anticipated, and the brethren are much more numerous.'[48] Miller, who had visited the Eastern Townships in June 1845, returned again in the fall of 1846. He was then too ill to attend the conferences or leave his sister's home, causing great disappointment in Waterloo, where John Porter wrote: 'The Sisters are so anxious to see you they say if Bro. Buckley would only bring you to Shefford *for exhibition* they would ask no more, if no more was for them ... The curiosity of many beside the Brethren and Sisters was high in regard to the man that has turned the world up side down.' Miller did return to the Townships for a last visit in July 1848 before he died in December 1849.[49]

But neither the Albany conference's rejection of antiformalism nor these tours by the established leaders could entirely prevent the radical sectarianism that was emerging in the United States from developing in the Eastern Townships as well. No Perfectionist cults, or Shaker or Mormon societies, would emerge from the 'great disappointment' in this region, in contrast to New England and New York, but the millennialism and pietism that helped make Adventism a mass movement also ensured that it would not easily be controlled.[50] While adherence to the insititutional structure erected by the General Conference implied that Christ's second coming was not imminent, Hutchinson continued to insist in 1845 that 'the end of all things is just upon us,' and that it would certainly take place before the end of 1847. The *Stanstead Journal* attributed the same belief to Himes and Miller based on the latter's sermon in neighbouring Derby Line in September 1846. It is not surprising, therefore, that Adventists in Stanstead adopted the same belief.[51]

While the clergy of most denominations in the region complained about a spiritual decline during the later 1840s, the Adventists were clearly becoming inured to failed prophecies, for the latest disappointment in 1846 touched off another wave of radical behaviour, manifesting itself in trances, visions, spiritual marriages and gifts of the spirit.[52] Adventism in the Eastern Townships continued to be supported by visits from American itinerants such as I.R. Gates, who preached to a congregation of about five hundred in Dunham Flat in January 1847. In the fall of 1848 a camp meeting held in Barnston with about fifteen preachers (who had obviously ignored the Albany conference's resolution against such meetings) was reported to be a glorious success.[53]

But such manifestations of enthusiasm were not widespread enough to attract attention from the missionary reports of the other churches, and the 'orthodox' Adventist leadership was able to forestall the Spiritualizers who taught that Christ had returned in a non-literal sense on 22 October. During his four-week tour of the southern part of the region in 1848, Josiah Litch advocated an itinerant ministry in order to reach the most people possible. With Hutchinson's assistance, Litch organized the Advent Conference in Eastern Canada (the first in Canada) in 1848, but it did not meet again until 1851 when Vermont was added to its territory.[54] That same year the first Adventist churches were established in Waterloo and Danville. The rules and regulations were simple, as illustrated by the covenant signed by the founders of the Waterloo church:

> We believers in Christ, looking for his speedy appearing and kingdom, known as 'Adventists,' do agree to watch over one another in love, according to the teachings of the Holy Scriptures, which we receive as the sufficient and only rule of our faith and duty, as well as discipline. We are willing and anxious when we stray from that rule in word or deed, to be corrected, reproved, and instructed by each other, according to God's holy

word. And we cordially receive all as brethren, who are willing to walk by the same rule.[55]

Despite these halting steps toward institutionalization, it would not be easy to regulate a movement that had been born in rebellion against organized religion, and in anticipation of an imminent fiery apocalypse. Certainly, the efforts of Litch and other mainstream Adventists from the United States could not prevent dissension from beginning early in the Eastern Townships, where John Porter – the first Adventist pastor in the Eastern Townships – was known as a defender of the faith because of his active role in opposing religious fanaticism within his sect. In 1848, for example, Porter accused the Adventist leader, Levi Dudley of Derby Line, Vermont, of being a fanatic and of causing trouble among the Adventists in the Stanbridge area. And, in a letter published in the *Herald* in July 1848, the Adventist preacher Jonathan Cummings denounced Simeon Hall and warned Canadian co-religionists not to receive him because he taught heresies.[56] In October 1850 the Outlet's Ralph Merry, who had been sympathetic to Miller's prophecies as early as 1838, complained of the 'great deal of wild unreasonable talk' from a visitor who insisted that the end would come within two years from June or July 1853. Merry added that others pointed to the current month: 'thus we see that visionary and enthusiastical men continue presumptiously to pry into the secrets of the Almighty as though they belonged to his council.'[57] Joseph Bates had already become the first Adventist visiting the region to advocate observation of Saturday as the Sabbath, foreshadowing a split in the movement.[58] Like their American counterparts, the Eastern Townships Adventists eventually divided into three factions: the Evangelical Adventists supported by the Millerite leaders, the Christian Adventists, and the Seventh-Day Adventists.

The Adventists remained a marginal group in the Eastern Townships according to the 1851–2 census, which reported only 1,362 adherents, or 2.6 per cent of the Protestant population. But the Millerites had clearly made a dramatic impact on the region, and many of those who did not openly join them came to accept the premillennial belief that the last days lay not far off in the future. What explains this rather dramatic upheaval of Yankee revivalism after years of conservative British missionary activity in the region? The most obvious answer is that this movement had simply become too powerful in the neighbouring states for the American-settled border townships to resist, particularly given that they were targeted by Miller himself and his able disciple, Josiah Litch.

But the Eastern Townships had previously been relatively immune to much of the religious enthusiasm of the 'burned-over country' that lay to the south and southwest, and local conditions clearly had to be ripe for Millerism to make the major impact that it did. One might speculate that it provided an emotional outlet that was missing in the dominant Anglican and Wesleyan Methodist churches. Doan claims that Millerism's chief attraction was that it appealed to the need to undergo the conversion experience, to believe in the message of the Bible, to spread this message, and to prepare for the glorious reign of God.[59] The problem with this interpretation, as far as the Eastern Townships is concerned, is that a number of the evangelical denominations were already experiencing a religious revival in 1840-1, a year or two before Millerism made a significant impact in the region. Furthermore, while the British Wesleyans reportedly gave up considerable ground to Millerism, at least in the short run, the Anglicans did not. The denomination that declined the most was one of the most radical ones in the region, namely the Freewill Baptists, which saw several of its class meetings desert to the Millerite movement.

Also of limited value, as far as the Eastern Townships is concerned, is O'Leary's argument that the hostile reaction in the later 1830s by powerful vested interests against the temperance and anti-slavery movements resulted in the 'displacement of millennial optimism by a tragic sense of foreboding.'[60] There was no significant anti-slavery movement in the Eastern Townships at this time, and, even though the temperance movement was in a hiatus in 1843, this was due to flagging efforts on the part of the Congregational society that was its chief promoter, and not to local opposition. Members of Sherbrooke's entrepreneurial and professional elite would organize a major temperance campaign in 1845, and a year later the middle-class Rechabite temperance society would become very popular throughout the region.[61]

Finally, referring specifically to the Eastern Townships, Fortin points to the successive waves of American, British, and French-Canadian colonization, which introduced settlers of different social, political, and religious backgrounds who sometimes came into conflict with each other. He also mentions the social vacuum left by English-speaking emigration from the region. The result, he claims, was a fragmentation of cultural identity and a social instability which provided fertile ground for new religious groups. The problem with this explanation is that Millerism's appeal tended to be greatest in the homogeneously American-settled townships near the border. The villages of Waterloo and Danville did have mixed populations, but, more significantly, Waterloo was where the region's leading spokesman for Millerism, Richard Hutchinson, happened to be stationed as a Methodist minister at the time of his conversion. And Danville, which became the headquarters of John Porter, was an anomaly since the first Adventist meetings were apparently not held there until 1850.[62] As for the French-Canadian colonization mentioned as a contributing factor by Fortin, it had barely begun in the 1840s, and most of the contact between American, British, and French-Canadian inhabitants took place to the north of those border communities where Millerism made its greatest impact. Given that Millerism originated across the border in Vermont and New York, ethno-cultural tensions were hardly a prerequisite to its appeal.

To explain the rise of Millerism in certain townships, one must consider the more specific political, social, and economic conditions of the early 1840s. The factors that made the post-Rebellion French-Canadian parishes ripe for the ultramontane revival were also present to some extent in the Eastern Townships. Communities and churches had been divided by the 1837–8 Rebellions, the raids by arsonists from Vermont had continued well past the crushing of the Patriotes, and political tensions re-emerged with the introduction of tax-levying municipal and school councils. For those who felt threatened by the changes taking place around them, Miller's apocalyptic prediction and promise of salvation – based on the authority of the Bible and presented in the context of emotional revivalism – must have been difficult to resist. But the political pessimism of the early 1840s should not be exaggerated. The Rebellions had been over for five years, the subsequent border raids would only serve to consolidate local opinion against outside threats, and the protest petitions did not demand abolition of the new tax-supported institutions of local governance but rather their decentralization and improvement.[63]

Probably more significant than the contentious political climate was the fact that the economic crisis dragged on and unseasonable frosts were killing the grain crops. Wheat had rusted in the fall of 1840, and in 1841 a late June hail storm had cut the grass and grain to ribbons as well as ruining the corn and potatoes.[64] The following year, Josiah Litch wrote from Stanstead: 'The country here is most delightful, the soil good, the land gently undulating and well watered, but the climate cold and backward. It is now the 12th of June, and the apple orchards are just in bloom, and the corn hardly apparent as you pass the fields. Yesterday, the 11th of June, was a severe snow-storm all the forenoon ... Toward night it cleared off cold, and the result was a severe frost.' In 1843 winter came early, burying farmer's crops in the snow.[65]

To make matters worse, various contagious illnesses had begun spreading death throughout the Stanstead and Sherbrooke area in 1842. The epidemic was still active in the spring of 1843 when the Congregationalist Reverend Hall of Stanstead wrote that. Within 10 months we have followed 5 of the members of our church to their graves, and many of our numbers have been very sick apparently nigh unto death.'[66] It must have seemed to many that God's judgment was upon them, though a doctor in Stanstead suggested a reverse causation, speculating that the renewed outbreak of erysipelas (which Miller himself contracted) along the Vermont border in 1843 was due to the 'excitement and consequent exposure of the Millerites.'[67]

Religious historians have generally argued that Millerism was not a movement of the poor and dispossessed, and have rejected the Marxist notion that premillennialism reflects the 'chiliasm of despair' (to use E.P. Thompson's phrase).[68] Indeed, Harrison states that the millenarian movements of Britain and the United States prior to mid-century generally attracted artisans, small farmers, shopkeepers, tradesmen, domestic servants, and women – not the very poor.[69] This generalization is confirmed by a social analysis of the Second Adventists listed in Melbourne and Shipton by the manuscript schedules of the province's 1852 *Census Reports*, for the ratio of non-farmers and especially tradesmen was particularly high. The Second Adventists in these essentially rural townships included thirty-six farmers, six servants (three of whom were women), four blacksmiths, three labourers, three carpenters, two millers, one tanner, one clerk, one tinsmith, one cordwainer, one cooper, and one engineer. Further analysis of the Shipton manuscript census suggests that the Adventist farmers were of above average economic standing, for they occupied an average of 122.2 acres, as compared with the township mean of 108.0 acres, and they had improved an average of 50.3 acres, as compared with the township mean of only 32.3 acres. In contrast to what Roth found for the Connecticut Valley of Vermont,[70] most supporters in Shipton did not come from the poorer sectors of society, but neither did they include the more affluent or influential. Even if it was not the most marginal members of society who were attracted to Adventism, and even if the Millerite preachers did not focus on local signs (such as the inclement weather) of the 'latter days,' the basic concern for survival felt by many people of the Eastern Townships during the early 1840s must have been an inducement to seek refuge in the certainties and hope offered by Millerism.[71]

But why, then, did Millerism make such a relatively small impact on the region in 1844, the year it reached its zenith in the United States? The most obvious reason, aside from general exhaustion from the enthusiasm of the previous year, is simply that the prominent preachers all remained south of the border in 1844, focusing their efforts on the larger population centres. It is important to remember that while local conditions clearly had to be ripe for Millerism to attract adherents in the Eastern Townships, the doctrine was introduced by a military-like strategy of invasion. American preachers arrived in groups to deliver an apocalyptic message in carefully organized tent meetings that would almost inevitably produce a degree of mass hysteria. A less tangible factor lies in Rowe's theory that Millerism, along with Shakerism, Mormonism and the various manifestations of Perfectionism, reflected a deep-seated reaction against the libertarianism of Jacksonian politics and the materialism and social fragmentation associated with the rise of urban industrialism.[72] If this was the case, we should not be surprised that the movement faded rather quickly in the essentially rural Eastern Townships (aside from the small outbursts in 1848 and 1849) where the fate of Jacksonian-inspired radicalism had already been sealed by the suppression of the Rebellions of 1837-8, and where politics took a decidedly conservative turn in the 1840s in order to stimulate the long-desired integration into the market economy. If many people had turned towards Millerism in response to economic hardships and disillusionment with politics in the post-Rebellion era, it was only natural that they would turn away again as institutional reforms attracted their attention and as improved economic conditions restored their hopes. From this perspective, Millerism was a distinctively American phenomenon – a product of the radical sectarian and political culture that failed to take strong root north of the border.

Conclusion

Revivalism was a powerful force in early-nineteenth-century America, and the forty-ninth parallel was certainly not impervious to its impact, even after the War of 1812 interrupted New England missionary efforts, and the Methodist Episcopal preachers were withdrawn. But the flames of religious enthusiasm fanned by revivals tended to cool quickly, and some sort of institutional support was required to keep the embers glowing until the next conflagration could be ignited. The problem was that sects that placed a strong emphasis on each individual's relationship with God were not inclined to accept institutional regulation or centralizing controls. This was not an insurmountable obstacle south of the border, but the Yankee settlers of the Eastern Townships were too isolated to sustain churches without some means of local taxation, which all but the Quakers rejected, or outside support, which proved to be sporadic and limited in scope. Radical American sects were clearly not inclined to expend their efforts in a British colony, and to a lesser extent the same was true of the more mainstream Congregationalists. Perhaps greater efforts would have been made to sustain the American-origin churches had British missionary societies not made substantial support available. As we shall see, the offer of free clergymen and free churches (for the Anglicans only) was too tempting to refuse. We shall also see that conformity to the norms and regulations of the conservative British-based churches was another matter, for the American adherents tended to be independent-minded and affiliation somewhat unstable. In this respect, the New England sects continued to have a greater influence on the region than their membership numbers might suggest, but there is no mistaking that a more conservative religious culture was emerging north of the international border.

Part III
Postwar British Responses: The Wesleyan Methodists

7

Laying the Foundations

Replacing the Methodist Episcopal Missionaries

With the War of 1812 preventing the Methodist Episcopal Church from providing more than a couple of missionaries for Lower Canada, Methodists in Montreal appealed to Britain for help, and appointments were made to Montreal and Quebec without consulting the American bishop. To counteract this initiative, once the war had ended, the Genessee Conference of 1815 assured the Upper Canadians who were in attendance that the Canadas would soon receive suitable preachers, and that they would be warned to avoid political offence. The conference recognized de facto the British preachers' occupation of Montreal and Quebec, but appointed Henry Ryan as presiding elder of an enlarged Lower Canada district in order to rally the colony's neglected circuits.[1]

Nineteenth-century Methodist historian John Carroll states of Benjamin Sabin, who served the Stanstead circuit for the New England Conference from 1815 to 1817: 'All who remember him in the Stanstead country, pronounce him to have been a very good man,' but there was only a small increase in the number of Methodist adherents during his years of activity. By 1818 there were still only 229 members in the Stanstead and St Francis River circuits, which were now combined.[2] As for the St Armand circuit, the local Anglican curate wrote in 1816 that 'The Methodists have no Teachers from any society. A Farmer from the other side of the Province Line preaches to them generally once in the three weeks. Some years ago they were more numerous and had frequent visits from itinerant preachers.'[3]

Despite Methodist Episcopal assurances to the contrary, the field was clearly open for a British Wesleyan initiative. In 1817 the Wesleyan annual meeting in Montreal declared that no Wesleyan missionary 'shall be allowed to take into his circuit any place where the American Brethern have Societies, unless there is a regular invitation from a majority of the official members in that place; nevertheless, where the American Brethern only preach but have no Society our missionaries have full liberty to take such place into their circuit and attend them regularly.'[4] Consequently, the Wesleyans designated the Canadas as a separate British district and assigned Richard Williams to what they called the Melbourne circuit, with boundaries similar to those of the American missionary society's St Francis River circuit. Williams reported only sixty-one members in 1818.

The Wesleyans also established the St Armand circuit in 1818, even though the Americans still occupied the same area as what they called the Dunham circuit. The Wesleyan appointee for St Armand, Richard Pope, claimed that

> Religion once prospered in this neighbourhood, but the late unnatural and destructive war between great Britain and the united States of America, gave it a dreadful blow. Many pious persons who were inimical to our government moved away to other places, while others were soon engaged in the war and so disregarded all religion, and even persecuted the Preacher who laboured among them. Since the peace the American Preachers have been sent to some of the circuit as before, but in vain. The people retain their former prejudices, and by far the greater part will not come to hear them.[5]

But the Methodist Episcopal Church had not given the Dunham circuit up, for in 1819 and 1820 their missionary, Fitch Reed, visited each of his fourteen appointments (three of which were in Vermont) every two weeks, a distance of 150 miles. His only break was when he stayed with a Dutch-speaking family at St Armand from Saturday afternoon to Monday morning, once a fortnight. Reed's journal describes how, during the summer, families would travel by ox-team to hear him, 'the women and children riding on sleds, and the men and boys, – with their pants rolled up – wading through the mud, six or eight miles, so eager were they for the word of life.' Winter travel was easier: 'In the place of deep *mud* I had deeper *snow*; but, for the most part, the roads were kept open and passable by constant travel.' Reed needed his buffalo and bear robes to keep warm in the draughty log cabins where he spent his nights, usually in the loft to escape the 'room full of men, women, children, and dogs.' After one such night, he awoke to find his blankets covered with more than a foot of snow that had drifted in through the openings in the roof. On the spring circuits, the waterproof box on his one-horse sleigh enabled Reed to float 'through miles of water.'[6]

By his own account, on his first circuit Reed had initiated a revival at a funeral service in a 'large and flourishing settlement, – most of the people being from New Hampshire, and of much more than ordinary intelligence and refinement.' The enthusiasm persisted until his return visit two weeks later: 'Never did I see a revival progress so delightfully, and as I earnestly wished and prayed it might. Almost the entire population of adult age professed and gave good evidence of genuine conversion.' Reed claimed that he had added seventy-eight members by the end of his year's circuit. One of the settlers he met in St Armand was the eldest son of Philip Embury, the first Methodist preacher to go to America. Much to Reed's surprise, Samuel Embury willingly sold him the autographed Bible his father had brought from England in 1760 and used throughout his life.[7]

According to Methodist Episcopal records, membership in the Dunham circuit had increased from 165 in 1819 to 247 in 1820. For what was effectively the same circuit, the Wesleyan, Richard Williams, reported only sixty-eight members in 1820.[8] But the British Wesleyans had to face much weaker competition from their American counterparts in the Stanstead circuit. After a visit to Stanstead Township in November 1819, the Guernsey-born John DePutron reported that the Methodist Episcopal Society had failed to assign a minister there for nearly a year. In DePutron's view, even where American preachers were active, their influence was minimal or harmful: 'They remain about 7 or 8 months in the year, and preach once in 3 and sometimes 6 weeks in some part of the Townships. Several Townships are included in the one circuit so that at the Best very few persons can hear them unless they travel many miles.' DePutron added that because married Episcopal Methodist preachers had to remain in one place 'in order to provide necessities for their families, the missionary society had to resort to young men 'who previous to their conversion had never studied Divinity.' These young men were 'doubtless possessed of piety and zeal, but with ideas[?] very inadequate to the task, the sacred work has suffered from their well-meant endeavours.'[9]

The British Methodist missionaries obviously perceived their American counterparts as competitors. Conflict was, nevertheless, largely confined to Upper Canada where the Methodist Episcopal Society was more strongly committed. John DePutron reported in 1820 that the American society had completely vacated Lower Canada, having no men to send. In February 1821 the Americans agreed that they would give up part of the Dunham circuit within three months, and that the British would take charge of the Stanstead and the St Francis River circuits immediately.[10] Later the same year the two branches of the church finally declared that Methodist Episcopal Society would confine its efforts to the economically promising Upper Canada, and the Wesleyans would confine theirs to the other colonies (Kingston excepted).

The local population was clearly disappointed when the American preachers formally withdrew from the region. In the spring of 1821 DePutron complained from his new station in the St Francis Valley:

> These Townships are chiefly inhabited by Americans, many of whom have always been bitter enemies to the English government, they are protected by our laws, they prosper under them, they pay no taxes, and yet they are cruel enough to calumniate the British Constitution, and reject British Missionaries, because they are faithful to their King and Country. In attempting to establish a Sunday School last summer a few narrow souls opposed me and at last, finally counteracted my attempts, because I was not an American.[11]

From the Shefford circuit, Thomas Catterick reported that 'Many of those who belonged to the American Methodist Societies were in a very low state of mind when I arrived, and altho' several have been quickened according to God's word, yet nevertheless there are still some whose minds are in a weak and sickly state.'[12] This uncertainty about the spiritual state of the circuit presumably explains why the first page of the Shefford quarterly meeting minute-book states that of the 130 members, only eighty-five 'professeth to be justified.'[13]

Methodist Episcopal spokesman, William McKendrie, asked the Lower Canadian members to forgive his society for 'our seeming to give you up,' and stated: 'It is a peace offering. No other consideration could have induced us to consent to the measure.'[14] The British branch of the Methodists had several disadvantages as far as the North American environment was concerned. Not only were their missionaries less inured than the Americans to the hardships of the frontier, but Carroll states that other specific advantages of the American connection were 'efficient oversight' by a presiding elder, and the bestowing of orders on local preachers.[15] We shall see that the Wesleyan effort in the border townships would be considerably weakened by the movement of some of the leading local preachers across the border where their official status would be increased.

While Carroll suggests that it was deemed more expendable by the Methodist authorities to risk losing support in Lower Canada and the Maritimes than in the rapidly growing Upper Canada, the fact was that Methodist Episcopal missionaries had simply been far more active in the latter colony than had the British Wesleyans, who were therefore in no position to dictate terms.[16] The Wesleyan missionaries were informed by their sponsoring association that:

> The only reason we could have for increasing the number of missionaries in that province was, the presumption of a strong necessity, arising out of the destitute condition of the inhabitants, the total want, or to great distance of Ministers. On no other ground could we apply money raised for missionary purposes for the supply of Preachers to Upper Canada. The information we have had for two years past, has all served to show, that the number of Preachers employed there by the American brethren, was greater than we had at first supposed, and was constantly increasing.

Upper Canada was, therefore, a less needy missionary territory than Lower Canada, 'where much less help exists, and a great part of the population is involved in Popish Superstion [*sic*].'[17]

Paradoxically, the Methodist Episcopal Society may well have focused much less attention on the Eastern Townships because the settlers of this region were less self-sustaining. The rapid development of Vermont had come to an abrupt end, Methodist growth in New England remained relatively slow, and the church's financial resources were stretched to the limit. The preacher's 'allowance' in the New England Conference was supposed to be $100 a year, paid quarterly, plus an equal amount for his wife or widow, and $16 to $24 per child, depending on his or her age. (A Wesleyan missionary received a similar stipend of £30 per year, plus £20 for a wife.) The stewards of each church also submitted expense accounts for fuel, rent, and 'table expenses,' and the preacher could claim his travelling costs. Anything contributed locally was to be deducted from these accounts, but the Conference's debts mounted quickly. In 1814 the debt to the thirty-six men who had received $1,359 was $2,766, and a mere $438 was available to meet it. By 1821 the deficit was $11,062 out of an estimate of $16,487, and there was only $863 to meet it.[18] Historians have not been sufficiently aware of the degree to which it was these financial considerations that determined the nature of the 1821 agreement.

Organizational Structure

According to Semple, 'Methodism was first and foremost a connexion, not a group of quasi-independent congregations.'[19] The institutional structure established by John Wesley was, nevertheless, based on local societies divided into class meetings under class leaders, with each adherent given a membership ticket and required to participate in prayer, singing, and testimony. Arising naturally out of the quarterly examination of the Methodist classes by the principal circuit preacher, the quarterly meeting of itinerant preachers, local preachers, class leaders, and stewards reviewed the work of the circuit. While women had served as preachers for the Methodist Episcopal church, and they generally dominated the membership roles of all evangelical denominations, there is little evidence that they were welcomed to take part in local governance. In 1837 Rebecca Blunt became the first woman to be listed as a class leader in the Shefford circuit book, but she rarely attended quarterly meetings.[20] In any case, much of the governing power remained centralized in the hands of the annual conference, which was composed only of the itinerant preachers within the district. It was their collective role to discipline each other, settle doctrinal issues, and examine the work of the church as a whole.[21]

Of the nine stations (the Wesleyan term for circuits) remaining in the Wesleyan Methodists' Canada District after 1821, the four in the Eastern Townships were known as St Armand, Stanstead, Melbourne, and Shefford, named for the chief township in each of them. New Ireland would become a separate circuit in 1835, Compton and Hatley in 1836, Dunham in 1840, and Sherbrooke in 1847, but the Wesleyan missionaries continued to have very large territories to cover.[22] As a result, most stations rarely received the services of these men on the Sabbath, which was perceived to be a particular hardship because of that day's spiritual significance.

Unlike their Methodist Episcopal predecessors in the region, the Wesleyan missionaries each had a home base which received more of their attention than did any of the outlying communities. John DePutron reported from the Melbourne circuit in June 1819 that he preached in each of ten 'appointments' every two weeks, except in the townships of Melbourne and Shipton which he served two Sundays in three. His successor, Henry Pope, claimed in 1821 that he spent three-quarters of his Sundays in Melbourne and Shipton, with occasional forays into Brompton to preach in the evening. There were four other 'preaching stations' within a seven-mile radius, and every fourth Sunday he travelled to the back part of Shipton, twelve miles north of the river, where he preached 'to a good congregation, 24 of whom are in Society.' Twenty miles down the river there was 'a very pious local preacher who labours faithfully on the Lord's day to serve his ungodly neighbours,' but he was the only such individual mentioned in the report.[23]

On the Shefford circuit, Thomas Catterick reported in March 1822 that 'There are seven Townships in which I regularly preach once a fortnight when my health and the roads will permit, ... In each of these Townships we have a small society, and the work of the Lord is prospering in many of their souls.' By 1836 there were four preaching places in Shefford Township, three in Granby, two in Stukely, two in Bolton, and one in Farnham; recently added were one in Brome and one in Milton. Demonstrating the Wesleyans' continuing deference to the Church of England, Thomas Turner alternated his preaching in Stukely with that of the Episcopal clergyman who resided near him in Shefford Township.[24]

While it included the oldest settlements of the region, the St Armand circuit was no less challenging. Having previously spent four years on the difficult Shefford circuit William Squire complained that 'I could have wished for a little relaxation, from such severe exercises, as on my last station I traveled about four thousand miles each year, with only one horse, without roads, or at least any worthy of being called so, and here my circumstances are not much improved in that respect, whilst I have to superintend more than double the number of members.' The St Armand circuit of 150 miles and upwards of four hundred members was travelled every fortnight, and Squire also felt obliged to visit the nearby Caldwell Manor Station, on the west side of Missisquoi Bay, which had not had a missionary for some time.[25]

While a number of them were married, the Wesleyan missionaries felt socially isolated in what was, to them, a foreign environment. Noting that the closest clergy were the two Anglican ministers twenty-five miles down river in Drummondville, and twenty-three miles upriver in Sherbrooke, respectively, a lonesome Henry Pope complained from Melbourne in August 1842 that the missionary society had failed to acknowledge the letters he had been sending during the previous two and a half years. He added: 'While attempting to penetrate these almost pathless woods, upwards of 3000 miles from my native country and dear

Friends – excluded from a hundred blessed animating privileges which I once enjoyed, to be informed that my Letters how uninteresting soever they may be, have been duly received is deemed no small favour.'[26]

Most of the Wesleyan missionaries were dedicated and self-sacrificing individuals, but probably none more than John Brownell, whom a local historian recalls as 'a popular and powerful preacher.'[27] Brownell contracted inflammation of the lungs and pleurisy in 1842, and he continued to suffer from the weak heart that had terminated his labours in the West Indies. He wrote from Dunham in 1843, the year he was accused of spreading the Millerite heresy:

> Three times lately I have all but expired instantaneously – twice in the Chapel, and once whilst on my way into the circuit. In the latter instance I was in my sleigh proceeding to a place called 'Sutton.' In a moment a spasm seized my heart – pain of the most excruciating character was the result – and in another instant I was wholly unconscious of every thing. How long I remained so I can not say, but for some moments after consciousness returned I could not call to mind where I was nor what my object in being on the road.

Obviously, then, to continue 'to preach five times a week besides performing all other duties connected with a circuit would be suicidal; and yet if I can not do this I can not have a circuit in this district.' To demonstrate his submission to the Missionary Committee, Brownell left 'entirely in your hands' the decision as to whether he should continue in Dunham, move to an easier station in the Maritimes, or take some time off. But Brownell could ill afford to take a break from work, because his wife's four-week visit to Saratoga Springs to cure a protracted illness had cost $40, plus travelling expenses, and the sending of his son to England to study at Wood house Grove had 'involved me in great expense.'[28]

The Wesleyan missionaries rarely mentioned politics in their reports, but they clearly saw themselves as agents of acculturation as well as religious conversion. The moral and spiritual danger came from the more radical sects and not the Church of England, which was criticized largely for its lack of zeal.[29] The Wesleyans saw themselves as filling a vacuum left by the too comfortable and too complacent – but also too few – Anglican clergy. The Methodist clergy of Lower Canada were therefore shocked in 1828 when Judge Sewell of the Quebec Court of King's Bench declared that they could not keep marriage registers. They obviously were aware that the enabling bill passed by the Legislative Assembly in 1825 had been rejected by the Legislative Council,[30] but James Knowlan, as chair of the Canada District, declared that keeping the registers was 'a legal right – a right which we once enjoyed – but which was wrested from us by a crafty Chief Justice.' Knowlan protested further:

> if our value even in a political point of view was known to the Government that ample assistance would be afforded us. The Church of England does not now and never can in Canada, as in England, possess a commanding control over the great body of the people. That Church is now most warmly opposed by all the other Churches, ourselves only excepted, and the leaders of the Upper Canada Methodists are very conspicuous in that opposition. In that Province the members of the Church would hail our return with joy.

Knowlan nevertheless counselled the Wesleyan Missionary Society (WMS) that it should not consider returning to Upper Canada until the Methodists' rights were restored in Lower Canada. A bill satisfactory to Knowlan was passed by the Legislative Assembly several months later, and forwarded with the support of the governor in the spring of 1829.[31]

In contrast to their Anglican counterparts, the Methodist missionaries were instructed to remain aloof from secular concerns. Most particularly, while their conservative sympathies were doubtless obvious, they were strictly forbidden from taking a public stand during elections. In 1841, when Shefford's John Tomkins was criticized by the district meeting for attending what it termed a political meeting, he explained that it was actually a supper for a defeated candidate who was 'a gentleman strongly attached to our Protestant Monarchy.' Furthermore, he had regarded it solely in the light of an expression of neighbourly good will to a worthy individual and not in any respect as a political feast.' The district meeting noted that 'This departure from our usual practice in such cases was so unanimously disapproved by all the Brethren, accompanied by expressions of regret from Br. Tomkins that by a misapprehension on his part he should have compromised our connexional character, that we feel confident it will never again be repeated.'[32]

Even the temperance movement was avoided by the Wesleyan missionaries. While conceding that temperance and total abstinence societies were strongly supported by other denominations, who 'on that account become attractive to some of our members,' the 1838 district meeting added that 'some of our best friends and most pious Leaders are Wine and Spirit merchants, particularly in Quebec.'[33] The strategy of the Wesleyan missionaries was essentially to ignore the temperance movement in order to prevent controversy and the alienation of some of their more influential followers.

The restriction of each Wesleyan missionary to two or three years per circuit assignment further discouraged the growth of local attachments. The community role of the Methodist Society would, instead, be largely filled by local preachers who maintained their secular vocations. French claims that this arrangement 'provided a sense of continuity and a degree of intimate supervision which the itinerants themselves would have found it difficult to provide,'[34] but the system was not particularly well adapted to the frontier environment of the Eastern Townships. Nor did it develop satisfactorily even after the early settlement period had passed, though the main reasons appear to have been the Wesleyan missionaries' reluctance to rely upon a local leadership, as well as the ease with which local preachers could be ordained if they moved to the American side of the border. Still, none of the Wesleyan missionaries recommended adoption of the Methodist Episcopal practice of ordaining local preachers, or establishing the office of presiding elder.

When union with the Upper Canadian Methodist Episcopal Society was being discussed in 1832, Lower Canada's Wesleyan missionaries opposed adoption of the more democratic structure of the church in Upper Canada. In the spring of 1834 Egerton Ryerson attended the Canada Eastern District meeting in Montreal to reassure the British missionaries about the role of presiding elder. He denied that this position usurped the powers of the circuit superintendent (the minister), who remained responsible for appointing class leaders, though only with the approval of the majority of the local members. But the presiding elder did chair the quarterly meeting, which could hear appeals against the class leaders. While Ryerson also pointed out that only the minister had the power to determine when a love feast (communal meal of the Eucharist) would be held, and to dispense the sacraments, a number of the missionaries remained concerned about the potential loss of clerical authority.[35] As a result, the union did not take place at this time.

The Methodist system had originated in densely-settled and socially-stratified England, and some of the Wesleyan missionaries began to question its efficacy in the very different social environment of the Eastern Townships. For example, Richard Pope complained concerning Stanstead in 1823 that 'We suffer much loss from a want of a few capable, pious and zealous Leaders of our Classes.'[36] William Squire, based on his many years of experience in the Eastern Townships, would develop the most consistent critique of the Methodist system. In December 1825 he reported that the necessity of travelling 130 miles every fortnight on the Shefford circuit to visit all the 'Preaching Places' was diffusing 'the rays of influence' too widely for him to make much of an impact.[37] Squire remained discouraged a year later, when he reported:

> the sanctity of the Sabbath is little regarded, the time being spent either in ordinary business, in useless visits, or idleness, not having any religious service of a public nature for several weeks together ... My labours seem almost lost when divided among fifteen small congregations, with ... very little local assistance. It is not sufficient that we preach to them on the ordinary days of the week, because their business will then prevent many from attending, and giving them only seven or eight Sundays in a year, which is all I can do for the majority, is not sufficient to preserve the good impressions which are made.[38]

Squire repeated the same refrain from the Stanstead circuit nine years later, in 1835 when the Wesleyan Missionary Society counselled its Lower Canadian appointees 'to encourage suitable young men to offer themselves as Assistant Missionaries, for in this way only can we hope to supply the want which is felt.'[39] He explained that the reason for not having more local preachers was that 'so soon as an individual is raised up, he is invited into the United States to enter the regular Ministry; or if he stays in Canada to join the Reformed Methodists, Baptists, or some others where if the pay is poor, the discipline is lazy, and he may act as he pleases as to the place and quantity of his labour; and such is the demand for men that very moderate talents will suffice if there be zeal and self-denial.'[40] Squire may have had the Stanstead-born Jason Lee particularly in mind, for, after being active as a local preacher in his home area for several years, Lee had left for the Amerindian mission in Oregon as soon as he was ordained in 1833. Squire's reference that year to 'the difficulties which were in the way of receiving Mr Jason Lee,' may help to explain Lee's decision to leave the Townships. If so, he certainly had his revenge, for he played a major role in winning the Oregon territory for the Americans.[41]

Also revealing is the treatment of Barnabas Hitchcock, who had been ordained for Vermont's Methodist Episcopal itinerant ministry after becoming a local preacher in the Eastern Townships in 1823. William

Squire reported in 1836 that 'the appointment of Br. Hitchcock to the Melbourne circuit continues to be attended with Divine blessing,' and Carroll claims that he 'was everywhere characterized as a soul-saving preacher.' Similarly, an early local historian recalled that Hitchcock had 'a clear musical and powerful voice; and he rarely allowed bad roads or storms to keep him from his appointments.'[42] Hitchcock worked on contract for the WMS, but it decided in 1838 that it would not accept him as an assistant missionary because he was too old, at fifty-two, and he was married.[43] Hitchcock was not the only such case, for the fact that John Borland of Quebec was also married made the district meeting hesitate to ordain him, despite his youth and his four years of experience as a local preacher. The twenty-six-year-old Borland was received on trial as an assistant missionary in 1835, but the meeting made it clear that this was not to be considered a precedent. He also had to promise to give up the letters of ordination if anything occurred 'to prevent him from being received into full connexion.'[44]

Assistant missionaries served the outlying areas of large circuits such as that of Quebec which included the northeastern periphery of the Eastern Townships. In 1833, four years after British families began settling this area in substantial numbers, the Quebec circuit was granted a second missionary in order to serve them. He visited only once every quarter, however, and while the Quebec report to the district meeting of May 1835 stated that the area had seen 'some gracious awakenings and conversions to God,' it added that 'they are earnestly desiring the word of life to be more frequently and extensively preached among them.'[45] In addition, a petition claimed that there were eight preaching stations on the circuit, 'and many more might be added should a Preacher be stationed here.' The settlers requested that he be an ordained minister, not an assistant preacher, 'for the purpose of administering unto us the Lord's Supper, Baptize Children, Solemnize Marriage, Bury the Dead, hold Love Feasts and regulate the affairs of the growing societies.'[46] This isolated area did become a distinct circuit known as New Ireland soon afterward, but Edmund S. Ingalls complained in 1840 that more missionary labour was desperately needed to do 'any very great additional amount of good.' There were eighteen settlements to visit every three weeks, only six of which could be served on Sundays. The missionary often had 'to travel over mountains, through rivers, swamps and wilderness a distance of a hundred and twenty miles and preach eleven times in one week.' Two years later, Ingalls wrote that the circuit's decline in numbers from 230 in 1839 to 213 in 1842 could be explained 'in part by the fact that the labors of the Missionary are so largely divided as to render it impracticable for him to visit the various settlements oftener than once in three weeks while ministers of other denominations preach in the same places once a week.'[47] To make matters worse, the local Methodists were again without a fully-ordained minister in 1847. Their quarterly meeting noted that John Hutchinson, a former preacher from England's New Connection Methodist Society, was to be commended for his assiduous labours, but his 'Ecclesiastical disabilities' had 'greatly militated against the Intrests [*sic*] of Methodism in this circuit.' Hutchinson apparently did not have the legal right to perform marriages, and the quarterly meeting of April 1848 insisted that his successor be able do so.[48]

One advantage New Ireland did have over Stanstead and other circuits was its number of local preachers. In 1837 John Borland reported that Upper Ireland, with only forty-two society members, had three local preachers and two exhorters; Lower Ireland, with twenty-three members, had one local preacher; and Inverness, with seventy-six members, had four local preachers and two exhorters. Borland added that the main road was the only one that could be safely travelled on horseback, making it necessary to visit many of the classes on foot: 'this evil however is considerably mitigated by the zeal and faithfulness of the local brethren and exhorters, who, thus efficiently co-operate with your missionary in sowing and watering the seed of the Kingdom.'[49] New Ireland's local preachers clearly helped to fill the gap left by the infrequency of visits by the circuit preacher, but it is doubtless also significant that this circuit was far removed from the American border, and that most of the settlers were British. Not only would their local preachers be less mistrusted by the Wesleyan missionaries, they would also not be so tempted to take advantage of the greater opportunities in the United States.

In the opposite corner of the Eastern Townships, the minutes of the St Armand quarterly meeting reveal that there were only seven local preachers on that densely-settled circuit in 1825. Furthermore, in March 1826, one of them was suspended for three months on the charge that he had neglected his appointments, and a class leader was required to make a public confession in the chapel for preaching without permission from the minister and quarterly meeting.[50] After being appointed to the St Armand circuit in 1837, Squire reported that it had been 'in a declining state for several years,' and he felt that it was, 'at least for the present in a state of hopelessness.' This he attributed to the 'Great political excitements' which had culminated in the Rebellion, the secession of a considerable number of local preachers and members to the Reformed or Protestant Methodists 'under the pretense of seeking a greater degree of religious liberty,' and, above all, 'the inconvenient and unprofitable size of the circuit' which 'effectually prevents the Preachers from doing much in the way of pastoral visitations.' Squire argued that while 'I am aware that solitary stations have their disadvantages,' nevertheless 'I am equally satisfied that such is the state of this part of the Country, that we shall do little permanent good until this circuit is divided into *three*.'[51]

Other Wesleyan missionaries also criticized the itinerant system as it operated in the Eastern Townships. In explaining the advantages enjoyed by the Congregational missionaries, Edmund Botterell of the Compton and Hatley circuit wrote in 1838:

> These good men *settle down in villages* to which they give *regular and frequent preaching on the Sabbath*. Thus they get meeting houses erected, form and conduct Sabbath schools and become the most influential persons of these places. The people prefer attending on a Preacher they can hear every Lord's day, they prefer placing themselves under the pastoral care of one who is with them constantly whilst they cheerfully subscribe to his support. Owing to our system of itinerancy (good altogether but perhaps not best when extreme) we have not been hitherto so much in the villages as the people needed and desired. Hence we have no chapel on either the Melbourne or Sherbrooke circuit, nor can we with any lasting advantage establish Sunday schools, not being on the spot to take the superintendance of them. Your missionaries have laboured here and others have entered into their labours.

Botterell warned that, unless the WMS adapted its system 'to the altered state of the country,' its missionaries would soon be preaching to only the most isolated settlements:

> If the object of our mission is to preach occasionally to those who seldom or never hear any other Ministers, that is, if we are required to do the least good by the largest amount of labour and inconvenience, we have only to act as hitherto we have done, but if it be our object to witness the utmost fruit of our labour – to gather around us societies that may flourish and create an influence that shall be equally permanent and beneficial, we should give more attention to the villages than has yet been done on these circuits and visit the remote settlers and scattered inhabitants as we may be able.[52]

Botterell returned to the same theme two years later, arguing that one of the chief disadvantages of the current system 'is the almost inappreciable benefit we are of to the youthful population who far outnumber the adults' because of the inability to operate more than a small number of poorly-conducted Sunday schools: 'Many of the young are not properly guarded by their parents nor are they brought under the salutary care of Christian Ministers. They are hence liable to be led away by vicious example and corrupted by pernicious opinions of politics, morality and religion.' Reducing the size of the circuits would also make it possible for pastoral visits 'to eradicate the strong prejudices which many have against us, and increase the union, foment the zeal, and guide the piety of such as are better minded.' Having travelled three thousand miles since the previous district meeting, Botterell had little time for such work, and the class leaders were of little assistance.[53]

Finally, the Melbourne circuit still included nine or ten townships in 1848 when Benjamin Slight wrote to the WMS making an impassioned plea for more missionaries:

> although we have stretched ourselves to our utmost tension in traveling, & that to the partial neglect of other, & important duties, yet we cannot ... meet the wants of the country. When I pass through it, & contemplate the wants & destitution of the great proportion of the rural districts in every direction, my spirit is stirred in me, & my feelings are of a distressing nature. ... British, Irish Methodists! here are your children, your neighbours, members of your congregations, passing years of their probationary existence without ever seeing the face of a minister of any kind – spending silent sabbaths – passing week after week without the means of grace! Years roll round, and many of them are growing grey without spiritual culture; and many are sinking into a state of almost perfect indifference, while many others are plunging into the grave exclaiming, 'No man careth for my soul!'[54]

William Squire had written in 1836 that 'From the number of Assistant Missionaries on trial, and recommended to be received, it appears to me probable that the work of the Ministry will soon principally, if not wholly, pass into the hands of individuals raised up amongst us. The sooner this can be done with safety to the interests of our cause the better.'[55] But the fact that little further progress would be made in this direction by mid-century suggests that the Wesleyan missionaries remained too conservative in their attitudes to encourage local vocations. Instead, they continued to demand additional support from England so that the circuits could be increased in number and reduced in size. Consequently, local preachers failed to become a significant source for ordained clergy from within the region.

If the Upper Canadian Methodist preachers had become Canadianized by the 1820s, as French claims, those in Lower Canada remained profoundly British in loyalty. While the Canada Western District left the Methodist union in 1840 due to what it felt was interference in its internal affairs,[56] there were no such complaints from Lower Canada. Indeed, when Canada District annual meeting was asked in 1843 to consider a union of all five Wesleyan districts in British North America, it agreed to do so only on condition that the new body remain '*subordinate* to the British Conference *and in perpetual connexion with it*,' and that each district deal independently with the WMS. When union did come in 1854, it was because the London-based missionary society had finally decided to cut the umbilical cord with Lower Canada.[57]

Institutional and Material Support

The Wesleyan Missionary Society had been established in 1818, with its funds managed by a large lay and clerical committee which entrusted routine operations to three secretaries, one of whom devoted his time exclusively to the missions.[58] The missionaries were stationed according to the recommendations of this committee which exercised firm doctrinal and disciplinary authority over them. But the main source of conflict with the Lower Canadian missionaries, who were embodied in the Canada District, was the committee's enforcement of a prudent financial policy. Initially, the missionaries were simply allowed to draw on the missionary society, with the district meeting checking the accounts, but the supervisory committee also encouraged self-reliance. It questioned disparities between the contributions of individual circuits, insisted on the rental of pews, and avoided occupying any station that would cost the society more than £50 a year.[59]

The initial reports from the Eastern Townships were optimistic as far as material support was concerned. While serving the Melbourne circuit in 1819, John DePutron claimed that 'In these parts the necessaries of life are not wanting, but there is little money in circulation,' so his supporters provided produce which was converted into money towards the end of the year. Fresh provisions were seldom seen, and there were few fish in the St Francis River, but 'Tea and tobacco are here in high repute, the former is presented in many places three times a day; many an old matron has recourse to the [.?.] pipe after every meal because she reasons it helps her.' Little assistance would therefore be required from England. DePutron's successor, Henry Pope, persuaded the settlers, many of whom were in debt for their farms, to subscribe upwards of $200 towards his support. He, too, noted that '*money* is out of the question here,' but added that each subscriber contributed a part of his farm produce. From the Stanstead circuit, Daniel Hick reported in 1821 that even though the people could not provide him with money, 'provisions of various kinds have been amply and cheerfully supplied, so that we have not suffered want.'[60]

It did not take long, however, for comments about local support to become distinctly negative. Thomas Catterick on the Shefford circuit reported in 1823 that 'Sometimes we have more provision [*sic*] brought in by our friends than we can keep from spoiling; and at other times we find it difficult to purchase.' This problem was to be somewhat alleviated by the purchase of a house for the missionary situated on three acres of land 'which will be nearly sufficient pasture for a horse, and cow during the summer season.'[61] The people of Stanstead were less charitable, according to Hick's successor, Richard Pope. He complained in 1823 that they could easily support the two ministers that were needed, if they wished to do so, but they 'were all divided into seven or eight different persuasions, many of whom think that the minister is under as great an obligation to preach as they are to hear, and consequently contribute nothing towards his living.'[62]

The Wesleyan missionaries were under much greater financial constraints than their Anglican counterparts, for the secretary of the WMS, Joseph Taylor, objected as early as the spring of 1821 that the Canada District was drawing bills that greatly exceeded the allowed maximum of £50 per station. Taylor did not mince words: 'Is it a wonder that the English Preachers in Canada are preferred to the Americans? In the last two months the English Preachers in those Provinces had drawn £1147.10.3.' He refused to meet any further bills until a decision was reached concerning whether to pay for the previous years' expenditures. In response, the nine Canadian missionaries held a special meeting at which they protested vociferously that 'we are represented as deceivers and impostors.' They declared that 'if we are found guilty of the things charged against us we are not worthy of retaining a name or place in a Christian Society much less of being employed in the sacred office of the Christian Ministry.' In defence of their expenditures, the missionaries argued that the 1815 regulations simply stated that no more than £50 could be withdrawn at one time without previous advice and explanation. While a maximum of £60 per missionary, exclusive of children (who qualified for an additional £5 each), had admittedly been fixed in 1820, the missionaries did not realize that this limit was to apply to the current year. Seven months' experience had shown that it was too low for some of the circuits, which would therefore have to be abandoned. If the WMS persevered in its determination to dishonour the bills the missionaries had drawn, 'there is no alternative but our going to Prison as our people are unable to extricate us from such a difficulty and we are utterly unable to meet them ourselves.'[63]

As for the greater economies of the American preachers, the Wesleyan missionaries stated that they often owned farms 'which are generally cultivated by themselves or at least under their directions by which means they with families derive great part of their support, their collections among the people being altogether inadequate to their wants.' After a few years they usually married and retired from the ministry, but in the meantime

> to obtain the necessaries of life they frequently buy and sell Horses – carry about with them various kinds of provisions – also wool stockings and cloths [sic] for sale and even pitchforks have been left by our American Brethren to be disposed of. But after all their exertions in thus trafficking they are seldom able to abtain [sic] decent (clothing) apparel. Such proceeding being contrary to our Rules and in our opinion derogatory to a Christian Minister as well as injurious to our spiritual warfare [sic] we therefore unanimously reject.[64]

If only because he had a family to support, James Booth was a particularly vocal complainant while he was on the St Armand circuit during the early 1820s. He repeatedly asked to return to England if the WMS could not help pay off his debt. He explained that because the farmers were unable to sell their produce at a profit, they focused on subsistence. As a result,

> if a friend present us with a pound of butter, or a Fowl, we have to account for it, as Cash received, according to the market price, and in this way, the greatest part of contributions are made for our support in wheat – rye – barley – oats – corn – hay – peas – beans – wood – leather – pork – beef – mutton, etc. Now whether we want them, or not, we must take such things

as are offered, and account for them as Cash, and unable to sell the surplus, if any, we lose at least 25 percent towards having the whole of our allowance in Cash.

Booth added that the cost of items such as clothing was high, and that 'Out of our little pittance, we have to give frequently towards the erection of Chapels – establishing of benevolent institutions, or we could not succeed in the Country.' The small amounts collected from baptisms and the sale of books were simply directed towards necessary expenses.[65]

To make matters worse, St Armand, like the rest of Lower Canada, had been experiencing economic hardship. Fortunately, Booth's successor, John DePutron, was able to report in 1823 that the spring thaw and rain had brought a great many logs into Missisquoi Bay, 'an acceptable present to the Inhabitants.' Also, the fish that had once offered many settlers a great part of their subsistence, suddenly returned after six or seven years' absence from the Pike River. A year later, however, DePutron reported that 'many of our Members ... are not able to give any thing towards supporting our Mission. Last September a severe frost destroyed the greater part of their corn, and the Summer being very dry, the hay was worth but little. Several persons have lost cattle this winter from want of hay – An old man, who has 5 of his family in Society, declared last Winter that they had been 3 days without Bread.' Fortuitously, the fish had again returned to the Pike River, which 'will prove a great blessing to many of the inhabitants in this circuit.'[66]

As it became clear that the British immigrants were bypassing the Eastern Townships for Upper Canada, the disillusioned Wesleyan missionaries declared in 1824 that the American delegate, John Emory, had misled their church in suggesting that Lower Canada presented as extensive a field for missionary operations as the upper province.[67] The sense of disillusionment was exacerbated by the London committee's determination to limit the costs of the Canada district. In 1826 it declared that it would return all bills beyond a £60 annual limit for each missionary. The missionaries responded through the minutes of the district meeting that on accepting their assignments 'we were of opinion, and still are of that opinion, that should not the People among whom we were appointed to labour be able to support us, we had an undoubted claim upon the Mission Fund to make up the deficiencies in our several accounts.' They protested further that 'the direction now before us evidently implies either that we have not made all the efforts in our power to obtain from the People a competent support, or that we claim more than is necessary for that purpose; but neither is the case; we have done our utmost in our several stations, and our allowances are not more than is indispensably necessary to enable us to live, and to appear with becoming decency before the public.' The minutes concluded that 'sending back any part of the deficiencies of the circuits to be charged to the personal accounts of the Preachers ... has a direct tendency to damp the zeal, and embarrass the minds of these Preachers, and we therefore most respectfully request the Committee not to urge the measure upon us.'[68]

Constraints imposed by the missionary society's decision to limit the year's grant to £500 were such that when the Melbourne circuit's leaders and stewart purchased a horse, harness, sleigh, and buffalo robe for William Faulkner's use, paying with 'produce of the country,' the district meeting deducted this amount from his quarterage of £15. The Shipton committee protested that the horse and equipment were purchased exclusively for the use of the station's preacher, and that the District Committee had no claim to them. The situation was reduced to comic opera when, in anticipation of Faulkner's return to England on the recommendation of the district meeting, the chair, James Knowlan, attempted to collect the books and desk, worth £21, that had been provided by the WMS. Faulkner refused to surrender the property until his arrears for the previous six months were paid. When Knowlan, in turn, refused to return the horse and sleigh he had borrowed from Faulkner, the local magistrate confined him to jail for fourteen hours for horse stealing. Faulkner finally left Melbourne in the spring of 1829. Two years later the local Methodists, still without a preacher, sold the horse, sleigh, and harness for £14 in order to reduce the circuit's expenses.[69]

Meanwhile, the Canada District had managed to keep its budget under the allowed maximum of £500 in 1826–7, but the annual meeting protested once more against the principle of an annual ceiling. When the London committee suggested fixed annual grants in 1828, the Canadian missionaries protested that they had already limited their board allowance to £52 currency per year, with the result that their income was now reduced 'to the lowest sum possible in justice to ourselves, our families and the church of God.'[70] The district chair, James Knowlan, made the constructive recommendation that the society acquire sufficient land in each country circuit 'to maintain the missionary and his family & feed his horse and a cow & furnish food: the land to be cultivated by the voluntary labor of our friends.' Not only would this reduce expenses in the long run, but the mission would be given 'a permanence in future years ... when the fostering care of England is withdrawn from this country.' But the society was in no mood to increase its short-term expenditures. It imposed a district maximum in 1829 when it rejected £83.15.11 in expenses, causing the annual meeting to respond bitterly: 'Would any young man at home come out to us if he knew, not merely what they were to suffer, by bad diet, bad roads, bad beds, and a bad climate, in the company of men, many of whom are little more, except in the Towns, than half civilized?' They had been told that their needs would be met, not that the missionary society 'would limit and threaten us,' and they were resolved 'never to submit to it.'[71]

The rhetoric became even more heated at the next annual meeting, when the minutes declared: 'Whether our own destitute poor are not to be first supplied in preference to foreigners or even the heathen is a question which we think would soon be decided by a British Public.' Rather than continuing to strangle the mission 'by slow degrees' by failing to replace preachers, it would be 'more manly and honourable to us as a body' if the society were to abandon it 'to Calvinists and spurious Methodists as you have done in Upper Canada.' Questioning whether 'even the secretaries give due attention to our minutes and representations,' the district asked for permission to send a delegation to England: 'In truth we have not been treated as Brethren and equals but as Servants – nay worse than Servants for a contract with Servants is considered sacred until it is altered with their consent.'[72]

Chairman Knowlan also expressed increasing frustration in his own reports with what he felt was the neglect of his district. Finally, in the spring of 1831, he formally charged the WMS secretaries with persuading the committee as a whole 'to carry into effect, arbitrary principles and measures in the payment of the Missionaries, in the employment of said Society.'[73] The committee's response, according to the minutes of the district meeting, was to accuse the missionaries 'of *petulance, haughtiness*, of *treating the committee* in the most *disrespectful manner*, of *assuming false principles*, of dictating to the *committee* as if their wisdom and judgment were not equal to our own.' Knowlan had been singled out for particular rebuke by the chief secretary, to which the district meeting responded by asking what his reaction would be 'if various new financial measures were attempted to be forced upon him which would compel him either to forsake his missionary work after perhaps a quarter of a century of service and with a constitution ruined in that service or abandon a most important civil right?'

The district meeting also denied that its members were demanding 'to be the sole Judges of our own allowances,' or 'to interfere with your right to the appointment of missionaries.' They had in 1826, however, asked for the right to determine where each missionary would be assigned, and they were now requesting a voice in settling the amount of the annual grant and 'in the introduction of new financial measures.' The meeting even challenged the right of the WMS committee to abdicate its authority by granting lump annual sums to the district rather than disbursing funds on the receipt of 'vouchers specifying services for which such money is required.' Because the district meeting was aware of the financial circumstances of each circuit, it had been able under the old system to judge the legitimacy of the accounts, 'and could and we believe would as effectually guard the funds of the Missionary Society from abuse on this system as on yours, and would be stimulated to do so for their own honour and credit, and would be enabled to do so as they would then be acting upon known and fixed rules and checks.' As for the secretaries' request that the WMS call upon the Wesleyan Conference 'to exercise its discipline upon us without affording us an opportunity of being heard in defense before that Body, it is of too grave a nature to be commented on in a district meeting.'[74]

The Wesleyan missionaries' promising beginning in the early 1820s had deteriorated by the start of the next decade to what was effectively a labour dispute. There was no withdrawal of services, but the missionaries' enthusiasm was certainly waning, undermined by their home society's budgetary restrictions and the slow growth of the Eastern Townships as compared with Upper Canada. By 1831 there were still only 857 Methodist members in the region, slightly more than half the total in Lower Canada (see appendix, table A.5), and far fewer than the 12,563 in Upper Canada.[75] But the nadir had been reached, as far as relations between the Lower Canadian missionaries and the London committee were concerned, for they changed dramatically with the replacement of James Knowlan by Robert Alder as chair of the district meeting in 1833.[76]

The restoration of harmony was probably not so much due to a change in local leadership, however, as to the increased confidence brought by the first attempt at union with the Upper Canadian Methodists in 1832 and the more generous funding formula that ensued. The initial step in this direction had come with the Upper Canadian separation from the American Genessee Conference in 1828. The Lower Canadian missionaries, looking for any excuse to gain access to Upper

Canada, argued that this separation rendered the 1821 arrangement that had removed them from that colony no longer valid. Their hopes promised to become a reality in 1832 when the WMS decision to send thirteen missionaries to the Canadas threatened Upper Canada's Methodist Episcopal Society with the prospect of renewed competition. It therefore agreed to a union under the discipline of the British connection, but with provincially separate districts. An undated memorandum filed with the minutes of the district meeting suggests that the Canadian Wesleyans had driven a hard bargain, for only they would have access to the funds of the WMS. In return, the WMS would be responsible for all the new settlements as well as all the Amerindians.[77]

The new arrangement left more funds available for the discontented missionaries of the Eastern Townships. Now, rather than deducting the money raised locally from the district's annual grant of £500, the WMS agreed that local donations would be added.[78] With good reason, a resolution was passed in 1832 stating that the Lower Canadian missionaries 'cheerfully acquiesce ... in those plans by which the Committee is guided in appropriating the Monies placed at its disposal for Missionary purposes in district grants ... believing that, as has been stated to us, they have been found from experience to be well adapted to promote the personal comfort of the Brethren employed and the prosperity of Methodism.' As for the charges Knowlan had laid against the committee secretaries, a resolution was passed to the effect that 'this meeting was entirely ignorant of the existence of those charges until they were read by the Chairman and they now beg to disclaim all participation in the sentiments they contain.' The missionaries also apologized for the language that had been employed in questioning the motives of the secretaries, leaving Knowlan little choice but to do likewise.[79]

Despite adopting the formula of a fixed annual grant, however, the WMS continued to check all accounts carefully, and it turned a deaf ear to consistent pleas to cover deficits. Concern about the application of the funding formula surfaced briefly in 1837, when the district meeting noted that the year's grant had fallen short of the anticipated amount. It complained that if the locally raised funds were deducted from the fixed grant, it would be 'unable to extend the work in the district of pressing calls for help.' The time had arrived when 'we must advance or recede as the most zealous efforts are being made by our Baptist and Congregational Brethren to occupy the ground so imperfectly cultivated by us and a large number of Ministers is expected this summer to be stationed in different parts of the Country.'[80]

There would be no complaint about finances the following year, after the WMS promised to send three more missionaries, and, in 1839, it complimented the Canada District for the state of its accounts. The WMS had some reason to be pleased, for its grant could finally be reduced to £400 stg due to the £651 collected on the Lower Canadian circuits.[81] But local concerns emerged again in 1841 when the total budget was limited to £900 stg (for colonial purposes variously estimated at £1000 cy and £1100 cy), an amount the district meeting stated was insufficient to meet its obligations. It estimated that £1,483 would be required, the increase being largely due to the need 'to provide for the families of the newly married Brethren.'[82]

The ceiling would, nevertheless, remain at £900 stg for the remainder of the decade. Given that the district collections for the mission fund consistently exceeded £800 cy as of 1842 (when £251 were subscribed in the Eastern Townships and £554 were distributed there – see appendix, tables A6 and A7), there was not a large amount left for the WMS to provide. But there certainly remained areas where the population continued to be reliant on outside support. On the New Ireland circuit, Thomas Campbell reported in 1843 that the 'protracted commercial distress of the country at large appeared to be more painfully felt here than in any other part of the country, because of the circumstances of the people who are generally poor.' They were, according to Campbell, very anxious that they would not be able to contribute enough to justify the district meeting sending them a missionary the following year. To make matters worse, a hurricane had destroyed the largest chapel on the circuit, that in Lower Ireland, with the result that Sunday congregations had been reduced by half due to the 'uncomfortableness and danger of sitting in the comparatively open shell of a house' which was being used temporarily. One woman had caught cold and died as a result of this experience.[83]

In 1849, with a commercial recession hitting the three Lower Canadian cities particularly hard, the district meeting pleaded more strongly than usual for extra funding. Echoing the supporters of missions within Britain itself, it stated that 'We can understand and appreciate the sympathies of the Committee and our Christian people at home for the heathen portions of our world. Nevertheless we would respectfully request you to consider *if it be not more desirable to prevent a country from sinking into barbarism* than even to raise a Country from barbarism.'[84] The plea became even more insistent in 1852, with the focus this time on the large deficiencies accumulated during the previous three years by each missionary, ranging from £29 to £52. In preparation for the coming reunion of the Western and Eastern Canada districts, independent from the WMS, the £900 stg grant had been reduced by a third. William Squire, chair of the district meeting, assured the missionary society that there was no possibility of the circuits making up this shortfall: 'the agricultural portion of the inhabitants of Lower Canada is generally an embarrassed people, many of their farms are mortgaged, and most of the farmers are involved in debt; ... the protestant population is constantly on the move, seeking in the United States or in western Canada, a more genial home; and, moreover, ... we are completely hemmed in by Papists. We are, indeed, in a sense in which it could not be affirmed of any other North American district, a Missionary district.'[85]

French claims that the similar situation in the Maritimes reflected the fact that 'neither preachers nor people were really encouraged to accept full responsibility for their own welfare.'[86] While this may be true to some extent, it is nevertheless doubtful that the Wesleyan Methodists and Anglicans would have been remained the two largest Protestant denominations in the Eastern Townships had their British-funded missionary societies not provided substantial support for their clergy. One of the main reasons that the Church of England was more successful than the Wesleyan Society, as we shall see, was that it devoted more resources to the region, including most of the money to build local churches. There was little other reason for the people of the Eastern Townships to be attracted to denominations most of whose clergy did not share their national origin or cultural outlook, and whose rather rigid views about denominational discipline tended to clash with local community-based values.

Building Chapels

While the Wesleyan Methodists failed to embrace outdoor camp meetings, construction of chapels was not an initial priority for a society that focused on the circuit system of preaching. Local schools appear to have been the most common sites of worship for most of the evangelical denominations in the early years, but in the southwestern corner of the region the Church of England used its influence over the Royal Institution of Learning to bar the Methodist preachers from access to its schools. The Anglican incumbent of St Armand, James Reid, reported in 1823 that James Booth 'gave us great deal of trouble, before we got him out of Mr Ayer's school house' upon the archdeacon's orders.

Because Methodist meetings were continuing in the Stanbridge school, and probably in the one in Dunham, Reid recommended that a circular be sent to every schoolmaster informing them of the Church's wishes.[87] Matthew Lang, who was appointed to the Shefford circuit in 1823, complained that because only three or four school houses were available, meetings generally took place in log houses, '& those in unfinished state which render it inconvenient for the people & distressing for the speaker & destroys much of the solemnity of the means of grace.' Sixteen years later, in 1839, John Selley complained about the lack of suitable places to worship on the Melbourne circuit. He claimed that only small school houses were available, 'and a great part of the population being emigrants from Britain can neither feel themselves comfortable or safe in these ill constructed and every way unsuitable places.'[88] Attempts to gain a foothold in Sherbrooke were given up in 1840 because the Congregationalists refused to share their meeting house, and the Methodists had been denied access to the academy as well as the British American Land Company's school house.[89]

The Wesleyan missionaries tried to ensure that when new chapels were built they conformed to what was called the conference plan (meaning essentially that they would be owned by the Methodist Society), in order to prevent the local communities from exercising control over them. Construction of the region's first Methodist chapel, which remains an impressive white stone structure with a gallery, began in Philipsburg in 1819.[90] While it conformed to the conference plan, this was not the case for the chapel that was completed in Dunham two years later, because it stood on public ground, which may explain why it was built of logs.[91] Not surprisingly, the missionary reports reveal that there was considerable popular resistance to rescinding control over their chapels. In 1824, for example, Joseph Stinson held a public meeting at the rear of Shipton Township in order to encourage church construction, but the people insisted that they would determine who would preach in it. Only one of the twenty 'respectable' inhabitants who were present favoured building on the conference plan: 'they prefer Methodist ministry to any others – but they want us in their own way,' and they wished to adhere to 'their own peculiar modes of church government.' In 1833 there was a mini-rebellion by the Methodists in Shefford who demanded deeds for their pews, which was clearly another manifestation of the struggle between local and institutional control of the church.[92]

Union chapels presented a problem to the Wesleyan missionaries because of what they claimed was the inherent instability of such arrangements. While he was serving the Stanstead circuit in 1831, James Booth stated that he was placed 'in difficult circumstances' because the Congregationalist members of the union church had withdrawn to build 'a good brick Church' in the village of Stanstead Plain. Remaining in the union church was 'an amalgamation of free will Baptists, Calvinists, Episcopalians, etc. which is denominated the Methodist Society. This circumstance, connected with the fact, that we have not a single house on the whole circuit, in which we can worship God in, that we can call our own, you will see that there is little probability of a well-organized Society on this circuit.'[93]

Booth set out at once to raise money to build a Methodist chapel, 'by means of which our dicipline [sic] may be inforced [sic] and the society organized in a Methodistical way.' The main obstacle was that 'the principal part of the little support we obtain on this circuit, comes from persons unconnected with our Society, and a Preacher has to go like a Pauper from one to another for any thing he wants, and should he not meet the people's views, they will not subscribe towards his support.' As an initial step towards independence from the whims of the people, Booth had acquired a lot in Stanstead Plain and had it deeded on the conference plan, as well as raising over $2,000 in subscriptions for construction of a brick chapel measuring sixty by forty-eight feet. This sum would be paid in lumber, stones, bricks, nails, labour, and so on, and a local historian claims that 'at the time of building, this house was considered rather in advance of the times, at least for this country.'[94]

By the early 1840s, there appears to have been little local resistance to the conference plan. On the Dunham circuit, for example, John Brownell took advantage of the religious revival in 1842 to encourage 'a few of our members and friends' to build 'a very handsome stone chapel' at Abbott's Corner costing $1,300. The following year Brownell had opened another chapel worth $500, as well as pegging the ground for two others which would cost from $1,200 to $1,500 each. The deed for one of these buildings declared that it would not 'in any sense of the word be private property, but will be deeded to Trustees, put in trust, on behalf of the Wesleyan Methodist Connexion throughout the world.' Ministers of other 'orthodox' denominations could preach in it only with the consent of the majority of trustees, in conjunction with the local Wesleyan minister. The pew rental system would also undoubtedly make non-members feel more like outsiders.[95]

Bennett argues that, while church structures 'may appear linked to material advancement,' this aspect should not be over-emphasized because they were increasingly assumed to be instruments 'through which Christians could spread the word of God's salvation.' Furthermore, while Methodists did not believe that God was particularly present within a specific part of the building, 'the church was progressively perceived as channeling agent for the grace of God.'[96] In contrast to Upper Canada, however, the region's Methodists and other evangelical denominations were not quick to copy the Church of England's example in building neo-Gothic churches.[97] While Anglican churches began to adopt medieval-inspired features during the early 1830s, the Methodist stone chapel built in Knowlton in 1855 had a tower on its roof instead of the ground, inward-turning eves, a large entry on the front central axis, and high side walls to allow for large rectangular windows and internal galleries (see illustration 5). The chapel built in Hatley in 1836 does have pointed arches over the windows and main entry, in apparent imitation of the Anglican church erected in the same village several years earlier, but otherwise it is of strictly classical design (see illustration 6). This would remain the case for most non-Anglican churches built in the region during the pre-Confederation era.[98]

One might conclude that such resistance to change reflected a failure on the part of the Wesleyan missionaries to alter the religious outlook of their flocks, for the New England concept of the meeting house was, in the words of Benes and Zimmerman, 'an architectural expression of the Reformed point of view that "the house of God" was not a sacred place,' since it combined municipal and religious functions and was erected and supported by public taxes.[99] While Upper Canada's annual Methodist conference recommended the adoption of standard plans for new churches as early as 1845,[100] however, there is little evidence from our study period that the Wesleyan clergy took much interest in the architectural design of the chapels they preached in. Their chief concern appears to have been that such chapels be built so that religious services would no longer have to be held in schools or even less desirable quarters. It was also important to the missionaries that control of these chapels would lie strictly with the Methodist Church rather than the local congregations, thereby preventing transfers of ownership to rival denominations. In this sense, the Methodist institutionalization process appears to have been gaining ground, but we shall see that localism remained a powerful force at mid-century.

1 Eaton Corner Congregational Church, 1841. Author's collection, 2003

2 Congregational Church, Melbourne Village, *c.* 1839. Author's collection, 2001

3 Baptist Church, Stanbridge Ridge, 1842. Author's collection, 2001

4 Universalist Church, Huntingville, 1845. Author's collection, 2003

5 Knowltan Methodist Church, 1855. Brome County Historical Society, 71–52; postcard by M.E. Robb, Granby, Quebec.

6 Hatley (Charleston) Methodist Church, 1836. Author's collection, 2003

7 Holy Trinity Anglican Church, Frelighsburg, 1809–80. Parish of St Armand East Archives

8 St. James' Anglican Church, Hatley (Charleston) and Charleston Academy, 1829. Author's collection, 2003

9 All Saints' Anglican Church, Dunham, 1849. Author's collection, 2001

10 St Paul's Anglican Church, Sydenham, Kingsey Township, 1846. Author's collection, 2001

8

Revivals, Reversals, and Shifting Strategies

Revivalism in the Pre-Rebellion Era

Most of the Wesleyan missionaries in the Eastern Townships, as in the Maritimes, would come to take a somewhat sceptical view about the benefits of emotional revivals, but their initial arrival in the region was marked by a notable rise in religious fervour. It would seem that the situation was ripe for such a development, for waves of revivalism in which 'thousands were prostrated with religious fervour' swept neighbouring Vermont in 1810, 1816, 1821, and 1826.[1] Most revivals were initiated at quarterly meetings that were transformed into what were known as protracted meetings. Richard Pope's description of one such event in Shefford in 1824 is one of the most detailed for the region. Pope opened the meeting with a sermon on the theme, 'O Lord revive thy work,' then several exhorters stirred the congregation further. In the evening, there was 'a most numerous & live prayer meeting,' and the following morning began with the love feast to which over one hundred were admitted and fifty spoke 'very feelingly.' The love feast, restricted to members of the society and any outsiders who were deemed to be serious about conversion, had been introduced by Wesley as a means of celebrating fellowship through the sharing of bread and water, but in the United States the ceremonial aspect came to be overshadowed by the 'personal testimonies.' At 11:00 a.m. Pope preached again, a number of exhortations were delivered, then several adults and a child were baptized, and the sacrament was administered to about sixty persons. (Unlike the love feast, the sacrament was available to all members of other Protestant denominations.) Finally, one of the ministers addressed the leaders, exhorters, and members, and at 2:30 p.m. brought the end to 'a meeting long to be remembered by all present.'[2]

This was the pattern followed repeatedly, sometimes with more success than others, as the Wesleyan missionaries slowly but steadily expanded their influence throughout the region. A protracted meeting could last many days, but it differed in one important respect from the Methodist Episcopal practice, for the proceedings took place indoors. Richey has described how, at the turn of the nineteenth century, the American Methodists' quarterly meetings adopted the form of the camp meeting, which he claims became 'a national, quasi-official institution,' but Britain's Wesleyan society had condemned open-air meetings in 1807.[3] From Stanstead, James Knowlan reported in 1828 that protracted indoor meetings 'have a decided preference, in the minds of our friends, to camp meetings.' He added that 'the desired good effect is produced, without any of the inconveniences attending Camp meetings,' by which he clearly meant that the people in attendance could be controlled more easily by permitting a drawing of lines that would have dissolved in the outdoor space.[4]

There appears to have been considerable backsliding after the spring 1824 revival in Shefford. By 1828, the Wesleyan missionary could only report that 'the work of God on this circuit is both deepening & spreading, though not at present either powerfully or rapidly.' Shefford does not appear to have had a regular Wesleyan missionary from approximately 1829 to 1834.[5] A similar pattern unfolded in the other Wesleyan circuits. The lower St Francis Valley's Melbourne circuit was the scene of a revival as early as 1821, when Henry Pope reported that:

> In the course of the last summer the Lord has graciously favored us with many refreshing seasons. Many backsliders have been reclaimed and believers excited to diligent perseverance in their holy calling, while several, in different parts of the circuit have been awakened to a sense of their awful condition as sinners, and are now regular attendants on the means of grace; but, I am sorry to add, that there are many who, though constant hearers of the word, appear extremely hardened.[6]

The impact of the Melbourne revival appears to have been short-lived, for Joseph Stinson (described by Carroll as youthful, strong, comely, a fearless horseman, and 'just the man for the country')[7] experienced a sharp culture shock when he arrived there in 1824. He wrote that 'when

I first came to this place the gloomy appearance of the country, the irregularity of the society, and the badness of the roads were depressing beyond description.' To make matters worse, Stinson found 'no proper account of the persons in society – and not a leader or local preacher in the circuit.' He had endeavoured to establish regular classes, but found 'no where near the numbers in society that is mentioned in the last minutes.' Many had moved to other parts of the country, and several had died. Stinson added that while the congregations at his eleven preaching stations 'are generally very good and attentive [...] when I consider – the labour – the time – and the money that has been spent in this circuit for the last eight years – and see its present state – I am very much pained. There is no chapel – no regular means of supporting a preacher – and not forty persons that are *real* Methodists in the whole circuit.'[11] Melbourne soon ceased for a time to be a separate circuit, and a visiting missionary reported in 1825 that the people were 'labouring under great discouragement for want of constant preaching.'[8]

The St Armand circuit was also the site of a revival soon after the withdrawal of the Episcopal Methodist missionaries. The new Wesleyan appointee in 1821, James Booth, reported that 'Religion was very low when I first visited the classes,'[9] but this state of affairs changed dramatically when a revival followed Booth's first quarterly meeting in October of the same year. He described how, following the evening prayers, early morning love feast, and public preaching, many were 'convinced of their awful situation as sinners and never rested untill their souls were happy in God.' The stimulus for this revival clearly came from south of the border, for it began among the people of nearby Highgate, Vermont where 'upwards of 90 souls were added into their societies within the sphere of 8 or 9 weeks.' Between December and February, thirty-one souls were 'brought to God' in the St Armand circuit (which also included Dunham and Stanbridge Townships), and, from then until April, eighty-five had been received on trial. One of these was a French Canadian, which was a relatively rare occurence.[10] To the annual district meeting in February 1823, Booth reported that out of the 155 members added during the previous year's revival only five had been expelled for immorality. Impressive as the results of this revival may have been, however, it would be the last of Booth's career in the Eastern Townships.

After being appointed to the St Armand circuit in 1827, William Squire reported that the excitement of the previous years had entirely subsided before I entered upon my labours, and since then it has been little else beside the performance of painful duty.' Squire added:

> In our revivals in this country there is considerable mechanical excitement; and the constitutional temperament of the people strongly favors it, and this will account for the frequent and sometimes great decrease of members after the exciting causes cease to operate. It is a matter of regret that in some of the Societies, on this circuit proceedings were not so orderly in the late revival of religion as could have been wished, nor could my worthy predecessor prevent it as he would seldom meet the same Society oftener than once in two weeks, and sometimes only once in four.[11]

Echoing the sentiments of the Anglican clergy, Squire observed that the Methodists were often 'satisfied with a little occasional religious excitement instead of daily walking with God.' Indeed, the Anglican minister for St Armand East, James Reid, wrote in 1829: 'Three or four years ago, there was some appearance that Methodism would sweep the whole country, where I live, before it; but at the present time, there is hardly any meeting of that denomination within the Parish. A boisterous Preacher sets them all in motion, but when one of sober sense and correct ideas, such as the person on this circuit for the last two years, succeeds, all subsides.'[12] Squire did not criticize his fellow Methodist missionaries, however, explaining that their numbers had remained the same while their circuits were constantly increasing in size. They were told that no reinforcements would be sent until they could be locally supported, but 'this is impossible in the present state of the country, and probably will be for some time to come, and thus, after arduous conflict, the fruits of victory are frequently taken from us, and we have no remedy left us but that of making our complaint to you.'[13]

Squire was no more optimistic a year later. While he had converted a few people on the St Armand circuit, 'several of our members have fallen into gross immoralities, and many are becoming faint in their minds – discords are frequent between brethren, and trifling circumstances produce evasion.' Squire again blamed the revivals, for many who 'make a profession of experimental piety do not sufficiently understand the nature of their profession.' Furthermore, because the settlers were Americans who had come in search of land, 'they have ... imported the high feeling of personal importance which distinguishes many of their countrymen, and to this may be attributed much of that litigiousness which they discover after [they] become professors of religion.' Squire assured the Wesleyan Missionary Society, however, that 'I have generally enjoyed as much of their confidence as usually falls to the lot of one individual, and hence have no reason to complain of any thing personal.' Nor was he 'weary of this blessed work, only I desire to be more useful – to know the will of God concerning me, and to appear at last before the eternal Throne pure from the blood of all men.'[14]

Squire was clearly not exaggerating about local unruliness, for the July 1829 quarterly meeting noted that 'the disorderly conduct of some individuals' had prevented the love feast from being held a year earlier. Having been informed that the same individuals 'intend to act in the same manner tomorrow,' and in order to avoid prosecuting them, the meeting resolved to ask a justice of the peace, a militia captain and a sergeant to station themselves at the door 'in the hope that the presence of the King's officers may prevent disorder.' The minutes also note that 'This precaution had the desired effect.'[15] Squire failed to mention what the basis of this conflict was, but it may have stemmed from the Methodists' exclusion of non-members from the love feast, an exclusion which certainly raised considerable resentment in the latitudinarian American communities.

Revivalism would play a greater role in Stanstead than in the other three circuits. John Hick reported in June 1821 that, even though the Methodist Episcopal minutes stated that there were two hundred members in the Stanstead and St Francis River circuits, he had found only eight in Stanstead, and they had not held class meetings in two years. There were also a few pious Congregationalists, but 'the striking characteristic of the inhabitants is forgetfulness of God and excepting their attraction to the public means of grace little or no religion is to be seen amongst them.' For several months, the people continued to be 'kind, the congregations good, and apparently attentive, but, alas! religion, in its spirit and practice, was attended to but by a few.' A turning point for the better came in May 1822, on the day appointed by the district meeting for 'fasting & special prayer for the revival of religion.' At that point 'the Lord ... began to pour out of his Spirit on this part of his Vineyard, so that in the space of five weeks eight persons have been brought into the enjoyment of Christian liberty, and several others appear to be impressed with a conviction of the vast importance of serving God ..., and are determined to seek him while he may be found.'[16]

Hick's initiative came to an abrupt halt when it was discovered that he had been negotiating with the Anglican missionary, Charles Stewart, to join the Church of England, but his successor, Richard Pope, was also disposed towards the revivalist approach. He reported in 1824 that, despite his failing health, he had preached upwards of three hundred sermons and ridden nearly two thousand miles, besides attending between thirty and forty funerals for the people of all ages who had died of measles and 'throat distemper.' His fellow Wesleyan missionary, John DePutron, had resisted the people's expectation that he would preach at all the funerals, 'for when a man dies without signs of repentance what can a preacher say,' but Pope felt that burial services presented an ideal opportunity to impress religion on the unconverted. He was impressed with the local burial custom, which differed from that in England:

> The funeral service is attended either at the House of the deceased, or at the nearest School House. And as a discourse is always expected, the concourse of the people is generally large & deeply attentive, while the Preacher is called more especially to impress their minds with the solemn & momentous subjects of *Death, Judgment* & *Eternity*. Having explained & applied the doctrine of the text to the congregation at large, he is expected to address the mourners, all standing, in particular. As in this new country the people are extensively connected, the last part of the ceremony is frequently very impressive, interesting and useful. Divine service being over, the corpse is taken out side the door, and the face uncovered, when the congregation first & then the mourners are invited to take the last look at the dead. This being attended to, we proceed in procession to the place of interment where everything is dispatched with the greatest regularity & nothing is said but[?] a word of thanks to the Assembly for their kind & respectful attendance upon the[?] mournful occasion.[17]

In short, Pope felt that to win popular support the Wesleyan missionaries would have to accommodate themselves to the local customs. He added that, due to the lack of 'suitable persons for leaders, etc. every thing devolves upon the Preacher who must visit every department of his work himself.' But Pope's efforts were paying off, for he described how, at a meeting in late May 1824, 'many wept & mourned for their sins,' and, when the two who were accepted 'into communion on trial' continued to be 'happy in the Lord,' this 'excited a spirit of enquiry in the neighbourhood.' The third Friday in June, which was set aside by the district meeting for fasting and prayer, 'was kept by the inhabitants in the vicinity of the Church generally as sacred as a Sunday.' At the love feast on the following Sunday, 'a goodly number spoke of the goodness of God,' Pope read the Methodist discipline, and four 'of the most respectable inhabitants of the village' were accepted on trial.[18]

In his journal Pope reported that three months later, in September

1824, about one thousand people attended the public service in which 'a Brother from the States preached a useful sermon,' and nine people were accepted on trial. Some of the wealthiest inhabitants had now joined the Methodists, and Pope's strategy was to concentrate on the village and surrounding area, leaving Barnston Township largely without services for the time being, though he urgently requested an assistant to serve the outlying townships in his station.[19] More frequent prayer meetings were now held, and, 'for a long time we scarcely had a meeting but one or more persons were brought under good impressions.' Twenty-six members were added at the December quarterly meeting, and 'Our meetings through the winter became crowded to overflowing.' Seven hundred attended the New Year's Eve watch-night which took place for the first time in the chapel, and approximately five hundred were admitted to the love feast at the March 1825 quarterly meeting. Nearly a thousand participated in the public worship, 'a sight never before seen in the woods of this new country.' Again, the service would have taken place indoors rather than in the woods, however, for the Stanstead chapel was said to be large enough to hold nine hundred to a thousand people. At the close of the meeting, two hundred received the Lord's Supper 'in the presence of the whole congregation, who seemed affected with the sight.' Since the previous May, 146 new members had been added to the Methodist society in Stanstead. According to Pope, they included 'some of the most opulent, and a few of the abandoned in the town,' 'a few aged,' and 'about forty young persons,' but most were 'middle-aged' and undoubtedly of middling social status. This appears to have been a family-based revival, for Pope stated that fifty heads of family had 'commenced the too much neglected duty of family prayer during the year.'[20]

The protracted revival persisted into Pope's next term. This time many of the converts were young people, and Pope declared that 'It is a most pleasing sight to see men, long addicted to habits of inebriety, profane swearing, and Sabbath-breaking, bending before the throne of sovereign grace, seeking mercy; and this literal wilderness and solitary place becoming glad, and this desert rejoicing and blossoming as the rose.' Pope claimed that of the approximately three hundred persons 'savagely' brought to Stanstead during the previous three years (presumably meaning they had migrated there), more than two hundred had joined the Methodist society.[21]

This revival was not confined to the area surrounding the village of Stanstead, for in 1827 Pope's assistant, Thomas Turner, reported from another section of Stanstead Township that 'very many both old and young have been the subjects of converting grace.' Turner claimed to have travelled 1,250 miles during the previous year, and his report included the journal of his trip to Shipton Township on the deserted Melbourne circuit where he stimulated a revival at a place called the Ferry. He described some of the proceedings in vivid terms:

> we had not prayed long before the cry of those in distress became so loud as to drown the voices of those who engaged in prayer; ... before the close of the meeting three persons professed to have received a clear sense of pardon, and two sanctification ... One young woman, as soon as she had received the blessing went immediately and kneeled down by her father who was in unconverted state, and began to pray for him with uncommon earnestness. We were not able to close this meeting till between 1 and 2 o'clock in the morning although I had made an appointment to hold another meeting at 8.[22]

With Thomas Turner, the Irish-born James Knowlan continued Richard Pope's enthusiastic efforts on the Stanstead circuit, reporting in October 1828 that he, Turner, and Brother Peck from Vermont had held a four-day meeting which had launched yet another revival. Since then, 'awakenings' had begun in every part of the circuit, 'So many are the calls upon us, that if we do not take care, we may be led to extend ourselves too much, and injure our health; but what can we do, when the people all around are saying, come and help us.'[23]

But James Booth, who replaced Knowlan on the Stanstead circuit in 1829, painted a very different picture, stating in his first report that he had found 'the Society with respect to the life of God in the Soul as wretched as in Kingston.' Booth's assessment may have been coloured by the fact that Knowlan had been the chair of the committee that had recommended his recall because of a conflict with a local preacher in Kingston,[24] but a period of religious declension was, no doubt, inevitable after the remarkable three years of revival. William Squire, who succeeded the unpopular Booth in 1832, found that two classes of about thirty members had recently defected to the American-based Reformed (Protestant) Methodists, and he reported at the end of the year that 'The state of the circuit on which I am now stationed is such as to occasion humiliation before God, and deep regret that so little holy fruit has arisen from the Ministry of our Missionaries.' While the May 1832 report had claimed 215 members, Squire stated a year later that there were only about fifty regular class attendees in the circuit.[25] In August 1833 he wrote despairingly to a friend that 'I am by no means satisfied with my station; indeed, it is in so wretched a condition as to render it doubtful whether it should be occupied another week. A very suitable place to break the heart of a man of my sensibility! We have nominally twelve classes, and, out of these only one in the habit of meeting; all the rest, I may say, are formally given up.'[26]

The main reason for the deterioration, Squire later wrote, was 'the dividing influence of the Freewill Baptists, and the Reformed Methodists from the United States,' but he also noted dissatisfaction with the location of the recently completed Methodist chapel in Stanstead Plain. Not only was it more inconvenient for some families than the union chapel had been, but there was also resentment against the replacement of pew sales by annual leases.[27] Clearly, this step was seen as a means of diminishing popular claims to 'ownership' of the building. There may also have been some disgruntlement about the fact that rents were fixed by the trustees, for the treasurer would later offer to have a committee examine the accounts. Squire commented condescendingly that, frivolous as some of these objections might be, 'with a people so utterly unused to business, and who have seen so little of the world as they have, the merest trifles are regarded as difficulties of great magnitude.'[28]

People's minds would soon be distracted from 'trifles,' however, for Squire wrote in August 1833:

> to increase our misery, there is a great want of food among the people, – it is not to be had for *money*, – owing to the failure of last year's crop. The coming harvest is expected to be even more deficient from the failure of Indian corn, which is the principal dependence here. Our houses are nightly searched by thieves in quest of food. I once lost all the meat I had; and no wonder, while some of the poor people are living on green potato tops. I find the greatest difficulty in procuring necessary food for my family. We cannot now get a potato to eat, and all our flour we have had to procure from Montreal, at an enormous expense for transportation.[29]

The fall crop failed, as predicted, for in December Squire wrote that there was now very severe distress, and even threatened starvation, but there had as yet been no beneficial spiritual effect on the people. Finally, Squire referred to his personal sense of isolation due to the removal of the Barnston preacher, but he concluded that Stanstead could not be 'safely entrusted' to the revivalist sects 'for they are profoundly ignorant both of God's truth, and common decency.' He was not entirely closed-minded, however, for he favoured the expansion of the Upper Canadian Conference's mission efforts to the unoccupied places in Lower Canada, though he felt that their immediate assignment to the old circuits would be disastrous.[30]

The following spring, Squire reported to the district meeting that he had not established a missionary society to raise funds in Stanstead because of the partial famine and 'the uncomfortable prejudices of the Inhabitants, regarding the Chapel.' In 1835 only £2.11.0 were raised in Stanstead, necessitating a £95 grant from the funds collected elsewhere in the Canada District. Religious conditions had begun to improve dramatically, however, for Squire – who had roundly condemned the revivals in St Armand, as we have seen – reported that a protracted meeting in January had initiated 'a revival of Religion which to us has been as life from the dead.' With the assistance of two preachers from Montreal, the result of the forty-day meeting was that 'about 280 souls including a considerable number of backsliders recovered, professed to have obtained peace with God thro' believing in Christ. We have now great simplicity, unity and love in the Society; and about 170 persons on probation for membership.'[31]

Unlike Squire, the report of a witness named William S. Lock, published in *Zion's Herald* of Boston, emphasized the role played by a local figure. Lock wrote that on the first day 'Among those who addressed the congregation was Bro. Elias Lee, the venerable father of the Rev. Daniel, and brother to the Rev. Jason Lee, our worthy missionary to the far West.' Lock reported that at the love feast on the morning of the fourth day, 'One circumstance was very striking. Brother Lee ... arose, thanked the Lord for his goodness, and for the bright prospect before him, although two nights previous he was alarmed by fire, which wholly destroyed his dwelling house and much of its contents, and he was turned into the street with his family, without a dwelling of his own on earth; yet he gloried in the thought that he had a building in the heavens – a house not made with hands.'[32] Squire may not have entirely approved of such emotional testifying, for he would later chastise members of his circuit in Upper Canada 'for their extravagant conduct when engaged in their religious services.' Furthermore, he would not have approved of the Lees' politics, for Elias's second son (also Elias) was editor of the *Frontier Sentinel*, a pro-Patriote newspaper. Two years later, he would be arrested for fomenting unrest during the Rebellion.[33]

Meanwhile, in December 1835, Squire reported that 'many of our young members have been visited house to house, our doctrines misrepresented, and our discipline caricatured in the most unwarrantable and unchristian manner, for the purposed of decoying them.' Due to the 'great diversity of judgment, not to say licentiousness of opinion cherished here, we are compelled to see some torn from us who appeared to have been given us by God.' But Squire consoled himself with the thought that his efforts had saved their souls, and they would all meet in heaven 'although they walk not with us on earth.' The Baptists were the main rivals to the Methodists in Stanstead, and, as a result of their influence, 'infant baptism is seldom used, and of those whom I have baptized this year about one half have been baptized by immersion; but this does not satisfy, our Baptist Brethren contend *in the midst of our Society* that we should do it in no other way, to the injury of many.' The effects of the great revival had held, however, for 'a large proportion of those who professed to be justified through faith in the Lord Jesus during the last spring, remain steadfast in their profession, and many of them encourage the hope that they will be steady useful characters.' Squire stated that 'a more than usual prominence has been given in our Ministry to the doctrine of entire sanctification,' and seventy-eight more people had joined the Methodists during the previous quarter.[34]

In contrast to the 1820s, when the more enthusiastic missionaries in the Townships occasionally had to defend their tactics to the WMS, its directors were now encouraging emulation of their Methodist Episcopal brethren. The WMS message for 1835 stated: 'What are called Protracted meetings have been so eminently owned of God in America that we are induced to direct your attention to them in order that you may form some plan for holding them in your district generally.'[35] As in the 1820s, the popular climate was receptive, for deteriorating climactic conditions were again causing crop failures, and the flamboyant former circus performer Jedidiah Burchard was leading a dramatic revival in Vermont. It was probably no coincidence, then, that in 1835 Edmund Botterell of the Compton and Hatley circuit organized one of the first and only Wesleyan camp meetings to be held in the region. Thanks to assistance of four preachers from the New Hampshire Conference, the congregations were 'unexpectedly large,' reaching about five thousand at one point. Botterell gave no further details, simply concluding that 'the meeting has increased a religious excitement which had existed for some months in Hatley from which I hope our Society will derive extensive benefit.' According to a report in the *Wesleyan*, however, the outbreak of political disturbances prevented the society from receiving any additions at this time.[36]

Finally, from Shefford, which had been effectively abandoned for four years, Adam Townley reported in the spring of 1835 that 'the circuit is in general in a prosperous condition; indeed we have not been without some more than ordinarily gracious outpourings of the Holy Spirit at a four or rather five day meeting held in October and again at a quarterly meeting held in January.' As a result, weekday prayer meetings were now held 'in one or two of the principal places,' and classes were regularly attended 'which is the more striking when we consider the scattered state of the population and badness of the roads in these comparatively recently settled districts.' The increase to 154, with 25 on trial, would have been larger if not for people moving elsewhere. A missionary society had finally been established, and Townley assured the meeting that 'to those who know the state of things here the sum raised here £12.6.9 will not be thought despicable as a commencement.'[37] As on the other circuits, however, trying times would lie ahead following the outbreak of the Rebellions of 1837-8.

The Impact of the Rebellions

In the spring of 1838 the Canada District meeting boasted that 'notwithstanding the different national origin of our people, and their considerable number in proportion to the Protestant population of the Province, not one instance has come to our knowledge of their being accused of participating in the recent insurrection while almost the whole of them cheerfully contributed their part to the defense of the Country.'[38] This statement was presumably in response to a request by the president of the Canadian Conference that the missionaries identify all who had compromised their loyalty, a step which caused a good deal of resentment in Upper Canada, and helped to precipitate the break-up of the Methodist union.[39] While there were no rebel strongholds in the Eastern Townships, there certainly were pockets of Patriote sympathizers, among whom were a few Methodists, but the main impact of the Rebellions would be to divert popular attention from religion towards political and military concerns. As with the Congregationalists, the ensuing community divisions would deal a lasting blow to the Wesleyan Methodist strength in the Eastern Townships.

The outbreak of hostilities in the fall of 1837 left the largely defenceless Philipsburg under the threat of destruction by rebels who had taken refuge a short distance to the south in Vermont. Twice, William Squire had removed his family's furniture and buried some of their possessions, and three times they had 'fled to the woods with our little ones for protection, in the frost and snow of December.' The rebels had been repulsed by the local militia when they did attack, but the impact of the crisis was that 'many of our people are scattered, some doing militia duty, many failures by temptation; and every way we are tried by the dangerous and melancholy condition in which we are placed.' Squire concluded that 'I fear this exposed situation will have to be abandoned, as there appears very little probability of doing any good by living here in case of a war.'[40]

The following May, Squire reported that continued threats of attack had kept tensions alive on the border, with his family having to flee for safety and their house turned into a mess hall while the chapel served as a barracks for the militia. He felt that he and his colleagues had acted 'both in the spirit of the instructions to the missionaries on the subject of our political duty, and in that of the Circular recently received.' Diplomacy was clearly required, for Squire wrote that 'the majority of those around us are doubtless loyal, but there are many who would rebel could they see any probability of success. As it is, we are treated only with a little reviling, a few false reports have been circulated concerning us, and a few individuals have left the place of worship when we have prayed for the Queen, and the Authorities of the Country.'[41]

Squire explained that rebellion 'is rather regarded as a virtue than otherwise, seeing it has always been commended, and extravagantly lauded by our republican neighbours. Hence a little to the south of us we have found our most bitter enemies in Methodists and Methodist Preachers, with some of whom we have been heretofore on terms of personal friendship.' Squire also criticized the leniency of the government, which he felt had misjudged 'the deep animosity of the Canadian French, and their very general disposition to revolt,' and hoped that when Lord Durham arrived he would adopt 'those vigorous measures which appears to us to be absolutely necessary for the pacification of the Country.' In the meantime, he took pride in the fact that only one member of his circuit, an American, had been charged with sedition, and this individual 'was discharged after examination, having confessed his error.' Aside from political divisions, however, the Rebellion had caused some members to fall into sin, 'especially that of intemperance.' In addition, class and prayer meetings 'have been painfully neglected, although the attention of our people has been repeatedly called to these subjects.

The frequency and harassing nature of their Militia duty, and the distressing necessity existing for many of our People to embody in the volunteer companies of horse and foot, will best account for this.'[42]

Despite his belief that a revival would serve little purpose without being followed with the 'vigilant pastoral care' that the lack of assistance from either local preachers or class leaders made difficult to provide, Squire did resort to a protracted meeting in October 1838. As a result, sixty to seventy people were either 'reclaimed from a backslidden state, or converted from the errors of their way.' But the timing was poor, for the reopening of hostilities ended all spiritual progress. The western part of his circuit was briefly invaded from Alburg, Vermont, with the result, Squire wrote in February 1839, that two chapels were occupied as barracks, and religious meetings were largely ignored. All hopes of a successful revolution had passed, but the rebel exiles and their American sympathizers were resorting to a campaign of terrorism and arson along the border in order to incite war between Britain and the United States. Squire could not venture far from his home for fear of leaving his family defenceless, and he feared that the border area 'will soon probably be a wilderness again, as it is impossible for us to live in this fearful state of alarm and danger.'[43]

The situation had not improved by the spring, when Squire reported:

> As this circuit embraces a large proportion of the most disturbed part of the frontier, we have been called to suffer the painful consequences of the rebellion by frequent alarms and invasions, mid-night burnings, and attempted assassinations. The mental excitement, the constant military occupation of our people, and the harassing nature of the duty, have had a most unfriendly influence upon their character and our work, too plainly evinced in their frequent backsliding and general apathy in respect of religion. In only a few cases have our troubles been sanctified so as to awaken a spirit of repentance. The greater part of the people have yielded to the almost overwhelming temptations presented to them, and there has been a distressing increase of Sabbath-breaking, drunkenness, and profanity.[44]

Squire remained pessimistic a year later, reporting in the spring of 1840 that the once flourishing society in Philipsburg, which had become the headquarters of the first Regiment of volunteer militia, had 'painfully declined, principally through political excitement, and intemperance.' There had also once been a large society in Stanbridge East, but it had been 'reduced to a very few by divisions, removals, and death. Political principles, Universalism, etc. prevent us from being useful to the People.' In Phelp's Settlement, there was 'a small dull class ... and the probability of doing good is limited.' Lower Falls and Pike River had a 'better society' and 'an interesting though small congregation,' but the 'French Canadians were 'gaining upon our own People in the settlement of the Country, and will limit our field of labours.'[45] Conditions were not a great deal better on the neighbouring border circuit to the East.

While the economic hardship caused by climate change in the early 1830s had been an important factor in Stanstead's powerful 1835 revival, the crop failure of the following year had a rather different effect. William Squire, who had not yet moved to Philipsburg, complained in May 1837 that this trial by the Almighty 'has not produced that penitence of heart and reformation of life required by God, but more of impatience and murmuring against the Country by a winter of uncommon severity in its length, quantity of snow, and force of wind, thereby preventing the people from assembling themselves together and using the appointed means of grace, and which has also prevented us from employing any protracted meeting for arousing the Spiritual energies of our Societies.'[46] Popular adherence to religion would be tested even more severely by the ensuing political turbulence.

Thomas Turner wrote in November 1837 that in order to maintain union within his congregation he had avoided making political comments, but this stance became increasingly difficult as tensions mounted. In March 1838 he reported that he had attended and voted at a public meeting called to support the government's efforts to suppress the Rebellion, though he did not address it, 'nor should I under ordinary circumstances have identified myself with it in any way.' Turner claimed that had he not acted 'with great moderation, such has been the high state of excitement we have been in that I have reason to fear some of our Societies would have been torn to pieces.' He also reported that men from Stanstead, Barnston, and Hatley had been among those who had gathered at Derby Line, Vermont, on the night of 26 February to attack Stanstead Plain while everyone was sleeping, though they had aborted the plan when the expected arms did not arrive until the following day. He assured the missionary society, however, that 'our congregations are ... large and attentive,' and that 'not one of our members that we know of on this circuit has been in any way concerned in aiding or abetting the late Rebellion.'[47]

By June, Turner was able to write that with the decline of political excitement there were signs of a renewed interest in religion. The situation would change again in November when the inhabitants were once more said to be in 'a state of very great excitement and alarm.' Captain Kilborn had been shot and wounded on his way home from attempting to arrest 'the leaders of the disaffected' in Barnston.[48] As a result of the near panic, several 'of the most respectable families' in Stanstead Plain were moving to 'places of greater safety an attack upon this place being expected in the course of a few days. Even our places of worship are being put into a state of preparation for defending the place.'[49]

A week later, Turner assured the WMS's secretaries that the expected attack had not materialized, probably due to the defeat of the rebels at Odelltown and Napierville, to the west, as well as to the prompt arrival of troops in Stanstead. The Methodist chapel had been occupied by soldiers for the previous three weeks, producing 'a most lamentable influence upon our congregation. The sight of implements of war, and military stores etc. etc. in the house of God is what many of our people cannot endure, and the consequence is our congregations are comparatively very small.'[50] In addition, among the families who had moved away were 'some of our best friends and most able supporters.' These included Ichabod Smith, who had been asked to join Sir John Colborne's Special Council, and Marcus Child, Stanstead's pro-Patriote MLA. Smith had been the principal subscriber for the church built in 1833, and Child was the society's longstanding treasurer, but 'the former fled from fear of assassination and the latter from fear of being made a state prisoner.'[51]

In January 1839, Turner reported that martial law had quieted some of the local excitement, but 'the disaffected and the well-affected' were quite evenly balanced in numbers, and there was still concern about invasion and incendiarism from across the border. The Methodist missionary had, nevertheless, been successful with his protests against the continued use of his chapel as a barracks on the grounds that it had become not only 'most offensively filthy but lousy too.' The following November, with incendiary border raids still taking place, Turner reported that in Stanstead Township there were eleven to fifteen hundred who attended the Methodist ministry, and in Barnston from three to five hundred. The Methodists had fourteen regular preaching stations in Stanstead, the Close Communion Baptists had six (he presumably meant the Freewill Baptists), the Universalists four or five, and the Congregationalists one, but Turner estimated that only half the population attended Sabbath services regularly. In Barnston, where services were more irregular, only a third attended most Sundays.[52]

The report for 1840 again admitted that there had been little growth in numbers, though the exodus of members from the region had decreased to fourteen. Great hope was expressed for a revival in the near future, but the Rebellions did have a negative long-term impact on the fortunes of the Stanstead circuit. The Irish-born former Catholic, Robert Cooney, would later report that during his first two years as the Methodist incumbent in Stanstead (1840 and 1841), his chief obstacle was the 'political dissensions and family feuds' that were 'the dregs of the late rebellion.' In addition, his report for 1841 stated that 'The falling off in income of this circuit was occasioned by the removal of our most liberal supporters during the rebellion of 1838, and who did not return when peace was restored.'[53]

The Rebellions had a much less powerful impact on those circuits that did not share a common boundary with Vermont. The Hatley report for 1838 referred to the 'injurious effects' resulting from the 'excitement, agitation & alarm' caused by the Rebellion, yet claimed that there was a gross increase of 126 members, which meant a net increase of seventy-three due to thirty-five departures, fourteen expelled or dropped from the class book, and five deaths. The same year's report from Shefford declared that 'What God has been graciously pleased to effect on this circuit during the past year cannot fail to excite emotions of gratitude in every pious heart.' The net increase in the society was fifty-four, 'and would have far exceeded this number had not the late rebellion driven many of our old members to a more peaceful part of the country.'[54]

In early 1839, however, John Tomkins wrote from Shefford that 'nearly the whole of the English part of the population are under arms; the country resembling one great military station in which nothing is seen but sentinels, bodies of soldiers marching, and companies learning the discipline, etc.' Shefford was more secure than the border circuits of Stanstead, St Armand, Odelltown, and Russeltown, but the interests of religion had suffered: 'The community being made up of persons from different countries and political sentiments, unanimity of feelings and desires could not be expected; neither do they exist, and the consequence is that friendly intercourse had been interrupted, and friendly feeling in many instances destroyed; ... many therefore have become cold in their minds and others have fallen from their steadfastness.'[55]

The Melbourne circuit was still farther away than Shefford from the border raids, but John Selley reported in 1839 that the church was 'in a discouraging state,' with class and prayer meetings discontinued because most of the male members were serving as militia volunteers 'doing regular duty.' Several of them had fallen prey to the temptations they were thereby exposed to, and had become 'stumbling blocks in the way of others.' On the New Ireland circuit, where the local militia was assigned to help defend Quebec during the Rebellions, John Borland's report to the WMS sang a rather different refrain. He claimed that he had received no bad reports of their behaviour, and that there had been a spiritual revival among those who had remained behind. At the quarterly meeting in early January 1838, the Watch Service had been followed by a prayer meeting which 'continued till near morning light,' and resulted in ten conversions, including a young French-Canadian woman.[56]

Borland was obviously disposed towards providing the missionary society what it wanted to hear, for his annual report to the district meeting admitted that 'Several cases of moral delinquency have appeared amongst us, by some we felt compelled to apply the painful sanction of our discipline, expulsion.' The circuit minutes reveal that one exhorter had been removed from his position because 'certain unpleasant differences' had arisen which were 'prejudicial' to his character. He was finally expelled in June 1838 for 'continuing to retain an unchristian spirit and conduct.' At the same time, two brothers who were church officials were expelled because of 'a gross violation of the Sanctity of the Lord's day,' and a local preacher was suspended for neglecting to attend his appointments.[57] Even in areas where the Rebellions made little direct impact, then, the later 1830s were discouraging years for the Wesleyan missionaries of the Eastern Townships.

The Impact of Millerism

The 1840s would prove to be even more troubled for the Wesleyan cause in the Eastern Townships, which at this time had half the Canada Eastern district's fourteen circuits and approximately half its members and adherents.[58] Progress continued to be hindered by a shortage of preachers, which was in turn partly due to a lack of local financial support. As late as 1841, the district report stated that local collections were affected by 'the disadvantages arising out of the late political troubles.' The report for 1842 noted that additional preachers were urgently needed for at least six townships, 'but we have neither men nor means to extend ourselves and to the Committee alone must we look for such help as may save us from shame and defeat.' A year later, in 1843, the collections were down due to 'the depreciation in value of produce, the commercial failures, and the general stagnation of trade,' in addition to 'the prevailing delusion which has existed on some of our circuits.'[59] This was a reference to the rise of Millerism, a movement which would quickly undermine the benefits the Wesleyan Methodist Society was beginning to realize from its own widespread revivals after 1841.

While the Millerite revival certainly represented a diversion from worldly concerns, it is far from certain that it signalled a widespread reaction against the conservatism of the established religious denominations, as is commonly suggested. The following examination of each Wesleyan circuit in the Eastern Townships will reveal that Miller's movement essentially accelerated a revivalist momentum that was already beginning in the southern parts of the region. Seeing no need to establish a new sect, given the imminent Apocalypse, the Millerites focused on infiltrating and converting the existing congregations. While its main impact was on the region's Baptists, the movement did attract many Methodists, including one of the Wesleyan missionaries, and it appears to have tempted at least one other.

Scattered revivals began on the Dunham circuit in 1840, the year it was separated from St Armand. The middle-aged newcomer to Canada, John Brownell, reported the following spring that there had been an addition of approximately one hundred members, as well as 'an increase of piety among the generality of our people.' Continuing his efforts in the fall of 1841, Brownell chose 24 November 'as a day for humbling ourselves before God and for special prayer for the descent of the Holy Ghost as a spirit of conviction, conversion, and edification.' On the following Sunday, 'A spirit of deep conviction was indeed poured out, and the alter [sic] was crowded with penitents earnestly and fervently calling upon God for present salvation, whilst believers rejoiced greatly in the reviving and cleansing influences of the Holy Ghost.' These services were continued for thirty-one days, 'and resulted in upwards of one hundred professing to find peace with God through our Lord Jesus Christ.'[60]

Uncharacteristic of the Methodist missions as such enthusiasm had become since the 1820s, it was not confined to Dunham in the early 1840s. While the gap in neighbouring St Armand's circuit minutes suggests that there were no quarterly meetings there between April 1838 and January 1841, the number of members increased significantly from 312 in 1840 to 380 in 1841. The energetic new missionary Richard Hutchinson reported in 1841 that 'The past year may be regarded as one of considerable prosperity. Our Society is in a truly peaceful and happy state, its members generally advancing in internal holiness and in practical conformity to devine requirements. Hutchinson held eighteen-day protracted meetings at Clarenceville, west of Missisquoi Bay, and at Pigeon Hill in St Armand. He reported that fifty were converted at the former place, and 'though converts were not numerous' at the latter, 'yet a more genuine work of God perhaps was never witnessed.'[61] In 1842 Hutchinson reported that there were fifty-three people on trial as a result of his labours during the winter, but deaths and removals had brought a slight decline in membership. Hutchinson was clearly not exaggerating, for the number of Methodist baptisms in St Armand increased steadily from thirty-one in 1839 to sixty in 1840, sixty-nine in 1841, and 102 in 1842.[62]

Eighteen-forty also brought renewed religious enthusiasm in Melbourne. The annual report for that year claimed that 'the Lord has graciously revived his work throughout the circuit, but more especially in Durham where many have been awakened to a just sense of their condition as sinners.' Forty-six had been received on trial, and the Melbourne chapel, which would seat upwards of three hundred persons, was nearly completed. Two more chapels would hopefully be completed within the year. In January 1841 John Borland held a protracted meeting which lasted twenty-two days instead of the planned eight, 'and even then the number of penitents was not diminished.' Sixty-eight people had given 'scriptural evidence of their being the subjects of pardoning grace,' and meetings were still being held in late February 'in special reference to those who groan for redemption through the blood of the Saviour.'[63]

Edmund Botterell reported a year later that the number present at the recent sacrament and love feast was unprecedented. The protracted meeting begun soon afterward, in February, followed the set pattern of having a prayer meeting in the mornings, sermons in the afternoons, and then more forceful sermons in the evenings when the 'congregation was mixed and far more numerous.' The result was twenty-three conversions, and Botterell concluded that while assistance from neighbouring ministers was very desirable for protracted meetings, it was apparently not indispensable. Botterell believed that the membership would increase from the 176 that had been reached under his predecessor to at least three hundred. He warned, however, that 'either a second Preacher must be appointed to the circuit, or we must lose, *we had better give up*, some places where the Brethren have laboured for years, and classes have long been formed.'[64]

From the Stanstead circuit Robert Cooney wrote that the Methodist cause was finally recovering from the disruption caused by the Rebellions and the 1841 election: 'The Congregation increased, the receipts were augmented, the chapel which had been for a long time out of repair was thoroughly renovated.' The Sabbath school was also revived, 'and our connexional principles began to diffuse themselves among the people.' Cooney expressed the postmillennialist hope 'that the day is approaching when the Lord will pour out his spirit upon this part of his inheritance, so that the thirsty Lands may become springs of water; and the wilderness rejoice and blossom as the rose'[65]

Shefford witnessed fewer signs of a religious revival than the foregoing circuits during the early 1840s. The missionary's report for 1840 lamented the 'fickleness' of some minds, and their 'improper views of Christian duty and obligation.' Two elderly members had withdrawn 'in consequence of having imbibed antisabbatic and other notions contrary to those received by our body,' and another had become a Universalist. But the report concluded that 'the Society generally continues to live in peace and harmony firmly attached to our doctrines and discipline,' and noted that there had been a slight increase in membership. In September of the same year, John Tomkins reported that he had visited East Bolton several times, and found that the cause of the Reformed Methodists (Protestant Methodists), 'has nearly dwindled to nothing.' Some of the local people had remained faithful to the Wesleyans and more would do so 'could we but extend to them the means of grace.' In 1842 Thomas Campbell complained that because he had to cover a territory forty miles long by thirty miles wide, he could only visit half the preaching places once a month: 'consequently the little religious feeling that may be from time to time excited is in general on our re-visiting in a great measure subsided.'[66]

The situation was still more discouraging on the Compton and Hatley circuit. John Tomkins reported in July 1842:

> On this circuit I find much to discourage me in my work. The people are mostly of American origin, and in their feelings generally hostile to every thing British, and as the greater part of the members on the Hatley side of the circuit have trained under the ministry of the Fr[ee Will] Baptists, a people in this country remarkable for laxity of doctrine and discipline, and they are but very poor materials a Methodist society; indeed, I must say that during the fifteen years of my missionary labours, I have never found a society so objectionable.[67]

Finally, the largely British-settled New Ireland circuit was too far from the American border to have been much influenced by the Rebellions, or the wave of revivalism taking place on some of the border circuits to the south. Nor would Millerism reach this far north, as we shall see.

From the Dunham circuit, however, Brownell wrote in April 1843 that the Millerite doctrines 'have threatened to overrun my circuit as they have done some other of our circuits; and to prevent wh. has required all the wisdom and prudence gained from past experience.' He added that 'This line of conduct has given rise to various reports wh. have been carried to the Chairman of the district & some others of my Brethren on the different circuits and for *a season* gave rise in their breasts to the idea that I was being led away by the specious arguments of Mr Miller and was consequently preaching doctrines contrary to Wesleyan Methodism.' As a result, Brownell had faced a dilemma: 'Either to alter my line of policy & thus stand well with my Brethren, but ruin my circuit by permitting Millerism *to flood* it; or maintain and pursue my line of policy – increase or at least permit to exist my Brethren's' suspicions – but save my circuit. Under these circumstances I *did not* – I *could not* hesitate a moment wh. difficulty to prefer.' Brownell claimed that the state of the circuit proved that 'I have the sanction of the Great Head of the Church, and I trust at our ensuing district meeting my brethren will not withhold their silent (if they will not give it openly) "well done".' His report to the district meeting added that the public services, prayer meetings, and class meeting 'have been better attended than in any previous period during the last four years.'[68]

Brownell had some impressive statistics to support his claim. There had only been 108 members listed for the circuit when he arrived, and thirteen of these had died or left, but now there were more than four hundred 'in Society.' The number of baptisms had jumped dramatically from forty-two in 1841 to 129 in 1842, declining only slightly to 115 in 1843.[69] The Canada District meeting of 1843 reported, nevertheless, that the Dunham preacher had 'in some degree, and on some occasions, given at least an apparent sanction to the opinion promulgated respecting the second advent this year.' While Brownell denied this, the meeting recorded that 'it is evident he has sometimes sustained perplexity in the consideration of the subject.' It resolved that he had 'betrayed a lamentable error of judgment,' but that he had also 'most fully freed himself from all suspicion of any further leaning towards that delusion,' and 'fully restored him to his former place in our affections and confidence.'[70]

Despite serious health problems, Brownell remained on the Dunham circuit until 1844, when he reported that 'the very questionable excitement which prevailed on this circuit the winter before last was succeeded by a culpable languor which depressed its subjects far below the scriptural standard of duty and privilege.'[71]

In the end, Brownell's revivalist efforts did not prevent Millerism from having a negative impact on the Dunham circuit, for the movement was far from dead, even in 1847. That year, Brownell's successor, Matthew Lang, complained of opposition 'from those who have embraced the Millerite delusion with respect to the second Advent.' Those Millerites who had remained within the Methodist Society in 1843 were now answering the call to establish their own church. Others had been expelled due to 'apathy and unfaithfulness.' Lang felt that this exercise of discipline had been salutary for the remaining members, and he reported that the congregations were generally large and attentive. At Dunham Flat (the head of the circuit), the dilapidated old chapel was being replaced by a new one, and the number of Sunday schools had increased to six. But the number of baptisms on the circuit dropped sharply after their sudden surge upwards to over a hundred a year in 1842 and 1843, for they now ranged from nineteen in 1844 to only eight in 1848.[72]

If John Brownell had only flirted with Millerism, there was no question about where his St Armand colleague, Richard Hutchinson, stood by 1843. The annual report for that year declared that while Hutchinson 'has been zealously labouring for the conversion of souls during the year, he has sanctioned to that end the erroneous doctrine that the world would this year be destroyed by fire.' At a meeting with the chairman in February, Hutchinson had agreed 'to abstain from any further advocacy of his new opinions, either publicly or privately, until he had further re-considered the subject,' and he had been granted a leave from his mission until the district meeting took place in May. In the meantime, however, he was said to have left the Methodists 'and attached himself to the advent party in the United States.' While recognizing Hutchinson's 'utmost sincerity of mind and uprightness of purpose,' the annual meeting expressed its 'deep regret that his judgment has so unhappily failed him in the course he has adopted ... They particularly regret that he should have felt more congeniality of mind with men characterized by the most loose and unsound principles of Scripture interpretation than with those natural friends and protectors by whom he was plentifully and providentially surrounded in that church which was the instrument of his conversion.'[73]

The district meeting's second resolution was aimed at preventing further defections by recognizing 'the sacred duty of every minister of our body not only, most conscientiously and scrupulously, to abstain from all appearance of sanctioning any novelties of religious opinion, which may at any time arise, but also in the fear of God, most fearfully and uncompromisingly to banish and drive away all erroneous and strange doctrines contrary to God's word, from the flock committed to his charge.' To reinforce this point, the third resolution condemned, 'most heartily, the unscriptural opinions which Mr Hutchinson has embraced and disseminated during the past year, opinions which have inflicted so great an amount of injury, upon the peace of some of our Stations as well as laid the foundation for future evils to which they cannot but look forward with the most painful apprehension.' A set of sub-resolutions drove these points home by declaring that no matter how much 'a missionary may feel at any time exercised in mind on novel points of religious opinion,' he was bound 'to abstain from any reference to such points in his intercourse with the people of his charge, whether in public or in private, as would be adapted to produce in them similar exercises and perplexities.' Instead, such missionaries must 'seek the aid of those Chief Ministers unto whom is committed the charge and government over him, and to follow with a glad mind and will their Godly admonitions.' Hutchinson was to be particularly condemned because he had been promoting Millerism while still in the employ of the WMS.[74]

Not surprisingly, then, when Hutchinson later asked for the £66.6.1 owed to him as a Methodist missionary, he met with a flat refusal from the district meeting. It based this refusal on the charges that he had neglected his pastoral duties, and that his promotion of the notion that the world was about to end had made it 'very difficult for your successor to raise contributions for that year.' Hutchinson was still attempting to collect his money four years later, when he argued that prior to his resignation he had followed the district meeting's instructions not to preach adventism, and that at least two other missionaries had asked him to present his views on the doctrine to their circuits: 'one of these gave about as much countenance to the doctrine as I did. Another wrote me expressing his faith in the doctrine and his purpose to teach it privately. I have his letter now.' The dispute was being played out in the public by 1850, but Hutchinson would never receive his money.[75]

In the meantime, Hutchinson's successor in St Armand, Hugh Montgomery, stated in 1843 that many of the local Methodists had 'adopted the same erroneous opinions and have, some in part, others altogether, withheld their usual pecuniary aid.' Montgomery took a leaf from the Millerite book by holding one of the region's only recorded Wesleyan camp meetings in September 1843.[76] It was followed by a series of protracted meetings in different parts of the circuit during the winter, 'the pleasing result of which has been the conversions of many souls, the reclaiming of many of those whose affections were alienated from us through the Millerite delusion, and the still further upbuilding of believers.' But baptisms declined from ninety-seven in 1843, to sixty-three in 1844, thirty-six in 1845, seven in 1846, and none the following two years.[77] Church membership also reached a peak of 531 in 1845, but declined precipitously thereafter (see appendix, table A.5).

W.E. Shenstone's report to the district meeting in 1847 stated little more than that 'Several causes have contributed to promote the spiritual apathy, and the financial defalcation, over which we mourn.' In the minute book of the quarterly meeting, Shenstone noted that no records had been kept since July 1844. He commented: 'The circuit appears to be all but ruined – and perhaps it would have been more agreable [*sic*] and profitable to have opened up an entirely new field of labour than to enter upon the duties of the Superintendency of this.' There were only four men, including himself, at the quarterly meeting in January 1847, and no subscriptions were deposited. The sole business undertaken was to censure the 'highly discreditable conduct' of one of the class leaders.[78]

The Millerite movement also made a dramatic impact in Stanstead. Robert Cooney reported that while he had been presenting his optimistic report to the district meeting in the spring of 1842:

> A host of preachers called 'Second Advent Lecturers' rushed in upon us from various parts of 'the United States,' and in a short time the whole circuit became infected with their crude and pernicious tracts. The doctrines taught by these misguided men are in substance as follows. Jesus Christ will make his second appearing during the present year. The great event will be associated with the general conflagration, the destruction of the wicked, the resurrection of the saints, and the establishment of the *Messiah's Kingdom in the 'the new Earth.'*[79]

By the fall, Cooney was lamenting that more than half of his flock had adopted this view. The Millerite lecturers were not Cooney's only challenge, however, for he also complained that the circuit was 'absolutely covered' with a variety of preachers, including Reformed Methodists and Freewill Baptists, 'many of whom cannot read our Common Bible without spelling the large words.' In Stanstead Township alone, the population of four thousand was served by thirteen Protestant ministers and one Catholic priest. Cooney claimed that six or eight of the former 'are soliciting to be heard – and in every respect accommodating themselves to the views and feelings of the people.' He himself had 'been obliged to resort to a kind of religious mendicity that is degrading to a Wesleyan minister; and that makes him appear like a *hireling* or a *pauper.*' The frustrated Cooney concluded emphatically: 'They say in Ireland, "He's *not the man for Galway*," and perhaps a more correct delineation of myself I cannot give ... than this: "*I'm not the man for the Eastern Townships*".'[80]

Millerism was at a fever pitch in January 1843 when Cooney wrote:

> The people here are almost exclusively *Americans*; and their views of civil and religious institutions are really incompatible with proper submission to pastoral authority, or any particular reverence for God himself. Their levelling, and indeed inverting sentiments reduce ministers to mere hirelings; and most of those that are called preachers in this part of the district cherish these principles, and do all in their power to propagate them. For these, and other reasons which might be mentioned, to enforce our excellent discipline is utterly impracticable. Very few are exclusively attached to Methodism.

The Stanstead minister continued: 'were you to witness the scenes which I have witnessed, and to see Methodism burlesqued as I have seen it burlesqued, your Wesleyan hearts would be pierced, and your insulted understandings would be prompted to exclaim in the language of one of our poets, 'O Judgment, thou art fled to brutish beasts: and men have lost their reason.'[81]

A particular threat to Cooney's church was that three of the Millerite lecturers were ordained Methodist Episcopal preachers, with the result that 'Special efforts are now being made by some of our people to support these very men; and those who have never been distinguished for liberality have become very generous.' To make matters worse, as far as collections were concerned, 'both the agricultural and commercial interests are suffering under an unprecedented depression, and to increase the embarrassment consequent upon such a state of things, the unusual changes in the weather during the winter has greatly impeded the travelling, and to a great extent rendered it impossible for the farmers to bring their produce to market.'[82]

The distraught Cooney had taken a leave of absence from Stanstead by this time, and a local church official wrote of his temporary replacement, a man named Graham, that 'his talents, good sense, and aparent [sic] piety and sincerity of manner seems to promise well for country circuits.'[83] But Graham was unable to counteract the fallout from the Millerite revival, for James Brock reported the following year, 1844, that the Stanstead circuit 'still suffers from the baleful effects of Rebelism and Fanaticism. The former has raised a very hostile feeling against the Wesleyan Church. The latter like a pestilence has spread desolation over many parts of [the] circuit not only involving the deluded in fatal error, but has also excited in the minds of others an awful irreverence towards the word of God, especially among the youth.' Brock lamented that no 'effectual barrier' had been erected 'against these evils' by distributing Wesleyan literature: 'The consequence of this paucity of Methodist works is a deep ignorance of Wesleyan doctrine and economy, which painfully exposed the members to the craft and design of wicked men.' Still, he concluded that a number of moribund classes had been revived, and the membership had increased by twelve.[84]

Three years later, in 1847, E.S. Ingalls wrote that his Stantead congregations had been 'respectable in point of numbers, and there has been some improvement in their attention to the preached word, and several have been converted and added to our society.' But he added that 'even among our own members the peculiar and scriptural institutions of our beloved Methodism are not more fully appreciated.' With numbers down slightly from the previous year, he could only pray that God would 'revive his work among us and cause a brighter day to dawn.'[85]

On the Melbourne circuit, Edmund Botterell had become somewhat discouraged as early as 1842, when he wrote that some of the classes were not prospering.[86] He would have greater reason for pessimism the following year. According to his report to the WMS, 'The spread of Millerism on the circuit has been productive of the utmost disregard of Christian order; and on the part of many a total forsaking of those means of grace which before they had professed to.' The apostates included a circuit steward, two trustees, a local preacher and a class leader, but Botterell's report to the district meeting declared that the membership had only declined by seventeen. Like his colleagues elsewhere in the region, he did admit that a beneficial result had been a greater appreciation for 'the preaching of the truth as it is in Jesus.'[87]

Botterell's successor, John Rain, was not as despairing of the aftereffects of the Millerite enthusiasm as some of his colleagues. He reported in 1844 that, on arriving in Melbourne, he had found the 'unhappy and deluding principles' of Millerism 'spread generally throughout the circuit.' He had attempted to reclaim the apostates without much success, but reported optimistically that the 'quarterly Love feasts and Sacramental services have been times of refreshing from the presence of the Lord,' and the 'public religious services connected with the Fast day which was appointed by the last district meeting were, to very many, services not soon to be forgotten.' But three years later, in 1847, conditions had not improved for the Melbourne Wesleyan circuit. According to John Borland, 'The peculiarities of Millinerianism as taught by the "Plymouth Brethren," of Millerism, Universalism, and Puseyism have been urged against us with considerable determination.' Borland claimed that 'our people generally have not been moved,' but he admitted that there had been a decline in membership, with sixteen backsliders and eleven removals, but only eleven new candidates on trial.[88]

The spread of Millerism was not entirely dependent on the preexisting revivalist wave that shook the border circuits, for it made considerable inroads among Shefford's Wesleyan Methodists, as well. E.S. Ingalls reported in 1843 that the year had been one 'of very painful anxiety, arising principally from the prevalence among our people of the mistaken opinion that the present year will finish the probation of the human family.' The main damage, however, had been done to the collection of funds, since many had purchased 'the ephemeral productions of the prevailing error,' and this during a year of partial crop failure, but 'our Societies have improved both in number and in piety.'[89]

The popular cynicism that followed the Millerites' 'great disappointment' was particularly strong in Shefford where Ingalls reported bitterly in 1844 that 'the stability of our people's faith and affection has been assailed from different quarters and many, alas, have been alienated not only from our beloved Methodism but also from the God of all their mercies, and shew by word and deed that they ardently wish for the entire extirpation of Methodism from the earth.' The decline by thirty-seven members was partially due to Millerism, and partially to 'the influence of Ministers of other denominations, who have come among us during the year.' The minutes of the quarterly meeting for July 1844 record that 'with a few exceptions the class papers are very old and no account kept of the attendance or non-attendance of the members and in several neighbourhoods neither prayer meeting or class meeting regularly kept up – in short the circuit is in a very discouraging distracted state.'[90] Two years later, the local missionary reported that a number of members had been expelled during the previous twelve months. Also, 'A few others having either become weary in well doing or fallen victims to the prevailing error in regard to the end of the world, have gone out from us, while not a few have removed to ... better their temporal circumstances in other parts of the country.' At least the circuit was no longer losing ground, for Matthew Richey reported that 'the places of all these have been filled up and nineteen additional members added to the society.'[91]

As in Shefford, there was no post-Rebellion Methodist revival on the Compton and Hatley circuit. Membership numbers continued to decrease in 1843, when only 155 were reported, partly due to emigration but mostly because of 'the delusion of Millerism.' In April of that year, John Tomkins wrote that one leader and forty members had become Millerites, and added that 'myself and brethren who have discountenanced the delusion have been stigmatized with a liberal profusion of opprobrious epithets, such as blind guides, Dumb dogs, and builders that daub with untempered mortar, etc.'[92]

Tomkins had become discouraged enough to argue that the Eastern Townships 'afford but a very uncongenial soil for our system. The greater part of the people of these Townships emanated from the States, and are with a few exceptions strongly opposed to every thing British; nor are they more favourably disposed towards our useages and discipline.' By 1844 he was almost reduced to despair:

> The religious state of the society on this circuit is discouraging, the congregations small and fluctuating, and not a few of the members of the Society appear to have no fixed religious principles, and of course the attachment to us is very slender. They are therefore ready to be carried away by every kind of doctrine. Indeed among the people around us almost every form of religious error exists, such as Socinianism [which denied Christ's divinity], the doctrine of anihilation [sic], Universalism and Millerism.

Tomkins added that the many who had been captivated by Millerism were, 'either from shame or alienation,' refusing to re-enter the fold. He concluded, however, that 'these people have souls to be saved or lost to all eternity and were Methodism removed little would be left to stand against the overflowing of destructive errors.' He could only hope that 'as the delusion is abated and people learn wisdom by the things they suffer,' the circuit would 'see better days.'[93]

Tomkins's hopes would be disappointed, for two years later, Benjamin Slight recorded in his journal that 'I found this circuit in the utmost degree of prostration. Perhaps some part of it may be imputed to the deleterious influences of Millerism.' The entire circuit had been reduced to one class, which 'had not had their Tickets renewed for 3 quarters,' and there had been no love-feasts for three years. Slight had been given one year to improve matters, or the circuit would be abandoned. He noted six months later, however, that 'we have not one Local preacher in the whole circuit & but three persons meeting classes.' He concluded that 'with so little help of this kind it would surely be best either to abandon such stations altogether, or to provide more ministerial labour.'[94] Yet another six months later, in June 1847, Slight again confided to his journal that 'of all the circuits I have been on, surely this is the most deficient. Here we can have no regular Church organization. We have scarcely any class meetings, to which to invite any who are impressed with the necessity of working out their soul's salvation. I go around & preach, impressions I know are made; but they are either lost again, or the subjects of them are picked up by the Baptists, who have 12 ministers operating within the space of country I alone occupy, & whose church members are ever ready to lay hold of any advantage they perceive.'[95]

Unlike the other circuits, the rise in religious enthusiasm that New Ireland experienced in 1843 had little or nothing to do with Millerism. Thomas Campbell reported that year that, largely as a result of six protracted meetings throughout the circuit, 'believers in general have been quickened, backsliders reclaimed, and sinners converted.' To attend the two-week protracted meeting in Lower Ireland, Campbell wrote, 'Some of the poor women, even those with infants, would walk three or four miles and return the same night, though the roads were covered with water and saturated snow.' In Upper Ireland, 'the young and thoughtless' scoffers 'had soon either to retire from the meetings, or stand in silence, gazing on those who formerly led them in the ball-room and dance, now trembling before their much offended God.' The rather large number of twenty-two 'backsliders' had been more than offset by the seventy-six people who remained on trial, but Campbell insisted that the revival had nothing to do with the Millerite movement: 'Lest it should be supposed that our late revivals have been produced by Millerism, I would just mention, that I have heard of only one person on this circuit who believes it, and he declares, 'if the Second Advent do not take place in 1843, he will burn his Bible.''[96]

Even without the influence of Millerism, however, the New Ireland circuit would continue to be plagued by divisiveness because of its relatively recent settlement and mixed population. In 1844 Campbell reported 'a withering curse hanging over a few neighbourhoods' due to 'old bickerings of two or three years standing.' These had caused some expulsions and threatened to result in more. To encourage a revival, the quarterly meeting decided to hold two 'grove meetings,' clearly the British version of the American camp meeting, but there was only a slight increase to 293 members the following year (see appendix, table A.5).[97]

One reason that Millerism became as briefly popular as it did in much of the Eastern Townships may have been that a revivalist impulse had already begun in many of the Methodist congregations in 1840-1. It may not be a coincidence that this was the year of the Caughey revivals in Montreal and Quebec City, but Caughey apparently did not visit the Eastern Townships.[98] The number of Wesleyan members in the region's seven circuits during these years of economic hardship and out-migration increased by 206 between 1839 and 1840, 152 between 1840 and 1841, and 117 between 1841 and 1842. The peak years of the Millerite craze brought only modest increases of 146 between 1842 and 1843, and thirty-four from 1843 to 1844, after which there began a steady decline.

Not all the losses were due to religious apathy, for the Adventists had finally decided to establish their own church, and the Methodist report in 1847 stated that Millerism 'still continues rampant' in the country districts: 'The latitudinarian views of a large portion of the people in these parts supply material for their operations and thus, proportionally, prejudice our cause.' The report explained the stagnation in membership numbers by noting that at least 250 had left the fold due to Millerism in the previous year, and two hundred had moved from the district.[99]

The tide began to turn in 1848 when the district letter stated that 'the Millerite eruption has done its work – and the Lord is now evolving good out of the evil. The people see the folly of yielding up their judgment to every spiritual empiric who may come amongst them. Our Ministry has been well tried – its stability duly tested, and now they desire the old wine which is better.'[100] There had been a very limited attempt to fight fire with fire by holding two or three camp meetings in 1843 and 1844, but the emphasis was shifting towards establishing a firmer base for such revivals by nurturing and educating the young through Sunday schools. The Wesleyan missionaries would, however, have relatively little success in exercising control over this movement.

Sunday Schools

The Sunday schools movement had been launched in the colony by Thaddeus Osgood, who had opened one in Stanstead around 1819. Five years later, the Sunday School Union of Canada sent two agents to the Eastern Townships where they reported that they had distributed ten shillings in books to each of two schools in Stanstead, two in Hatley, and two that had been moribund in Barnston. They also established a Sunday school in Stanbridge Mills, and revived others in Sutton and Schoolscraft.[101] While the Wesleyan missionaries supported this movement, they preferred to control their own Sunday schools as a means of tying children and families to their church. On the Shefford circuit, for example, Thomas Catterick had by 1822 established two of them, one with thirty students and the other with twenty-five. A year later, the same circuit had four Sunday schools with 'above 100 Scholars, many of whom are now under serious impressions.'[102]

As with the Congregationalists, indoctrinating the young was not considered to be an alternative to evangelical fervour, and preachers such as John Borland and Edmund Botterell promoted both Sunday schools and protracted meetings. Borland reported from the New Ireland circuit in 1837 that, due to the 'scattered state of the population and ... the imperfect manner in which the children are clothed,' only one Sunday school had been maintained. But in this one, 'some of the elder children are under serious impressions and are met in class by their superintendent previous to the commencement of the regular business of the school.' Such an approach made perfect sense, the historian Whitney Cross argues, because 'Sunday-school pupils, temperance advocates, and Antimasons all had a training in religious enthusiasm which would make them easy targets in the next revival.'[103]

Sunday schools were envisioned as a means of avoiding the fluctuations in enthusiasm produced by a more exclusive focus on revivals, but this initiative also proved difficult to sustain. Catterick's successor in Shefford reported that there were so few qualified to be teachers on the circuit that he had only been able to establish four or five small Sunday schools.[104] In 1823 St Armand reported nine Sunday schools with upwards of four hundred students and fifty teachers, but they were only open during the summer due to 'the poverty of the people with the want of proper persons to engage in them.' Also in 1823 Melbourne reported only two Sunday schools of twenty children each, 'particularly from the want of suitable teachers.' Stanstead had one Sunday school, with eight male students and twenty-eight females, but this gender imbalance was not universal for there were seventy-two boys and seventy-three girls in Shefford's three schools.[105] Table 8.1 reveals that the genders remained quite evenly balanced in all the circuits during the 1840s, which may have been considered another advantage of the Sunday schools over an exclusive focus on revivals, which apparently tended to be more effective with females than males.

But there was still no progress in 1824, when Shefford reported four very small Sunday schools 'owing to the badness of the roads, and the inability of the parents to provide cloathing for their children that will enable them to attend.' Melbourne reported two, with few children in attendance; Stanstead one, with four teachers and thirty-seven children; and St Armand six, with no other information since DePutron had fractured his leg on the way to the annual meeting. Only two stations submitted Sunday school reports in 1826, with Stanstead now reporting five, and 'two or three female children having become pious.'[106]

Still, the Wesleyan missionaries expressed less concern with sustaining Sunday schools than with asserting exclusive denominational control over them, for this had become a priority in England during the early nineteenth century.[107] On the St Armand circuit, which had seven Sabbath schools in 1835, only one was exclusively affiliated with the Methodists by 1840 because of 'an aversion to Sabbath schools being under the management of any one denomination.' Similarly, William Squire lamented in 1835 that he was unable to convince the Stanstead Methodists to establish their own institutions: 'From the conflicting views and jealousies of the people upon religious subjects there is an aversion among them to Sabbath schools being placed under the controul of any one particular body of Christians, and unity in any one of our thinly inhabited neighbourhoods is necessary to a school being sustained. Hence, there has been as many as seven schools on this circuit principally conducted by our principals, but over which as a body we had not controul.'[108] Another interpretation might be that the local communities preferred to cooperate with each other in instilling common Christian values in their children. By 1837, however, the Stanstead Methodists had taken control of three small schools numbering about eighty children, but which were suspended during the winter because of the weather. After peaking at only four in 1838, the number of exclusively Methodist Sunday schools on the Stanstead circuit would decline steadily in the early 1840s.

The same pattern unfolded elsewhere in the region. John Rain noted

TABLE 8.1
Female and male Sunday School students, Eastern Townships Wesleyan Circuits, 1843–52

	St Armand	Dunham	Shefford	Stanstead	Hatley	Melbourne	Ireland	Sherbrooke	Total	District
1843										
F	81	–	–	32	–	70	66	–	249	1,025
M	92	–	–	22	–	52	60	–	226	1,114
1846										
F	116	80	61	52	55	40	49	–	463	1,495
M	135	79	66	50	65	40	67	–	502	1,521
1847										
F	98	109	65	62	35	30	55	32	486	1,577
M	100	93	71	40	33	20	57	23	437	1,585
1848										
F	46	121	56	53	25	38	49	37	425	1,532
M	45	97	47	60	20	40	75	18	402	1,535
1849										
F	25	115	38	50	30	59	36	32	410	1,555
M	25	95	46	45	20	71	72	21	395	1,525
1852										
F	30	25	75	70	30	96	27	89	449	1,438
M	34	25	75	77	20	90	30	70	414	1,381

Source: NA, MMS, Synod Minutes, Lower Canada/Canada East

that there was still no Methodist Sunday school anywhere on the Hatley and Compton circuit in 1837 due to 'the scattered state of the population of the Country and the mixed character of the people.' The first one would not be opened until two years later, but, in the meantime, the missionary reported that 'To meet these and other existing difficulties over which we had not controul it has been our endeavour when practicable to blend catechetical instruction with our pastoral visitations.' In Shefford, there was said to be only one small Sunday school as late as 1840 and a year later, even it was no longer operating, 'nor is it possible, at present to establish any, for want of suitable persons to conduct them.'[109]

The situation was more promising on the more British Melbourne circuit where three Sunday schools were reported in 1841, the teachings of which had 'resulted in the conversion of nine of the children, and who have joined the Society.' All but one of the teachers was a Methodist member. The following year, the number of Sunday schools had increased to five, four of which were in Durham Township. Edmund Botterell stated that 'some of the children in these schools have given evidence of their conversion to God, and others are deeply serious in reference to their salvation.' He complained of a shortage of suitable books, but this problem was solved by the acquisition of a library a year later, in 1843.[110] The fact that the Wesleyan missionaries obviously considered Sunday schools to be potentially powerful instruments of conversion helps to explain why they wanted exclusive denominational control, but this would prove elusive.

While in 1844 there were six Sunday schools in Melbourne, with an average attendance of 165 boys and 105 girls, most of whom were said to 'have made praiseworthy proficiency in their studies,' a definite decline had set in three years later. John Borland reported that there were now only two Sunday schools, one of which was closed during the winter 'in consequence of various and antagonistic influences against which we could not controul.' And while these schools were 'decidedly Wesleyan in opperation,' efforts to introduce 'our excellent Catechism' had met with little success. By 1852 the Melbourne Methodists were reported to be in charge of only three Sunday schools.[111]

On the Dunham circuit, as well, the religious revival of the early 1840s was accompanied by increased interest in Sunday schools, but not ones exclusively identified with the Methodists. John Brownell, who became tainted with Millerism, as we have seen, reported the opening of a Sabbath school with sixty-one children and nine teachers in 1841. He noted that some of the teachers were members of other churches, and also that one of them was able to communicate in French with those who were children of 'habitans'. By 1842, there were eighty-two students, with an average attendance during the summer and autumn of sixty, and, in 1843, a library of 150 volumes was procured. An open-air celebration of the school's anniversary had attracted over 1200 people, but Brownell had been unable to open a second one. There were still only two Sunday schools on the circuit in 1844, and only one with a library because efforts to increase the number had been 'less successful than could be desired.'[112]

Sunday schools were more popular on the New Ireland circuit where there was strong resistance to the government's public school reforms of the 1840s.[113] By 1841, there were two Sunday schools in New Ireland, with thirty males and twenty females attending, but the Methodist missionary reported that because there were no 'week day schools' in these areas 'little more can be taught in them than reading the scriptures.' A year later, however, the number of Sunday schools had increased to five, with fifty-two females and fifty males. E.S. Ingalls noted that 'in the absence of almost every other means of instruction these schools are producing many good results by enabling the children to read and understand the word of God.'[114]

The chief objection the Methodist clergy had to union Sunday schools, which in practice they had considerable influence over, was the inability to teach their Catechism. A greater threat than local control over the schools came from the Anglican Church's somewhat belated interest in them, for it began to apply its well-tested method of offering money as an incentive to taking them over. In 1842 the Methodists' district meeting suggested that Sunday school teachers be paid in special circumstances because the Church of England was making great gains in the poorer settlements by this means. The Methodist synod of 1842 reported alarmingly that, in return for £10 to £15 per year, a teacher would instruct the children in the Anglican Catechism, 'keep a "High Church" Sunday school, and act as clerk to the clergyman in his *endeavours to form* a congregation! chiefly among our own people!' The Lower Canadian Methodists therefore requested the establishment of an education grant and a supply of school books and Catechisms: 'Had this been earlier done the country would have been in many places entirely our own.'[115]

The renewed effort to establish exclusively Methodist-controlled Sunday schools after 1842 made little progress. The thirty-eight Sunday schools and 2268 students of 1843 had decreased sharply to twenty-seven schools and 955 students by 1846. The decline continued for at least three more years, by which time there were only twenty Methodist Sunday schools and 780 students in the region. The Millerite movement, and the ensuing religious divisions and exhaustion, had clearly undermined all aspects of the Wesleyan missionary effort. By 1852, however, there was a slight recovery to twenty-two schools and 863 students (see appendix, table A.8).

Wesleyanism at Mid-Century

Following the decline that effected most of the Protestant denominations and churches in the Eastern Townships during the later 1840s, the pendulum began a somewhat tentative swing back towards a renewed interest in religion, including Methodism. From Stanstead, John Borland reported in 1849 that a revival had begun in a part of the circuit where his predecessor 'had laboured in much hope.' The revival produced about seventy conversions, including several backsliders who 'had been for years estranged from the church.' Far from all of the converted had joined the Wesleyan Methodists, however, for their net increase in numbers that year was a mere eight people, plus thirty-three on trial.[116]

It also appears that Borland's initiative was not followed up by his successors, for John Tomkins's report of two years later was a model of brevity and vagueness. He wrote that there were still three Sunday schools, some of which 'have done well,' while others 'have been poorly conducted,' and added little more than that many of the Methodists 'ought to be in a better state of grace than they are, ... yet we thank the Lord for many among us, who are walking in the fear and enjoyment of the love of God.'[117] What the missionary reports failed to reveal was that there had been a major hemorrhaging from the Wesleyan ranks to at least one other Methodist society, for in Stanstead and Barnston Townships the 610 people who reported themselves as Wesleyans to the census enumerator in 1852 were outnumbered by the 718 New Connection Methodists (who had succeeded the Protestant Methodists in the region) and 2,140 'Other Methodists.' As previously stated, it is likely that certain enumerators, and even certain adherents, failed to distinguish between the branches of Methodism, making it necessary to record them as 'Other Methodists' in the printed census reports. The fact remains that identification with the conservative British-based organization was far from firm in what was the region's main centre of Methodism.

In St Armand, William Scott was a popular minister who remained longer than the regular three years due to the insistence of the quarterly meeting,[118] but there does not appear to have been any major revival on the circuit. E.S. Ingalls reported in 1852 that there was only one Sunday school, and the society suffered from 'great want of unity and Godly charity.' There were twelve new members, in addition to the twenty-three transferred from the Dunham circuit, but twelve had moved away, one had died, and thirty had been dropped 'for neglecting the means of grace.'[119]

From Dunham, John Tomkins's 1849 report suggested that the circuit was still catching its breath from the Millerite craze. The scattered nature of the membership discouraged 'regular attendance upon the means of grace, which for want of labourers are but sparingly dispersed among them.' There were now only three Sunday schools, rather than the six of two years earlier, but there had been a few more converts, 'and after a painful season of delusive and destructive excitement the people are returning to a better mind and we hope to see better days.'[120] Further progress was hampered, however, by the district meeting's decision to remove the assistant missionary in 1851. The impact had been softened by the transfer of one of the classes to St Armand, and the assistance of the salaried agent, Barnabas Hitchcock, but the highly dedicated John Borland still had to travel thirty to forty miles and preach nine times each week.

At Dunham Flat, early in 1852, Borland held 'protracted services of preaching and prayer, for about six weeks, which resulted in the conversion or reclamation of about sixty persons.' These included two French Canadians (a young man and an elderly woman), which had 'excited attention on the part of their country people who are, many of them at least, much impressed.' Borland felt that a minister to serve the French Canadians would meet with considerable success, and the WMS began to recruit French-Canadian missionaries in 1854 even though it had more than it could do to serve the region's Protestants.[121] On the Dunham circuit itself, there were only 297 Wesleyan members as of 1852, though the 1852 census lists 1,428 individuals as Wesleyan Methodists in Dunham and Sutton Townships alone. The distinction between full membership and mere adherence was clearly an important one.

On the Shefford circuit, the minutes for the July 1850 quarterly meeting reported that the state of religion was 'Painfully low, with a general neglect of the social meetings of the church.' In April 1851, however, the circuit's minutes stated that 'while the meeting is still called upon to mourn over appathy [sic] in some of the classes, it is upon the whole encouraged.'[122] A year later R.A. Flanders noted that his obligation to serve fifteen 'preaching appointments' meant that 'Pastoral visits must be almost entirely neglected, and the regular visitation of the Society interrupted.' Now that the 'disorganizing excitement which like a mighty scourge has passed over this district of country has expended its violence,' the WMS had the opportunity 'to occupy a position and exert an influence upon the population of these Townships it has never before possessed.' That, however, would require a second missionary for the circuit.[123] In the meantime, prospects were not promising for membership had declined from 243 in 1849 to 215 in 1852.

The number of Wesleyan Methodists in the Compton and Hatley circuit began to increase slowly in 1848, and Thomas Campbell reported the following year that the 'religious state of this circuit is decidedly improving.' Progress might not be as rapid as hoped for, 'but that it is at all rising above the deleterious effects of past events affords matter for gratitude to God and encouragement to his Ministers.' In 1852, when there was still only one Sunday school, Malcolm McDonald wrote that 'our efforts to promote the cause of God have not been without evident tokens of the Divine sanction and approval,' though he lamented the impact on 'the religious state of the societies ... by the spirit of California adventure.' McDonald added that 'in the pursuit of gold we have been called to sustain the loss of some of our most efficient and useful members,'[124] but he reported an exodus of only six people.

While assigned to the Melbourne circuit, Benjamin Slight recorded in his journal during the summer of 1849 that 'our congregations in most places are very good & a good deal increased.'[125] The impact on membership numbers had yet to be felt, however, for Slight reported to the district meeting of 1849 that seventeen people had been received on probation, but twenty-five had been expelled for missing class meetings, five had died, eleven had moved away, and two had quit the church. Slight appears to have been unduly optimistic once again with his journal entry for March 1851, when he wrote that 'this circuit has evidently been for some time increasing in good feeling & attendance on the means.' He later admitted, however, that there had only been an increase of eight members since he had taken up the Melbourne circuit three years earlier. The modest results were not for want of effort on his part, for Slight recorded that he had preached 'on this circuit each year about 350 sermons, special church & other meetings from 130 to 150.

Pastoral visitations numerous. Baptized from 45 to 50 persons. Funeral sermons 8 or 10. Marriages 8 to 10. Received on trial about 30 to 40; travelled 5000 miles or more, about 150 nights from home, & about 300 days.'[126]

The first surviving report for the Sherbrooke circuit (later known as Sherbrooke and Eaton) was not submitted until 1847. John Douglas then wrote that 'notwithstanding the operation of many circumstances of a discouraging nature, God has been pleased to vouchsafe a measure of prosperity, which is indicated, both by the deepening of the piety of our people and by the increase in the number of members.' Douglas claimed that the 'congregations at *all* the appointments are large and attentive.' Ten had been dropped for non-attendance at class meetings, and fifteen had moved away, but forty-five had been added and five new members had arrived, leaving an increase to 115 full members. There was still only one small Sunday school in Sherbrooke in 1849, but, as in Stanstead, this was a year of revival, with sixty people being added to the Methodist Society. Gifford Dorey's report of that year claimed that 'the Spirit of the Lord has been poured out upon us and the result has been peace within our walls and prosperity within our palaces. Sinners have been awakened, backsliders have been reclaimed, penitents have obtained a sense of pardoning mercy and believers have been established in their most holy faith.'[127]

Unfortunately, there are no district reports available for the rather turbulent two following years, when construction of the St Lawrence and Atlantic Railway brought large numbers of impoverished Irish navvies to the Sherbrooke area. However, Benjamin Slight entered the following observation in his journal, after being assigned to the circuit in June 1851: 'Prayer meetings nearly deserted; spiritual feeling & enjoyment at a low ebb; & the zeal & energy put forth in furtherance of the cause exceedingly deficient.' Slight's annual report a year later did suggest, however, that progress had been made, for there were 113 members in Sherbrooke and 112 in Eaton. He added that, while this was only an increase of 8 members from the previous year, the size of the congregations had grown substantially, especially in Sherbrooke, and subscriptions throughout the circuit were 'considerably in advance of former times.' The Methodists would soon stop meeting upstairs from a shop and build their own chapel.[128]

From the exceptionally challenging circuit of New Ireland, R.A. Flanders reported in 1849 that he had 'little of an encouraging character to report.' The circuit was 'in a very low and in some respects in a very disordered state.' Flanders added that 'All who were known to be disorderly in their lives have either been expelled or admonished while many of the Backslidden in heart have either withdrawn or have been dropped for not attending class.' He had expelled 'the senior local preacher, and leader of the largest class upon the circuit' because 'a difficulty of seven or eight years standing' had divided the society. Flanders was clearly referring to Lower Ireland's controversial Joseph Redfern, who had been criticized by a temperance supporter for attending a public dinner in a tavern. Redfern had not been expelled, however, rather he had resigned when ordered to present himself to a leaders' meeting for a disciplinary hearing.[129]

Flanders attributed the low state of the circuit primarily to the 'want of suitable persons for class leaders which makes it difficult and in some cases quite impracticable to maintain that religious influence and order which are necessary for the preservation and prosperity of our people.' A case in point was the small number of Sunday schools due to 'the want of suitable persons to act as Teachers, and a supply of books.' This problem stemmed in part from the crop failures 'of the last few years,' and the subsequent removal of some of our most substantial and influential families to other parts seeking to improve their temporal circumstances.'[130] The situation had evidently improved somewhat by 1850, however, when the quarterly meeting passed a resolution recognizing 'the labours of the Rev. R.A. Flanders on this circuit as being under Gods blessing greatly calculated to raise its spiritual tone and also to increase its finances.'[131]

New Ireland's Wesleyan Methodist membership of 227 in 1852 remained lower than what it had been in 1844, and all 476 Methodists recorded for Megantic County in the 1851-2 *Census Reports* are identified as 'Other Methodists.' Because it is highly unlikely that the New Connection Methodists penetrated this far north, it seems clear that the enumeration is mistaken. Certainly, Gifford Dorey still had Wesleyans to serve in 1852 when he reported that 'a better state of Christian unity exists in most of our Societies' in what was now known as Leeds circuit. On one occasion, the 'Spiritual influence' was so strong at a love feast that it had to be turned into 'a penitent prayer meeting. The power of Christ to save was then displayed in the emancipation of six precious souls from the thralldom of sin and satan.' As in the past, however, the impact of such local revivals would remain limited as long as 'our class meetings cannot be attended with that regularity which is so desirable, nor can the amount of pastoral care be given, which the wants and interests of the church demand.' In the July 1851 and March 1852 quarterly meetings, two class leaders were warned to meet their classes more regularly, and a third was suspended. Not surprisingly, there were still only three Sunday schools, which Dorey claimed had made little advancement.[132]

Conclusion

After William Squire toured the Eastern Townships in 1852 as general superintendent of the Eastern Canada district, he reported that 'our cause has greater influence upon the population than I had expected; I went with forebodings, – I have returned with joy.'[133] This somewhat ambiguous statement reflected the Wesleyan Methodists' rather disappointing record in the region since the early 1840s. According to the 1851–2 Canadian census, there were 13,545 Methodists in the Eastern Townships, an increase to 14.5 per cent of the population from 8.8 per cent in 1831, when they numbered only 3,364. While most of the 5,206 'other' Methodists listed in 1852 were undoubtedly Wesleyans, there were also 3,442 New Connection Methodists, and the Wesleyan records reveal that adult membership numbers declined from a peak of 2,078 in 1844 to only 1,637 in 1852 (see appendix, table A.5). The Methodists as a whole may have been close to outnumbering the Anglicans in the region but, as the missionaries were constantly lamenting, adherence to Wesleyan Methodism was evidently not deep-rooted.

In December 1850, shortly after a wave of American annexation sentiment had swept the southern townships, John Borland complained from the Stanstead circuit that 'the unsettledness of political and commercial matters – together with the many inducements to the West and South, tend very much to keep up a spirit of emigration. It is very trying to have vacancies created in various localities by the removal of first one and then another influential member of our Church. Vacancies that we sometimes find it extremely difficult to fill.'[134] This was a growing handicap faced by all the non-Catholic denominations in the region, yet the recently arrived New Connection, which was based in Britain, had made an impressive number of converts. Those numbers would soon decline due to a lack of missionary effort, but this sect's sudden success was built on its radical approach and affiliation with the local American Protestant Methodists. Despite the removal of the Episcopal Methodist missionaries in 1821, American-style Methodism continued to have a strong appeal in much of the region.

One reason was clearly that the Wesleyan missionaries remained almost entirely British at mid-century, but the population had quickly adjusted to the Wesleyan newcomers during the revivals of the 1820s. Another important factor was that the early evangelical zeal of most of the Wesleyan missionaries had soon given way to a more institutionalized approach, yet there continued to be major revivals thereafter. For example, while no missionary was more rigorous about reining in 'excesses' than William Squire, his forceful style of preaching helped to stimulate an enduring revival in Stanstead in 1835. According to his biographer, Squire's ability to 'dissect' the human heart 'and to lay open the latent corruption of its various parts, often left both backslider and ordinary sinner trembling and appalled.'[135] Admittedly, his approach elicited an enthusiastic response only in times of crisis, and it was no accident that his Stanstead revival took place during a period of near famine, but the economic depression of the early 1840s provided an opportunity for another wave of revivals among the Wesleyan Methodists of the region.

In light of these revivals, Carroll's charge that the Wesleyan approach in Lower Canada was characterized by 'plodding diligence'[136] seems rather unfair. By the early 1840s membership was growing steadily and more Methodist chapels were being built. But the sudden upsurge of Millerism in 1843 brought a dramatic reversal, one which the Wesleyan missionaries' own renewed interest in revivalism was powerless to prevent; indeed, it may have helped pave the way for the Millerite preachers. Much of the radical enthusiasm passed away with the failure of the Apocalypse to arrive as predicted in 1843, or again in 1844, but the Wesleyan Methodists, particularly in their stronghold of Stanstead Township, were slow to recover from the fallout.

Semple has argued concerning the Wesleyan missionaries in the Maritimes that their 'sense of evangelism was often diminished since they did not need to relate to the priorities of their members or to expand membership in order to receive their pay.'[137] He would presumably apply the same argument to the Eastern Townships, but we have seen that the Wesleyan missionaries were still promoting revivals at mid-century, well after this approach is said to have gone out of fashion in Upper Canada. The fact is that the failure of the WMS to increase funding meant that a small number of missionaries each remained responsible for as many as a dozen widely dispersed communities in the Eastern Townships. And, as they pointed out year after year, their influence was diluted accordingly. The aim is not to shed blame on the WMS, which had its own financial problems as well as more exciting obligations in the 'heathen' world than in a district that included the growing commercial and industrial centres of Montreal and Quebec. The point is that, as our examination of the Anglican experience in the following section will illustrate, external funding did make a positive difference in the competition for souls in the Eastern Townships.

Semple also criticizes the Wesleyan missionaries in the Maritime colonies for gravitating towards a semi-settled rather than an itinerant ministry,[138] but, as we have seen, Edmund Botterell argued convincingly in 1838 that there were strong advantages to the Congregational and Anglican system of a settled village ministry. The experienced Benjamin Slight also pointed to the weakness in the Methodist system when he recorded in his memoir in 1847 that it was entirely dependent upon 'efficient class leaders, local preachers, and prayer leaders.' One man, 'however earnest and desirous to save the souls of men, can do but little. He visits a place once in two weeks, preaches, etc., and passes on to another, and without this co-operation all the improvements he makes evaporates before he comes around again.'[139] To rely on such a local lay leadership made good sense in an old settled society such as England, but with missionaries turning over ever two of three years in a relatively unstable environment, the WMS's expectations were rather unrealistic. It was clearly also the case that the British missionaries generally felt that the local social leaders were too ignorant and too radical to be trusted with religious authority. Consequently, as in the Maritimes, they failed to develop more than a token native-born ministry, and other more evangelical denominations, including other Methodist societies, took advantage of their weakness.

Henry Lauton illustrated this problem in March 1841 when he reported from the Stanstead circuit that 'persons from the United States calling themselves preachers make frequent invasions upon our circuit and disturb the people; no less than four of these have annoyed us since we came here.' For example, in one of the more distant locations, where the Wesleyans could preach only once a fortnight on weekdays, a Protestant Methodist (who had been a Wesleyan local preacher) had arrived 'promising them more preaching and allowing them liberty or rather licentiousness.' As a result, the Wesleyan missionaries had been forced to withdraw. Another 'interloper' was an Episcopal Methodist preacher who had come to live with his father in one of the most populous places, and 'insinuated himself into the affections of his people partly by holding meetings in that and other places much more frequently than it was in our power to do, and partly by giving them "more liberty" than we could consistently with the character of the christian church.' He had asked to be employed by the Wesleyans to preach on the Sabbath, had circulated subscription papers for the support of himself and his family, and 'without license baptized as many as he could persuade.' When Cooney and Lauton explained 'the impropriety and evil of such proceedings,' some members withdrew from the society, and 'many who regularly subscribed to our funds will not now give a cent.'[140]

Paradoxically, one reason the Wesleyan missionaries failed to develop a solid lay leadership within their extensive circuits may have been that religion and community were clearly seen to be inextricably interlinked in the Eastern Townships, as they had been in Puritan New England. Because power had been exercised largely at the local community level, denominational exclusivism would undermine community ties and influence. Such an analysis is supported by Lauton's March 1841 report from the Stanstead circuit:

> As the people are principally from the United States, and have brought with them their republican peculiarities, *they are not and I fear never will be British Wesleyan Methodists*. This will appear when I inform you that our excellent discipline is almost universally disregarded by those who consider themselves members of our Society. We have only one Lay-preacher, and over him we have no control, he preaches when he pleases, for other congregations as well as ourselves, even for those who oppose us; he receives subscriptions from the people; he is called by some 'a minister' and by others 'The Rev — although he can hardly read a chapter in the easiest part of the Scriptures. And if we move at all to correct any of these errors, we are said to be proud, tyrannical, etc., etc.

Lauton also complained that many people did not attend the class meetings regularly, 'and others who occasionally come relate very little of their religious experience, doing little but exhort others:– the class papers are seldom used, although we supply the leaders with them, so that at the quarterly visitations we cannot tell who has attended or who has not.' In addition, the love feasts had to be held with open doors 'caused partly by different members of a family coming in the same vehicle to the preaching which is either before or after the love feast; some of these people are members of the society, others are not. The latter, if kept out, must sometimes stay in the open air exposed to all the contingencies of the weather.' Furthermore, people with no connection to the society 'consider it a part of their liberty to come to our 'feasts of charity,' and if we attempt to prevent them we are charged with destroying their Christian fellowship; and even many of our own members contend for such open doors. The same difficulties lie in the way of *meeting the society apart by themselves.* So that we can seldom address them except in the public congregation.'[141]

Stanstead was not unique as far as popular resistance to Wesleyan formalities was concerned. From the Compton and Hatley circuit, Benjamin Slight reported in 1847 that the local Methodists had a repugnance for what they called closed class meetings – that is, ones in which Baptists and other non-Methodists did not share 'an equal priviledge with themselves.' They pointed out to Slight that his predecessors had followed the open policy, and they insisted that 'the original intention was not to keep out any sincere Xns, but only to exclude the mocking, hypocritical Episcopalians – that it is Popery – that it has an injurious effect – that the Baptists are good men, & are as worthy to meet as they are.' In reply, Slight informed them that 'the establishment of Class-meetings was intended to be the basis of a Society or Church, & that the meeting in Class is the test of membership.' The sacraments and union public prayer were open to all Christians, but the class meetings were what distinguished Methodists from other churches. Slight also argued that the practice of open meetings 'contained the seeds of their own dissolution as a religious body, & has tended to their present deadness.'

Slight concluded that since non-Methodists could 'enjoy all our priviledges, they have no inducements to become members of the Church, & we can exercise no discipline over them.' He went on to lament that 'we have no Congregations of our own. The School House system militates against it. We may, in the first instance, visit a neighbourhood, & gather a congregation, but from that moment it is open to all. The Universalists, Millerites, Baptists, etc., etc. press in & vend their errors. We have no compact, regular & combined phalanx to carry out aggressive warfare. We have no sufficiently efficient Class-Leaders, Prayer-Leaders, or Local-Preachers ... The good seed is not sufficiently nourished & cultivated, & any good impressions are in a good degree lost ... It is like writing on the sand, or engraving on the liquid wave.'[142]

Six years later, in 1853, William Squire's biographer also concluded that the Methodist system 'is little understood and less practiced.' And in his memoirs Robert Cooney recalled of his three years in Stanstead that 'the people generally, are very exemplary in their morals, and steady in their habits, ... warmly attached to the Wesleyan ministers, and ... as generous in their efforts to sustain them, as any of our people similarly circumstanced are in other places.' Yet he concluded that 'Methodism was never properly established here, owing probably to the character and religious views of the original settlers, the greater part of whom came from the New England States. In doctrine they are sufficiently Wesleyan, but in many instances our peculiar institutions are not particularly admired.'[143]

Aware of their weak hold over the membership, many of the missionaries argued the need for greater pastoral care through weekly Sabbath services and Sabbath schools, but the WMS adhered to the tactic of spreading them thinly over large areas, and uprooting them every two or three years. Under these conditions, even those itinerants who were as conservative as William Squire had little choice but to resort to revivalism in order to maintain a foothold in their circuits. In short, between 1821 and 1851, the Wesleyan missionaries of the Eastern Townships operated on a borderland where they were caught between radical revivalism, on the one hand, and well-endowed religious conservatism on the other. It is not surprising, then, that they lost ground during the Millerite revival, and that the Church of England still outdid them in terms of membership numbers at mid-century. That said, it is important to note that Adventism ultimately failed to establish a strong permanent presence in the region, and the Anglican clergy also complained loudly about persistent non-conformity to their rituals. For the majority in the Eastern Townships who were of American origin, identification with a hierarchical, British-based church was still to be largely on one's own terms. Constructing Wesleyan Methodist chapels would eventually lead to a more exclusive denominational identity, though the ongoing American influence was reflected by their persistently classical design. Despite the lamentations of the Wesleyan missionaries, however, affiliation with their church did mean that a significant step had been taken towards assuming a new more conservative cultural identity north of the border.

Part IV

Postwar British Responses: The Anglicans

9

Building a Colonial Church

While there is no census identifying religious affiliation in the colony prior to 1831, it is clear that few of the settlers who migrated from southern New England to the Eastern Townships during the late eighteenth and early nineteenth centuries were Episcopalians. Furthermore, this was the era of the Second Great Awakening, when the pioneer settlements in the neighbouring hill country of Vermont and New Hampshire became centres of religious radicalism. Since the revivalist approach to proselytization was not compatible with Anglicanism, the Church of England would appear to have been at a considerable disadvantage on the northern frontier of American settlement. Many Canadian historians of religion have assumed, as did Clark, that membership in the Anglican Church was confined to what he calls the 'respectable' segment of the population.[1] Referring specifically to the Eastern Townships, Kesteman has recently written that the Church of England was 'mal préparée à une mission itinérante de prédication, car elle s'appuie sur des pasteurs résidants, qui doivent loger dans un presbytère distinct. Le système de la paroisse anglicane est donc peu adapté à un pays pionnier.'[2]

The fact is, however, that the Church of England was the largest Protestant denomination in both Upper and Lower Canada throughout the first half of the nineteenth century. In the Eastern Townships, self-declared Anglicans outnumbered their closest Protestant rivals, the Methodists, by more than two to one in 1831. Twenty years later they continued to be the most popular Protestant denomination in the region, albeit by a much reduced margin. While Canadian historians of religion have written a good deal about how the Church of England lost its quasi-official status in the Province of Canada by mid-century, the following two chapters will focus on how this denomination succeeded in becoming entrenched in such an unpromising environment as the Eastern Townships, and what the ramifications were for popular religious and cultural identity.

Missionary Recruitment

The Society for the Propagation of the Gospel (SPG) and Society for the Promotion of Christian Knowledge (SPCK) had been established at the turn of the eighteenth century as responses to increasing pressures from nonconformists in England and a resurgent Roman Catholic Church abroad. Doll writes that in addition to promoting the common interests of church and state, the two societies were characterized by 'a rigidly orthodox doctrinal stance, and a commitment to upholding a sacramental episcopalianism in the Church.'[3] The SPG missionaries who were selected to serve the Eastern Townships during the first half of the nineteenth century generally conformed to these High Church standards, though the Church of England's assimilating ambitions encouraged the bishops of Quebec to be somewhat flexible in recruiting clergy from the local population, including ministers from other denominations.

The conservative Jacob Mountain was less inclined to be as flexible in this regard than his successors, perhaps in part because he had a smaller population from which to choose. In 1800, when the Duke of Portland encouraged him to look to his own diocese for reinforcements, Mountain replied that while he had recently ordained two men without English theological training, locally born settlers were not suitably educated and there was still no institution in the colony to provide that education. The solution Mountain proposed to the governor general was 'a respectable, & effectual Establishment of the Church of England.' This step would not only 'go very near to unite the whole body of Dissenters within its pale,' thereby consolidating 'sentiments & interests' behind the government and sovereign, it would also facilitate the recruitment of clergymen:

> Where there is no hope of advancement, there can be little expectation of engaging the services of men of ability, & worth. Respectable, & useful ministers of our Church, will not easily be induced to fix themselves in the wilds of this Country without hope of emerging to such more convenient & more honourable stations, as their labours, & their merits, may be found to deserve.[4]

Despite Mountain's entreaties, the government felt that the Church of England had too few adherents to warrant granting it similar powers to the Roman Catholic Church. But the bishop did not remain entirely dependent on missionaries sent from England, for local candidates were assigned to study under various clergymen within the diocese. This pragmatic approach was described clearly and succinctly in 1821 by his son and secretary, Archdeacon George Jehoshaphat Mountain. The young Mountain explained to the SPG that without a divinity school the diocese was not in a position to train candidates for holy orders, yet 'the evil of leaving the people unprovided for is increased by the instability & want of religious attachments which ... prevail among them to a very considerable extent.' Those fluid circumstances could be 'turned to the account of sound religion & loyalty,' but only if the church took advantage of 'the only resource *upon the spot*' by accepting candidates from among '*irregular* persons who apply.'

George Mountain assured the SPG that strict requirements were enforced, and that the number who applied was greater than the number who were put forward for the missionary society's consideration (to be trained at its expense). His father had recently decided to exclude all former military men because of two unfortunate experiences, and because a number 'whose expectations in life were disappointed by the Peace concluded with America, have looked to the Church as to a refuge & maintenance.' Also excluded were the physically handicapped, for in 1824 a young man with a wooden leg was rejected as 'a lame and blemished sacrifice,' and because 'the effect in mounting the pulpit, administering the Eucharist, etc, etc. must be very bad.' To disguise the truth, the applicant was simply told that there were no vacancies because the SPG was continuing to send missionaries from home.[5]

As for recruiting clergymen from other denominations, Archdeacon Mountain explained that some of them had the same disregard for 'religious preferences' as the people in general. While promoters of the frontier thesis argue that the Church of England was too formal and too inflexible to adapt to new settlements, Mountain had a different view of the frontier's impact. He wrote that non-Anglican ministers

> have been divested, in some degree, of their religious prepossessions by their removal to this country – they are more at liberty, at a distance from their friends & from the connection in whose service they may be employed, to examine & to compare with impartiality; & the Lutheran, the Scotch Presbyterian or the American Congregationalist, finding that the

Church of England, from her connection with the Government, & from the pious bounty of the Society, affords means of greater usefulness to her Ministers & more respectable provision for the spiritual wants of the people, than the communion to which they belong, – are led to look more favourably, & thence more closely into her Constitution & her Ordinances; & this terminates very naturally in conviction of her superiority.

Mountain assured the SPG that 'reasonable and sufficient evidence of such conviction' had been required from all such candidates, and that none of those recruited had given cause for regret. He also added that they sometimes brought their congregations with them. At the same time, he made it clear that the bishop would be careful to limit such recruitment in order to 'sustain the character of the Church of England in the eye of the public.'[6]

Because requirements for the Anglican ministry were obviously somewhat relaxed in the colonies, a British statute declared in 1819 that candidates ordained there would not be able to officiate in any English or Irish church or chapel. Upon the recommendation of Oxford University, this principle was expanded in 1821 to ordinations by colonial bishops, even when they were in England. Jacob Mountain complained vociferously about the double standard: 'How can it be thought otherwise than degrading to the whole body of Clergy in the Colonies, – Bishops as well as Rectors, & missionaries – that persons ordained for those Colonies may be *excluded*, however deserving, from being employed, or holding preferment at home, by any Eng. or Ir. Bishop, who may happen not to be disposed to accept them?' Mountain protested that 'at present, many more persons, not being of either University, & usually called *Literate*, are ordained in England, than in the Colonies.'[7]

Wounded professional pride aside, Mountain was concerned that the restrictive egulation would diminish the supply of clerical candidates in the colonies: 'Many a man would pass his whole life contentedly in the Colonies, who yet would be miserable, if he were told that he shd. never go home.' Samuel Simpson Wood of Drummondville proved Mountain to be right, at least as far as missionaries from England were concerned. Wood, who claimed to have invested £1,500 in seven years of studies at Richmond School in Yorkshire and at Cambridge University's Trinity and Corpus Christi colleges, had been asked by Mountain in 1819 not to wait for ordination before sailing for Quebec. Only on his return to England for a visit in 1827 did Wood learn 'of the interdict which prevents me from assisting even a sick clergyman, a friend, or it may be a ci-devant fellow student.' He objected that 'it has caused me to appear in a questionable light, it has given rise to continual inquiries, and has wearied me with incessant explanations, which, after all, are unintelligible to many, and unheard of by many more.' After protesting that the regulation was 'unsound and anti-Catholic in its principle,' Wood reluctantly resigned as missionary so that he could be re-ordained in England. But he added that he would accept another SPG appointment, and he was subsequently assigned to Trois-Rivières.[8]

Bishop Mountain also chafed under the SPG's insistence that he wait for its authorization before ordaining anyone trained in his diocese, even to missions the society had already approved, though this was not required for missionaries sent from England. He protested that during the six- or seven-month interval required for approval of his recommendation for ordination, the opportunity could well arise for 'some Methodist Preacher, from the States, to step in, & secure a situation for himself.'[9] Despite Mountain's complaints, the Anglicans were more successful than the Wesleyans in recruiting clergymen from the local population. By the early 1840s the Anglicans also had the advantage of SPG financial support for the training by local clergymen of four students for the ministry,[10] a strategy superseded by the founding of Bishop's College in 1843. By mid-century, then, the diocese was in a position to begin supplying most of its own clergy, though several aging incumbents would have retired earlier had more funds been available for pensions, and had local contributions for their successors been more forthcoming.

Institutional and Material Support

Since the eighteenth century the British government's financial support for the Anglican Church in the North America had reflected its belief that to ensure loyalty to the mother country, the colonies should be modelled on the English constitution, with a close connection between church and state.[11] In the opinion of the 'dissenters,' however, the Anglican clergy were not supported by the people among whom they laboured. One Wesleyan missionary stated in 1821 that 'those who love money and a form only are generally desirous of receiving them ... The people do not like unconverted men in their pulpits whose life and doctrines are continually at variance, and who preach for a living.'[12] But many settlers obviously overcame their assumed distaste for Anglican formality, for twenty-one years later the Congregationalist Committee of

Danville reported that the recent visits of an Episcopalian minister were leading some to hope 'that they can get preaching ere long at less expense or without paying anything.' The local Congregationalist minister, Ammi Parker, also complained that, given the proximity of Episcopal preaching, 'I almost wonder that people hold upon ... the voluntary principle even as well as they do.'[13]

In addition to receiving state subsidies, the Anglican clergy collected fees for performing burial and marriage services, though apparently not for baptisms. James Reid of St Armand East stated in 1823 that only marriage fees were charged in his parish, and half the ten shillings went to the clerk whose sole duty was to give the responses during the Sunday services.[14] Each Anglican minister depended almost entirely on the salary paid by the SPG, which was a generous £200 a year after 1815, but it, in turn, depended largely upon a grant from the British government which was to be terminated in several steps from 1832 to 1835. In 1834 the British government agreed to extend its financial assistance for the clergy already resident in the colonies, and the SPG revised its salary schedule so that those appointed before 1833 were to receive £170 annually, and those appointed after that year would receive only £100 annually.[15]

As a result, in 1834 Bishop Mountain's successor, Charles Stewart, asked his clergy to raise money locally to compensate for the loss, explaining that where the reduced salary scale was 'confessedly inadequate to the decent and respectable maintenance' of a minister and his family 'according to his station in society, it will be expected that an addition shall be made to his income by the voluntary contributions of his hearers.'[16] To encourage members of the congregations to open their purse strings, Stewart made the SPG grant conditional on such a contribution, varying from £25 to £100 a year. Since it would be beneath the Anglican clergy's dignity to solicit or collect this money, however, and since the wardens could not do it alone, Stewart recommended that each congregation elect a vestry of four to ten people for the purpose. But he also hoped that this would be a temporary measure until the clergy reserves began to generate more income.[17]

Jacob Mountain had stated that he opposed having the clergy rely on local contributions for their support, presumably because it would undermine their respect and authority in the parish. And Mountain's son George, who succeeded Stewart as bishop of Quebec, made it clear that he did not rely on local promises of support or approve of Stewart's system: 'upon the whole, the voluntary system in that form in which the

Minister receives contributions directly from the people over whom he is set in the Lord, besides its being in itself vicious, proves always, in this country, either totally or partially, a failure.'[18]

The position taken by Mountain reflected his High Church leanings, but also the failure of Stewart's experiment, at least in part due to crop failures.[19] But the economic crisis did not prevent the British government from terminating all direct subsidies for the Church in Lower Canada in 1836, necessitating a further 25 percent cut in salaries.[20] Bishop George Mountain asked the governor, Lord Gosford, to endow a parsonage or rectory in each township, as well as in each missionary station in the seigneuries, but this he refused to do.[21] Mountain was subsequently authorized by the SPG to draw £500 to meet the cases of great distress among the clergy in the Quebec Diocese.[22] In 1840, when the SPG raised the salary of the new Quebec chaplain to £150 per year, Mountain objected that this long-time family friend and highly qualified clergyman should not be favoured over the rural clergy: 'I see more & more the ill effects of the poverty of the Missionaries, who, in point of respectability in the eyes of the world, are fast sinking below those of the Wesleyan connection.' The missionaries, some of whom had been reduced to taking in pupils or farming in order to survive, should be the ones to receive a raise from £100 to £150.[23]

Mountain realized that the missions would eventually have to become independent of the SPG, so in 1841 he appointed lay and clerical commissioners in different districts of Lower Canada to purchase parcels of land to serve as local endowments for the Anglican clergy.[24] Two years later a more decisive move was taken towards greater self-sufficiency with the founding of the diocesan Church Society whose goals included contributing to the salaries of clergymen as well as funding travelling missionaries. It in turn established district associations, composed of clergy and twelve annually elected laymen, as well as providing for parish subcommittees consisting of the local clergy and churchwardens.[25] The first lay committee of the St Francis Association was comprised of the most prominent members of the office-holding Sherbrooke-Lennoxville elite, including Judge John Fletcher, the Honourable Edward Hale, crown lands agent John Felton, Lieutenant-Colonel William Morris, and court clerk (and future sheriff) G.F. Bowen; there would be little change in the coming years.[26]

While the bishop required that half the funds raised for general purposes be forwarded to the central board, the St Francis Association requested that the ratio forwarded be reduced to a quarter, which subsequently became policy.[27] Referring to Upper Canada, Fahey states that placement of the funds in the hands of the central board and the district associations, rather than with the parochial branches, ensured that the voluntary system did not submit to localism. As a result, in contrast to Stewart's system, the independence and status of the clergy was protected.[28] This was the theory, but in practice a crucial concession was made to localism in the diocese of Quebec, for funds that were targeted by donors exclusively for local purposes were to remain under the control of the parish subcommittees.[29] The result of this provision was that, in the earlier years at least, the wealthier parishes were generally able to target most of the funds raised within their boundaries towards local church and parsonage construction.[30] Within the St Francis District, nearly all the money came from three of the nine parishes – Lennoxville, Sherbrooke, and Hatley – which managed to avoid heavy subsidies to the poorer parishes, just as better-off local school districts subverted government regulations by directing local taxes exclusively to their own schools.

For the St Francis Association in 1846, general contributions amounted to £99.0.10, and locally targeted funds were £35.0.0. Contributions then began to increase dramatically, but only for specified local projects. The St Francis Association increased its fund to £534.0.0 in 1849, and again to £829.6.10 in 1850. All but £81.11.10 of the latter amount was targeted at local church building projects. Of the £184.10.0 raised in Compton, £37.10.0 was for the new church site and £124.5.0 for construction. Only £2.15.0 went to the society's general revenues. Lennoxville provided nearly half the St Francis Association's fund for general purposes, but also targeted £127.10.0 for church lamps, an organ, and a new bell 'of superior tone & power.' In Sherbrooke, £75.0.0 went to the purchase of an organ, and £150.0.0 to church expenses and contingencies, leaving only £15.11.3 for the society. In Eaton, the congregation raised £112.10.0 towards the cost of the new parsonage, and £21.10.0 to paint and repair the church. Rather than contributing to the society's funds, Eaton received a grant of £20.0.0. Hatley, which was in serious decline, raised only £11.15.0; and Stanstead, which shared Hatley's minister, contributed £20.0.0 towards his salary and £5.0.0 to the society. Bury reported £8.0.0, but nothing was forthcoming from Kingsey, Melbourne, or Dudswell.[31]

Within the Missisquoi District Association, Joseph Scott of the recently established church in Brome reported in 1845 that £30.9.6 had been raised nominally for the Church Society that year, but effectively all was to go towards completion of the parsonage. He declared that, while the people took a personal interest in the welfare of the minister, 'scarcely anything could then have been done for the Church Society in *the abstract.*'[32] The District Association as a whole reported in 1850 that £91.19.9 was raised for the main fund, while £200 was contributed for local purposes. Subscriptions and donations had fallen short of the previous year's amount by nearly £500, which, Scott complained, would 'lower our character in the esteem of the Venerable Society for the Propagation of the Gospel, and induce them to think that their bounty would be better bestowed elsewhere.'[33] But the older James Reid of St Armand East complained privately that the assumption of a begging role was demeaning. He confided to his diary in April 1851 that 'it being my Master's business I was not ashamed to go collecting, but if it was for myself, they would not have seen me that day or any other.' While very critical of his parishioners' parsimony towards the support of the Church, Reid was angered a few months later when the Church Society rejected his request to keep all the year's collections to pay for the shingling of the parsonage. Informed that this was the parishioners' responsibility, he wrote that St Armand East had not once, to that point, asked for funds despite contributing to the society since its inception. Reid added to the minutes of the Missisquoi district, 'I think they have treated me unfairly,' but Judge McCord, the chairman of the Lay Committee, was not sympathetic. He argued that there were missions unable to complete their churches because of a lack of financial assistance: 'Now with these applications unsatisfied before us, shall we vote money for the repairs of Parsonage houses and outbuildings in one of the oldest and richest of the rectories?'[34]

Concerns had heightened in 1845 when the SPG declared that in permanently settled colonies grants would only be made in aid of contributions raised by the colonists themselves, and they were ultimately to be extinguished entirely. The following year, the SPG decided to focus its support on Bishop's College in Lennoxville so that Lower Canada could produce its own clergy.[35] But the future for the local clergy remained bright because additional amounts could be drawn from the clergy reserves fund which was generating £942 by 1839 and well over £2000 by 1848 when Church Society land produced £15,000. In 1846 the SPG had devoted the £812 it saved in salary payments (supplemented by £200 from the clergy reserves fund) to appointing ten additional missionaries in the diocese of Quebec. As a result, Anglicans in more established parishes were still expected to make financial contributions, and the Church Society accepted Mountain's suggestion that the district associations levy an assessment 'proportional to the resources of each mission.' The timing was poor, given popular resistance to the government's recently introduced school and municipal taxes, but Mountain declared that any parish that failed to raise the prescribed amount would lose its minister. Any, that is, except those with long-established clergy, for Mountain stated that exceptions would have to be made 'in some of the old Missions where clergymen have so taken root, with their families, that it would be ruinous to displace them' should their congregations fail to make the payments.[36]

In 1849 the SPG categorized parishes according to their ability to support their ministers, with most of those in the Eastern Townships required to pay half the amount. George Slack of Granby complained to the SPG two years later:

> oh if you could but see the materials, with w^h we have to work you would soon see that there was but a very faint prospect of the Society's expectations being realized of any well sustained effort at self support being put forth by our people – ... in practice – the Soc^y says to the people – You must raise so much. The people reply – we want to know, who is the man you are going to send us before we can subscribe – and after all the most that can be done is a subscription for *one year* – pledges beyond that time are valueless in most instances – and even as to the yearly subscription – there are to[o] many, who if they take offense, will repudiate – What clergyman with a family can feel safer resting upon such ground for their support?[37]

Westfall emphasizes the degree to which the Church of England had become a voluntarist institution by mid-century,[38] but, compared to the clergy of the other denominations, the Anglican ministers could hardly be said to be dependent on local good will or financial resources. The SPG continued to provide a matching subsidy up to at least £100 per year, with six of the longer-established incumbents each collecting £150 or more.[39] Not all the clergy felt that this arrangement was inadequate. The youthful Robert Lindsay of Brome recommended that the Missisquoi Church Society dedicate most of its funds to the appointment of more missionaries, beginning with Potton and Bolton Townships. Lindsay felt that £100 was an adequate income, but the more jaded James Reid advised him that, once he was married, his wife would soon let him know what to do with his salary. As for convincing the people to support a missionary, Reid declared, 'he would as soon get the snowbirds to do it.' Much to the older clergyman's annoyance, Lindsay's motion was, nevertheless, approved by the Church Society meeting.[40]

The fact that the government-funded SPG would guarantee a substantial salary to every minister assigned to a parish in the diocese represented a strong incentive for the bishops to sustain the missionary effort. The Anglican Church's missionary zeal persisted, however, long after external funds had begun to diminish. After visiting the 'very small cluster of houses' in Dudswell Township in 1848, Bishop George Mountain supported their request for an Anglican minister, reasoning that

> Nothing else but the Church, in her distinctive solidity, can stand in the tossings and agitations of opinion, which, on every side, are stirred up in the place; and here, as elsewhere in the townships, the more sober and reflecting members of the community would take refuge in her, as in an ark of safety inscribed with the name of Christ; while others of a susceptible temperament, weary at last of a succession of strange and irregular excitements, would find repose, once for all, in her bosom.[41]

In neighbouring Ham, Mountain preached to about twenty-five people, children included, and declared that 'There is a comfort, a great comfort, in carrying our ministrations to these churchless settlements in the woods, where at least they are kindly and thankfully received, and we have no cause to shake off the dust of our feet for a testimony against the people because they will not hear us.' Mountain recommended that a missionary be assigned to Dudswell, with Ham as a dependency, and the Church's travelling missionary, Thomas Chapman, was subsequently given this assignment.[42]

Sacralizing the Landscape

According to Bennett, 'in popular perception a denomination that invested resources in the construction of a church building was more inclined to remain or at least return to the community and would probably be more inclined to provide stable spiritual service.' The Methodist spokesman Nathan Bangs went so far as to state in 1844 that the desire to worship in a building specifically dedicated to that purpose was so strong that many people were prepared to change their denominational affiliation in order to do so.[43] The Church of England enjoyed a considerable advantage in this respect, due to its patronization by the powerful and wealthy in England as well as the colonies. Between 1815 and the early 1820s Charles Stewart was able to collect enough money in England to build a number of the first Anglican churches in the Eastern Townships. A second wave of church building began after 1839, the year that the SPG committed £500 towards that end, and it continued to make contributions for that purpose during the 1840s. Prosperous landowners also donated church sites and glebe lots, as in the case of the three Quebec women who, between 1839 and 1841, granted 1,500 acres to endow a church being built in Upper Ireland. Another donor was Major-General G.F. Heriot, founder of Drummondville, who gave 400 acres to the newly-established Church Society in 1843.[44]

The policy of erecting a physical structure as soon as possible reflected the Anglican belief that public worship should take place in a sanctified space, a space that would not be shared with other denominations. Noting in 1816 that there were twenty thousand Protestants in the region bordering the United States, but no churches except in St Armand, Charles Stewart's public circular promoting his English fund-raising campaign declared: 'In the early stages of society, in a newly settled country, it is of the first importance to introduce sound religion, and to afford to all classes an opportunity of worshipping God in public; by which vice and infidelity are checked, and habits of piety, morality, and industry are promoted.' According to Stewart, the people were willing to build churches, but unable to do so without financial assistance. Neglecting to mention that relatively few of the settlers were Episcopalians (or even that they were Americans),[45] he excused the lack of Anglican churches in the Eastern Townships:

> When it is considered that twenty five years ago the greater part of this country was an uninhabited wilderness: that all the settlers in it were either labourers or poor farmers: that it was necessary to build houses for themselves, and barns for their stock and grain: that roads were to be made, and schools erected, and all this without the least assistance from any public fund, it cannot be a matter of surprise that there are scarcely any churches; and that in order to encourage the erection of them some foreign aid should be required.[46]

Stewart's campaign was launched when the archbishops of Canterbury and York, with the bishops of Oxford, Lincoln, Durham, London, and Carlisle, donated £62 5s. The subscription list printed in 1824 reveals the degree to which Stewart's project depended upon support from the British elite and clergy. Of the 697 subscriptions, fifty-four were by individuals with aristocratic titles and many others were by military officers; twenty were by bishops or former bishops; 167 were by clergymen; and forty-eight were by individuals associated with Oxford or Cambridge. Illustrating how heavily women were involved in religious charity, 186 donors whose gender could be identified were females, and the £100 donated by the Countess Dowager of Rosse was much greater than any other. The fund had already reached £2,547 by 1820, by which time it had supported construction of twenty-five churches, nine of them in the Eastern Townships.[47] It had also been extended to Upper Canada, which remained within the diocese of Quebec until 1839. Claiming that he had contributed £1,000 of his own money for churches in Lower Canada alone, Stewart petitioned Lord Bathurst for a grant of land as compensation, and received 2,000 acres in Shefford Township in 1821.[48] He went on to establish a second church-building fund which raised the impressive sum of £2441.[49]

If the Yankee settlers were characterized by their republican leanings, they also clearly had a practical streak that encouraged many of them to take advantage of such donations rather than make financial sacrifices for the support of a dissenting preacher and construction of a meeting house. But they would prove even less willing to supplement the Church of England's external funding. Bishop Jacob Mountain admitted in 1821 that he had found several of the churches (including those in Upper Canada) which had received the largest subsidies to be 'in a state more or less unfinished, &, in remote country missions, almost invariably destitute of some decent appendages, which the usage of the Church of England requires: such as a set of Communion Plate, a bell, a font, & even a proper Bible & Prayer Book, & a surplice.'[50] In Compton the Anglican congregation refused to purchase a stove for their church several years after it was built on the grounds that the school house was closer to the village, and the other denominations who used it on winter Sunday mornings left it warm for Anglican afternoon service.[51]

Because the buildings funded by Stewart were constructed shortly before neo-Gothic architectural design came to be considered the only proper one for Anglican churches, there was little to distinguish them from New England meeting houses. Holy Trinity, the church built in Frelighsburg in 1809 while Stewart himself served as the incumbent, was a roughly designed, unpainted frame structure, with high walls, wide square windows, and no tower or spire. The main entrance, at the side of the building, had a classical roof with Greek columns, and inside the fifty-five-foot by thirty-nine-foot building were seventy box pews with three aisles between them. A cupola with a little bell was added in 1812.[52] In 1874 an article in *Harper's New Monthly Magazine* referred to the 'high square pews placed at every angle to the pulpit,' and 'the old windows of seven by nine glass' as showing that 'a New England meeting-house can be adapted to the needs of the Church of England.'[53] It would not be replaced until 1880, outlasting the region's other early Anglican churches by many years (see illustration 7).

Of a similar design, the large wooden building serving neighbouring St Armand West was, in the words of George Mountain, located 'in a bleak place' one and a half miles from the village of Philipsburg.[54] The result, according to the incumbent in 1838, was that the average Sunday attendance in a congregation of 560 adherents was only ninety.[55] As for All Saints', the church built in Dunham in 1821 with the assistance of a £50 grant from the SPG, George Mountain later described it as 'very roomy, but ill arranged and unsightly,' It would be painted for the first time in 1834, and by the mid-1840s the exterior had rotted to the extent that it was not considered worth repairing.[56]

Further east in the region, the two original Anglican churches begun at opposite ends of Eaton Township in 1820 were also far from orthodox in style, for their communion tables were placed under the west gallery facing the backs of the congregations.[57] The arches atop the windows of the plain white clapboard church built in neighbouring Hatley in 1829 do make a slight reference to the neo-Gothic, but it was the positioning of the church on the village square beside the Royal Institution of Learning school that spoke most clearly to the Anglican Church's symbolic dominance of the village (see illustration 8).

The Sherbrooke church, which would not be completed until 1827, was also classical in design with heavy wooden pillars flanking the front steps.[58] The delay in construction was caused by the hesitation of British-born William Bowman Felton, who owned most of Sherbrooke's mill sites, to fulfill his promise to donate sufficient land for the church and burial ground.[59] As a result, nearby Lennoxville gained a head start in building a church and claiming the primary services of Ascot township's Anglican minister. The first service was held in it in 1823, but the contractor, Jason Wright, found that he could not sell any of the twenty-four pews he had been given in payment to complete the building. While the average price per pew was £15, he informed the bishop that he would settle for two thirds or even half that amount.[60] The incumbent of Sherbrooke and Lennoxville, Clement Fall LeFevre, reported that Wright was suffering from bad health and had no means of recovering financially from this 'unfortunate speculation.' He could therefore petition 'as an act of charity, but by no means as one of right' because, with the capacity to hold one thousand people, the Lennoxville church was much too large. LeFevre added that the expectation of a separate ministry there 'has acted most unfavourably to my usefulness.'[61]

The Lennoxville Anglicans attracted some sympathy from Charles Stewart, who wrote that if Lennoxville and Sherbrooke were to be joined, the latter should not be the mother church.[62] Archdeacon Mountain, on the other hand, was not impressed with Lennoxville's over-sized church, declaring in 1829 that it was 'out of all proportion to the numbers & resources of the Congregation.' He suspected that 'some of the leading people who engaged in the undertaking' were interested primarily in 'augmenting the value of property by planting a standard which shall be the rallying-point for a new Village.'[63]

Westfall claims that examples of medievalism were rare and tentative in the design of Upper Canadian churches prior to 1840, and Bennett states that the earliest known example of an overtly Camdian interpretation of medieval Gothic did not appear in the Ottawa Valley until the late 1850s. This is not surprising since the Cambridge Camden Society's public programme of Gothic advocacy did not begin until 1841 with the publication of *A Few Words to Church Builders*.[64] In Lower Canada, however, George Mountain began to promote the Gothic style considerably earlier. In 1829 he registered his disapproval of the former school used as an Anglican church in Drummondville, reporting that it 'is of a good size but it wants all the distinctive characteristics of a Church. The Windows are square, there is no kind of steeple or cupola, & all the wood-work within is of unpainted deal. These are considerations immeasurably subordinate to those which relate to the actual religious improvement of the hearts & lives of the worshippers, but it is impossible not to wish that the House of God should bespeak reverence in its exterior, & exhibit its proper distinctions to the eye.'[65] Mountain would be happier with the church planned for Stanbridge East that same year, when a contract was drawn up for a brick building at the considerable cost of £1372. The design featured a tower the same height as the church (for the later addition of a spire), and windows 'in the Gothic Order with one Venetian Window over the Altar.' On this same 1829 tour, Mountain also reported that construction had commenced on a brick building in the town of Richmond, complete with cupola, belfry, and arched windows.[66]

Decay of the hastily constructed Stewart-funded churches provided

Mountain with other opportunities to place his stamp on the region's Anglican church architecture. Plans to replace the old church in St Armand West with a new building located in the village became urgent in June 1843 when the steeple was catapulted by a stiff wind through the roof, causing 'much destruction in the interior.'[67] As with other Anglican churches in the Missisquoi area, the new St Paul's remained more classical in design than those being built elsewhere in the region by this time, for it was a plain rectangular building with high sides, but it did have large arched windows and a very tall steeple.[68] From nearby Dunham, Mountain reported in 1846 that a new church was to be built of stone, following a plain and simple design, but delays were caused by local resistance to the bishop's prohibition of pews as private property, another reflection of his High Church proclivity. A compromise was finally reached whereby the pews were assigned according to the amount of contributions made, and taking into account individual interests in the old church. The new church, measuring sixty feet by forty feet, was completed in 1849 at a cost of £1,100.[69] It has a distinct classical profile due to its high walls, relatively flat roof, sharp returns on the eves, and generally earthbound appearance. But it also has arched windows with tracery, a relatively large chancel, a window directly above the communion table, a vestry, and a tower to which a spire was added at some point after its construction (see illustration 9).

Meanwhile, Sherbrooke's population had grown to the point that by 1839 approximately fifty persons had applied for seats that were not available in the town's overcrowded Anglican church. A meeting resolved to sell it and build a larger one, with those in attendance subscribing £385 on the condition that amounts over £5 were to be partially reimbursed at 6 percent a year from the pew rental income. The new church was still under construction in 1843, partially financed by donations of £200 from the SPG and SPCK, £205 advanced by incumbent Lucius Doolittle, £100 from the most influential member of the local elite, Edward Hale, and £150 from his brother Jeffery in Quebec.[70] According to Bishop Mountain, the church was built of brick in a 'plain gothic' style 'with tesselate windows.' In short, it was 'a very respectable structure and well placed.' An illustration reveals that the church had high sides and a low-pitched roof, but also buttresses and spires on each of the front corners as well as a tall steeple.[71]

By 1840 the Lennoxville Anglicans were also seeking external donations for a new church because, according to one of them, the old structure was already 'falling to pieces and in the winter the cold wind penetrates its decayed walls to such a degree that in spite of our Furs and a large stove, we sometimes suffer so severely that the service is obliged to be shortened.'[72] A new church was under construction three years later, and in 1846 Bishop Mountain wrote approvingly that it was built of brick (Doolittle claimed that there was no suitable stone in the area), 'with lancet windows, and a square tower projected from the front, upon which it is intended to raise a spire.'[73] A later incumbent would state that 'the interior of the church was painted a dark brown, one little sentry box on each side of the Altar for vestries, a huge pulpit on the north side, and reading desk on the south side, a small pipe organ in the choir gallery over the west door.'[74] While the size of the pulpit may have reflected Doolittle's evangelical leanings, Protestant church interiors were usually both bright and austere because their worship priorities were focussed on reading and preaching the word of God.

It would not be in a town that the most ambitious example of neo-Gothic architecture would be constructed, but rather in a rather isolated location in Kingsey Township. A plea by George Mountain in 1839 resulted in approximately £230 being sent from England for this project, then two well-to-do farmers and land speculators began to compete with each other to have the church located close to them. One of them, according to the Reverend George McLeod Ross of Drummondville, had received plans from England which 'embracing as they do the florid style of architecture, ... would be far too costly for this country, and indeed workers could scarcely be found to do them justice. It will I conceive be most consistent with correct taste to avoid all attempts at any thing of the kind, and build a plain, neat and unpretending edifice.'[75] But Mountain appears to have vetoed Ross's objections, for he observed in 1843 that while the unfinished building was unfortunately built of wood, 'a material not in harmony with its stile of architecture; it exhibits a nearer approximation to correct Gothic than almost any other in the Diocese; and, what is a great rarity in this country, although necessary to the good effect of a building with any pretensions to such a character, the panes of the windows are inserted in the diamond form.'[76] Despite opposition from those favouring a site closer to the St Francis River, more money was forthcoming from donors in England, and the Kingsey church was completed and consecrated in 1846. Mountain reported that the interior had been 'fitted up with the wood of the butter-nut, than which nothing can have a better effect in the woodwork of ecclesiastical buildings – and it has a raftered open roof.' He was so impressed with its appearance that he sent a drawing to the SPG to be engraved.[77] While the Kingsey church is a modest structure by later standards, it does have high narrow windows, buttresses along each side, a steeple topped by a cross, and eight small spires on each corner of the building (see illustration 10).

Despite G.M. Ross's concerns about the design of the Kingsey church, he obviously looked to Mountain for advice, for he thanked the bishop in 1842 for a lithograph that he would use as a model for the new church in Lower Durham. According to the Reverend Thomas Chapman in 1845, the Anglicans of Sutton Flat had also 'waited until they got a proper plan of building' before proceeding with construction. Chapman neglected to mention that the Anglican initiative had been taken by an absentee proprietor from Frelighsburg in order to raise the value of his land. The final product, in Bishop Mountain's words, was 'a plain, solid, stone building, of moderate dimensions, with a tower in front, and pierced with gothic arches for windows.'[78]

Granby was another community where the Anglican Church was slow to become established. Here Mountain found in 1846 that the new church, although built of wood, 'has, with its whole premises, an English style and air about it, not at all usual in the Canadian Townships.' At a cost of $1,600, the church had been completed largely through the efforts of the minister, George Slack, who had raised money from friends in England.[79] Even though Slack was on the Evangelical side of the spectrum, his church was in the neo-Gothic tradition, and Mountain felt that the way it was 'finished and fitted up ... would afford a model for our country Churches in Canada.'[80] Mountain was also delighted with the design of the Milton church, which Slack was instrumental in building, reporting that 'if it were only of stone,' it 'would be an excellent pattern for our Churches in the woods.' In Mountain's words, a 'square embattled tower projected from the building,' the gothic windows were fitted with 'panes in the lozenge form,' and, in true neo-Gothic style, its unpretentious but 'ecclesiastical' interior had open seats instead of pews because Slack had insisted that there be no leased sittings of any kind.[81]

Mountain's frequent repetition of the word 'unpretentious' would suggest that he was not an advocate of the more ornate features of Gothic revival architecture for the rural and small-town churches of his diocese. His main aim was to ensure that they conformed to certain basic interior and exterior design principles associated with the Anglican service and philosophy. Young clergymen such as Thomas Chapman shared the same views. Referring to Dudswell Township in 1851, Chapman complained that 'We cannot forbear remarking how detrimental the assembling in schoolhouses is to the solemnity and decency of Divine Service – most of them being so constructed that there is not even room to kneel at the time of prayer.' Dudswell's most central school had, nevertheless, been 'fitted up with a decent reading desk, Chancel railing & Communion Table' for the monthly Communion service. In neighbouring Ham, according to Chapman, the fourteen families were 'chiefly Church people,' and they had 'proved their liberality & zeal for the cause (not by contributing money, for of that they have none),' but 'by fitting up a block building, erected for a schoolhouse, by boarding & battening outside, by lathing & plastering inside and by adding a spire & pinnacles, so that they now possess a decent looking structure, very church-like in appearance and suitable to the day of small things.'[82]

In contrast to the New England Puritan tradition, in which a church was a covenanted body of people rather than a building, public worship in a sanctified space was an integral part of the Anglican religious identity. That space should be aesthetically pleasing, while also representing tradition and stability. In a sermon preached at the dedication of All Saints Church in Dunham in 1849, James Reid advised the parish to imitate the beauty 'profusely scattered over your fields, your woods, and forests.' He added:

> even your swamps, the sides of your travelled roads, abound with all manner of beautiful ornaments. Look at the gay clothing of your woods and vales, and the sloping mountains up to their summits, of which many are yet untrod by the foot of man, washing their beauty on the desert air – take a glance at the plumage of thousands and thousands of the feathered tribes, altogether independent of the care of man, and then say, if you can, whether God has not regard to order, and beauty and harmony in his works.[83]

In a less poetic tone, George Mountain wrote in 1829 that 'A smaller Church well-finished, with all the decent appendages characteristic of the Church of England, such as a bell, font, altar cloth, surplice, etc, and with a respectable enclosure, is much preferable to a building ambitiously large & beyond the wants of the Congregation, which remains incomplete & perhaps encumbered with debt.' The type of building Mountain preferred would probably be more expensive than the region's first simple structures, built with the ambition of attracting large congregations. Half empty on Sundays, and of a secular design, these original churches were an embarrassment to George Mountain who was well aware that, in Vaudry's words, churches were 'cultural artifacts that conveyed a myriad of social, political, and religious symbols.'[84]

The Gothic revival had clearly not completely transformed the region's Anglican church landscape by 1850, when the newly ordained Bishop Fulford of Montreal made his first visit to the townships that lay within his diocese. Fulford wrote that he was 'very much pleased with the clergy,' and 'charmed beyond measure' with 'the most romantic & picturesque scenery,' but the churches were 'all of a *very* inferior kind, as to materials & style & ornament.'[85] Certainly, most churches were built of wood, and there is little mention of the stained glass which dramatically recast the interior space into what Finley describes as 'the form of an ancient English sanctuary.'[86] But Fulford was writing as a recently arrived Englishman, judging what he saw by Old World standards and apparently blind to how different the designs of the newer Anglican churches in the region were from those built earlier in the century. The landscape was becoming dotted with neo-Gothic churches, symbolizing the cultural expansion of the British empire.[87] There appears to have been little local resistance to this transformation, perhaps because much of the funding came from elsewhere, though some congregations did cling to a measure of control through pew rentals.

Organizational Structure

According to Clark, the failure of the Anglican Church 'to build up an adequate body of itinerant missionaries and to integrate an itinerant system into the regular organization of the Church,' were two of the greatest mistakes it made in the colonial era. To him, 'the inherent weakness of the Church lay in its general failure to depart from principles of church government which had developed out of very different circumstances.'[88] Aside from the fact that the Church of England was much more successful in the Canadas than Clark gives it credit for, he fails to appreciate that the Methodist itinerant system was itself the product of a densely settled environment with a well-established local lay leadership that could assume a religious role. Also, the fact is that most Anglican clerics preached at several places within their parishes rather than confining their services to one church, though there were limits to how far they could stretch their services.[89] Bishop George Mountain made this clear in 1836, when he reported to the SPG that James Lynne Alexander of Leeds was

> faithful & pious, & he divides his labours as he best can; but he experiences the same difficulty which is experienced by many others, servants of the Society: if he concentrates his exertions upon the head-quarters of his Mission, he leaves many out-posts neglected, & exposes the Church in his person to many complaints; if he attempts to spread his ministrations over the face of the surrounding country, his principal & immediate congregation suffer by necessary consequence, & no decided fruit & effect of the Gospel ministry among his people are seen any where within the limits of his charge.[90]

Furthermore, the Anglicans did take a leaf from the Methodist book when Stewart ensured, while on his first return to England, that 'serious persons of good character, who were disposed to do so, might read the Liturgy to their neighbours (where there is no Clergyman) on Sundays.'[91] To reach a broader territory, Bishop Stewart also convinced the SPG in 1829 that catechists should be appointed with the authority to act as lay readers.[92] Catechists were to serve two or more stations on a regular rotation and to establish lending libraries and Sunday schools, superintending the operations of at least one of the latter. Their chief role was to promote religious instruction of the youth, including the promotion of family prayer and Bible reading, but they could also read the burial service when a minister was not available. Also, during public worship they could read a selection from the church service, together with a printed sermon approved by the bishop or archdeacon. In 1832 Stewart asked for authorization to elevate a small number of catechists to the level of deacon without additional cost to the missionary society. His reasoning was that their exertions made people more eager for the services which they were not authorized to provide. Furthermore, local prejudices against the delivery of printed sermons acted as 'a bar to the acceptableness of the Catechist among people otherwise well disposed to profit by his ministrations.'[93]

There were apparently still no catechists in the Eastern Townships in 1832, but the following year W. Harvey, from Leeds, reported that he had opened three Sunday schools, and was holding public worship in two stations where the congregations were large.[94] In 1838 Bishop Mountain reported that Harvey's 'range of labours' was very large, and he had 'unquestionably been an instrument of much spiritual improvement among the people.'[95] Harvey was replaced by the Orkney-born Robert G. Ward. To prevent Ward from being attracted to some other denomination, the Anglican minister for Leeds, James Alexander, recommended that he be ordained despite his lack of education. Alexander attributed Ward's greater popularity than his own largely to the fact that he received a smaller salary, and lamented that 'it is common, both at home, & in the colonies to commiserate the case of the poor curates, & declaim against wealthy Bishops & rectors.' In addition, (contrary to regulations) Ward preached 'ex tempore,' and Alexander confessed that 'instead of envying his superior talents in public speaking, we ought to take shame to ourselves, & endeavour to emulate him.' Seven months later, a petition signed by 125 residents of Inverness was submitted in favour of Ward's ordination, but the bishop may have suspected his orthodoxy, for he never did become an ordained clergyman.[96]

Another catechist, the English-born Fred S. Neve, had been the curator of the diocesan SPCK depository in Montreal before opening a school in Philipsburg. Neve was effectively doing all the work of a minister in St Armand West between 1840 and 1843 due to the incumbent's ongoing health problems.[97] By 1841, however, Mountain had decided not to make any more appointments to the office of catechist.[98] But there were still deacons, such as the former Methodist, Captain Henry Evans of Kingsey, who was appointed to this position in 1844. The local Anglican minister, John Butler, reported that Evans's literary qualifications were 'not very much below mediocre,' but after nine months reading he might be able to pass 'a tolerable examination.' He knew some Latin, very little Greek, a good deal of the Holy Scriptures, and was 'not unacquainted' with Ecclesiastical history. Evans was also a regular attendant at church and Holy Communion, and, while Butler felt that 'he has not that decision of character so necessary in clergymen especially at the present day,' he added that 'he has in *Mrs Evans* an influence which would very materially tend to counteract any thing that might be in danger of misleading him.' Finally, Butler felt that Evans was likely not applying from pecuniary motives as he had enough land to support his family. His knowledge of the country, Butler felt, would make him 'a very useful missionary.' Evans became the assistant of the aging and ailing Charles Cotton of Dunham, where his arrival quickly reversed a gradual decline in Anglican strength. While Cotton reported in 1845 that there were only about three hundred in his congregation, Bishop Mountain preached to five hundred souls in August 1846, a much larger audience than three years earlier. There were also thirty-seven on the confirmation role as compared to nineteen on the previous visit, but Evans died within a year of his arrival.

The Church also resorted to travelling missionaries to a limited extent. Charles Stewart had been assigned to this role during the 1820s, and in 1835 the Society for Propagating the Gospel to the Destitute Settlers and Indians in Lower Canada was established. Its activities in the Eastern Townships appear to have been confined to a small number of visits in the Leeds mission, but more active in the region were the two missionaries appointed by the diocesan Church Society in 1845.[99]

In the final analysis, Clark is right in stating that the Anglican mission fell largely on the shoulders of a parish-based clergy, but he underestimates their messianic motivation and effectiveness. The Anglican Church also benefited from a stronger and more stable leadership than its Protestant rivals. Aside from Charles Stewart's crucial role even before he became bishop, George J. Mountain was indispensable to both his father and Stewart as archdeacon from 1821 to 1836, when he in turn became bishop. One of the archdeacon's most important roles was to help administer an episcopal see too extensive for the management of one man, and in this capacity he acted as the bishop's emissary, ministering to the more isolated settlements and checking the missionaries' activities, as well as encouraging their efforts.[100]

Despite their genteel British backgrounds, Bishop Stewart and the two Mountains did not shrink from the discomforts of regular visitation tours throughout the Townships during an era when travel conditions were arduous at best. The poor communications link between the townships west of Lake Memphremagog and those to the east was described graphically by Jacob Mountain during his episcopal tour of 1816:

> From St Armand to the river St. Francis, (a sort of zig-zag diagonal of all these townships), we travelled in waggons, over high mountains, rocks and roots, only exchanged, occasionally, for ... deep, black, swampy soil. Nobody would believe, before I tried it, that it could be so accomplished; but, thanks be to God, it *was* so accomplished, although we sometimes could not advance more than twelve miles a day, and though we ourselves thought the obstacles insurmountable.

Approaching seventy years of age, Bishop Mountain boasted to his son that 'I never took cold, though wet through on the water, and sleeping on the shores of the lakes, six times in a tent, and often in strange houses. I had preached at every place where I stopped, and found it practicable to hold divine service (four times, for instance, in five days), and made arrangements for the establishing of future churches.'[101]

British Tories though they may have been, the three successive bishops clearly felt they had to show some sensitivity to the democratic sensibilities of the American-origin majority in the region. One such occasion arose when Colonel Nickle, commander of the British armed forces in the region since the onset of the Rebellion, arranged for a military escort for the bishop in 1840. George Mountain wrote to his daughter that 'I should have been escorted all the way from Waterloo to Abbotsford & back, by mounted troopers – & should have come this morning (12th) after my return to Waterloo with a fresh escort till within a dozen miles of Charleston where about 30 troopers were to have followed me into the village, where again, I believe, some military honors would have awaited me.' But Mountain declined the honour, noting that 'I don't think it would have recommended the Church in the eyes of the township population to see the Bishop & his acting Chaplain scouring the country with dragoons as their attendants.'[102]

Conclusion

It would appear that the willingness of the Anglican Church hierarchy to adapt to local conditions, within limits, was an important factor in keeping it the first-ranked Protestant denomination on this frontier of largely American settlement. Perhaps the most important concession the bishops made was to ordain local men, including those of different denominational backgrounds, for crucial to the success of any church was the degree to which its clergy were able to establish a rapport with the people. But the major advantage the Anglican Church had over its competitors was the external funding of its clergy and churches, the construction of which left a distinctly unAmerican mark on the landscape. This support could be a double-edged sword, however, discouraging local congregations from a sense of commitment through personal sacrifice. To take one example, in January 1851 James Reid recorded in his diary that there was much discussion as to whether to repair the old church or build a new one:

> Talk however will effect nothing, and nothing can be done because no two persons can be found to agree in what should be done; and with the human materials we have in this Parish, especially in this Village, I have no faith to believe that any thing will be done. I have long foreseen this. They

have had the ministry free for the last 43 years, and they are so far from having learned their duty of honouring the Lord with the first fruit of their increase and prosperity as if they had never been taught the value of the Gospel.[103]

But Reid could not express these sentiments openly. While his diary criticized the unduly rosy picture painted in the diocesan history written by the secretary of the SPG in 1849, Reid reported to him in May 1850: 'My Congregation keep up very regular. The hateful stir about annexation has not troubled my parish or mission. I have a good Sunday School, and a Bible class of young exemplary persons, to whom I expound a Chapter of the New Testament &c every Tuesday evening. In this exercise we take much pleasure, and find it very profitable.'[104] This statement does not directly contradict Reid's diary entries, but it certainly presents a contrasting interpretation of the situation in his parish. In the following chapter, we will examine more closely the degree to which those in the Eastern Townships who claimed to be Anglicans actually conformed to the rules and regulations of the Church.

10

Messianism and Popular Response

The Sense of Mission

In his study of the Anglican Church in Upper Canada, Fahey argues that it held a strongly messianic outlook from the 1790s until disestablishment became a reality in the late 1840s and early 1850s. He also states that since the Church in Lower Canada was on the periphery of that colony's religious life, 'its clergymen were not driven by the same sense of mission that inspired their brothers beyond the Ottawa River ... Put simply, their major concern was not charting the course of their society's evolution, but survival.'[1] Thus, clergymen of essentially the same social, national, and educational backgrounds, financed by the same missionary society and directed by the same bishop until 1839, are said to have had two sharply contrasting outlooks. While Fahey's statement echoes the standard Ontario-centred excuse for ignoring Quebec when writing 'national' histories of the Protestant churches – namely that Protestantism was doomed there in any case – it fails to ring true as far as the Eastern Townships was concerned. Neither Protestantism nor Anglicanism were on the defensive in this region during the first half of the nineteenth century.[2]

The position of the Church of England was that, in return for protection and support, it had surrendered a degree of freedom and independence to the state, and was advancing the state's interests by teaching people to venerate order. It was natural, then, for the Anglican Church to see itself as the ecclesiastical branch of Britain's colonizing mission in British North America, at least until the era of responsible government and disestablishment in the later 1840s.[3] The Church of England's main instrument was the SPG which had been established to keep the European settlers within the fold rather than to convert the surrounding 'heathen' populations. But the great majority of the families were from a dissenting tradition, and their conversion was perceived to be crucial to retaining this region – like the rest of British North America – within the British Empire.

James Reid of St Armand East made this clear in 1839 when he argued that the appointment of a missionary to the border township of Sutton 'would greatly tend to preserve the people in their duty of allegiance and loyalty to the Government.' Christopher Jackson of Hatley echoed the same point in 1839:

> In Barnston, Bolton, & Potton, the only ministers they have amongst them are uneducated men of the methodist or baptist persuasion, principally from the U. States; & it is in such places, where ignorance, poverty, & irreligion prevail that disaffection to the Government chiefly manifests itself in these townships: whereas wherever an Episcopal Missionary is stationed, the people are found to be loyal, in such numbers at least, as to over-awe the disaffected.[4]

Finally, Bishop George Mountain reported to the SPG in 1841 that the site for the proposed theological college had been moved from the old and largely Catholic town of Trois-Rivières to the young and mostly Protestant Sherbrooke-Lennoxville area because 'it would be highly desirable to bring directly to bear upon the rising population of this new tract of country, part of which skirts upon the American frontier, the moral, religious & political influences of which the proposed Institution would naturally become a focus.'[5]

To those who challenged the exclusive right of one church to the clergy reserves, the reply was that not only would Anglicanism ensure loyalty and order, for these feelings and principles were 'vitally interwoven with the system of the Church,' but sectarian affiliation had become weakened on the settlement frontier, and denominational divisions were retarding the spread of the Gospel.[6] Referring to Upper Canada as well, Bishop Jacob Mountain argued in 1810 that 'a respectable, & effectual Establishment of the Church of England, would have the advantage of going very near to unite the whole body of Dissenters within its pale, & thus to consolidate that uniformity of sentiments & interests, that attachment to our Government, & to our Sovereign, & that community of zeal for the support of both, which the circumstances of the time so peculiarly call for.'[7]

In an essay written for a British publication in 1821, George Mountain engaged in similar wishful thinking concerning the American colonists: 'There never was a population more malleable, ... in terms of Religion than the mass of the Protestant population in the more nearby settled parts of this Diocese. They are very generally speaking, loose and disengaged from any strong religious preferences ... and ready to close with any overtures from Protestant bodies which are advantageously recommended and supported.'[8] Twenty years later, when the Millerite craze was at its height in the region, Mountain insisted further that the Church of England served as a barrier to 'the impetuous flood of fanaticism, rushing at intervals through newer parts of the country and those especially which lie along the frontier. Nothing else can stand against it. The irregular sects are frequently seen either to yield, through policy, and mix themselves with a stream which they cannot turn, or to be forcibly carried along where it leads them, and finally to lose the stand which they had held.'[9]

Impractical as this messianic vision may have been, it was not without some popular support, for in 1841 a petition from Brome with 107 signatures declared that 'the Inhabitants of this Township are divided into a great variety of Religious Sects or Denominations, and the undersigned humbly believe would more readily unite with the Episcopal Church than with that of any other if a Pious and Worthy minister of the Established Church was settled among them.'[10] In fact, the 1831 census does reveal that a high ratio of the Eastern Townships population failed to identify with any particular religious denomination.

While the pragmatic strategy of paying generous salaries to its missionaries, and providing most of the funding for the construction of local churches, was interpreted as simple bribery by members of other denominations, the Anglican Church clearly felt that exposure to its liturgy as well as its doctrines would make a profound impact on a population that had been prejudiced against all things British and formally ritualistic. The 1824–5 report of the SPCK expressed confidence that the people of the Eastern Townships, 'having arrived ... at some settled notions on the subject of Religion, may gradually be brought within the fold of the establishment, and the Church of God be built up, in all its beauty, in the desert places of the wilderness.'[11]

While the religious sects that were proliferating in the democratic society south of the border emphasized individual salvation and spontaneous communion with God, the Anglican emphasis, even for someone as moderate as Charles Stewart, was on communal rituals. To this end, in 1814 he published a lengthy collection of prayers to be used on a wide variety of occasions. Defending the use of forms for prayer in one of the sermons that introduced the collection, Stewart stressed their unifying effect as well as arguing that they would assist 'in carrying on our devotion decently and in order ... serving the Lord in fear, and rejoicing unto him with reverence.' To those who might object that 'as God knows our wants, we need not tell him of them, or ask for his assistance,' Stewart answered that the role of prayer was 'to make us sensible of our own wants and interests, and of our dependence upon him.'[12]

But Stewart's main aim with this publication was to promote family prayer, a goal which reflected an evangelical orientation as well as the fact that the family's social and religious role was particularly crucial on a settlement frontier with weak institutional foundations. In the first of the two introductory sermons, Stewart argued that 'family prayer gives dignity and importance of a sacred and fatherly nature to heads of families, and adds to their authority and influence in all their advice and commands. It contributes good order and regularity in a house in many essential points, by calling them and bringing them together in a decent and respectful manner at appointed hours.' The chief benefit, however, was to further the religious education of the children. Anglicans felt that the inculcation of religious faith and rituals at an early age was crucial, and that the family was in the best position to do this effectively. Stewart declared that 'family prayer is precept and example, instruction and increase in all righteousness, afforded and combined together more perfectly than can be embraced in any other mode of shewing forth good faith and works.'[13] This message would be repeated in much greater detail by Stewart's successor in St Armand, James Reid, when he published his 'Fireside' essays during yet another political crisis, the Rebellions of 1837–8.[14]

One major shortcoming that the university-trained Anglican ministers undoubtedly had in terms of popular appeal was the formal nature of their sermons. The Anglican combination of rationality and paternalism was nicely summed up by Charles Cotton's sermon on the resurrection in which he simply declared that the possibility 'that a number of persons of sound understanding, & honest character, should unanimously combine to attest & support a falsehood, in opposition to all their interests and prejudice ... would be as astonishing & as strictly miraculous, as any interruption or violation of the common course of nature.' Jasper Nicolls, principal of Bishop's College, went still further when he admonished his congregation in 1845 that they came to church to pray, not to hear sermons. But James Reid took his sermons seriously enough to consider publishing them, and Richard Whitwell left a collection of 196 that he had written between 1819 and 1854.[15]

The problem, in the view of the Anglican clergy, was that the exercise of sermonizing had been debased by the dissenters. Reid complained in 1839 that if the local preacher 'can pour out a torrent of words, which every native of America can do much easier than to hold his tongue, he is sure to obtain credit for religion, talents, and gifts with which the regular ministers of God's word can never cope in the estimation of that stuff which constitutes our society.'[16] But apparently not everyone appreciated *ex tempore* preaching, for in 1849 Reid noted privately that the Stanbridge congregation had complained that the sermons of the former Methodist preacher, James Jones, 'are frequently interlarded with stories and unprofitable anecdotes, but that when he keeps himself to the scriptures he is very good.'[17]

Disdainful as the Anglican clergy may have been towards the religious enthusiasm displayed by their more evangelical rivals, they were not unaware of the need for religious zeal. While touring the Eastern Townships in 1829, George Mountain wrote that the missionaries must be 'exemplary in their conduct & faithful in dealing out the breath of life; awake themselves to the awful and glorious truths of the Gospel & deeply concerned to excite the same regard for them in others.' Mountain described for his wife the close rapport he himself felt with the settlers at a social gathering in the back part of Melbourne:

> It was a very humble cottage but there were plenty of hot cakes & a most cordial welcome, which with the opportunity of a kind pastoral conversation with people who rarely see a clergyman & gladly avail themselves of it, made me feel happy as a king. I have indeed often felt that if I had not other duties marked out for me, I could gladly devote myself to such scattered sheep as these about the country, & I am well-persuaded that a clergyman who would give himself to the work, & engage at once with kindness & zeal in guiding & gathering them together, would decidedly fix them by degrees in regular habits of religion & compliance with all the ordinances of the Church.[18]

A good deal depended upon the personality of the minister. In some respects, Charles Cotton was the stereotypical Anglican curate with his lack of evangelical zeal and his concern for external appearances and comforts, and in 1823 he earned a sharp rebuke from Charles Stewart, then serving as ecclesiastical commissary to the bishop. In a message to Cotton's Dunham parishioners, Stewart wrote:

> I advise you to state that you feel it to be your duty to yourselves, your families, & the Church, to represent to his Lordship the low estate of the interests of the Church in this township in consequence of the Reverend Mr. Cotton's inattention to the performance of his duties; that his remissness in visiting the people in general & the sick in particular, & in affording them spiritual comfort and advice, & his frequent refusal to attend funerals, have given great & general dissatisfaction: that his refusal to bury the corpse of a young woman, in November last, after it was brought to the Church, he being in the immediate vicinity of the Church, on the plea that she had been baptized by a Minister of the Dissenters & not in the Church, alleging that he had orders from your Lord^P not to bury persons so baptized, had hurt the feelings of every one who attended the funeral, & caused most of the people, since that time, to absent themselves from Public Worship: that owing to these circumstances & other grounds of discontent arising from the conduct of Mr. Cotton & the deficiency of his ministerial services, a Stove has not been procured, & the Church has not been used during the winter; that its use & the interests of the Church in this place are in a measure destroyed: that you are sorry to trouble his Lord^P, or to injure the character or the feelings of Mr. Cotton, but that your concern for the Church, & your own best interests, oblige you to make the above statement to throw yourself on his Lord^P's candour & mercy, and that you humbly request his Lord^P to take your memorial into consideration.[19]

James Reid delivered Stewart's letter to Dunham, leaving it there to serve as a petition 'for copying, signing, and forwarding,' but he reported that 'after all their fuss, when it came to the point, I believe they became faint-hearted.'[20]

Four years later, in 1827, Stewart expressed greater satisfaction with Cotton, reporting that the Dunham minister 'appears to have taken much pains of late,' having presented sixty-one persons for confirmation.[21] Cotton admitted that the number of Anglican adherents had declined slightly 'arising from the impetuous altho' blind & ignorant zeal of some members of the Methodist laity (we believe their present Clergy may be acquitted of this charge) and this alienation of some members of our Congregation has been effected by exciting & confirming prejudices against our National Church, leading greatly to produce false and unjust impressions of her character, as possessing the form, with but little indeed of the power of godliness.' Some of this 'ill will, violent hatred and animosity' against the Church of England had subsided, but Cotton was not optimistic about an increased 'preference for our own or any other national Church.'[22]

Despite the antagonistic tone of his report, Cotton began taking Stewart's conciliatory approach to heart, for he wrote in 1830 that his policy of 'avoiding religious controversial subjects with the numerous Dissenters in this place, and its vicinity, seems to have operated very beneficially, in allaying those strong animosities, which had so long subsisted.' In February 1836, he claimed that, due to 'our endeavours to promote Christian peace and a spirit of brotherly love towards all who differ from us in religious opinions, the attendance at the Church, of those who properly belong to the Methodist Society, has increased.'[23] In 1843, Bishop Mountain reported meeting a sizable congregation of three hundred in Dunham, though James Reid of St Armand noted in his diary that 'Mr. Cotton, honest simple man, was in the habit of going from house [to house] to engage people's attendance, on that day, in order to make a respectable appearance.'[24] Mountain was aware, however, that Cotton's 'very feeble health' had caused 'great interruptions of his public duty,' leaving the congregation to be held together by a lay reader.[25]

The English-born but American-raised Joseph Scott of the new Brome mission subsequently took over much of the work in Dunham, where he was transferred after Cotton died in 1849. The bishop reported that Scott was 'a very laborious, zealous and successful Missionary,'[26] but the number in Dunham who declared themselves to be Anglicans was considerably lower in the 1852 census, when they were 996, than in the one taken in 1831, when they had been 1,237. Much of the loss was to the Methodists, but the number of active adherents had probably not changed much, and Dunham still had the largest number of declared Anglicans outside Ascot Township.

As we saw in chapter two, the contrast between Charles Cotton and Charles Stewart illustrates how dangerous it is to generalize about the 'typical' Anglican clergyman. After returning from his fund-raising trip to England, Stewart decided to move from St Armand to the well-populated area east of Lake Memphremagog, which was yet to be served by an Anglican clergyman. He chose Hatley in 1818, perhaps because of its central location.[27] Stewart wrote to his sister during his first year in this parish that 'I have got not only to make people Christians, but also Churchmen, for they are in general prejudiced against our Church, and imbued with Baptist and enthusiastic notions.' He added, however, that 'my experience suits me for the business; and I do not after all mean to say that my situation is an unpleasant one.' According to a later report by Stewart, 'the people had built a place of Worship without deciding to what Sect it should be appropriated, but upon my removal thither as a Missionary of the Society, they made it over to the Church of England.'[28] But the church had been far from complete on Stewart's arrival, for he gave the parish £100 from his subscription fund and loaned it an additional £150, trusting that the SPG would add £50.[29] Though he was ambitious enough to wish to succeed Bishop Mountain, who was anxious to retire, Stewart continued to live in what a visiting George Mountain described as a one-room garret. He spent three days each week visiting and exhorting from house to house, and Fridays were devoted to meditation and prayer in his room, with a single meal restricted to potatoes and salt.[30]

Rather than becoming the permanent incumbent of Hatley, Stewart was appointed in 1819 to be the bishop's ecclesiastical commissary, charged with opening new missions throughout the diocese, and given full power to regulate those already established. Stewart informed his sister that 'My being single is a great advantage to me as a Missionary on a large scale. This consideration indeed chiefly determines me to continue so ... I am always ready to go or to stay anywhere for a long or a short time, and no place, and every place is my home.' Because he and his servant could live on £250 a year, Stewart was able to dedicate the remaining £400 of his annual income to 'public and private beneficial purposes.'[31]

While he enjoyed strong material and political advantages over other missionaries in the Eastern Townships, including his fellow Anglicans, Stewart's popularity and success clearly reflected his extraordinary dedication and spirituality, attributes which Canadian historians have generally not associated with the Anglican clergy. By confounding the stereotype of the complacent and indifferent Anglican cleric, by recruiting local non-Anglicans (including the Congregational minister of Compton) who would become long-serving parish clergy, and by establishing a material foundation through the funding of a number of church buildings, Stewart was perhaps the most significant factor in the Church of England's firm entrenchment in the Eastern Townships, particularly in the southwest. Had he not begun to divert his energies to

Upper Canada after 1819, Anglicanism would undoubtedly have gained a stronger foothold in the townships east of Missisquoi County.

It is difficult to judge the validity of Clark's assertion that the Anglican centralization of authority, combined with inadequate supervision, discouraged a spirit of individual initiative and zeal,[32] but it is somewhat contradictory to claim that the Anglican clergy had both too little independence and too much. Also, the Wesleyan preachers were themselves far from independent as long as they relied on funds from their missionary society and were required to change locations every two or three years, yet they had no bishop, archdeacon, or ecclesiastical commissary to inspect their efforts or offer encouragement. Furthermore, the Anglican missionary impulse was still alive in 1850 when John Carry visited the Irish labourers (most of whom were Catholics) on the St Lawrence and Atlantic railway line, then nearing Sherbrooke. Despite the violence (often unfairly) attributed to these workers, Carry reported that 'they were remarkably attentive and devotional in their conduct, and very thankful for my services, earnestly requesting that I might come again.'[33] The railway that these workers were building may have ended the region's external isolation, but internal travel could still present challenges, as Carry's description of trying to reach Hatley after a late December snow storm illustrates:

> we travelled in the day with great difficulty nine miles, and then horse and all were glad to rest. Next day we started through the unbroken snow, which was of extraordinary depth, and having gone 3½ miles, on a road which we had not before travelled, we became alarmed at our position. We had been 4 hours going this distance, and, as well as the horse, were perfectly exhausted. We determined on returning to the Tavern we had left; but, after proceeding one mile, I was overcome with fatigue, and Mr. Boyle, having unharnessed the horse, rode back to send a fresh one for me, I meanwhile covering myself up in my sleigh, and all dripping with perspiration. After 2½ hours I was relieved.[34]

Church Adherence, Attendance, and Communion

Many of those in the Eastern Townships who identified themselves as Anglicans resisted conformity to certain Church rituals. Indeed, many identified as Anglicans by the state census appear not to have attended church services at all, for assuming an affiliation with the Church of England cost nothing, required no strong spiritual commitment, and signalled conformity with the state's desires. Thus, Charles Cotton's estimate of 469 Anglican adherents in his Dunham parish in 1827 was very modest in comparison with the 1,237 (of 2,220) inhabitants of Dunham Township who declared themselves to be Anglicans in the official census four years later. Similarly, David Robertson of Stanbridge Township reported in 1833 that the 1,170 Anglicans recorded in the census two years earlier were largely a fiction, for no more than one hundred had been baptized. The average church attendance at Robertson's Bedford church was 140, and at St James (Stanbridge East) it was only sixty-five.[35] G.M. Ross of Drummondville made a similar comment about the 1852 census, stating that number of Anglicans reported in his jurisdiction was not accurate because 'it is well known that there are those who have so returned themselves who appear not to care whether they ever see the inside of a Church from one year's end to the other; and who seem to cloak their indifference to religion by a mere tacit declaration of adherence to a Church which is considered respectable, and their nominal connexion with which costs them nothing. My ministry being without charge is very generally availed of by all those within reach who go under the name of Protestants.'[36]

Not only did the clergy not recognize all of those who identified themselves as Anglicans to the census enumerators, but many of those the ministers did report as adherents were not full communicants. Ross reported in 1833 that there were approximately 795 Anglicans (the 1831 census reported 882) within his charge of Grantham, Wickham, Durham, Kingsey, Simpson, and Wendover, which was certainly a large territory for a settled Church of England minister to cover. Not surprisingly, perhaps, many of these were wavering, and Ross reported only sixty communicants. Most of those who had been Presbyterians appeared to be genuine converts, but he did not trust the Methodists who called themselves members of the Church of England, 'seeing no difference.' Ross charged that 'they are mostly extremely ignorant & uneducated people, governed by impulse & *animal passions*, in many instances, fit materials for plausible & pretending Preachers to work upon. *They* cannot be depended upon, for could they find any Preachers to humour their fancies & make them pleased with themselves, they would probably refuse "to walk with us".'[37]

In his parish report for 1851, John Carry of Leeds stated that there were sixty-three adherents in the neighbourhood of the Leeds village church, another fifty on the fourteenth range, and two hundred in the region of Lambly's Mills (Kinnear's Mills). Of all these adherents (and the 1852 census listed the much higher number of 545 Anglicans in Leeds Township), only thirty-five were communicants. The ratio of communicants to adherents was much higher in the neighbouring mission of Inverness and Upper Ireland, for Samuel Hoare Simpson reported 110 adherents and forty-five communicants in the former church, and eighty adherents and fifteen communicants in the latter, but this was not the norm in the Eastern Townships.[38]

Furthermore, many of those identified as communicants failed to partake in the Lord's Supper on a regular basis. Charles Fleming of Shipton and Melbourne reported in 1838 that the number of communicants had doubled to one hundred since four years earlier, but the average number actually taking Communion at any one time had changed little, varying from twenty to forty.[39] The small numbers were not for lack of urging, at least on the part of Lucius Doolittle of Lennoxville and Sherbrooke. The recent English immigrant, Lucy Peel, recorded in her letter-diary in 1833 that 'Mr Doolittle is indefatigable in his duties as a Clergyman, he calls on the families before the Sacrament requesting their attendance and last Sunday in his discourse, he hoped all would remain, even if they did not partake of the Holy communion, hoping that the solemnity of it would induce many to wish to prepare themselves to take it next time. I am sorry to say many persons left notwithstanding all he said.'[40]

Most of the clergy appear to have administered communion only four times a year, perhaps in deference to the puritanical sensibilities of their parishioners. G.M. Ross of Drummondville appeared to share the same reservations, at least on their behalf, for he reported in 1851 that he would like to introduce monthly Communion but he had been 'restrained by the fear that such frequency might tend to lessen among the more ignorant and unlettered the veneration in which the holy mysteries should be held and cause a negligence in the duty of self examination & preparation. The people generally speaking being of those who are to be fed with "mild & not with strong meat".'[41]

In most of the parishes, then, the majority of those who claimed to be Anglicans actually did not conform to the Church's most basic regulations. Disinterest in formal religious affiliation was, perhaps, the main explanation. For example, Christopher Jackson reported in 1831 that after the original Hatley church was transferred to the Baptists, and a new Anglican church built in the village of Charleston, those who had not sold their pews in the old church or purchased in the new 'prefer attending Divine Service in the former, where they have property, when an itinerant preacher attends it, w^h is about once in five or six weeks.'[42] But hesitance to be confirmed and take Communion also suggests that these steps were not taken lightly in the minds of the Eastern Townships population. The transition to what was, in many respects, a Catholic tradition would not occur within one or, in many cases, two generations.

Sunday Schools and Catechism

Faced with a population that had, for the most part, been raised in a dissenting religious tradition, the Anglican clergy tended to place much of their hope in the Canadian-born generation. Sunday schools offered the best opportunity for indoctrinating youths with Anglican beliefs, and James Reid of St Armand boasted in 1823 that he had established one 'conducted purely on the national system, by a person who understands it well.' Reid was presumably referring to the system devised by the recently established Sunday School Union Society of Canada. Within a year his school had ninety-five scholars, and an average attendance of fifty-four. The classes clearly served a serious pedagogical function, as Reid reported that 'the time is occupied, after commencing by prayer, in reading, spelling, reciting portions of scripture, and catechising.'[43]

But efforts such as these would be frustrated by the popular preference for interdenominational classes. Charles Cotton apparently made little effort to resist this preference. He reported in 1824 that a Sunday school had been established in Dunham in response to the Methodist offensive there: 'This plan, besides the good effect which it must produce in supporting orderly behaviour, restraining habits of idleness and vice, among the younger part of our people on the Sabbath, will it is really hoped, have the additional good effect of lessening religious prejudices, which are among the greatest obstacles that we have to encounter.' Ironically, nine years later, Cotton made it clear that the Sunday school had been a joint Anglican-Methodist project, and left the impression that the recent amicable separation had not been his idea.[44]

The problems were somewhat different in peripheral areas of more recent British settlement. John Kemp of Bury reported in 1851 that only one of the three churches he served had a Sunday school in operation, due to a lack of children within reach of the other churches, as well as suitable teachers. Similarly, John Carry reported in 1852 that there were not enough Anglican children in the vicinity of the Leeds village church to operate a Sunday school, and he had been unable to find suitable teachers for other areas where 'there is a great need, & a large number of children.'[45] Even in the older community of Drummondville, many families were said not to be able to dress their children adequately to send them to Sunday schools as late as 1851. The more urban areas had a distinct advantage in this respect, and in 1851 Isaac Hellmuth of Sherbrooke reported 150 Sunday school students. That same year Lucius Doolittle of neighbouring Lennoxville reported one hundred attending four classes 'in operation as teachers can be provided.'[46]

But Sherbrooke and Lennoxville were exceptional cases, and the failure to establish more Anglican Sunday schools presumably had an impact on the number of confirmations. In 1833 Charles Fleming reported for Shipton and Melbourne – where the only Sunday school was no longer in operation, allegedly due to a lack of competent teachers – that he did not instruct the youth in catechism during the service because it was objected to by the people. He intended to do so, however, immediately after the Sunday service had ended. Fleming was forced to take up teaching a public school the following year in order to supplement his salary, and he reported in 1838 that he taught catechism in this school every Saturday. There was still only one Sunday school in 1851, but Fleming's successor, D.D. Falloon, also held special meetings to teach catechism.[47]

Without regular Sunday schools, then, the teaching of the catechism became largely the clergy's responsibility, but this was not always fulfilled. David Robertson of Stanbridge reported in 1833 that he had not yet had a chance to catechize the youths because most of them attended the Sunday school established by the dissenters.[48] George Salmon of Shefford stated the same year that catechism could only be conveniently taught on Sundays, when he was too busy. Consequently, there had been no confirmation service since 1827, and only twelve were now ready for it. Five years later, in 1838, Salmon was still not instructing the youth of his parish in the church catechism. Samuel Simpson of Inverness and Upper Ireland made the same admission in 1851.[49] Christopher Jackson, on the other hand, wrote in 1838 that he occasionally instructed youth in the catechism in the Charleston church, where there were twenty-one students attending a Sunday school operated on Church principles. Bishop Mountain confirmed thirty people in Charleston five years later, in 1843, when he reported that the Sunday schools were 'small and interrupted efforts.'[50]

In short, like their Wesleyan Methodist counterparts, the Anglican clergy were largely frustrated in their attempts to encourage exclusivist Sunday schools. The result was obviously to limit opportunities for catechization and confirmation, although Charles Cotton, for one, distributed catechism booklets to the parents in his congregation so that they could teach their own children. Also, Charles Fleming was not the only teacher to include the Anglican catechism in the week-day school curriculum, for James Reid reported that it was taught in St Armand's Royal Institution schools.[51] When he first arrived in Hatley in 1831, on the other hand, Christopher Jackson found that, 'owing to the different religious tenets of their parents,' there was no religious instruction in the local Royal Institution schools, except when teachers, who were mostly from the United States, happened to be religious. Then, 'the ex tempore kind of prayer & instruction they use, to say the least of it, preoccupies the tender mind & enlists the prejudices of the children in behalf of Dissent.' As an official visitor of twenty-one schools, Jackson insisted 'on the great importance of every child [...] committing to memory the Lord's Prayer, the Creed, & the 10 Commandments; & as an inducement to the children to learn the other parts of the Church Catechism, I have offered two prayer Books & a few Tracts, as rewards, to those who say it the best in each.'[52] But many people resented the Anglican influence over the Royal Institution schools, and the Anglican clergy would have less influence in the Assembly schools that began to eclipse them after 1829. James Reid did report, however, that the catechism was taught in even some of these schools in his parish.[53]

Baptism and Godparenting

While one needed to learn the catechism and be confirmed by the bishop in order to become a full member of the Church of England, the first step in that direction was baptism, and the Anglican clergy found that popular notions concerning this ritual often conflicted with their own.[54] In 1810, soon after his arrival in St Armand, Charles Stewart asked Bishop Mountain if he could accommodate the wishes of a 'respectable man' who wished to be baptized by immersion. Stewart explained that 'the errors of the Baptists even on points of the first importance I often find troublesome with persons not belonging to that Sect.' Mountain's reply was that baptism must be performed in the church and at the font only. The man in question 'either means to be bonâ fide a member of the C. of E., or he does not. If he does not, there can be no reason why he sh^d receive baptism from one of its ministers; if he does, & thinks himself already wiser than his teachers, he can not be in a fit frame of mind to be received into that church.'[55]

Stewart was not alone in reporting popular preference for adult baptism, though Samuel S. Wood of Drummondville reported in 1826 that 'the prejudices against Infant Baptism which I at first found to prevail among a considerable part of the American population appears now to be fast losing ground.' Christopher Jackson submitted a less optimistic report from Hatley in 1830, when he claimed that five-sixths of the local people were unbaptized, with some being indifferent and others entertaining 'the wildest notions of being born of the Spirit.' Edward Cusack also observed in Brome in 1834 that the Freewill Baptist preachers 'have succeeded in frightening the people against baptism so effectively that when I speak to an adult about being baptized the answer I invariably get is this, "I am not good enough".'[56]

Baptism was presumably a legal requirement in Lower Canada, since there would otherwise be no certificate of birth, yet the clergy of most denominations did not gain the right to keep parish registers until 1834. It would seem to follow, then, that the parents of many of the infants baptized by Anglican ministers prior to that time did not consider themselves to be Anglicans. This might help to explain why there was considerable parental resistance to having infants baptized in church – resistance that the Anglican clergy generally felt compelled to give in to. In Dunham, Charles Cotton wrote in 1833 that he baptized only in church except when the infant was very ill or the family lived far away or lacked 'decent clothing.' But in neighbouring Stanbridge, David Robertson reported the same year that he felt he had to baptize wherever requested to do so, and Charles Fleming of Melbourne and Shipton also admitted that some baptisms were administered privately.[57] Furthermore, this popular pressure continued even after other denominations gained full civil recognition, for Fleming followed the same practice in 1838, and, in Shefford, George Salmon reported the same year that he frequently administered baptism in private on the grounds that it was not convenient for the parties to attend church, where there was no font in any case.[58]

Elsewhere, however, slow progress was evidently being made towards church baptisms. In 1838, Hatley's Christopher Jackson wrote that he christened children at home 'rather than suffer them to remain unbaptized,' but, five years later, he claimed that he did so only 'occasionally when people object to bring [sic] their children to Church.' There had apparently never been any resistance to church baptisms in British-settled Leeds, and D.D. Falloon reported from Melbourne in 1851 that he almost always baptized in church.[59] In Lennoxville also all baptisms reportedly took place in the church by 1851, though, like most others in the region, it still had no baptismal font.[60]

Even more difficult for the Anglican clergy was to convince the members of their congregations that infants being baptized needed to have godparents, commonly known as sponsors at this time. Charles Stewart reported in 1810 that it was sometimes impossible to find three suitable sponsors for a baptism because the promises required of them 'are generally regarded here in a very difficult point of view.' Reasoning that the 'Primitive Church' had allowed the use of parents as sponsors, and that the Anglican Rubric did not exclude them, Stewart had resorted to this contingency in some cases. Bishop Jacob Mountain replied tersely that the twenty-ninth Canon expressly forbade people from acting as baptismal sponsors for their own children, but this practice became commonplace throughout the region.[61]

The available documents do not indicate exactly why godparenting was resisted, but one factor may have been the relatively small number of adult Anglicans to act as sponsors in the early years of settlement. Stewart's successor reported that no more than two or three families in the congregation had been raised within the fold prior to the establishment of the parish. Furthermore, infant baptisms consistently far outnumbered those of older people. Between November 1810 and May 1811, for example, Stewart baptized four adults and twenty children in the two St Armand parishes. But the number of Easter communicants did increase significantly, from forty-five in 1810 to sixty-two the following year. Stewart also claimed that many more were eligible to take Communion, for 'there are many causes in this new & thinly settled country which often prevent the attendance of the members,'[62] which suggests a reasonable number of possible sponsorship candidates.

Stewart claimed that the promises required of sponsors were the main deterrent to non-parental sponsorships, which suggests that social ties were still insufficiently developed on this young settlement frontier. As already noted, during the early years many parents who resorted to Anglican clergy for their infants' baptism did not consider themselves to be Anglicans. But popular resistance to Anglican baptismal requirements would persist throughout the region as late as mid-century. In 1843, for example, Bishop George Mountain reported that, while John Butler observed 'the strictest regularity in his manner of performing the public service,' with all baptisms taking place in church, he was still unable to insist on more than one sponsor in addition to the parents. In 1851 D.D. Falloon of Melbourne and Shipton reported that he was seldom able to find the full number of sponsors, necessitating the use of at least one of the parents. While giving no reason why this was so, he insisted that it was not due to a popular prejudice against the use of sponsors, 'not even among the Scotch who apply to me for baptism.' The same year G.M. Ross of Drummondville explained that 'in country parishes there is not much choice, & it frequently happens that I am obliged to yield the point, and baptize the child without sponsors, the parents being addressed as assuming that relation & obligation.'[63] In the final analysis, however, the resistance to godparenting, as to church baptisms, clearly reflected not only how Yankee individualism remained strongly resistant to communal-oriented ritualism, but how difficult it was to eradicate the settlers' deep-seated antipathy to any practice associated with Catholicism.

Churching

It was a bold move, then, to attempt to introduce the practice of churching into the region. While the official position of the Church of England was that the formal churching of mothers after childbirth represented thanksgiving for a safe deliverance, and that women might return to church whenever they wished, Keith Thomas argues that in England it was traditionally viewed as 'a ritual of purification closely linked with its Jewish predecessor.' Resistance to churching consequently became 'one of the surest signs of Puritan feeling among the clergy or laity in the century before the Civil War.'[64] None of the missionaries in the Eastern Townships openly questioned the need for mothers to be publicly blessed after childbirth, but neither is there much evidence in their responses to the questionnaires circulated by the Quebec bishops that they placed a great deal of emphasis on the practice.

The question posed by the 1833 circular actually left the clergy a way out, for it asked only if the thanksgiving ritual took place in church. By answering yes to this question, ministers were not necessarily stating that churching was commonly practised. Despite Charles Cotton's affirmative response in 1833, for example, Bishop George Mountain reported after his visit to Dunham ten years later that churching was only partially in use. He also found that there was much American prejudice against churching in St Armand West. And, while Charles Fleming of Melbourne and Shipton had answered the same question in the affirmative in 1833, D.D. Falloon of the same mission wrote eighteen years later that 'I regret to say that perhaps not more than one family of the mothers in our congregations can be prevailed upon to attend to this duty at all.'[65]

Indeed, most ministers freely admitted that the ritual was not observed in their churches. In Hatley, Christopher Jackson reported in 1833 that 'the people are averse to this service, & no woman ever returns thanks in Public.' Five years later, he stated that public thanksgiving after childbirth was still 'very seldom offered,' and in 1851 Henry Burrage of the same parish reported that his efforts in this direction had not produced 'very favorable results, – the Americans with whom I have particularly to do are averse & their prejudices very great.' Even in Lennoxville, all that Lucius Doolittle could report in 1851 was that 'this duty is urged.'[66]

Only in some of the settlements with substantial English populations were new mothers reported to be churched without difficulty in 1843.[67] In Leeds, however, John Carry was informed in 1851 that one of his predecessors had told the new mothers 'not to mind – 'twas an old rite out of date.' The other two predecessors had also ignored it, 'and it will be long before the people are brought into the habit again.' Similarly, in neighbouring Inverness and Ireland, the incumbent admitted failure in 1851 when responding to the query as to whether he guarded 'against the introduction of any habit of laxity or negligence among the mothers in your congregations, respecting the solemn duty of *publicly* returning thanks to God, in the *prescribed form*, after the mercy of safe deliverance in *child-birth?*'[68] As with baptismal sponsors, then, it was not only the parishioners close to the American border who resisted conforming to this Anglican ritual.

Public Worship

The most frequent ceremony that Anglicans were required to participate in was the vocal expression of worship and praise during the Sunday services, and here the clergy were more successful once they were able to distribute enough prayerbooks. From Drummondville in 1819, Samuel Simpson Wood reported that the lack of prayerbooks meant that the congregation would be unable to join in the singing of psalms, 'if it can be introduced.' Also, one man 'who reads tolerably well' appeared to expect payment for leading the congregation in singing.[69] Wood's successor, G.M. Ross, reported in 1828 that some of the older and 'more respectable' inhabitants were now buying prayerbooks, and audible responses could be heard during the church services. Also, some had begun kneeling during prayers. Five years later, he was still more sanguine: 'The responses are made by almost every member of the Congregation audibly and reverently.' However, he could not 'boast of our singing. It appears impossible to form the voices of the greater part of the congregation to the purposes of Psalmody.'[70]

Eighteen years later, in 1851, Ross still found the singing in his churches to be 'very deficient.' Worse still, the decorum that had once characterized church services in Drummondville had been undermined by 'an influx of strangers' who remained standing during prayers, and with their backs to the altar: 'These annoyances, with a habit of coming in late for the sermon, and leaving abruptly which has crept in of late years, greatly destroys the solemnity of Divine worship.' Ross added that early prejudices against 'forms & ceremonies' persisted even among those who 'have from habit imperceptibly glided into our way of worship.' On the positive side, 'There are however still a good proportion of the Congregation who conform in kneeling, and make audibly the responses.'[71]

Most of the ministers were less critical than Ross of their American-born flocks, particularly where there was an adequate supply of prayerbooks. In Shipton, Charles Fleming expressed great satisfaction with both the singing and responses in 1833, even though George Mountain had found in 1818 that no one in this parish had a prayerbook, obliging him 'to read responses and all.' Mountain had been relieved, however, that there was 'no chiming in of groans,' as the Quebec military chaplain had reported after a still earlier visit.[72] When Christopher Jackson of Hatley and Compton served outlying areas, he carried a number of prayerbooks with him 'to put into the hands of the children & people to make the responses, & thus insensibly & without opposition, habituate them to the use of the Liturgy.' In 1833 he reported that there was generally singing and the responses were made well.[73] After Compton became a separate parish in 1840, C.P. Reid reported that, thanks to Jackson's efforts, 'no where in the Diocese are the responses better made than in the Church at Compton.' But Jackson's Hatley successor, Henry Burrage, had apparently raised the standards by 1851, reporting that 'my people are seemingly devout in their behaviour at church, but the responses are not as audibly made as I could wish, although I have taken pains to prevail upon them to do so.' As for the outlying areas however, only a few at best participated due to the unavailability of prayerbooks.[74]

The singing of hymns would have been more familiar to settlers from New England, and Jonathan Taylor of Eaton reported in 1833 that many of his congregation joined in this part of the service even though few took part in the responses, 'not having been accustomed to it.'[75] As we have seen, Charles Stewart had established an impressive choir in Frelighsburg as early as 1809. Also, Charles Cotton reported from Dunham in 1836 that his parishioners had hired 'an efficient Teacher of sacred musick' to instruct the youths. Cotton added that 'Psalmody has been much cultivated among us during the present winter and the good effects have been very apparent in the public singing during the performance of Divine Service.'[76] From Stanbridge, however, David Robertson reported in 1833 that while those who owned prayerbooks 'join in the devotions of the church well – as well as I could possibly expect,' he had 'not succeeded in introducing congregational singing among them. They too generally leave that to the choir in the gallery, yet some join, and the number is increasing.' Similarly, from isolated Tingwick, the travelling missionary reported in 1851 that 'there was tolerable responding' from the thirty-five who attended his service, though 'of singing, in these back places, there is little chance.'[77]

If there was some reticence about joining in the public responses and singing, Bishop George Mountain's attempt to encourage chanting was undoubtedly regarded by many adherents as an unwelcome Catholic-inspired initiative. Despite the anti-Tractarian stance of Isaac Hellmuth, however, he reported that 'chanting and psalmody' had been introduced to Sherbrooke as well as Lennoxville by mid-century.[78] Only three other ministers mentioned the chanting of the *Venite* and *Jubilate*. John Kemp noted the practice in his Robinson church, which was attended by English immigrants; Falloon did likewise for a small choir in one of his of Melbourne and Shipton churches; and Carry claimed that some progress had been made in that direction in British-settled Leeds.[79]

If the Church hierarchy was not inclined to water down the liturgy in order to accommodate puritanical or evangelical sensibilities, there were still areas of religious radicalism that the Anglican missionaries had failed to penetrate. John Carry reported of his visit to the Outlet (Magog) in 1850: 'It was the first time I ever heard our Service (shall I say, celebrated?) without a single response, – not even one solitary Amen! I cannot describe my feelings as I read our Confession and versicles, and Prayers, and Psalms, and Hymns, – not hearing a voice but my own, while the people *sat* from the beginning to the end of the prayers.' To avoid a repeat performance, Carry brought along his own accompanist on his next visit of January 17, 1851, when he wrote: 'Not a move from the people during service, and no responses, save from a little boy whom I brought with me, and whose tiny voice could scarcely be heard above the wind which whistled through the dilapidated school-house.'[80] But this evocative description also reminds us that the Anglican service represented a fundamental change in deeply entrenched religious practice for most of the settlers of the Eastern Townships, a change that had long been under way in many parishes.

Burials

Before other denominations had gained full civil status, Anglican ministers were expected to officiate, when requested, at the funerals of those who had not been baptized in their church. This expectation on the part of the public apparently did not end in 1834, for in January 1849 James Reid buried a two-week old infant despite the fact that its parents were 'not a Church going people' and there had been no baptism. In his diary, Reid wrote that 'I only read the 39th Psalm, and a prayer out of Dr. Stewart's Book. Had I refused, there would have been an offence. The people think they are entitled to whatever they ask from the Clergy, but themselves bound to do nothing.'[81]

Local communities also ignored the Anglican requirement that they establish denominationally exclusive cemeteries. In 1820, for example, James Reid reported that while the Frelighsburg burial ground legally belonged to the Anglican Church, it was also used by other denominations. In 1822 S.S. Wood reported running into the problem of people (including those from outside the parish) taking as much space as they chose, and where they chose, for burials in the Drummondville churchyard. He planned to establish a vestry for the management of church affairs, 'but I do not see how it can effect much unless it has the power of enforcing its decisions.' While visiting Eaton in 1843, Bishop Mountain observed that the cemetery, 'which appears to have passed by deed to the Church of England, has by some means, become common for the use of different denominations.' And Henry Burrage admitted in 1851 that, while the Hatley cemetery had been consecrated by Bishop Stewart, it had never been exclusively used by Anglicans. The cemetery for St Anne's in Richmond, on the other hand, had not been concentrated as of 1851 because it was being used by several denominations. Even in Sherbrooke and Lennoxville there was no separate Anglican burial ground at mid-century.[82] As with popular resistance to other church requirements, the clergy failed to explain the popular insistence on interdenominational cemeteries. Perhaps the answer is obvious, however, for death was a universal experience, cemeteries were communal spaces, and extended families who might belong to different denominations probably preferred to have their dead close to each other.

Conclusion

Westfall has recently pointed out that, in the Anglican view, worship was a public act, therefore 'baptisms, marriages, the churching of women, and funerals were celebrated in a church in order to transform something that was private into something public, bringing these deeply personal moments into public view, and by so doing conferring upon them official (and often legal) status.'[83] From this perspective, the Anglican clergy's role was to create a stronger sense of community, but as of the middle of the nineteenth century they still had far to go, given the ongoing popular resistance to frequent Communions, godparenting, and the churching of women. Resistance to denominational Sunday schools and cemeteries, on the other hand, clearly was in the interest of a broader-based community. Perhaps, then, the majority of those who identified themselves as Anglicans were simply resisting High Church pressures to make them more distinctive from the other Protestants in the region.

The temptation on the part of the Anglican clergy to adopt a latitudinarian stance must have been great. As Woolverton has stated of the Anglican missionaries in pre-Revolutionary America, 'they had to appeal to the heterodox many rather than to the loyalty of the homogenous chosen few.'[84] Stating in 1829 that the clergy of his diocese needed 'to combine the wisdom of the Serpent with the innocence of the dove,' Archdeacon George Mountain admitted that they might occasionally have 'to do what is unusual, if not irregular,' but he insisted that 'any too free & frequent deviation from our rules & forms' would only reinforce the objections to them. Mountain criticized Richard Whitwell and George Salmon in 1829 for their compromising strategies while serving Shefford. He felt that in attempting to render

> their ministrations more acceptable & thence more beneficial to persons unaccustomed to our Church-service, they stretched the spirit of accommodation – a wise and christian spirit in itself when kept within due limits –

farther than I humbly conceive to have been warrantable; & won some of
the people no doubt more readily to hear them, but in the mean time, if
they did not retard, failed at least to advance the introduction & accep-
tance of our established & regular forms.[85]

While a recent study claims that by the 1830s the aristocratic High
Church attitude of the Anglican Church was dépassé in the Eastern
Townships, and the missionaries were becoming more 'middle church'
in orientation,[86] there is no evidence that this was so. The Church hierarchy appears to have been generally successful in preventing any liber-
alizing tendencies on the part of the clergy, and their questionnaires
reflect the degree to which Tractarianism was beginning to have an
influence in the bishop's palace. In 1851, for example, the clergy were
not only asked detailed questions about churches, parsonages, burial
grounds, and vestry-rooms, but whether there was 'a bell – a font – a
Communion-service – a surplice, an altar-cloth and pede-cloth – a fair
linen cloth, for the administration of the Communion, and another for
covering what remains of the consecrated elements – a proper set of
Church-Service books? And if there is a deficiency of any of these articles, what is the reason of it, and what the prospect of supplying it?'[87]
Significantly, there was no mention of crosses, candlesticks on the altar,
or other Anglo-Catholic innovations, yet the introduction of chanting is
somewhat remarkable as is the fixation with the churching of women
after childbirth, given that English bishops had ceased to ask questions
about this ritual as long ago as the 1680s.[88]

It is probably safe to assume that forms and rituals were a deterrent to
the Anglican Church's expansion, particularly in the early years of the
settlement frontier. Of course, the settlers needed someone to baptize
their children, sanctify marriages, and bury the dead, if nothing else,
and Butler argues that in the American colonies 'the *Book of Common
Prayer* furnished stability amid the confusion engendered by new landscapes, new settlements, new economies, new elites, new labor, and new
forms of government.'[89] The fact remains, however, that some of the
Anglican rituals represented a major move away from the Puritan and
evangelical beliefs and practices that most of the New Englanders were
familiar with before settling in the Eastern Townships. And the Anglican
hierarchy did its best to ensure that religious formalities did not become
overly diluted, or the sanctity of the church buildings compromised, for
central to the claim of the Book of Common Prayer was that its rituals
conveyed truths of the early Christian church.[90]

While Bishop Stewart may have been somewhat more inclusive in his approach than the two Mountains, he would certainly have agreed that altering the forms and rituals of Anglican worship would mean succumbing to the levelling and disintegrating impact of the North American frontier. In a sermon printed in 1814, Stewart denied being prejudiced against any denomination of Christians, 'but at the same time, I would walk in the old paths, and point out the good way, which the Saints and heroes of the Reformation, and the Martyrs of our Church, were raised up by God to repair and establish.'[91] In 1832 Bishop Stewart advised Lucius Doolittle that he would leave to his discretion future ministrations to the Presbyterians, adding that: 'I wd. not refuse them when requested, but, generally speaking, it is not consistent with good order to administer the sacraments to persons, or children of persons who will not join our Church, especially if they have ministers of their own denomination.' Stewart was more forceful with James Reid when he learned the same year that a Methodist preacher had been allowed to conduct a funeral service in the church at Stanbridge Mills. Stating that 'every religious Society has its own rules and principles,' Stewart declared that 'we must have the same right to object to any violation of ours as any other religious body has to the maintenance of any principle or practice in which it dissents from us – I wish the principles of the Church to be always upheld in a spirit of meekness and charity, but we have no right to compromise them.'[92]

Yet most of the Anglican clergy were not very zealous about insisting on separation of Sunday schools and cemeteries, or refusing burial to those who had not been baptized. Even in England, conformity could be negotiable in practice, with much of the detail of worship left to local discretion or custom.[93] And popular resentment against Anglican exclusivism was overcome to some extent by the clergy's doctrine of usefulness, especially as long-term incumbencies provided Anglican ministers with a distinct advantage over their evangelical competitors in forging bonds with their parishioners. They played a particularly prominent role in the larger community by promoting public schools and temperance societies. For example, James Reid served as official of the local school district for over thirty years, and he was also an active supporter of the temperance movement. Even the easy-going Charles Cotton reported in 1830 that he had helped to establish a local temperance society, a surprising move for someone who had once purchased a liquor patent! Cotton was clearly motivated not so much by a disapproval of alcohol as he was by the hope that it would 'have a great influence in lessening the unreasonable prejudices entertained by many of the Dissenters against the Established Church – diffusing a more general spirit of brotherly love, and awakening a more conciliatory disposition than has ever yet existed among us.'[94] Involvement in secular affairs ran the risk of sacrificing moral authority, but Westfall argues that the Anglican clergy 'sustained a code of virtuous conduct that was supposed to guard the moral character of public life.' Certainly, there were no gentrified hunting parsons in the Eastern Townships, as in England, nor is there much evidence of the indolence and immorality referred to by Clark, or the social frivolity referred to by Grant.[95]

Religion was, nevertheless, at a low ebb by the late 1840s when James Reid confided to his diary: 'Any one may despair of our success in the Eastern Townships. There is neither religious nor moral principle to depend upon among the bulk of our population. The spirit of Slumber and indifference prevails over all, and nothing has hitherto been effectual enough to put a Stir among the dry bones.' The revivalists might blame the Anglican Church's influence for such religious complacency, but to Reid the villain was the democratic mindset that lay behind radical sectarianism: 'All men they say are born equal and ought to be free to worship God according to the dictates of their conscience. And this amounts to the same thing, as fancy prompts, to worship God when they please, and to neglect it when they please; and being led by such notions, it is found to be true in fact, that most of them neglect it altogether.'[96]

Whether or not Reid was exaggerating, it seems that far from all those identified as Anglicans in the census were actually adherents. The clergy reports for 1845 suggest that there were approximately 4,500 adherents in the region's eighteen parishes, which was less than a third of the 15,109 residents of the Eastern Townships who were reported to be Anglicans in the 1852 census. It is not clear, however, whether most clergy included as adherents children who had not been confirmed. If not, much of the discrepancy in numbers is explained, though several ministers did note that some people claimed to be Anglicans simply because this affiliation was considered respectable, and it demanded little sacrifice on their part. Reid made the latter point clear in 1839: 'When the coming of the Bishop is announced we have sometimes to baptize whole families, and prepare them for confirmation that had little or no thought of coming forward till they heard that the Bishop was arriving. The Churches are full. Every thing looks like devotion and zeal. The Bishop is of course pleased, and goes away with an impression that matters are in a better state than they are in reality.'[97]

The Church of England might have had greater appeal in the Eastern Townships had more evangelically-inclined missionaries been sent to the region, but one of the Anglican Church's strengths in the colonies prior to mid-century was the lack of doctrinal and political infighting that was taking place in England even before the rise of Tractarianism in the 1830s.[98] Furthermore, men like Richard Lonsdell of Kingsey were not lacking in messianic zeal. His journal entry of 26 January 1842 states that he had travelled more than forty miles on 'chiefly wood tracks, within the last two days.' Snow storms were a major obstacle, and on 14 February Lonsdell wrote: 'Divine service at the back of Kingsey; catechised the children; drove to the back of Shipton; got into a drift; had to unharness the horse, and try and lift him out; a man came to look for me; reached my evening appointment an hour after the time; an attentive congregation, chiefly Irish.'[99]

High Church as his orientation may have been, George Mountain, did more than emphasize the observance of religious holidays, proper ecclesiastical dress, and conformity to ordinances such as the institution of sponsors, and the churching of women. He also stressed the importance of Sunday schools, catechising, family devotion, pastoral visits, and preaching at outposts.[100] The Church of England strategy was a long-term one, based not only on establishing a solid footing in each parish but also on molding the minds of future generations. From this perspective, the Anglican clergy of the Eastern Townships were strictly within the Church's mainstream, for Walsh and Taylor state that most of their counterparts in England 'saw themselves first and foremost not as priestly mediators between God and man, dispensing the sacraments, but as pastoral educators, spiritual and moral teachers and guides ... In this respect there was little difference between Evangelicals and their brethren.'[101] Despite the periodic outbreaks of revivalist enthusiasm spreading north of the American border, it was religious indifference, not religious enthusiasm, that mostly concerned the Anglican clergy. Clearly, then, the cultural identity of the largely American-origin people of the Eastern Townships had become markedly different from that of their radically sectarian cousins and neighbours on the other side of the forty-ninth parallel.

Conclusion

In December 1811 'A Poor Farmer' in Shipton Township wrote the following plaintive words to the editor of the *Quebec Gazette*:

> Eleven years have elapsed since I first entered these woods, with my family, and seven years since my residence in this Township ... On my first arrival in these woods, with my wife, both of us about the age of Twenty, we had one child, at present we have six, and have lost three. Our first care and inquiry was, in what manner shall we have our children Baptized, Educated, and taught the true Religion of Christianity. Hope led us to believe, living under so good a Government, we shall shortly have men placed among us for these purposes. Alas, Eleven years are now gone over, and I dont see the least prospect of these blessings.
>
> With what sorrow do I declare that in the Townships, in this District, it is estimated that near Two thousand Children live without Baptism, upwards of Six hundred men and women live together without lawful marriage; and that the greatest part of these people have not, for the last Ten years, heard the Word of God on a Sabbath day; as for our dead, they are disposed of in the same manner that most people dispose of a favorite Dog who dies, by placing him quietly under a Tree.[1]

New England's religious institutions had failed to keep up with the extension of its settlement frontier as it crossed into British territory, and war was about to interrupt the small degree of progress that had been made by itinerant preachers. Noll writes: 'The chance that Canadian Protestantism might follow the populist, sectarian, fragmenting ways of the United States – certainly a real chance in the early decades – came to an end because of the War [of 1812].'[2] But the war itself probably had less of a long-term impact than the fact that the American missionary societies would naturally come to consider their own country's rapidly expanding western frontier to be a priority. The result was that in the 1831 census the largest cohort in the Eastern Townships declared no religious affiliation whatsoever. By this time, however, British missionary societies had been attempting to fill the religious vacuum for more than a decade, and the Anglicans and Wesleyan Methodists had become the largest two denominations in a region that was still largely American in origin. Many who declared affiliation with the Church of England were probably doing so because it was the only one available to provide the basic services of baptism, marriage, and burial. Furthermore, the Anglican and Wesleyan Methodist ratios would decline by mid-century due to the influence of American revivalism. But the Congregationalists, Baptists, and dissident Methodists were falling under the influence of their own British missionaries, and the border that divided this northeastern borderland of American settlement had become more than an arbitrary line drawn on a map as far as religious and political values were concerned.

The influx of British settlers had been largely confined to the outlying townships, and attempts to impose a British oligarchy on the region had only intensified political radicalism in the pre-Rebellion period, but the Society for the Propagation of the Gospel and the Wesleyan Missionary Society, both based in London, had been more effective imperial agencies. Such a conclusion should hardly be surprising, given the fundamental importance of religion to the popular world view in pre-industrial societies, but liberal historians of empire have, in Bayly's words, propagated the myth 'that religion played only a small rôle in British imperialism which was a pragmatic construction of hardy entrepreneurs and agnostic statesmen.'[3] Similarly, English-Canadian historians have stressed social control and state formation as the instruments for creating a disciplined society, a society which – they generally fail to acknowledge – reflected the Anglican view that a 'loyal and ordered population was the basis for a Christian society.'[4]

Religious historians themselves have tended to minimize Canada's cultural distinctiveness from the United States by stressing the triumph of evangelicalism. Thus, Wise states that the Anglican Church's promotion of the 'providential mission of the Elect Nation' was 'too narrowly conceived, too deeply rooted in the defence of the dying order to catch the imagination of the people, and to provide the basis for an emergent Canadian nationalism.'[5] Doll's recent study on imperial Anglicanism in

British North America concludes that the Church of England's policy of church-state unity 'did not go far towards effecting the desired Anglicization of colonial society.' While French does concede the persistent strength of the Anglican Church in Canada, he emphasizes its evangelical character. Moir even argues that, prior to Confederation, anti-Americanism was 'a minor and in some areas insignificant factor in the development of Canadian Protestantism.' Finally, while Gauvreau rejects this Whiggish interpretation by emphasizing that 'order' and 'respectability' were the most influential concepts 'in forging the values and institutions of the maturing English Canadian society,' he adds that these were provided by evangelicalism.[6] It would seem highly likely, however, that the conservative, pro-imperial message of the Anglican Church played at least as important a role in forging the values and institutions of a country in which 'peace, order, and good government' became the basis of the constitution, the Orange Lodge was the most popular voluntary society outside Quebec, and English-Canadian nationalism was expressed largely through the imperial federation movement.[7]

The Church of England's failure to achieve its goal of becoming the officially established church, and of incorporating the majority of Protestants within its fold, did not prevent it from playing an important role in developing the English-Canadian cultural identity. The myth of an Old World church failing to meet the challenge of the New World frontier has survived so long largely because research on Protestantism in pre-Confederation Canada has remained focused at the institutional and elite level, with the embittered Strachan and the triumphant Ryerson receiving the lion's share of attention.[8] But the concessions towards creating what Westfall calls a common Protestant identity in Upper Canada were largely on the part of Ryerson and the Methodists, for their clergy became less evangelical while the Anglicans were being influenced by Tractarianism. The Anglican Church's relinquishment of its goal of incorporating all dissenters into a single national church may have eased tensions over the clergy reserves issue, but Westfall, himself, admits that it strengthened the impulse to establish a denominational identity that was sharply distinct from that of the evangelical churches.[9] And, while the Church of England may have disassociated itself from direct state ties during the 1840s and 1850s, imperial patriotism remained a key component of Anglican ideology, as it did that of the Wesleyan Methodists and, presumably, the other increasingly British-influenced Protestant churches. Stanstead's locally born Congregational minister R.V. Hall is a case in point, for he took a strong stand against the Rebellions in 1837–8, as well as distancing himself from his American colleagues.

The Presbyterian churches certainly played their role in promoting loyalty to the British empire, but they have not been included in this study because they were generally not interested in converting the American settlers. There were one or two American Presbyterian ministers, but they were virtually indistinguishable from the Congregationalists. As for the Church of Scotland, it focused almost exclusively on Scottish settlements because its claim to equal status with the Church of England was based on its role as a national church. There were very few such settlements in the Eastern Townships, where only 5 per cent of the population was Scots-born in 1844.[10] The Scots Irish, who were more numerous, were largely neglected because the Irish Presbyterian Church had agreed to confine its efforts to the Maritime colonies. Even the evangelical Free Church, established in 1843, would remain interested only in the Scots, as Edinburgh's *Home and Foreign Record of the Free Church of Scotland* admitted in September 1846 when it declared that 'Presbyterianism has done comparatively little for this fine section of the country; and it is more owing to the attachment of Scotchmen to the faith and forms of worship of their fathers, than to the fostering care of the Presbyterian Church, that so many are still within her pale.'[11] Crofters arriving from the Hebrides during the 1840s may have helped push Presbyterianism to the third largest Protestant category in the Eastern Townships by 1852, when 5,527 individuals claimed affiliation with it, but they were served by only two or three resident clergymen.[12]

To use a scientific metaphor, the Eastern Townships can be approached as the equivalent of a control group as far as analysing the origins of the English-Canadian identity are concerned. Focusing on Upper Canada, social scientists and historians have emphasized the role played by the Loyalists, the War of 1812, and British immigration in creating a predominantly conservative political culture.[13] All these factors were obviously important, keeping in mind that a strong liberal and even radical strain persisted,[14] but none of them were particularly decisive in the Eastern Townships where there were few Loyalist settlers, no major battles during the War of 1812, and the proportion of British immigrants was much lower and more marginally located than in Upper Canada. Yet in this most American of the British North American settlement regions, support for the Rebellions of 1837–8 failed to spread beyond a few isolated pockets (pockets of religious radicalism, it should be noted) despite the persistance of political grievances. And support for agrarian radicalism grew weaker in the 1840s despite ongoing resistance to centralized state control. The growing conservatism of the Eastern Townships obviously reflected the region's increased integration into the capitalist economy during the railway era, as well as the diminishing political influence of the English-speaking population within Lower Canada, but these developments set the stage – they did not provide the vocabulary.

A good deal remains to be done on popular religious culture in the Eastern Townships prior to 1850, work that requires careful reading of the local press, the personal letters and diaries of as many lay people as possible, and the relatively few collections of local church records that have survived. We can gain insights into popular spirituality by examining the degree to which adherents conformed to the regulations of their churches, or the frequency with which waves of revivalism swept through a community, but the average individual's concept of God, and how this affected his or her daily life, remain elusive. In addition, a clearer understanding of the role of religion in community formation calls for a microhistorical approach that would allow one to examine the influence exerted by local elites, the degree and effect of interdenominational apostasy and intermarriage, the role of women, the secular role of the clergy, and so on. Hopefully, this study will set the stage for such inquiries in the future, inquiries that will doubtless modify or challenge some of the hypotheses put forward here.

It is safe to conclude, however, that the efforts of the Anglican and Wesleyan Methodist missionary societies, despite their shortcomings, managed to fill a religious vacuum left by the failure of their American counterparts to exert a concerted effort north of the international boundary. The Millerite movement of the early 1840s represented the most serious American challenge to British religious hegemony over the English-speaking population of the Eastern Townships, but it was one that dissipated quickly when the predicted Apocalypse failed to take place in 1843 or 1844. In fact, by undermining the Baptist meetings that were beginning to establish a solid foundation in the region, and by contributing to the fracturing of Methodism, the Millerite movement probably strengthened the Anglican Church's position in the region. Not only did the Second Adventist Church – which emerged from the ashes of Millerism – have relatively few adherents in the Eastern Townships by mid-century, but the more radical Shaker and Mormon societies that profited greatly from the 'Great Disappointment' in New

England failed to spread north of the Vermont border. And even if the majority of self-declared Anglicans still rarely attended church, their religious apathy itself distinguished them from their more zealous neighbours south of the border, as did the fact that the overwhelming majority of the Townships population claimed a denominational affiliation at mid-century.

The victory of the forces of religious conservatism should not, however, be exaggerated. The ratio who declared themselves to be Anglicans was considerably lower in 1852 than in 1831, and Wesleyanism was (temporarily) losing ground to a more radical (albeit British) Methodist society. Bishop George Mountain lamented in 1840 that every village's energies were dissipated from 'the promotion of Religion,' and the diary of Magog's pedlar and mystic, Ralph Merry, reveals that premillennialism remained in the air at mid-century.[15] Visually, much of the religious landscape continued to be indistinguishable from that south of the border, for the Anglicans were largely alone in building the neo-Gothic churches that would become a distinctive feature of British North America, though this was less the case in the lower St Francis Valley than in the border townships. The tellingly named 'Magna Charta' of the Griffin's Corner union church in Stanstead Township is a good illustration of local independence from ecclesiastical authority. By declaring that 'the public worship of God and instruction in piety, religion and morality promotes the happiness and prosperity of any people,' the document, drafted in 1842, suggested that religion served a secular, community-building purpose. And the fact that the church was strictly operated as a corporation, with use by each member denomination being determined by the investment made in the purchase of pews, illustrates how the community had developed its own institutions, as well as why the people of the Eastern Townships might resent the imposition of state-controlled ones. Finally, the building's continued use as a union church until the 1920s illustrates how persistent localism remained in the rural communities of the region.[16]

To some extent, the Eastern Townships remained an extension of the northern New England frontier by mid-century. Smugglers continued to evade customs officers, counterfeiters continued to produce bogus American bank notes, bootleggers continued to ignore license inspectors, squatters continued to defy absentee proprietors, and there was overwhelming support in the border townships for the annexation manifesto of 1849. But the temperance movement – an American initiative, but one supported by Anglican clergy – was gaining in strength; decentralization of state authority was making law enforcement more effective; the absentee proprietorship problem was being resolved through municipal taxation rather than direct collective action; and the annexation movement quickly fizzled when economic conditions improved. Partly because the international border would continue to mean little to the many people who had personal and business ties in New England, political and religious radicalism would certainly survive beyond the first half of the nineteenth century. What it had always lacked, however, was the organizing force provided by sectarian religious movements and local democracy south of the border. The expansion, and even the survival, of radical religious movements in the Eastern Townships was also seriously handicapped by their members' resistance to formal organization, and by neglect on the part of their parent bodies in the United States. Generously supported by the imperial state, and strengthened by their own messianic convictions, the British missionaries took advantage of this situation to preach a conservative religious and political doctrine on this northern frontier of American settlement. In doing so, they played an important role in the making of a distinctively English-Canadian identity – an identity that represented a still somewhat lumpy synthesis of American and British values.

Statistical Appendix

TABLE A.1
Protestant denominations in the Eastern Townships and Upper Canada, 1852

	Eastern Townships No.	%	Upper Canada No.	%
Church of England	15,109	28.7	223,190	28.5
Wesleyan Methodist	4,897	9.3	96,640	12.3
Episcopal Methodist	–		43,884	5.6
New Connection Methodist	3,442	6.5	7,547	0.1
Other Methodist	5,206	9.9	59,585	7.6
Church of Scotland	152	0	57,542	7.3
Free Church of Scotland	–		65,807	8.4
Other Presbyterian	5,375	10.2	80,799	10.3
Congregationalists	3,364	6.4	7,747	0.1
Universalists	3,321	6.3	2,684	0
Baptists	2,781	5.3	45,353	5.8
Second Adventists	1,362	2.6	663	0
Protestants	854	1.6	1,733	0
Unitarians	261	0	834	0
Quakers	157	0	7,460	0.1
Mormons	2	0	247	0
Christians	2	0	3,093	0
Bible Christians	–		5,726	0.1
Lutherans	–		12,089	1.5
Disciples	–		2,064	0
Menonists and Tunkers	–		8,230	0.1
Other Creeds	3,380	6.4	7,805	0.1
No Creed Given	2,900	5.5	35,740	4.6
Not Known	33	0	6,744	0.1
	52,598		783,206	

Source: Province of Canada, *Census Reports*, 1851–52.

TABLE A.2
Agricultural variables related to religious affiliation of farmers occupying 10 or more acres in 11 townships of Lower Canada, 1831

	Church of England	Methodist	Church of Scotland	Presb./ Cong.	Roman Catholic	Baptist	Other	None listed	Mixed	Total
N (farms ≥10 acres)	459	184	80	55	117	115	48	149	119	1,326
Population	2,770	1,144	503	321	674	738	292	858	958	8,258
Mean family size	6.0	6.2	6.3	5.8	5.8	6.4	6.1	5.8	8.1	6.2
Mean acres	139.6	124.4	196.9	165.9	114.6	129.4	104.3	122.5	208.7	141.9
Mean improved acres	38.7	35.1	20.5	32.4	13.1	49.0	37.7	30.5	59.6	36.4
Ratio of improved acres	27.7	28.2	10.4	19.5	11.4	37.9	36.1	24.9	28.6	25.7
Farm servants (per family)	0.1	0.1	0.1	0.1	0.0	0.1	0.1	0.1	0.6	0.1
Wheat	23.4	18.7	25.1	15.1	12.3	19.0	18.4	17.2	37.8	21.5
Potatoes	166.4	173.6	209.7	149.7	111.6	269.4	196.1	162.7	300.4	186.1
Oats	26.3	22.7	17.2	15.5	5.8	30.0	11.0	12.9	32.7	21.8
Cattle	9.0	7.9	4.7	6.6	2.6	13.1	7.1	6.8	11.7	8.2
Horses	1.7	1.8	0.2	0.9	0.4	2.2	1.3	0.8	2.9	1.5
Sheep	12.2	11.5	2.3	8.2	1.7	19.7	10.5	8.7	15.2	10.9
Hogs	6.1	5.5	3.6	3.2	2.9	8.1	4.4	2.9	7.8	5.4

TABLE A.3
Agricultural variables related to religious affiliation of farmers occupying 10 or more acres in the Townships of Inverness, Ireland, Leeds, and Halifax, 1831

	Church of England	Methodist	Church of Scotland	Presb./Cong.	Roman Catholic	Baptist	Other	None listed	Mixed	Total
N (farms ≥10 acres)	121	30	57	22	44	5	1	1	25	306
Population	630	171	369	135	236	38	11	5	218	1813
Mean family size	5.2	5.7	6.5	6.1	5.4	7.6	11.0	5.0	8.7	5.9
Mean acres	167.7	172.7	217.6	218.2	159.7	180.0	250.0	50.0	366.0	196.3
Mean improved acres	15.8	12.4	17.7	15.7	14.0	22.6	50.0	4.0	58.3	19.2
Ratio of improved acres	9.4	7.2	8.1	7.2	8.7	12.6	20.0	8.0	15.9	9.8
Farm servants (per family)	0.1	0.1	0.1	0.1	0.0	0.0	0.0	0.0	1.0	0.2
Wheat	15.3	20.3	25.5	19.1	22.1	50.0	50.0	0.0	63.0	23.1
Oats	5.6	6.2	18.8	12.0	6.1	26.0	0.0	0.0	27.0	10.7
Corn	0.1	0.2	0.1	0.9	2.7	0.0	0.0	0.0	2.4	0.7
Barley	3.4	7.3	13.2	12.3	3.7	15.0	0.0	0.0	9.0	6.9
Rye	1.0	0.6	1.8	5.9	3.1	8.4	0.0	0.0	8.0	2.5
Peas	0.9	0.7	0.4	0.8	0.7	0.2	0.0	0.0	7.6	1.3
Buckwheat	0.0	0.0	0.0	0.0	0.0	0.0	0.0	0.0	0.0	0.0
Potatoes	117.6	126.3	193.0	186.4	152.2	300.0	100.0	100.0	394.4	167.9
Cattle	2.8	2.2	3.7	3.2	2.8	4.0	7.0	0.0	10.6	3.6
Horses	0.3	0.2	0.1	0.1	0.2	0.2	0.0	0.0	1.6	0.3
Sheep	1.4	0.2	1.1	1.8	0.8	2.6	0.0	0.0	15.2	2.3
Hogs	2.2	3.8	2.4	2.6	3.3	8.2	8.0	0.0	7.4	3.1

TABLE A.4
Agricultural variables related to religious affiliation of farmers occupying 10 or more acres in the Townships of Stanbridge, Shefford, Brome, and St Armand, 1831

	Church of England	Methodist	Church of Scotland	Presb./ Cong.	Roman Catholic	Baptist	Other	None listed	Mixed	Total
N (farms ≥10 acres)	274	130	4	29	22	105	5	148	70	787
Population	1829	834	18	165	138	663	36	853	526	5062
Mean family size	6.7	6.4	4.5	5.7	6.3	6.3	7.2	5.8	7.5	6.4
Mean acres	133.6	110.1	100.0	137.1	86.8	126.7	150.0	123.0	155.3	127.5
Mean improved acres	51.8	40.9	21.3	44.8	12.8	50.0	57.0	30.7	56.9	44.8
Ratio of improved acres	38.7	37.1	21.3	32.7	14.7	39.5	38.0	25.0	36.6	35.1
Farm servants (per family)	0.2	0.1	0.0	0.0	0.1	0.1	0.4	0.1	0.5	0.1
Wheat	26.8	19.8	22.5	12.9	2.9	16.9	8.8	17.3	27.3	21.3
Potatoes	181.2	167.1	75.0	122.3	71.4	267.0	250.0	163.1	231.3	186.0
Oats	39.3	25.8	3.3	19.3	5.1	29.2	2.0	13.0	31.1	27.9
Cattle	12.3	9.4	8.3	9.7	3.5	13.6	9.4	6.9	12.2	10.6
Horses	2.7	2.2	0.0	1.7	0.7	2.4	1.4	0.8	3.1	2.1
Sheep	18.4	14.6	5.0	12.9	2.0	20.7	17.2	8.7	17.9	15.5
Hogs	8.2	6.1	3.8	3.9	3.4	8.2	1.8	3.0	8.2	6.5

TABLE A.5
Wesleyan Methodists in Eastern Townships circuits, 1818–52

Year	Melbourne	Shefford	St Armand	Stanstead	Ireland	Hatley	Dunham	Total	District
1818	61	–	24	–	–	–	–	85	364
1819	46	–	68	–	–	–	–	114	585
1820	66	–	68	–	–	–	–	134	?
1821	71	–	79	–	–	–	–	150	464
1822	75	135	163	27	–	–	–	400	?
1823	72	156	313	43	–	–	–	584	1,081
1824	91[a]	162	260	52	–	–	–	565	1,113
1825	59	159	260	130	–	–	–	608	1,109
1826	59	187	366	174	–	–	–	786	1,301
1827	59	195	420	254	–	–	–	928	1,519
1828	90	192	422	200	–	–	–	904	1,532
1829	90	196	465[b]	220	–	–	–	971	1,540
1830	80	196	465[b]	205	–	–	–	946	1,560
1831	80	86	465[b]	226	–	–	–	857	1,535
1832	70	100	372[b]	215	20[c]	–	–	777	1,488
1833	70	151	400[b]	207	–	–	–	828	2,094
1834	70	141	373[b]	77	–	50	–	711	2,203
1835	70	154	371	99	–	50	–	744	1,956
1836	–	174	364	336	127	50	–	1,051	2,297
1837	365	171	297	315	189	–	–	1,337	2,520
1839[d]	150	234	332	294	230	181	–	1,421	2,644
1840	176	240	312	300	260	203	136	1,627	2,886
1841	218	248	380	296	252	195	190	1,779	3,227
1842	277	253	370	279	230	185	304	1,898	3,561
1843	260	293	486	211	236	155	403	2,044	4,036
1844	270	256	500	193	280	165	414	2,078	4,169
1845	261	210	531	186	293	165	373	2,019	4,115
1846	262	221	261	196	285	189	355	1,769	3,923
1847	257	240	261	152	285	198[e]	296	1,689	3,909
1848	263	239	187	145	275	206[e]	273	1,588	3,782
1849	271	243	145	153	234	275[e]	342	1,663	3,849
1852[f]	270	215	124	163	227	341[e]	297	1,637	3,740

[a] Includes Trois-Rivières
[b] Includes Caldwell's Manor
[c] Still part of the Quebec circuit
[d] No information reported for 1838. The district total was 2,784.
[e] Includes Sherbrooke Circuit
[f] No reports for 1850 and 1851

Sources: United Church Archives, Victoria University, Wesleyan Methodist Missionary Society, Minutes from Lower Canada and Canada East; National Archives of Canada, Methodist Missionary Society, Synod Minutes. Lower Canada / Canada East.

TABLE A.6
Apportionment of Wesleyan missionary grant (in £ sterling), Eastern Townships circuits, 1835–48

Year	Melbourne	Shefford	St Armand	Stanstead	Ireland	Hatley[a]	Dunham	Total[b]	District[b]
1835	–	80.0.0	25.0.0	95.0.0	16.0.0	–	–	216	881
1836	50.0.0	75.0.0	70.0.0	80.0.0	16.0.0	–	–	291	502
1837	50.0.0	80.0.0	80.0.0	20.0.0	–	–	–	230	1,006
1838	20.0.0	60.0.0	90.0.0	80.0.0	18.0.0	50.0.0	–	318	1,056
1839	95.0.0	85.0.0	90.0.0	80.0.0	15.0.0	25.0.0	130.0.0	520	1,194
1840	95.0.0	70.0.0	60.0.0	80.0.0	15.0.0	80.0.0	120.0.0	520	1,117
1841	77.6.8	60.0.0	37.6.8	46.13.4	16.0.0	71.6.8	76.0.0	385	1,000
1842	102.8.0	56.0.0	46.0.0	62.18.0	106.0.0	93.10.0	85.0.0	554	1,000
1843	95.0.0	56.0.0	40.0.0	90.0.0	110.0.0	95.0.0	100.0.0	586	1,000
1844	95.0.0	65.0.0	125.0.0	100.0.0	80.0.0	185.0.0	90.0.0	740	1,000
1845	110.0.0	65.0.0	70.0.0	85.0.0	35.0.0	90.0.0	128.0.0	583	1,000
1846	98.0.0	60.0.0	60.0.0	78.0.0	30.0.0	83.0.0	98.0.0	507	1,000
1847	–	40.0.0	65.0.0	83.0.0	73.0.0	85.0.0	79.0.0	425	1,065
1848	69.0.0	40.0.0	87.10.0	83.0.0	73.10.0	138.0.0	79.0.0	571	1,100

[a] Also known as Compton; includes Sherbrooke circuit in 1847 and 1848
[b] To the nearest pound

Source: National Archives of Canada, Methodist Missionary Society, Synod Minutes. Lower Canada / Canada East.

TABLE A.7
Wesleyan Missionary monies subscribed (in £ Halifax), Eastern Townships Circuits, 1835–50

Year	Melbourne	Shefford	St Armand	Stanstead	Dunham	Hatley[a]	Ireland	Total[b]	District[b]
1835	–	9.17.0	24.10.4	2.11.0	–	–	–	37	327
1836	–	18.0.2	17.19.11	–	–	–	–	35	391
1837	–	22.15.6	32.16.5	29.10.0	–	–	–	85	450
1842	19.0.0	26.3.8	100.0.0	39.7.0	28.19.5	28.4.11	8.0.0	251	972
1843	13.12.3	22.4.2	55.15.7	26.4.9	24.2.2	17.2.3	5.13.4	165	795
1844	18.2.8	21.0.3	66.5.6	27.15.10	33.11.5	23.1.2	7.4.2	197	880
1845	21.9.5	32.18.7	66.2.11	26.2.10	33.12.3	16.8.4	12.6.4	209	908
1846	17.18.6	32.12.7	70.0.0	31.15.6	42.5.0	29.18.11	10.12.10	235	968
1847	20.8.9	32.1.8	35.13.10	37.3.1	41.7.6	39.2.5	7.15.6	214	991
1848	25.11.2	27.1.3	34.17.6	52.10.4	31.11.1	40.5.0	15.14.7	227	1,064
1849	22.14.4	28.4.10	35.16.8	42.2.8	41.12.0	47.17.1	20.0.2	239	880
1850	24.1.2	33.4.5	30.0.0	35.7.2	46.4.0	38.16.7	23.9.7	231	870

[a] Includes Sherbrooke circuit from 1847 to 1850
[b] To the nearest pound

Sources: National Archives of Canada, Methodist Missionary Society, Synod Minutes. Lower Canada / Canada East; United Church Archives, Victoria University, *The Report of the Wesleyan Methodist Auxiliary Missionary Society of the District of Lower Canada*, 1844–50.

TABLE A.8
Wesleyan Methodist data, Eastern Townships circuits and Canada District, 1842–8

	1842 E.T.	1842 Dist.	1843 E.T.	1843 Dist.	1845[a] E.T.	1846 E.T.	1846 Dist.	1847 E.T.	1847 Dist.	1848 E.T.	1848 Dist.	1849 E.T.	1849 Dist.	1852 E.T.	1852 Dist.
Missionaries	8	17	8	18	8	7	17	9[b]	23	9	23	10[d]	23	10[e]	22
Members	1,898	3,561	2,047	4,039	2,028	1,769	3,923	1,689	3,909	1,587	3,782	1,662	3,849	1,637	3,740
Preached to	8,136	15,236	8,240	16,542	?	7,650	17,840	8,350	18,440	8,190	19,080	10,120	20,975	9,230	17,750
Local preachers	c	c	23	38	20	18	29	18	33	17	35	19	36	13	33
Class leaders	c	c	99	195	87	c	c	c	c	c	c	c	c	c	c
Sunday schools	c	c	15	38	26	27	58	23	54	20	54	20	53	22	53
Teachers	84	280	94	352	162	158	446	141	443	138	425	113	426	131	326
Students	537	1,751	604	2,268	1,030	955	3,016	1,431	3,162	827	3,067	780	3,080	863	2,224
Chapels				c	15		c		c	20	35	20	36	24	42

[a]No information for the district
[b]Includes one 'salaried agent' in New Ireland and one in St Armand
[c]Data not included
[d]Includes one 'salaried agent' in Melbourne
[e]Includes one 'salaried agent' in Dunham

Source: National Archives of Canada, Methodist Missionary Society, Synod Minutes. Lower Canada / Canada East.

Notes

Preface

1 Frye, *The Bush Garden*, and Harris, 'Canadian Archipelago.'
2 Rawlyk, 'Religion and Popular Culture,' 187.
3 There is little evidence to support Rawlyk's claim that Canadian evangelization was 'more radical, more anarchistic, and more populist than its American counterpart' in the early nineteenth century. Rawlyk, 'Introduction,' *Aspects of The Canadian Evangelical Experience*, xv.
4 For a recent study on this theme, see Hubert, 'Ritual Performance.'
5 Notable exceptions are Greer, 'L'habitant, la paroisse rurale et la politique,' 19–34; Acheson, *Saint John*; Marks, *Revivals and Roller Rinks*; Schrauwers, *Awaiting the Millennium*; Clarke, *Piety and Nationalism*; Stanley-Blackwell, '"Tabernacles in the Wilderness"'; Van Die, 'Marks of a Genuine Revival'; and Little, 'A Crime "Shrouded in Mystery."'
6 Little, *State and Society in Transition*.
7 See Little, 'A Moral Engine.'
8 See Nelson, 'Rage against the Dying of the Light'; Greer, *Patriots and the People*; Dessureault and Hudon, 'Conflits sociaux'; and Little, *State and Society*, chapter 7.
9 On this theme, see Gauvreau, 'Protestantism Transformed.'
10 McKinsey and Konrad, *Borderlands Reflections*, 4.
11 Adelman and Aron, 'From Borderlands to Borders.' For a recent Canadian overview, see Widdis, ''Borders, Borderlands and Canadian Identity.'
12 See Konrad, 'Borderlines and Borderlands.'
13 For brief overviews, see McGuigan, 'Administration of Land Policy'; and Little, 'British Toryism.'
14 The Eastern Townships also represented a borderland between a French

Catholic and an English Protestant culture, but social interaction was limited and the effects were felt largely by the French-Canadian newcomers to the region. See Hudon, *Prêtres et fidèles*.
15 Buckner, 'Borderlands Concept,' 156–7.
16 See, for example, Little, 'Mental World of Ralph Merry.'

1 Protestant Identity in the Eastern Townships

1 *Harbinger,* 15 June 1842, 87.
2 The following brief survey of population development is from Little, *Ethno-Cultural Transition*.
3 See, for example, French, *Parsons and Politics*; and Moir, *Enduring Witness*. The Lower Canadian Protestants are also largely ignored in Murphy and Perin, eds, *Concise History*; and Noll, *History of Christianity*.
4 Only 9.3 per cent were identified as Wesleyans, but examination of the manuscript census reveals that most of the 'other Methodists' (9.9 per cent) were not a distinct category. The more recently established New Connection Methodists (6.5 per cent) were also British-based.
5 Westfall, *Two Worlds* 13.
6 Cleveland, *Sketch of the Early Settlement*, 72–3.
7 Marini, *Radical Sects*, 4. A good brief description of the distinctions between Old Lights and New Lights can be found in Bassett, 'Cabin Religion,' 76.
8 Roth, *Democratic Dilemma*, 27.
9 Marini, *Radical Sects*, 5–6.
10 Ibid., 6–7.
11 Roth, *Democratic Dilemma*, 1–2, 12. In 1841 Vermont had 22,666 Congregationalists with 203 churches; 16,039 Episcopal Methodists with 92 exclusive churches and 40–50 others, which they shared; approximately 11,025 Regular Baptists with 139 churches; 4,423 Freewill Baptists with 100 churches; 92 Universalist societies with 62 meeting houses; between 30 and 40 Christian churches; and 4 congregations of Unitarians. Thompson, *History of Vermont*, 176–93.
12 Ludlum, *Social Ferment*, 17. Potash ('Welfare of the Regions Beyond') makes a sharp distinction between conservative southeastern Vermont and the radical territory west of the Green Mountains.
13 Quoted in Little, ed., 'Journal of Archdeacon G.J. Mountain,' 87–8.
14 Ludlum, *Social Ferment*, 51. Cross (*Burned-Over District*, 13) states that the grand climax for revivalism in western New York took place between 1825 and 1837.

15 Montreal Diocesan Archives (MDA), Reid Papers, J. Reid to Bishop of Quebec, St Armand, 18 Feb. 1839.
16 Marini, *Radical Sects,* 7.
17 On the economy and society of the New England hill country, see Marini, *Radical Sects,* 29–30, 39.
18 Marini, *Radical Sects,* 29–31; Barkun, *Crucible of the Millennium,* 106.
19 Kenny, *Perfect Law of Liberty.* Hatch (*Democratization of American Christianity,* 9–10, 44, 65) claims, more specifically, that early American religious dissent essentially reflected a virulent anticlericalism, or what he calls a 'crisis of authority.'
20 On the central role of town government in New Hampshire, and the rise of taxes during the revolutionary era, see Daniell, *Experiment in Republicanism.* On Shay's Rebellion in Massachusetts and the similar movement in rural New Hampshire, also in 1786, see Marini, *Radical Sects,* 34–5. On backcountry dissent in general, see Hatch, *Democratization of American Christianity,* 30–4.
21 Roth, *Democratic Dilemma,* 26, 30, 32–5, 77.
22 Cited in Labrèque, 'Les Églises,' 99.
23 Kesteman et al., *Histoire des Cantons de l'Est,* 182–3, 186.
24 The Dutch theologian Jacob Arminius (1560–1609) rejected predestination and stressed the universal availability of God's saving grace. See Semple, *Lord's Dominion,* 14.
25 Kesteman et al., *Histoire des Cantons de l'Est,* 188; and Kesteman, 'Au pays des "sectes,"' 22.
26 Quebec Diocesan Archives (QDA), series D, folder 91, C.J. Quebec to Rev. Sir, Quebec, 15 Nov. 1827.
27 Victoria University Archives, United Church Archives (VU/UCA), The Wesleyan Methodist Church (Great Britain). Foreign Missions: America ... Correspondence. 78.128c [hereafter Wesleyan Correspondence], box 15, file 94, no. 28, James Booth to James Townley, Stanstead, 2 March 1831.
28 Quoted in Stuart, 'Episcopate of Jacob Mountain,' 232.
29 Robins, 'Vernacular American Landscape,' 166. French ('Evangelical Creed,' 18) claims that the proportion was only 15.5 per cent.
30 As of November 1844, Freewill Baptist members had contributed $939.00, Universalists $681.50, and Methodists $267.00, with the result that the first group was assigned twenty-six Sabbaths, the second group nineteen Sabbaths, and the third group eight Sabbaths. The exact dates were selected a year in advance. By November 1845, Universalist investment was $741.75, Freewill Baptist was $547.25, Protestant Methodist was $424.00, and Wes-

leyan Methodist was $213.50. Stanstead Historical Society, BD-A-41.1, Minute Book of the Griffin Corner United [*sic*] Church, 37, 41.
31 Febvre, *Problem of Unbelief.*
32 In their additions at the bottom of each page the Compton enumerators lumped with religious denominations a number of people whom they had identified as free-thinkers.
33 Three exceptions are Greenlaw, 'Choix pratiques'; Darroch and Soltow, *Property and Inequality*; and Baskerville, 'Did Religion Matter?'.
34 The eleven townships, chosen in part for their distribution, are Stanbridge, Shefford, Brome, St Armand, Durham, Orford, Ascot, Inverness, Ireland, Leeds, and Halifax.
35 See Kesteman et al., *Histoire des Cantons de l'Est*, 127–45.
36 This is the theory referred to in Darroch and Soltow's denominational analysis. See their *Property and Inequality*, 48–9.
37 In the following comparisons, the mean for all the farmers in the township is followed by the mean for those farmers not declaring a religious affiliation. Shefford: average farm size (acres) – 118.6 vs 115.6; land improved (acres) – 30.6 vs 26.5; wheat (bu.) – 14.9 vs 17.3; oats (bu.) – 6.2 vs 6.2; potatoes – 114.9 vs 98.3; cattle – 6.7 vs 5.7; horses – 0.8 vs 0.6; sheep – 9.4 vs 6.8; and hogs – 2.3 vs 2.3. Brome: average farm size (acres) – 121.5 vs 127.1; land improved (acres) – 31.4 vs 32.7; wheat (bu.) – 16.1 vs 17.2; oats (bu.) – 16.6 vs 16.7; potatoes – 176.3 vs 197.6; cattle – 7.2 vs 7.5; horses – 1.0 vs 0.9; sheep – 10.0 vs 9.7; and hogs – 3.3 vs 3.3.
38 In Eaton Township there were only six mixed marriages among the 241 married couples listed in the 1852 manuscript census, and in Melbourne only eight among 269.
39 Darroch and Soltow, *Property and Inequality*, 48, 52.
40 This was nevertheless a slow process in the Eastern Townships until well into the twentieth century. See Kesteman et al., *Histoire des Cantons de l'Est*, 283, table 7.3.
41 See, for example, Grant, *Profusion of Spires*, 57.

2 The Pioneer Era

1 The information in this section on Joseph Badger is taken from E.G. Hubbard's *Memoir.*
2 According to Hubbard, elder was the term then commonly used for Baptist ministers, though it had become obsolete by mid-century. Badger does not mention Moulton's first name, but Avery Moulton of Stanstead received his licence to preach as a Freewill Baptist in 1804, and was ordained two years

later. As we shall see below, he helped lead a revival in the church in 1811–12. Hubbard, *Forests and Clearings*, 98.
3 See Epps, *Eastern Townships Adventure*, 108–11, 112–15, 118–21, 149–52, 170–3.
4 Badger does not mention Nichols's first name, but he was a justice of the peace in the early nineteenth century. See Little, 'William Bowman Felton,' 282. See also LaBrèque, 'Jesse Pennoyer,' and 'Gilbert Hyatt.'
5 See Rawlyk and Stewart, 'Nova Scotia's Sense of Mission,' 5–17.
6 Grant, *Profusion of Spires*, 32.
7 Wood, *Memory of Henry Wilkes*, 20; Eddy, 'Beginnings of Congregationalism,' 164–7.
8 Stuart, 'Episcopate of Jacob Mountain,' 241, 291–2; Channell, *History of Compton County*, 68. Wood (*Memoir*, 22) states that the Congregational church was established in 1815, and Taylor left it in 1821.
9 Marini, *Radical Sects*, 36–7, 172.
10 Fitch, *Baptists of Canada*, 101–2.
11 For some unknown reason, Baptist historians have stated that in 1796 the whole membership from Caldwell's Manor moved to Eaton Township where they became known as the Sawyerville church. This church was not organized until 1822. Terry, 'Sawyerville Baptist Church'; Fitch, *Baptists of Canada*, 103; Ivison and Rosser, *Baptists in Upper and Lower Canada*, 158–60.
12 Hubbard, *Forests and Clearings*, 97; Canadian Baptist Archives, McMaster University (hereafter CBA), Hatley Church Minute Book, 1799–1844; CBA, 'Memoir of William Marsh,' *The Register* (Montreal), vol. 2, 27 July 1843, 116. In contradiction to this memoir, on which they base most of their information, the Baptist historians mistakenly state that Marsh lived in Hatley from 1799 to 1811. Fitch, *Baptists of Canada*, 103; Ivison and Rosser, *Baptists in Upper and Lower Canada*, 158–60.
13 Quoted in Ivison and Rosser, *Baptists in Upper and Lower Canada*, 162–3.
14 Hubbard, *Forests and Clearings*, 97–8.
15 Carroll, *Case*, 1: 28.
16 'Memoir of William Marsh,' 117–18.
17 Hibbard, *Exercises*, 50–1; Crocker, *History of the Baptists*, 231–2.
18 For the floor plan, see Hibbard, *Exercises*, 73–4.
19 'List of Members,' in ibid., 67–9.
20 Crocker, *History of the Baptists*, 241, 242, 244; CBA, Barnston Baptist Church, parish records.
21 Quoted in Ivison and Rosser, *Baptists in Upper and Lower Canada*, 161.
22 See ibid., 161–3; and the table in Wright, *History of the Shaftsbury Baptist Association*, 369.

23 Crocker, *History of the Baptists*, 344–5.
24 On the Freewill Baptist theology, see Baxter, *History of the Freewill Baptists*, 124–37.
25 Marini, *Radical Sects*, 94; Ludlum, *Social Ferment*, 35. On the influence of Henry Alline on the Freewill Baptists, see Rawlyk, *Ravished by the Spirit*, chapter 2.
26 Robinson Smith was ordained by the newly established Hardwick (later Wheelock) Quarterly Meeting. Stewart, *History of the Freewill Baptists*, 1: 258–9; Hubbard, *Forests and Clearings*, 99.
27 Stewart, *History of the Freewill Baptists*, 1: 260.
28 Hubbard, *Forests and Clearings*, 98–9.
29 Archives Nationales du Québec à Sherbrooke (ANQS), P1000, 1A13-6603A, Fonds Lyster, William Hamilton, Rev., Compton Church Record, Free Will Baptist Church (hereafter, Compton Church Record), 1.
30 Hubbard, *Memoir*, 32.
31 Roth, *Democratic Dilemma*, 82.
32 Ward, 'Religious Enthusiasm,' 67–9, 105. The New England Methodist Conference had been established in 1796. Methodist conferences met every four years, and ensured that power remained evenly divided between the bishops and the preachers.
33 Semple, *Lord's Dominion*, 136–7.
34 Butler, *Awash in a Sea of Faith*, 237–41. See also Hatch, *Democratization*, 36–40, 50.
35 McNairn, 'Mission to Canada,' 54; Mudge, *History of the New England Conference*, 65; Grant, *Profusion of Spires*, 30. See also Playter, *History of Methodism*, 60–1; Findlay and Holdsworth, *History of the Wesleyan Methodist Missionary Society*, 1: 369–70.
36 [Dow], *Dealings of God*, 1: 33–4.
37 Playter, *History of Methodism*, 61.
38 Carroll, *Case*, 1: 74–5. McNairn ('Mission to Canada,' 54) states that Dow was succeeded by Elijah Hedding for a few months.
39 Clark, Potts, and Payton, eds, *Journal and Letters of Francis Asbury*, 3: 267; VU/UCA, 78.131C, Methodist Episcopal Church, Journals of the New York Conference, 1800–39, 4 July 1803, 18. A local history also refers to Roswell Bourn of Vermont who settled in Potton Township around 1803, and 'travelled and preached in the townships adjoing, and in Vermont,' even though he was too poor to afford a horse. Thomas, *Contributions*, 310–11.
40 Hubbard states that the New England Conference appointed the Reverend Joseph Fairbanks to Stanstead in 1804. Hubbard, *Forests and Clearings*, 84. A quarterly meeting held at St Armand on 25 September 1806 appointed a

presiding elder and a deacon, as well as licensing one man to preach and another to exhort on the Dunham circuit. Bishop's University, Eastern Townships Research Centre (hereafter ETRC), UCA, Quebec-Sherbrooke Presbytery, Dunham Civil Registers (Methodist) and Quarterly Board Records (hereafter Dunham Methodist Minutes), 3, 25 Sept. 1806. On the boundaries and dates of origin of each circuit in the Eastern Townships prior to 1851, see Noël, *Competing for Souls*, 130, table 8.

41 Carroll, *Case*, 1: 118; Bangs, *History of the Methodist Episcopal Church*, 2: 181. For the annual membership of the Methodist circuits in the Eastern Townships, see Noël, *Competing for Souls*, 139–41, table 9. The totals listed for each year are actually based on reports from the previous year.

42 Carroll, *Case*, 1: 139–40, 144; Mudge, *History of the New England Conference*, 56; *Minutes of the annual conferences*, I: 141, 148. McNairn ('Mission to Canada,' 55) mistakenly states that the Dunham and Stanstead circuits were both established in 1807 as part of the New England Conference.

43 Carroll, *Case*, 1: 191–2. Hibbard was twenty-two years old, and described as single, pious, and gifted. (VU/UCA, Methodist Episcopal Church, Journals of the New York Conference, 44. See also Findlay and Holdsworth, *History of the Wesleyan*, I: 373.) Semple (*Lord's Dominion*, 42) mistakenly locates the St Francis River northeast of Quebec City, but also states that its territory overlapped the disputed boundary with Maine.

44 Carroll, *Case*, vol. 1, 213, 215, 244–5. Hubbard (*Forests and Clearings*, 90) states that Kilborn was an itinerant preacher in New Hampshire and Vermont who frequently visited his brother's family in Barnston Township.

45 Hubbard, *Memoir*, 32; *Minutes of the annual conferences*, 1: 202, Carroll, *Case*, I: 279. The Wesleyan missionary John DePutron reported in 1821 that the American preachers remained on their circuits between eight and nine months, and delivered about twelve sermons to each place on their circuit. VU/UCA, The Wesleyan Methodist Church (Great Britain). Foreign Missions: America ... Correspondence. 78.128c (hereafter Wesleyan Correspondence), box 4, no. 9, John DePutron to Rev. and Dear Sir, Shipton, 18 May 1821.

46 Carroll, *Case*, 1: 275–6. Semple (*Lord's Dominion*, 14) mistakenly states that Montreal had the only American missionary active in Lower Canada during the war. Ashur Smith, an Episcopal Methodist preacher who had settled on a Stanstead farm, was convinced not to re-enter Lower Canada during the War of 1812. Thomas, *Contributions*, 349–51.

47 Carroll, *Case*, 1: 227, 278.

48 Quoted in ibid., 279.

49 Robert Hibbard was drowned while returning to the St Francis Circuit to

'encourage the young societies to hold fast' in 1812. Playter, *History of Methodism*, 112.
50 *Minutes of the Annual Conferences*, vol. 1, 210, 228, 245. These numbers differ significantly from the higher ones recorded in Noël, *Competing for Souls*, 139.
51 Hubbard, *Memoir*, 73–4, 77–8. There were few black settlers in the Eastern Townships, aside from some Loyalist slaves and servants in the Missisquoi Bay area, but a local history published in 1874 (Hubbard, *Forests and Clearings*, 90) states that Samuel Dunbar was a local preacher from Barnston Township (he had obviously moved eastward) whose 'labours in public, and in administering the consolations of religion for the sick and dying, were abundant and were attended with much success. He was greatly respected and beloved.' There is also a reference to Dunbar at the Outlet (Magog) in 1817. Stanstead Historical Society Archives, 'A Memoir of Ralph Merry IV, 1786–1863' (typescript), 8 Oct. 1817, book 1, 20.
52 VU/UCA, Methodist Episcopal Church, Journals of New York Conference, 24 May 1810, 52; French, *Parsons and Politics*, 12.
53 On this struggle, see Semple, *Lord's Dominion*, 45–52.
54 Ward, 'Religious Enthusiasm,' 61–4.
55 Marini, *Radical Sects*, 124–6; see also MacDonald, *Rebellion in the Mountains*, 3–5.
56 Miller, *Larger Hope*, 661–2. The regional associations had essentially all the powers of the New England Convention, and served, in effect, as the first jurisdiction for congregational disputes. Marini, *Radical Sects*, 126.
57 Badger does not mention a date, but his family arrived in Compton in 1801 and the Baptists were active there by 1808. Hubbard, *Memoir*, 30–1.
58 William Farewell was from Barre, Vermont. See Hubbard, *Memoir*, 52–3, 86; Hubbard, *Forests and Clearings*, 101.
59 Zielinski, *Story of the Farnham Meeting*, 15–18; Shufelt, *Nicholas Austin*, 9, 26–30, 121–3.
60 Zielinski, *Story of the Farnham Meeting*, 19–20. Dorland *(History of the Society of Friends*, 39) identifies the pioneer in question as Aaron Bull, and claims that he did become a Quaker.
61 Grant, *Profusion of Spires*, 28.
62 While St Armand was technically a seigneurie, it is located east of Missisquoi Bay and in practice the settlers did not become censitaires. Gendron et al., *Histoire du Piémont*, 45.
63 Stuart, 'Episcopate of Jacob Mountain,' 39–40, 62–3; Millman, *Jacob Mountain*, 104–6; Millman, *Life of Stewart*, 10–11.
64 National Archives (NA), MG24 J7, C.C. Cotton Papers, Cotton to Anna, Dunham, 9 Aug. 1810.

65 Millman, *Short History*, 8–9.
66 NA, MG24 J47, Cotton Papers, Cotton to My Dear Sister, Missisquoi Bay, 31 Dec. 1804.
67 QDA, B4, 53, Cotton to My Lord, Missisquoi Bay, 19 Feb. 1805, 3 April 1805.
68 Ibid., 3 April 1805.
69 Ibid., 21 May 1805.
70 Ibid.
71 NA, MG24 J47, Cotton Papers, Cotton to Frances Cotton, Missisquoi Bay, 3 Aug. 1807.
72 Ibid., Cotton to Mary J. Cotton, Missisquoi Bay, 27 July 1807.
73 Ibid., Cotton to father, Missisquoi Bay, 31 March 1807; Cotton to Louisa Cotton, Missisquoi Bay, 15 Nov. 1807; Cotton to Frances Cotton, Missisquoi Bay, 3 Aug. 1807.
74 Ibid., Cotton to father, Missisquoi Bay, 22 March, 18 April, 26 April 1808.
75 Cotton's father died in 1811 without his son having contributed anything to relieve him from debt. Ibid., Cotton to Anna, Dunham, 1 July 1811; Cotton to Mary J. Cotton, Dunham, 8 Sept. 1811.
76 Thomas, *Contributions*, 138.
77 Montreal Diocesan Archives (MDA), Jacob Mountain Papers, RG 1.3, J. Mountain to C. Cotton, Rosemount, 30 Sept. 1809 (draft).
78 NA, MG24 J7, Cotton Papers, Cotton to Fanny, Dunham, 24 Sept. 1811.
79 MDA, Cotton Papers, Mary S. Wisdom to Canon Kelly, Shawinigan Falls, 7 Mar. 1936; Reisner, *Measure of Faith*, 56.
80 NA, MG24 J7, Cotton Papers, Cotton to Sister Anna, Dunham, 20 July 1814.
81 Stewart's father was the seventh Earl of Galway. On Charles Stewart's early life, see Millman, *Life of Stewart*, 1–8.
82 Hawkins, *Annals*, 307. Henshaw met Stewart in 1811 when the former was a young missionary in northern Vermont. His memoir appears as Appendix A in Hawkins's book.
83 Hawkins, *Annals*, 308. In contrast to Reid, A.N Bethune, editor of *The Church*, stated that Henshaw's description of Stewart was substantially accurate. Millman, *Life of Stewart*, 172.
84 Hawkins, *Annals*, 38; Stuart, 'Episcopate,' 11–13; Millman, *Life of Stewart*, 8–9.
85 Quoted in Millman, *Life of Stewart*, 13.
86 *The Church*, 30 March 1839. Reprinted in *Canadian Church & Mission News*, July–August 1888, 164.
87 Quoted in Hawkins, *Annals*, 43–5.
88 QDA, Unbound Manuscripts, case 1, folder 5, 1807–15, Stewart, Delivered at Trinity Church on Trinity Sunday, the 21st of May 1815, and St Paul's Church, Sept. the 10th.

89 Seven subscribers, in addition to Stewart, committed themselves in March 1808 to having the church ready for services by the following 1 November, 'or sooner if possible, provided we are not prevented by War, which God forbid!' Brome County Historical Society, Frelighsburg Church, C. Stewart et al., St Armand, 26 March 1808.
90 QDA, D7, C. Stewart to Dr Morice, St Armand, 22 Apr. 1808; Hawkins, *Annals*, 41–3; Stuart, 'Episcopate,' 14–17, 22–3, 26, 51–4; Millman, *Life of Stewart*, 15–17, 22.
91 QDA, Unbound Manuscripts, case 1, folder 3, Jacob Mountain Letters, 1802–25 (Private and Personal), J. Mountain to Miss Brooke, Missiskoui Bay, 22 Aug. 1809. In 1829 Bishop Mountain's son George expressed quite a different opinion of the singing at Philipsburg and at Caldwell's Manor (Noyan), West of Missisquoi Bay. See Little, 'Journal,' 106.
92 A subscription in Quebec, Montreal, Chambly, and St Johns had also raised £150 for the two new churches in St Armand. QDA, D7, C. Stewart to Dr Morice, St Armand, 5 Nov. 1808, 1 May 1810, 1 Nov. 1810; C. Stewart to Bishop Mountain, St Armand, 1 Oct. 1810; D8, C. Stewart to Dr Morice, St Armand, 1 Nov. 1811; Hawkins, *Annals*, 48; Stuart, 'Episcopate,' 26; Millman, *Life of Stewart*, 20–1.
93 QDA, Bishop C.J. Stewart, 1807–36, 'The Honble and Rev. C.J. Stewart's Brief Journal of his 1st Voyage to Canada Aug. 1807, & of his arrival at St Armand Oct. 1807.' Despite the title, the journal continues to 1812.
94 Ibid., D8, C. Stewart to Dr Morice, 1 May 1813. For a brief description of the war in the Missiquoi Bay area, see Millman, *Life of Stewart*, chapter 3.
95 QDA, D8, C. Stewart to Dr Morice, 1 Nov. 1813; Millman, *Life of Stewart*, 28.
96 QDA, D8, C. Stewart to Dr Morice, St Armand, 2 May 1814.
97 Stewart, *Short View*, 9–10.
98 Gendron et al., *Histoire du Piémont*, 110.
99 QDA, Reid Collection, C. Stewart to J. Reid, Steamboat, River St Lawrence, 26 July [1815].

3 The Congregationalists

1 *Home Missionary*, Oct. 1833, 101.
2 Parker is being quoted by R.S. Storrs in *Home Missionary*, Dec. 1833, 141–2.
3 *Home Missionary*, Nov. 1833, 117. On counterfeiting in the Eastern Townships, see Little, *State and Society*, chapter 2.
4 *Home Missionary*, Nov. 1833, 118.
5 Cooper, 'Canada Education and Home Missionary Society,' 43; *Reports of the American Home Missionary Society*, 1836, 69.

6 Eddy, 'Beginnings,' 167–71; Millar, 'Thaddeus Osgood,' 665.
7 QDA, Diocesan Papers, vol. 1, 78, Bishop Quebec to Dr Andrews and Dr Gaskin, Quebec, 16 Nov. 1812.
8 Millar, 'Remarkable Rev. Thaddeus Osgood,' 59–76; Sweet, 'Nineteenth-Century Evangelicalism,' 884–6.
9 ETRC, UCA, Ammi Parker Papers (hereafter APP), 5/Par/4, 'Church History,' 1870, 33–4; For a more detailed study of Parker, see Little, 'Serving,' 21–54.
10 Parker, 'Church History,' 34–5.
11 Eddy, 'Beginnings,' 174–5. Information also kindly provided by John Scott of Georgeville, Quebec, based on his reading of the unpublished memoir of Gibb's granddaughter, Isabel Barrows, 'Chopped Straw, or the memories of three-score years'; and of James Stark, *John Murker of Banff: a picture of religious life and character in the north*, 2nd ed. (London: Hodder and Stoughton, 1887).
12 Archives Nationales du Québec à Montréal, United Church Archives, Montreal-Ottawa Conference, Canada Education and Home Missionary Society Papers (hereafter CEHMS), A.J. Parker to Perkins, 24 Nov. 1834; A.J. Parker to Sec. of Mont. Ladies Sewing Soc., Shipton, 21 Feb. 1835; A.J. Parker to Perkins, [n.a.], 8 Dec. 1835.
13 CEHMS, Rev. M. White to Perkins, Southampton, 12 May 1836.
14 Ibid., Lewis Sabin to W.F. Curry, Stanstead, 23 Sept. 1836.
15 Ibid., Lewis Sabin to Curry, Stanstead, 17 April 1837; W. Ritchie to Curry, Stanstead, 4 May 1837; Lewis Sabin to Curry, Stanstead, 5 June 1837.
16 Ibid., R.V. Hall to Curry, Stanstead, 13 Dec. 1837, 10 Jan. 1838, 19 March 1838,
17 Ibid., 24 July 1838, 31 Oct. 1838, 17 Dec. 1838.
18 Ibid., CEHMS, [R.V. Hall] to Rev. & Dear Sir, Stanstead, 14 Jan. 1839. The first contribution of the ladies' sewing circle was directed at spreading English in the French-Canadian settlements through the schools sponsored by the CEHMS. Mrs L. Colby to Rev. Sir, [n.a.], 3 Feb. 1839.
19 Ibid., R.V. Hall to Curry, Stanstead, 12 March 1839; R.V. Hall to W. Taylor, Stanstead, 8 Oct. 1839; R.V. Hall to C. Strong, Stanstead, 28 April 1840; 2 March 1841.
20 Ibid., R.V. Hall to Strong, Stanstead, 24 April 1841.
21 Ibid., 30 Aug. 1842.
22 Ibid., R.V. Hall to Secretary of CEHMS, Stanstead, 6 Nov. 1842.
23 ETRC, UCA, St Francis Association, 1836–66, Minutes, 28 Dec. 1842, 92.
24 CEHMS, R.V. Hall to Strong, Stanstead, 8 Jan. 1843.
25 Ibid., R.V. Hall to Strong, Stanstead, April 1843. See also Little, *Child Letters*, 37.

26 Ibid., Stanstead Church Committee to Strong, 9 May 1843.
27 Ibid., R.V. Hall to Strong, Stanstead, 28 Dec. 1844.
28 Parker, 'Church History,' 35–6, 38–40.
29 APP, A.J. Parker, 'For 35th Anniversary of my Introduction to the field, thru back of Shipton now Danville, C.E., March 8, 1864'; Parker, 'Congregationalism in the Eastern Townships.'
30 Parker, 'Church History,' 43.
31 APP, 5/Par/15, Report to Directors of Can. Ed. & H.M. Society, Shipton, 20 July 1829; 5/Par/23, E.S.P. to Miss Hazelton, Danville, 7 Feb. 1871.
32 Curtis is described in 'Rev. A.J. Parker,' *Canadian Independent*, March 1894, 55–6.
33 Ward, 'Religious Enthusiasm,' 111–14, 130–2.
34 Scott, *From Office to Profession*, 77–84.
35 APP, 5/Par/23, E.S.P. to Miss Hazleton of Sherbooke, Danville, 7 Dec. 1871.
36 Ward, 'Religious Enthusiasm,' 132–43. The phrase is from Sweet, 'Nineteenth-Century Evangelicalism,' 886–7.
37 ETRC, UCA, APP, 5/Par/25(4), 11 Nov. 1866; Parker, 'Church History,' 41–2; Parker, 'History of the Congregational Church.' Scott (*From Office to Profession*, 119) notes that ministers frequently fell into difficulty with their congregations after revivals because they could not meet the preaching standards that had been established by the visiting clergy.
38 Parker, 'Church History,' 43; Parker, 'History of the Congregational Church'; 'History of Danville Church,' 20; APP, 5/Par/16, A.J. Parker to Com. of Can. Ed. & H.M. Soc'y, Shipton, 31 July 1833.
39 CEHMS, A.J. Parker to G.W. Perkins, Shipton, 26 March 1833; Geo. Bangs et al. to Directors of CEHMS, Shipton, Sept. 1833.
40 Danville United Church Archives, Rev. 17, verse 16 [?], Shipton, May 1830.
41 ETRC, UCA, *Report of the Canada Education and Home Missionary Society*, 1834, 8–9. On the temperance movement in the Eastern Townships, see Little, 'Moral Engine.'
42 Ward, 'Religious Enthusiasm,' 114–21. See also Roth, *Democratic Dilemma*, 94.
43 CEHMS, Report of W.C. Lord et al. to Montreal Ladies Sewing Society, Shipton, 18 Aug. 1834.
44 APP, 5/Par/17, A.J. Parker to Montreal Ladies' Sewing Society, Shipton, 18 Feb. 1834. Of the nucleus of twenty-five, only six of the men and six of the women had died or 'removed' by 1850. ETRC, UCA, DPR, 10/Dan/20, Names of Church Members from Nov. 11, 1832 ... to Nov. 11, 1850, Danville Congregational Church; *Canadian Independent*, 19 (July 1872–June 1873), 201.
45 *Home Missionary*, March 1835, 186.

46 ETRC, UCA, Danville Civil Registers, vol. 1, 1834–52, 20–21 Aug. 1834. Parker had already baptized thirty-eight infants and attended forty funerals, but he did not dare officiate at marriages. Parker, 'Church History,' 46, 48.
47 See Veilleux, 'John Fletcher' 300; and Little, 'British Toryism.'
48 Eddy, 'Beginnings,' 164, 182–5.
49 According to Scott (*From Office to Profession*, 120–1), such means to get around the permanence implied by ordination and installation became increasingly common in the early nineteenth century.
50 Danville United Church Archives, Agreement made this 11th day of July 1839 between Rev. Ammi J. Parker on one part & Henry Barnard et al. on the other part. ETRC, UCA, Danville, Civil Registers, vol. 1, 1834–52; Sweet, *Religion in the Development*, 265.
51 'History of Danville Church,' 19–20; ETRC, UCA, *Report of the Canada Education and Home Missionary Society*, 1834, 6.
52 APP, 5/Par/10, Commission to Rev. Ammi Parker from American Home Missionary Society, New York, for missionary work in Danville Congregational Church, 21 Aug. 1837; ETRC, UCA, DPR, 10/Dan/13, Milton Badger to Rev. A.J. Parker, New York, 13 Sept. 1837.
53 Thus, the average payment had actually declined slightly, from $4.73 to $4.55. APP, 5/Par/9, Subscriptions for payment of salary to Rev. Ammi Parker at Shipton, 1832, 1834, and undated three items.
54 Danville United Church Archives, Agreement between A.J. Parker and Henry Barnard et al., 11 July 1829; ETRC, UCA, DPR, F.P. Cleveland to Rev. E.C. Woodley, Lorne, 7 Feb. 1910.
55 APP, 5/Par/7, Account Book, A.J. Parker, 1829–47.
56 APP, 5/Par/22, untitled address, Nov. 1850.
57 Landholdings under ten acres were excluded from these calculations.
58 *Home Missionary*, Nov. 1836, 129.
59 Quoted in Noël, *Competing for Souls*, 191.
60 Scott, *From Office to Profession*, 142–3.
61 Cleveland to Woodley, 7 Feb. 1910.
62 APP, 5/Par/17, A.J. Parker to Secretary Montreal Ladies' Sewing Circle, Shipton, 18 Feb. 1834.
63 APP, 5/Par/19(1), A.J. Parker to Rev. G.W. Perkins, Shipton, 9 Dec. 1833.
64 CEHMS, A.J. Parker to Dr Br Perkins, St. Albans, Vt, 25 Feb. 1833; G.W. Perkins to editor of *Vermont Chronicle*, 30 April 1833; A.J. Parker to G.W. Perkins, Shipton, 26 March 1833, April 1833.
65 APP, 5/Par/19(1), A.J. Parker to Rev. G.W. Perkins, Shipton, 9 Dec. 1833; CEHMS, G.W. Perkins to A.J. Parker, Montreal, 23 Dec. 1833.

308   Notes to pages 73–8

66 CEHMS, A.J. Parker to G.W. Perkins, Newport, Vt, 20 Jan. 1834; A.J. Parker's Report of Agency to Secretary of CEHMS [11 Feb. 1834].
67 *Home Missionary,* Oct. 1833, 99–103; CEHMS, R. Storrs to Rev. C. Perry, Braintree [Mass.], 21 Jan. 1834.
68 APP, 5/Par/18, R.S. Storrs to Rev. J.A. [*sic*] Parker, Braintree, Mass., 7 June 1834; CEHMS, J.J. Gilberte to A.J. Parker, Phillipsburg, 10 Sept. 1834; Henryville, 30 Oct. 1835; J.J. Gilberte to G.W. Perkins, Phillipsburg, 8 Nov. 1834; Henryville, 6 Jan. 1835; J.W. Curtis to G.W. Perkins, Compton, 16 Sept. 1834; [Apr. 1835]; Lennoxville, 13 Jan. 1835.
69 CEHMS, A.J. Parker to G.W. Perkins, Shipton, 8 Jan. 1835; 20 Jan. 1835, addendum 14 Feb. 1835; G.W. Perkins to A.J. Parker, Montreal, 1 Apr. 1835.
70 CEHMS, G.W. Perkins to W.F. Curry, Montreal, 6 May 1835, G.W. Perkins to A.J. Parker, Montreal 14 May 1835; 14 July 1835; A.J. Parker to G.W. Perkins, Shipton, 11 Aug. 1835.
71 APP, 5/Par/19, A.J. Parker to Rev. G.W. Perkins, Shipton, 5 Oct. 1835.
72 ETRC, UCA, Twenty-Second Annual Report of the Female Auxiliary to the New Hampshire Missionary Society, Concord, N.H., 1835, 7.
73 CEHMS, W.F. Curry to A.J. Parker, Montreal, 27 Jan. 1837.
74 CEHMS, A.J. Parker to W.F. Curry, Shipton, 6 June 1837.
75 Ibid., Danville, 8 Aug., 25 July 1837.
76 Ibid., A.J. Parker to W.F. Curry, Danville, 17 Aug. 1837; 20 Nov. 1837.
77 Ibid., Simeon Flint et al. to W.F. Curry, Danville, 11 Dec. 1838.
78 Ibid., A.J. Parker to Rev. Caleb Strong, Danville, 27 April 1840.
79 APP, 5/Par/3, Copy of Instructions to Rev. A.J. Parker, 30 Jan. 1841; C.S. to Brother Parker, Montreal, 30 Jan. 1841.
80 These stories are published in Little, 'Perils in the Wilderness.'
81 ETRC/UCA, St Francis Association, 28 July 1836, 6–7.
82 Ibid., 7 July 1836, 16; 29 Dec. 1836, 26. This forum was the origin of a number of the essays (including 'Why am I a Congregationalist?') still preserved in Parker's personal papers.
83 Ibid., 13–14 Feb. 1838, 39–41; 14 June 1838, 45.
84 Société d'histoire de Sherbrooke, Sherbrooke Total Abstinence Society, Minute Book, 8 Jan. 1846.
85 Sweet, 'Nineteenth-Century Evangelicalism,' 878.
86 APP, 5/Par/16,A.J. Parker to Com. of Can. Ed. & H.M. Soc'y, Shipton, 31 July 1833.
87 Hamilton, *With Heart,* 165.
88 CEHMS, Report of Rev. Gleed, Mar. 1833; Petition to Rev. Perkins, Granby, 26 March 1833.
89 Ibid., Rev. Gleed to Rev. Perkins, 21 Oct. 1833.

Notes to pages 78–84   309

90 Ibid., A.W. Burton, clerk, Shefford, Oct. 1833; Gleed to Perkins, 20 Dec. 1833 (with two undated enclosures).
91 Ibid., J. Gleed to Perkins, Granby, 10 Sept. 1834.
92 Ibid., 30 April 1835.
93 Ibid., J. Johnston to Perkins, Laprairie, 9 May 1835.
94 Ibid., John Gleed to Perkins, Granby, 30 July 1835; Perkins to J. Gleed, Montreal, 29 May 1835.
95 Ibid., Charles Sherman Report, Town of Granby, May 1836.
96 Ibid., Rev. M. White to Perkins, Southampton, 12 May 1836. Hamilton (*With Heart*, 165) writes that W. Holmes (who had been serving Potton) succeeded Gleed, but the Granby secretary reported that Holmes had decided to reject the appointment. See CEHMS, G. Childs to Sir, Granby, 7 Apr. 1836.
97 Ibid., H.B. Chapin to W. Curry, Granby, 15 July 1836.
98 Ibid., Rev. H.B. Chapin's Report, 12 Sept. 1836; *Home Missionary*, Feb. 1837, 177–81.
99 CEHMS, H.B. Chapin to W. Curry, Granby, 15 July 1836.
100 Ibid., Rev. H.B. Chapin, Waterloo, 21 Aug. 1836; H.B. Chapin to Curry, Granby, 26 Aug. 1836.
101 Curry stated that $250 could easily be raised in Granby and Shefford, the CEHMS would contribute $200, and $50–$100 could be raised from private sources. CEHMS, Curry to H.B. Chapin, Montreal, 20 Oct. and 9 Nov. 1836; Curry to Rev. White, Montreal, 21 Nov. 1836.
102 CEHMS, Chapin to Congregational Churches of Shefford and Granby, Westhampton, 3 Dec. 1836; Chapin to Curry, Westhampton, 5 Dec. and 26 Dec. 1836.
103 Ibid., H.B. Chapin to Curry, Waterloo, 30 Aug. 1837, 13 Oct. 1837.
104 Ibid., Report of H.B. Chapin, Shefford, 1 Feb. 1837. Chapin clearly made a mistake with the year, which should be 1838.
105 Ibid., H.B. Chapin to Curry, Waterloo, 3 May 1838.
106 Ibid., H.B. Chapin to Curry, Waterloo, 18 July 1838.
107 Ibid., H.B. Chapin to Curry, Waterloo, 22 Oct. 1838.
108 Ibid., H.B. Chapin to Curry, Shefford, 6 Jan. 1839. Chapin had complained in his daily journal that many of the Scots 'love the bottle.' H.B. Chapin to Curry, Waterloo, 18 July 1838.
109 Ibid.
110 Ibid.
111 Ibid.
112 Ibid.; H.B. Chapin to Committee of the CEHMS, Waterloo, 17 May 1839; H.B. Chapin to Curry, Waterloo, 7 March 1839.

113 Ibid., H.B. Chapin to Committee of the CEHMS, Waterloo, 17 May 1839.
114 Ibid., Horace Man et al., to C. Strong, Granby, 13 Nov. 1839.
115 Ibid., Rev. Fox to C. Strong, Granby, 28 April 1840; 3 March 1841. According to Hamilton (*With Heart,* 166) the Granby church cost $2,200.
116 CEHMS, Committee of Granby Church to Strong, 1 April 1841.
117 CEHMS, N.B. Fox to Strong, Granby, 15 April 1841.
118 Ibid., 5 April 1842.
119 Ibid., 28 Oct. 1842; 28 April 1843.
120 Ibid., 26 Feb. 1844.
121 Hamilton, *With Heart,* 166–7.
122 *Home Missionary,* March 1835, 185.
123 ETRC, UCA, St Francis Association, 23 Dec. 1851, 140.
124 CEHMS, H. Lyman to C. Strong, Granby, 27 March 1840; *Home Missionary,* July 1840, 62. By 1844, the resources for the CEHMS reportedly came almost entirely from the American Presbyterian Church in Montreal. *Reports of the American Home Missionary Society,* May 1840, 68–9; May 1843, 88; May 1844, 93; May 1845, 99; ETRC, UCA, St Francis Association, 1836–66, Minutes, 28 Dec. 1842, 92.
125 *Home Missionary,* June 1845, 46; Nöel, *Competing for Souls,* 194.
126 ETRC, UCA, St Francis Association, 3 June 1846, 116; 28 Dec. 1847, 121.

4 The Baptists

1 McMaster University Divinity College, Canadian Baptist Archives (CBA), Barnston Baptist Church, parish records; Hubbard, *Forests and Clearings,* 96. The Danville Association, established in 1809, chiefly covered Caledonia and Orleans Counties in Vermont, and part of New Hampshire. In 1824 it included sixteen churches and 555 members. By 1842 there were 1,127 members in twenty-one churches, now also including Bolton, Barford, Clifton, Compton, and Sutton. Crocker, *History of the Baptists,* 314–15.
2 Ivison and Rosser, *Baptists in Upper and Lower Canada,* 160–1, 167; Rev. Arnold L. Arms, 'Historical Address,' in Hibbard, *Exercises,* 3–5.
3 Pitman, *Baptists and Public Affairs,* 14–17.
4 Cox and Hoby, *Baptists in America,* 231.
5 Crocker, *History of the Baptists,* 314. Gorman, *Olivet Baptist Church.*
6 Montreal Diocesan Archives (MDA), Parish Reports, Frelighsburg, Report for St Armand [1816]; quoted in Millman, 'Rev. Canon James Reid,' 13.
7 Arms, 'Historical Address,' 5–7. The harmony may have been eased by the fact that Smith died in 1837. See Thomas, *Contributions,* 98.
8 Forty-two members had been added between 1820 and 1835. 'List of Mem-

bers,' in Hibbard, *Exercises*, 69–70; CBA, *The Canada Baptist Magazine and Missionary Reporter* (hereafter *CBMMR*) 4, no. 4 (Oct. 1840); 100.
9 Hibbard, *Exercises*, 69–70, 73–4.
10 Bennett, *Sacred Space*, 56. The original coloured glass windows were replaced in 1988 with modern stained glass panes. Hamilton, *With Heart*, 267–9. I found no records of the Stanbridge church in the Baptist Archives, but the 1852 census reports 221 Baptists in the township, 19 more than in St Armand.
11 Quebec Diocesan Archives (QDA), B7, 20, Thomas Johnson to Rev. Dr. Mountain, Hatley, 25 Oct. 1823; 27, Hatley Report, 15 Dec. 1827.
12 Hubbard, *Forests and Clearings*, 97–8.
13 CBA, Barnston Baptist Church, parish records.
14 Hubbard, *History of the Baptists*, 96–7.
15 CBA, Barnston Baptist Church, Parish Records. Barnston's Baptist minister, James Green, was a leader of the resistance to the school reforms. See Little, *State and Society*, 198–200, 221, 225–6.
16 *CBMMR* 4, no. 4 (Oct. 1840), 100; [J.H. Hunter], '1933. Baptist Church.'
17 Channell, *History of Compton*, 70; CBA, 'Eaton Baptist Church, as prepared by L.W. French, church clerk, May 1905'; *Canadian Baptist*, 28 Dec. 1922; Crocker, *History of the Baptists*, 254, 455.
18 'Eaton Baptist Church'; Terry, 'Sawyerville.'
19 'Eaton Baptist Church'; *CBMMR* 4, no. 4 (Oct. 1840); 99; Channell, *History of Compton*, 70.
20 Gillies served the community for thirty-eight years. 'Eaton Baptist Church'; Terry, 'Sawyerville.'
21 Quoted in Noël, *Competing for Souls*, 158–9.
22 *CBMMR*, 4, no. 4 (Oct. 1840): 100; no. 9 (March 1841), 222.
23 CBA, Canadian Baptist Historical Collection, Biographical file no. 815593, 'Titus Mooney Merriman, 1822–1903,' 53–8, 64; Hatley – Church Minute Book, 1799–1844; Hubbard, *Forests and Clearings*, 97–8.
24 'Titus Mooney Merriman,' 68–70; Hamilton, *With Heart*, 198.
25 *CBMMR* 4, no. 4 (Oct. 1840), 99–100; Noël, *Competing for Souls*, 159, 162, table 13. There is little record of this church aside from the register for 1842–4. CBA, Barford Township Register of Births, Marriages, and Deaths, 1842–4; Hubbard, *Forests and Clearings*, 97.
26 CBA, Beebe file, Mrs Sarah Lorimer to Dr J.G. Brown, Beebe, 26 May 1921.
27 The Baptists of the two townships had been joined under the ministry of Reverend William Hulbert in 1848, but it was dissolved shortly after Confederation. McKillop, *Annals of Megantic*, 111–12; CBA, Inverness file, Historical Sketch by J.H. Hunter, Sherbrooke, 29 March 1935.

312 Notes to pages 94–103

28 Edward Mitchell served Hatley and Stanstead; J. Baldwin served Barnston; S.B. Ryder served Bolton; and J. Ide served Barford and Compton. Without regular service by Baptist ministers were Eaton, Potton, Clifton, Stanbridge, and St Armand. *CBMMR* 4, no. 4 (Oct. 1840), 100. The Canadian mission was cut off in 1843. Crocker, *History of the Baptists,* 458.
29 *CBMMR* 5, no. 3 (Sept. 1841), 66.
30 Townships such as Stanstead, Hatley and Barnston, where there were significant declines in the Baptist numbers between the 1831 and 1852 census reports, also had the largest number of Adventists (a product of Millerism) in the latter year. Dunham, St Armand and Leeds, on the other hand, lost large numbers of Baptists without recording many Adventists in 1852. See Noël, *Competing for Souls,* 161, 168, 163, table 14, 171–3.
31 Badger claimed that two Ascot-based ministers named Bates and Grainger were forced to leave the province in the summer of 1812, when they refused to swear allegiance to King George, though it is not entirely certain that they were Baptists. Hubbard, *Memoir,* 67.
32 Marini, *Radical Sects,* 118; Compton Church Record, 2.
33 Compton Record Book, 2, 4–5; Marini, *Radical Sects,* 116–17.
34 Marini, *Radical Sects,* 117–18.
35 Ibid., 120–2; Hubbard, *Forests and Clearings,* 98.
36 Billington, 'Female Laborers in the Church,' 383.
37 University of Vermont, Bailey-Howe Library, Stanstead Free Will Baptist Quarterly Meeting, First Record Book, 1828–1847 (hereafter, Stanstead Record Book) (no pagination).
38 Stanstead Record Book, 16 Jan. 1829. On the origin and development of the plenary session, see Marini, *Radical Sects,* 121–2.
39 East Hatley reported sixteen members at the following meeting.
40 Compton Church Record, 22–3.
41 Compton Church Record, n. pag.; Marini, *Radical Sects,* 118.
42 Marks, 'Rattling, Tattling, and General Rumour,' 390–4; Marks, 'Christian Harmony,' 115–20, 124; Roth, *Democratic Dilemma,* 44–6, 210–12.
43 Hubbard, *Forests and Clearings,* 100.
44 On the Freewill Baptists and the slavery and temperance issues, see Baxter, *History of the Freewill Baptists,* 93–100, 109–13.
45 Wesleyan Correspondence, box 22, file 145, no. 5, John Rain to Rev. Alder, Charleston Village, 28 July 1838.
46 University of Vermont, Bailey-Howe Library, Stanstead Record Book, vol. 2. This volume is not identified as a separate one for the St Francis Quarterly Meeting, presumably because it continues with the minutes of the reunited meetings in 1847.

47 Stanstead Record Book, vol. 2, 30–31 Jan. 1846.
48 Rowe, *Thunder and Trumpets*, 24–6, 54.
49 Clark, *Church and Sect*, 313.
50 Matters were clearly no better in the Brome quarterly meeting (whose origins are unclear), for in February 1845 Stanstead delegates 'found a disorganizing spirit among them & advised them to join the Enosburg [Vermont] Q.M.'
51 Fortin, 'L'Adventisme,' 104–5, 117.
52 Thus, when Elder Folsom charged another member with selling ardent spirits in October 1853, he was dismissed as Compton's pastor, not because the charge was unfounded but because he was expected to be a mediator rather than an instigator. The offending member was later suspended, but discipline cases remained relatively few into the 1850s despite the strict requirements of the 1792 covenant which even banned unscrupulous business practices.
53 Marini, *Radical Sects*, 134–5.
54 By 1844 there were 119 churches belonging to the Vermont Yearly Meeting, whose boundaries crossed into Lower Canada. Ward, 'Religious Enthusiasm in Vermont,' 60.
55 Rowe, *Thunder and Trumpets*, 72.

5 Smaller Sects

1 Dechêne, 'Observations sur l'agriculture'; Roth, *Democratic Dilemma*, 81.
2 Hubbard, *Memoir*, 154–5.
3 Thompson, *History of Vermont*, 203–4.
4 Ham, 'Prophet,' 292–3.
5 Ibid., 293–7.
6 Thompson, *History of Vermont*, 203–4; Ham, 'Prophet,' 297–9.
7 One rumour suggested that they left after being charged with murdering an infant by giving it a drink made from poisonous bark. Ham, 'Prophet,' 290, 292.
8 Zielinski, *Story of the Farnham Meeting*, 3, 19–20
9 Schrauwers, *Awaiting the Millennium*, 6–7.
10 Zielinski, *Story of the Farnham Meeting*, 43. On the role of the Quarterly and Yearly Meetings, see Dorland, *History of the Society of Friends*, 3–5, 9.
11 On the large degree of control exerted by the elders, see Schrauwers, *Awaiting the Millenium*, 8–9.
12 Zielinski, *Story of the Farnham Meeting*, 43.
13 Bull, 'Sketch of Farnham Monthly Meeting,' 117; Dorland, *History of the Society of Friends*, 19–25.

14 Dorland, *History of the Society of Friends*, 27–8.
15 Zielinski, *Story of the Farnham Meeting*, 47.
16 Ibid., 46–8.
17 There may have been some resistance to this procedure on the part of the more affluent families, for several of them were missing from the evaluation of 1829, which was subsequently rejected. Ibid., 42.
18 Ibid.
19 Out of nine Preparative Meetings under the control of Ferrisburg, seven were divided on this issue, but there were apparently no dissenters from the Farnham Meeting's position. Zielinski (*Story of the Farnham Meeting*, 41–2, 54) states, however, that it is difficult to determine who decided what direction the Farnham Meeting was going to follow.
20 Braithwaite, *Memoirs*, 2; 156–7; Dorland, *History of the Society of Friends*, 16–18, 221–2; Zielinski, *Story of the Farnham Meeting*, 54.
21 Zielinski, *Story of the Farnham Meeting*, 25, 37–9, 44–5.
22 Ibid., 45.
23 Dorland, *History of the Society of Friends*, 212, 216–20; Zielinski, *Story of the Farnham Meeting*, 12, 43–6, 55; Bull, 'Sketch of Farnham Monthly Meeting,' 117.
24 Marini, *Radical Sects*, 122–3, 174.
25 United Church Archives in the Victoria University Archives (VUA, UCA), The Wesleyan Methodist Church (Great Britain). Foreign Missions: America. ... Correspondence, 78.128c (hereafter Wesleyan Correspondence), box 6, file 48, no. 36, Henry Pope to Rev. Richard Watson, Melbourne, 12 Aug. 1822.
26 QDA, Series D, folder 91, Bishop Quebec to Archdeacon Hamilton, Quebec, 10 Dec. 1829; B22, 13, Bishop to LeFevre, Quebec, 29 June 1829.
27 *Universalist Magazine*, 12 Sept. 1829, 42; 7 Nov. 1829, 74; 26 Dec. 1829, 103; Hewett, *Unitarians*, 74; Milner, *Huntingville*, 25.
28 *Universalist Magazine*, 18 Feb. 1843, 140.
29 QDA, D22, 14, A.H. Burwell to Venerable Sir, Lennoxville, 6 July 1829.
30 Ibid., 17, A.H. Burwell to Archdeacon Mountain, Lennoxville, 30 July 1829.
31 *Universalist Magazine*, 16 Jan. 1830, 114. On LeFevre's subsequent career, see 17 Jan. 1850, 126.
32 Milner, *Huntingville*, 93.
33 Miller, *Larger Hope*, 664. The association, which covered the counties of Shefford, Brome, and Missisquoi, obtained the services of Joseph Baker in 1835. Thomas, *History of Shefford*, 78.
34 Cross, *Burned-Over District*, 324.
35 Quoted in Milner, *Huntingville*, 94.
36 *Universalist Magazine*, 10 Nov. 1832, 78; Milner, *Huntingville*, 96.

37 Miller, *Larger Hope*, 662; Archives Nationales du Québec à Montréal, United Church Archives, Montreal-Ottawa Conference (ANQM, UCA), Canada Education and Home Missionary Society Papers (CEHMS), A. Ware to Rev. Perkins, Ascot, 13 Jan. 1834.
38 Milner, *Huntingville*, 96. Hewett (*Unitarians*, 73) states that Ward did not move from Stanstead until 1848.
39 The *Universalist Union* (2 July 1836) reported that Watson had moved to Stukely by 1836. His was apparently the first Universalist ordination in Lower Canada (Miller, *Larger Hope*, 664), though an account apparently based on memory in Thomas's *History of Shefford* (p. 78) claims that Thomas Wheeler was ordained in Frost Village in 1829.
40 *Universalist Magazine*, 19 Oct. 1833, 66; 12 Apr. 1834, 166.
41 Quotes are from Hewett, *Unitarians*, 73, 74. Arians taught that Jesus Christ is not of the same substance as God the Father.
42 NA, SPG Papers, Reel A199, part 1, box 29, folio 326, no. 81, C.C. Cotton to Rev. Sir, Dunham, 9 Sept. 1835.
43 Thomas, *History of Shefford*, 78.
44 NA, SPG Papers, Reel A199, part 1, box 29, folio 326, no. 83, C.C. Cotton to Rev. Sir, Dunham, 24 Jan. 1838; no. 84, 25 Feb. 1839.
45 VUA, UCA, Wesleyan Correspondence, box 20, file 129, no. 4, Thomas Turner to Rev. Alder, Shefford, 7 June 1836; *Methodist New Connexion Magazine* (Manchester), 1838, 76, John Addyman to My Dear Sir, Montreal, 13 Oct. 1837.
46 Butler, *Awash in a Sea*, 220.
47 *Universalist Magazine*, 1 Feb. 1845, 130; Miller, *Larger Hope*, 665; Milner, *Huntingville*, 60-1, 98-100.
48 NA, SPG Papers, Reel A199, part 1, box 29, folio 362, no. 77, C.C. Cotton to Rev. Sir, Dunham, 1 Aug. 1832.
49 On Smith see Kenny, *Perfect Law of Liberty*.
50 Rowe, *Thunder and Trumpets*, 85-6; Cross, *Burned-Over District*, 15; Hewitt, *Unitarians*, 66-7; Ward, 'Religious Enthusiasm,' 70-1.
51 NA, SPG Papers, Reel A199, part 1, box 29, folio 362, no. 77, C.C. Cotton to Rev. Sir, Dunham, 1 Aug. 1832.
52 VUA, UCA, Wesleyan Correspondence, box 20, file 129, no. 4, Thomas Turner to Rev. Alder, Shefford, 7 June 1836.
53 The context in which Tomkins makes this statement makes it appear that he is referring to East Bolton, but later in the letter he refers to the Christian Brethern of North Stukely and the Reformed Methodists of East Bolton. VUA, UCA, Wesleyan Correspondence, box 24, file 161, no. 16, John Tomkins to R. Alder, Shefford, 2 Sept. 1840.

54 Rowe, *Thunder and Trumpets*, 28–9, 86; Ward, 'Religious Enthusiasm,' 72; Hewett, *Unitarians*, 66–8.
55 NA, SPG Papers, Reel A200, part 1, box 29, folio 367, no. 98, J. Reid to Rev. Sir, St Armand, 14 Nov. 1831; ETRC, UCA, Baptisms and Quarterly Board Records, Dunham, 1825–61 (hereafter Dunham Methodist Minutes), 2 July 1831, 4 Aug. 1832.
56 NA, SPG Papers, Reel A205, part 1, box 35, folio 368, no. 198, C. Jackson to Rev. Sir, Charleston, 7 Jan. 1832.
57 Ward, 'Religious Enthusiasm,' 70, 110; Semple, *Lord's Dominion*, 111.
58 NA, Methodist Missionary Society, Synod Minutes, Lower Canada / Canada East, 1832.
59 *Christian Messenger*, 1 Jan. 1846, Memoir of Mr Thompson.
60 Burnside, 'Canadian Wesleyan,' 17–18; Semple, *Lord's Dominion*, 110–11.
61 Semple, *Lord's Dominion*, 110–11; VUA, UCA, Wesleyan Correspondence, box 21, file 137, no. 18, Thomas Turner to Rev. Alder, Stanstead, 30 Nov. 1837.
62 *Methodist New Connexion Magazine*, 1838, 76, John Addyman to My Dear Sir, Montreal, 13 Oct. 1837.
63 VUA, UCA, Wesleyan Correspondence, box 21, file 137, no. 18, Thomas Turner to Rev. Alder, Stanstead, 30 Nov. 1837; box 22, file 145, no. 32, Thomas Turner to Secretaries, Stanstead, 26 Nov. 1838. According to Addyman in 1837, Bolton's Protestant Methodist minister was an aging Yorkshireman 'of very humble talents, but I believe a very good man; and in every respect adapted for labour and hardship.' *Methodist New Connexion Magazine* (1838), 76.
64 Stanstead Historical Society, 'A Memoir of Ralph Merry IV, 1786–1863' (typescript), 13 June 1839.
65 VUA, UCA, Wesleyan Correspondence, box 26, file 178, no. 24, John B. Brownell to R. Alder, Dunham, 12 Oct. 1842. Addyman claimed that the four local preachers, who had originally been Protestant Methodists, had left the Wesleyans because of some unjust expulsions from that body. Ibid., Methodist New Connexion Church Fonds, 1814–41, Correspondence. 78.135c (hereafter New Connexion Correspondence), Addyman's Report, Montreal, 12 Oct. 1842; 'Canadian Wesleyan,' 33.
66 VUA, UCA, New Connexion Correspondence, Crofts to My Dear Brother, Montreal, 22 Feb. 1842.
67 Ibid., New Connexion Correspondence, Croft's Report, Montreal, 12 Oct. 1842; 27 May 1843; 19 Dec. 1843; Ward, 'Religious Enthusiasm,' 153.
68 VUA, UCA, New Connexion Correspondence, Crofts to Brother, Montreal, 21 Nov. 1843.

69 NA, Methodist Missionary Society, Synod Minutes, Lower Canada / Canada East, 1843.
70 Burnside, 'Canadian Wesleyan,' 68–9, 123–6.
71 *Christian Messenger,* 1 March 1846, 47, F.E. Powers to Dear Brother, 2 Jan. 1845; ibid., 1 April 1845, 52.
72 Ibid., 2 Feb. 1846, 36.
73 VUA, UCA, New Connexion Correspondence, quarterly accounts, Montreal, 19 Dec. 1845.
74 *Christian Messenger,* Nov. 1846.
75 VUA, UCA, New Connexion Minutes, 71, 2 Nov. 1848.
76 Hamilton, *With Heart,* 274. See the brief biography in *Yesterdays of Brome County,* 1 (1967): 57–8.
77 Burnside, 'Canadian Wesleyan,' 109–10.

6 The Millerites

1 'Miss M.A. Titemore Contributes,' 55.
2 Barkun, *Crucible of the Millennium,* 11–12.
3 Rowe, *Thunder and Trumpets,* 54. Sandeen argues that the American and British millenarian leaders felt embattled due to the growth of the Catholic power and influence in Britain, the rising power of the working classes, and the wickedness they perceived in their society. Most of the British premillennialists calculated that the next important events in the prophetic calendar would occur from 1843 to 1848. Sandeen, 'Millennialism,' 107–9, 116–17.
4 For useful discussions on the contrasting implications of pre- and postmillennialism, see Westfall, *Two Worlds,* 182–90; and Moorhead, 'Between Progress and Apocalypse,' 524–42.
5 Until recently, Millerism in Britain attracted more attention than that in Canada. See Billington, 'Millerite Adventists in Great Britain.' Westfall (*Two Worlds,* chapter 6) and Gauvreau (*Evangelical Century,* chapter 3) discuss millenarianism in Canada from an intellectual perspective, but only recently have two doctoral dissertations examined the Millerite movement within this country in some detail. See Fortin, 'L'Adventisme,' and Mussio, 'Communities Apart,' chapter 4.
6 The bishop had never heard of these lectures. Bishop's University, Quebec Diocesan Archives (QDA), B7, 18, Thos. Johnson to Rev. Dr Mountain, Hatley, 6 Aug. 1823.
7 Referred to in Stanstead Historical Society, 'A Memoir of Ralph Merry IV, 1786–1863' (typescript), 23 Jan. 1824.
8 Rowe ('Millerites: A Shadow Portrait') states that estimates for the United

States vary from 10,000 to 1,000,000, but he suggests that there were only 5,000 committed Millerites in the movement's centre of upstate New York. Ruth Doan argues that 'The connection between Millerism and decline in church membership is fuzzy and conjectural at best,' but this is certainly not the case for the Eastern Townships or Upper Canada, and Ward demonstrates its crippling impact upon the Baptist, Methodist Episcopal, and Congregational Churches of Vermont. Cross also points out that religious declension and internal schisms invariably followed outbursts of 'ultraism.' Doan, 'Millerism and Evangelical Culture,' 133; Westfall, *Two Worlds*, 176–7; Ward, 'Religious Enthusiasm,' 253–4; Cross, *Burned-Over District*, 257.

9 Cross, *Burned-Over District*, 291. On other American premillennialists of this era, see Ward, 'Religious Enthusiasm in Vermont,' 221–7.
10 Quoted in Fortin, 'World Turned Upside Down,' 42. For a clear summary of Miller's biblical analysis, see Ward, 'Religious Enthusiasm,' 215–20.
11 'A Memoir of Ralph Merry IV,' 27 June, 23 July 1835; 10 and 11 June 1838, 25 June 1838; Fortin, 'World Turned Upside Down,' 42, 43; Fortin, 'L'Adventisme,' 103–4.
12 See Muller, 'Trouble on the Border'; and Little, *State and Society*, 58–9.
13 Aurora College, Jenks Memorial Collection (hereafter AC, JMC), Millerites and Early Adventists, William Miller Correspondence, 1814–55 (hereafter Miller Correspondence), William Miller to his son, Hatley, 22 June 1840.
14 Knight, *Millennial Fever*, 933–8.
15 Archives Nationales du Québec à Montréal, United Church Archives (ANQM, UCA), Montreal-Ottawa Conference, Canada Education and Home Missionary Papers (CEHMS), R.V. Hall to Strong, 30 Aug. 1842.
16 *Signs of the Times*, 22 June, 13 July 1842; Fortin, 'World Turned Upside Down,' 45–6; Fortin, 'L'Adventisme,' 104–5. For a discussion of the Millerite camp meetings, see Knight, *Millennial Fever*, 99–105.
17 *Signs of the Times*, 13 July, 17 Aug., 20 July, 1842.
18 AC, JMC, Miller Correspondence, Edwin Adrion to William Miller, Fairfield, 12 Aug. 1842; ibid., Stanbridge Upper Mills, 16 Oct. 1842.
19 ANQM, UCA, CEHMS, R.V. Hall to Secretary of CEHMS, Stanstead, 6 Nov. 1842.
20 Victoria University, United Church Archives (VUA, UCA), Wesleyan Correspondence (Wesleyan Correspondence), box 26, file 178, no. 126. Robert Cooney to Secretaries, Stanstead, 9 Nov. 1842; NA, MG17 C1, Methodist Missionary Society, Lower Canada / Canada East, Synod Minutes, 1843.
21 NA, MG24 B141, Robert Hoyle Papers, Robert Hoyle to Eliza Hoyle, Stanstead, 13 Nov. 1842, 2 Dec. 1842; Fortin, 'L'Adventisme,' 108; ANQM, UCA, CEHMS, R.V. Hall to Strong, Stanstead, 8 Jan. 1843.

22 *Signs of the Times*, 4 Jan. 1843; Fortin, 'World Turned,' 46.
23 Hutchinson, J.V. Himes, and F.G. Brown set sail for England in June 1846. *Advent Herald*, 10 June 1846. Apparently based on the newspaper's mistaken date of 1845, Billington identifies the departure as June 1845. There is a letter from Hutchinson, whom Billington mistakenly refers to as Robert, dated Boston, 28 May 1846 in the same issue of the *Herald*. Hutchinson did not return from Britain until the spring of 1847. Billington, 'Millerite Adventists,' 65.
24 Himes also wanted to publish a pamphlet in French, which was done by July, and to target the Natives and the soldiers in Canada. *Signs of the Times*, 4 Jan. 1843, 19 July 1843, 13 Sept. 1843.
25 Twenty-five Americans had, as of March 1843, donated $113.97 for the Canada mission's publications, but Skinner stated that the expense of publishing was $22 a week, allowing nothing for the labour. The newspaper was still publishing in May, under the editorship of Richard Hutchinson and C. Green, but it was in chronic need of more funding. *Signs of the Times*, 5 Mar. 1843 (letter from Columbus Greene), 8, 22 Mar., 31 May 1843.
26 *Signs of the Times*, 2 Aug. 1843, 16 Aug. 1843, 12 June 1844; Fortin, 'World Turned,' 46–7; Fortin, 'L'Adventisme,' 105–7, 115–16.
27 Knight, *Millennial Fever*, 129; Fortin, 'World Turned,' 47; Knight, *Millennial Fever*, 103–5, 129.
28 Quoted in Fortin, 'World Turned,' 47.
29 *A Journal of Visitation to a Part of the Diocese of Quebec by the Lord Bishop of Montreal in the Spring of 1843*, 3rd ed. edition (London: Society for the Propagation of the Gospel, 1846), 76–7, 39–40.
30 McCord Museum, Hale Papers, Correspondence, Andrew Robertson to Edward Hale, Montreal, 11 Mar. 1843.
31 ANQM, UCA, CEHMS, R.V. Hall to Strong, Stanstead, Apr. 1843.
32 Quoted in Carroll, *Case*, 4: 381.
33 VUA, UCA, Wesleyan Correspondence, box 27, file 186, no. 15, John Tomkins to Secretaries, Compton, 18 April 1843.
34 Ibid., no. 16, E. Botterell to Rev. Alder, Melbourne, 18 April 1843.
35 Vansittart, *Lifelines*, 41.
36 See Rowe, *Thunder and Trumpets*, 66–7, 102–5, 108, 138; Cross, *Burned-Over District*, 305–7; and Westfall, *Two Worlds*, 178–9. For an entertaining embellished account of two such stories relating to the Outlet in 1854, see Shirley, *Buckskin Joe*, 15–16.
37 Lewis B. Hibbard, 'Centennial Discourse,' in Hibbard, *Exercises*, 55. On this theme, see Rowe, *Thunder and Trumpets*, 125; and Knight, *Millennial Fever*, 205–10.

38 *Signs of the Times*, 31 May 1843. On fanaticism in the American Millerite ranks, see Knight, *Millennial Fever*, 171–8, 211–12.
39 Rowe, *Thunder and Trumpets*, 133.
40 QDA, D17, folder 98, C.B. Fleming to Bishop of Montreal, Quebec, 1 March 1844 (typescript).
41 *Third Annual Report of the Missisquoi County Historical Society* (1908), 76–7.
42 *Advent Herald*, 3 Apr. 1844 (my emphasis); ibid., 21 Aug. 11 Sept. 1844; Fortin, 'L'Adventisme,' 78.
43 *Advent Herald*, 5 Feb. 1845; Fortin, 'World Turned Upside Down,' 50–1.
44 See Rowe, *Thunder and Trumpets*, 108–18, 139; and Knight, *Millennial Fever*, 151–8, 220–3.
45 MDA, Waterloo (St Luke's), Report of Rev. Andrew Balfour, Missionary at Shefford, 1 July 1845.
46 Fortin, 'World Turned Upside Down,' 50–2; Fortin, 'L'Adventisme,' 109–10. H. Buckley of Bristol, Vermont, would report in August, after a tour through Farnham, Shefford, Georgeville, Stanstead, Hatley, and Melbourne, that he had never seen 'people better prepared to salute our "King" with expressions of loyalty.' *Advent Herald*, 3 Sept. 1845.
47 Fortin, 'World Turned Upside Down,' 52; Fortin, 'L'Adventisme,' 111–12; Knight, *Millennial Fever*, 267–73.
48 *Advent Herald*, 5 Aug. 1848. Shipman's tour was followed by that of J. Gates in August and September; ibid., 19 Aug. 9 Dec. 1846.
49 Fortin, 'L'Adventisme,' 116; Fortin, 'John Porter,' 2.
50 Rowe, *Thunder and Trumpets*, 49. On the relationship between the Shakers, Mormons, Perfectionist cults, and Millerism, see ibid., 62–6; and Knight, *Millennial Fever*, 257–63.
51 *Advent Herald*, 10 June 1845; *Stanstead Journal*, 6 Nov. 1845, 1 Oct. 1846.
52 Fortin, 'L'Adventisme,' 90.
53 Fortin, 'John Porter,' 4. Three men also preached to large crowds in the region in 1849, and six hundred Adventists met again in Barnston in 1850, followed by five hundred in Shipton in 1851. Fortin, 'L'Adventisme,' 76, 143.
54 Fortin, 'L'Adventisme,' 39, 117–30, 143.
55 Other churches apparently adopted similar covenants. Fortin, 'L'Adventisme,' 123. The province's first Adventist chapel was built in Danville in 1852. Fortin, 'John Porter,' 6–7.
56 Fortin, 'John Porter,' 4; *Advent Herald*, 11 Mar. 1846.
57 'A Memoir of Ralph Merry IV,' 12 Oct. 1850. On 23 November, Merry entered into some chronological reckoning himself in relation to the theory of a local preacher that, rather than beginning with the time when Ezra built

the temple, 'they should have reckoned from the decree for Nehemiah to build Jerusalem.' This would start the millenium in 1855. Merry noted that the reign of three kings intervened between the two decrees, which would place the final days far beyond 1855.
58 Bates visited Eaton, Melbourne, and West Ely in 1848 and 1849, and returned again in 1850, when he was followed by James and Ellen White, the founders of this branch of Adventism. Fortin, 'L'Adventisme,' 152–3; Knight, *Millennial Fever,* 298–9.
59 Doan, 'Millerism and Evangelical Culture,' 118–38. Rowe (*Thunder and Trumpets,* 72) makes a similar argument, as does Mussio ('Communities Apart,' 210) for Upper Canada.
60 O'Leary, *Arguing the Apocalypse,* 97.
61 See Little, 'A Moral Engine,' 16–22.
62 Fortin, 'L'Adventisme,' 3, 167; Fortin, 'John Porter,' 5.
63 See Little, *State and Society,* chapters 4 and 6.
64 Milner, *Huntingville,* 37–8.
65 *Signs of the Times,* 29 June 1842; Little, *Child Letters,* 37.
66 ANQM, UCA, CEHMS, R.V. Hall to Strong, Stanstead, April 1843. See also Milner, *Huntingville,* 57–8; VUA, UCA, Wesleyan Correspondence, box 27, file 186, no. 18, Ichabod Smith to W.M. Harvard, Stanstead, 24 March 1843 (1 April 1843 postscript).
67 McCord Museum, Hale Papers, Dr James Johnson to E. Hale, Sherbrooke, 9 Feb. 1843. Erysipalis is defined as 'a febrile disease characterized by inflammation and redness of the skin and subcutaneous tissues.'
68 Sandeen, 'Millennialism,' 115–16; Rowe, *Thunder and Trumpets,* 106–7; Doan, 'Millennialism and Evangelical Culture,' 133; Schwartz, 'End of the Beginning,' 6–7.
69 Harrison, *Second Coming,* 221.
70 Roth, *Democratic Dilemma,* 218. Rowe (*Thunder and Trumpets,* 106) found his small sample of Millerites in Ithaca and Lockport, New York, to be of above average wealth.
71 Barkun's *Crucible of the Millennium* (103–23) also argues that the economy, climate, and epidemics of the 1830s and 1840s had a major impact on the rise of Millerism. Schwartz ('End of the Beginning,' 6) dismisses it as 'a bad book,' apparently largely on these grounds, but the position taken by Rowe (*Burned-Over District,* 317–20) as well as Roth (*Democratic Dilemma,* 218) is similar to that of Barkun.
72 Rowe, *Thunder and Trumpets,* 74–7. See also Barkun, *Crucible of the Millennium,* 8–9, 96–7.

7 Laying the Foundations

1 The result was a split in the Montreal Society. Findlay and Holdsworth, *History of the Wesleyan Methodist*, 1: 377–8; Victoria University Archives, United Church Archives (VUA, UCA), Methodist Missionary Society, finding aid no. 164, 9–10. The Stanstead and St Francis River circuits remained within the New England Conference, while Dunham remained within the New York Conference, attached to the Hudson River District. Carroll, *Case and His Cotemporaries*, 2: 189; *Minutes of the annual conferences*, 1: 281.
2 Carroll, *Case and His Cotemporaries*, 2: 70, 104, 189–90.
3 Montreal Diocesan Archives (MDA), Parish Reports, Frelighsburg, [1816].
4 VUA, UCA, 78.130C, Wesleyan Missionary Society Minutes from Lower Canada and Canada East (hereafter Wesleyan Minutes), 13 March 1817.
5 Quoted in Semple, *Lord's Dominion*, 49.
6 Carroll, *Case*, 2: 262–6.
7 Ibid., 2, 261–3. Before settling in St Armand, Samuel Embury had moved with his Loyalist mother and step-father to the Kingston area, where he is said to have become the first Methodist class leader in Canada. Moore, *Historical Sketches*, 81–4; Tucker, 'Brief History of Philipsburg Methodist Church,' 55. Dunham had been combined with Stowe, Vermont by 1817, but had its own preacher by 1818. *Minutes of the annual conferences*, vol. 1, 296, 312, 330, 336, 345, 351.
8 VUA, UCA, Wesleyan Minutes, 7 Feb. 1820; Wesleyan Correspondence, box 3, file 35, no. 24, R. Williams to Rev. J. Taylor, St Armand, 20 July 1819. The Anglican minister for St Armand gave higher numbers for the local Methodists, reporting that they grew from 322 in 1816 to 570 in 1820, but he was presumably not distinguishing between adherents and members. MDA, Parish Report, Frelighsburg [1816]; Report of St Armand, 2 Oct. 1820.
9 VUA, UCA, Wesleyan Correspondence, box 3, file 35, no. 30, J. DePutron to Rev. J. Taylor, Shipton, 15 Nov. 1819.
10 Ibid., box 4, file 40, no. 35, John DePutron to Rev. Jos. Taylor, Shipton, 12 Oct. 1820; Wesleyan Minutes, 12 Feb. 1821.
11 VUA, UCA, Wesleyan Correspondence, box 4, file 40, no. 9, John DePutron to Rev. and Dear Sir, Shipton, 18 May 1821.
12 See also ibid., Wesleyan Minutes, 4 Feb. 1822.
13 Archives of Ontario (AO), Church Records Collection, Ms 881, reel 2, Shefford Wesleyan Methodist Mission Circuit Book, 1821–56 (hereafter Shefford Methodist Circuit Book).
14 VUA, UCA, 78.131C, file 1–1, Correspondence, reports, addresses concerning Canada, 1816–1836, William McKendrie to members, trustees, etc. of

Methodist Episcopal Church in Lower Canada, Alexandria (D.C.), 16 Oct. 1820.
15 Carroll, *Case*, 2: 344. Because lay preachers were used to a greater extent in America than in Britain, the bishop began in 1792 to appoint presiding elders, each to take responsibility for the circuits served by the itinerant preachers in his district, as well as presiding over the quarterly meeting and administering the sacraments. French, *Parsons and Politics*, 18–21; Semple, *Lord's Dominion*, 23–6.
16 By 1820 the Wesleyans had only about 750 members in Upper and Lower Canada, while the Episcopal Methodists had rebuilt their societies to approximately six thousand members. Semple, *Lord's Dominion*, 52.
17 NA, MG 17, C1 (reel 252), Minutes of the Executive Missionary Committee and Copies of Letters on Missionary Business Begun Sept. 2, 1814 (hereafter Minutes of the Executive), Memo to Canadian Missionaries, 23 Aug. [1820].
18 Mudge, *History of the New England Conference*, 70–4.
19 Semple, *Lord's Dominion*, 19, 21.
20 AO, Shefford Methodist Circuit Book, 1 July 1837. The only meeting Blunt was recorded at was held in September 1838. She was no longer recorded as a leader in 1841, but neither was her resignation or replacement mentioned.
21 The annual district Meeting also became known as the Synod after 1793. VUA, UCA, Methodist Missionary Society, finding aid no. 164, 4.
22 In 1838 the Compton and Hatley circuit was said to include Hatley, the northwest corner of Barnston, Compton, Ascot, Orford, Brompton, Windsor, Melbourne, Shipton, Durham, and Kingsley. VUA, UCA, Wesleyan Correspondence, box 22, file 145, no. 5, John Rain to Rev. Alder, Charleston Village, 28 July 1838.
23 Ibid., box 3, file 35, no. 11, John DePutron to Secretary, Shipton, 2 June 1819; box 5, file 44, Henry Pope to J. Taylor, Shipton, 28 Nov. 1821.
24 Ibid., box 6, file 48, no. 19, Thomas Catterick to Rev. R. Watson, Shefford, 25 March 1822; box 20, file 129, no. 4, Thomas Turner to Rev. Alder, 7 June 1836; NA, Methodist Missionary Society, Synod Minutes, Lower Canada / Canada East (hereafter MMS, Synod Minutes), 1836.
25 VUA, UCA, Wesleyan Correspondence, box 12, file 76, no. 1, William Squire to Rev. Morley, St Armand, 4 Jan. 1828. Squire had begun his Canadian career in 1825, when he was twenty-nine years old and en route to England to recover from a fever acquired after several years' labour in the West Indies. For a summary of Squire's life, see Jenkins, *Faithful Minister*.
26 VUA, UCA, Wesleyan Correspondence, box 6, file 48, no. 36, Henry Pope to Rev. Richard Watson, Melbourne, 12 Aug. 1822.
27 Thomas, *Contributions*, 133.

28 VUA, UCA, Wesleyan Correspondence, box 27, file 186, no. 14, John B. Brownell to Dr. Alder, 18 Apr. 1843. As noted above, part of this letter was copied from one sent in November 1842.
29 Archbishop George Mountain took a less charitable view towards the Wesleyan Methodists, as John Borland learned on the New Ireland circuit. See ibid., box 22, file 145, no. 23, John Borland to Gen. Secretaries, New Ireland, 25 July 1838; no. 29, John Borland to Gen. Secretaries, New Ireland, 16 Oct. 1838. On the relationship between the Methodist and Anglican churches in New Brunswick, see Acheson, 'Methodism and the Problem of Methodist Identity,' 113–16.
30 Noël, *Competing for Souls*, 145–7. The annual District Meeting in 1818 reminded the Lower Canadian missionaries who had not yet obtained registers to apply to the judges of the King's Bench in their districts, and declared that 'the Judges now entertain a correct and high opinion of our Respectablity and importance as a Religious Body.' As of 1821, there were Methodist registers in Montreal, St Armand, and Melbourne (VUA, UCA, Wesleyan Minutes, 12 Feb. 1818, 12 Feb. 1821), but the District Meeting reported in 1823 that the registers in every station but one were illegally witheld, with the result that the missionaries could not baptize without risk of persecution. NA, MMS, Synod Minutes, 4 Feb. 1823.
31 VUA, UCA, Wesleyan Correspondence, box 12, file 76, no. 19, James Knowlan to Rev. Morley, Stanstead, 24 Oct. 1828; box 13, file 82, no. 10, James Knowlan to Rev. Morley, Stanstead, 26 March 1829. The Methodist Episcopal Church would not gain the right to perform marriages until 1831.
32 NA, MMS, Synod Minutes, 1841. For a summary of Methodist attitudes towards politics in the Maritimes and Upper Canada, see French, *Parsons and Politics*, 284–6.
33 NA, MMS, Synod Minutes, 1838.
34 French, *Parsons and Politics*, 8–9. Semple (*Lord's Dominion*, 73) states that distinctions between itinerating and local preachers were somewhat hazy in the pioneer era, but this was more true of the American Episcopal Methodist church than of the British Wesleyans.
35 VUA, UCA, Wesleyan Correspondence, box 18, file 112, no. 24, Minutes of several conversations at the Montreal District Meeting, 16[?] May 1834; Wesleyan Minutes, district letter following the 1834 meeting. Despite such concerns, the records do not support the statements by Bacon, echoing Reverend Benjamin Slight (who arrived in Canada three years later), that there was near unanimous opposition among the Lower Canadian Methodists to union with the Canadian Methodist Episcopals. Journal of Benjamin Slight,

1: 28–9; Bacon, 'Wesleyan Methodist Church,' 11. See also Semple, *Lord's Dominion*, 86–8.
36 VUA, UCA, Wesleyan Correspondence, box 7, file 52, no. 28, Richard Pope to Dear Fathers and Brethern, Stanstead, 23 Oct. 1823.
37 Ibid., box 9, file 59, no. 1, William Squire to George Morley, Shefford, 5 Dec. 1825; no. 17, William Squire to Rev. and dear Sir, Shefford, 16 June 1825.
38 Ibid., box 10, file 64, no. 14, William Squire to Rev. and dear Sirs, Shefford, 3 Nov. 1826.
39 NA, Minutes of the Executive, Robert Alder to Chairman of Canada District, London, 23 March 1835.
40 VUA, UCA, Wesleyan Correspondence, box 19, file 121, no. 19, William Squire to Rev. Alder, Stanstead, 8 Dec. 1835.
41 Ibid., box 17, file 106, no. 9, William Squire to Robert Alder, Stanstead, 6 Dec. 1833. Jason Lee was joined by his nephew, Daniel Lee, who was only three years younger. Carroll, *Case*, 3: 396–8; Hubbard, *Forests and Clearings*, 156–9. On Lee's role as the founder of Oregon, see Atwood, *Conquerors*.
42 VUA, UCA, Wesleyan Correspondence, box 25, file 129, no. 8, William Squire to Rev. Alder, Stanstead, 22 Dec. 1836; Carroll, *Case*, 4: 182–3; Thomas, *Contributions*, 45–6.
43 Thomas, *Contributions*, 45–6; NA, Minutes of the Executive, R. Alder to Chairman of the Lower Canada District, London, 22 March 1838.
44 NA, MMS, Synod Minutes, 1835, 1836; Carroll, *Case*, 4: 144–5.
45 NA, MMS, Synod Minutes, 1835; VUA, UCA, Wesleyan Correspondence, box 19, file 121, no. 4, to the Quarterly Meeting, Quebec, 9 Feb. 1835.
46 VUA, UCA, Wesleyan Correspondence, box 19, file 121, no. 4, to the members of the Wesleyan Committee in London [no date].
47 NA, MMS, Synod Minutes, 1840, 1842.
48 ETRC, UCA, Minutes, Quarterly Meetings, Methodist Mission, New Ireland, 1836–1904 (hereafter New Ireland Methodist Minutes), 4 and 22 April 1847.
49 VUA, UCA, Wesleyan Correspondence, box 21, file 137, no. 16, John Borland to Robert Alder, New Ireland, 6 Oct. 1837.
50 ETRC, UCA, Dunham Civil Registers and Quarterly Board Records, 1825–61 (hereafter Dunham Methodist Minutes), 31 Dec. 1825; NA, MMS, Synod Minutes, 1826.
51 VUA, UCA, Wesleyan Correspondence, box 22, file 145, no. 2, William Squire to Rev. Alder, Philipsburg, 12 Jan. 1838.
52 Ibid., no. 27, E. Botterell to General Secretaries, Lennoxville, 11 Oct. 1838.
53 Ibid., file 161, no. 3, E. Botterell to General Secretaries, Sherbrooke and Hatley Circuit, 10 Mar. 1840.

54 Ibid., box 32, file 226, no. 28, Benjamin Slight to Secretaries, Melbourne, 18 Oct. 1848.
55 Squire also recommended that married assistant missionaries be paid a salary close to that of the ordained preachers. Ibid., box 20, file 129, no. 8, William Squire to Rev. Alder, Stanstead, 3 Aug. 1836.
56 French, *Parsons and Politics*, 78–9, 188.
57 NA, MMS, Synod Minutes, 1843. The Upper Canadians had rejoined the British connection in 1847, and the Canadian Methodists became financially independent with the payment in 1855 of £10,000 as their share in the clergy reserves. French, *Parsons and Politics*, 196, 250; Methodist Missionary Society, 14–16; Semple, *Lord's Dominion*, 97–9. In 1855 the Canadian Eastern District was replaced by the Montreal, Quebec and Stanstead Districts. Bacon, 'Wesleyan Methodist Church,' 13.
58 For a brief history of the society, see finding aid no. 164 in VUA, UCA.
59 See French, *Parsons and Politics*, 56–7.
60 VUA, UCA, Wesleyan Correspondence, box 3, file 35, no. 11, John DePutron to Secretary, Shipton, 2 June 1819; box 5, file 44, Henry Pope to Taylor, Shipton, 28 Nov. 1821; no. 34, John Hick to Taylor, Stanstead, 12 Dec. 1821.
61 The £50 cost had been advanced by three local settlers on the promise that the missionary society would pay off the debt at £6 5s per year, though the local Methodists were also to contribute. Ibid., box 7, file 52, no. 7, Thomas Catterick to the Committee of the General Wesleyan Missionary Society, Shefford, 19 Mar. 1823.
62 Ibid., no. 28, Richard Pope to Dear Fathers and Brethern, Stanstead, 23 Oct. 1823.
63 Ibid., Wesleyan Minutes, 6 Sept. 1821.
64 Ibid., The annual meeting for the following year (4 Feb. 1822) repeated that £60 was insufficient and that the majority of the stations would have to be abandoned if this ceiling were not increased.
65 Ibid., box 6, file 48, no. 32, James Booth to Rev. Taylor, Philipsburg, St Armands, 20 Aug. 1822.
66 Ibid., box 7, file 52, no. 5, J. DePutron to Joseph Taylor, St Armand, 14 May 1823; box 8, file 56, no. 12, J. DePutron to Rev. James [*sic*] Taylor, 31 May 1824.
67 VUA, UCA, Wesleyan Minutes, 13 May 1824.
68 NA, MMS, Synod Minutes, 1826.
69 VUA, UCA, Wesleyan Correspondence, box 12, file 76, no. 12, William Faulkner to Rev. Morley et al., Shipton, 20 June 1828, no. 15, Arch'd Sloan et al., to Rev. Morley et al., Shipton, 21 June 1828; box 13, file 82, no. 1, William

Faulkner to Rev. Morley et al., Shipton, 26 Jan. 1829, and appendices; no. 6, James Knowlan to Rev. Morley, Stanstead, 14 Feb. 1829; no. 10, James Knowlan to Rev. Morley, Stanstead, 26 March 1829; VUA, UCA, Wesleyan Minutes, 20 May 1831; NA, RG4 A1, Civil Secretary's Correspondence, Incoming, vol. 285, James Knowlan to Col. Yorke, Stanstead, 30 April 1829; vol. 287, Daniel Thomas to Lt. Col. Yorke, Melbourne, 15 May 1829.
70 VUA, UCA, Wesleyan Minutes, 15 May 1828.
71 Ibid., Wesleyan Correspondence, box 13, file 82, no. 19, James Knowlan to Rev. Morley, Stanstead, 24 Oct. 1828; Wesleyan Minutes, 15 May 1829.
72 Ibid., Wesleyan Minutes, 13 May 1830.
73 Ibid., Wesleyan Correspondence, box 15, file 94, no. 3, St Armand, 10 March 1831.
74 Ibid., Wesleyan Minutes, 20 May 1831.
75 Carroll, *Case*, 3: 209, 309. With children included, the 1831 census records 3364 Methodists in the Eastern Townships, or 8.8 per cent of the total population.
76 Alder would serve as a secretary of the WMS from 1833 to 1851. On his career and ideology, see Semple, *Lord's Dominion*, 79.
77 VUA, UCA, Wesleyan Correspondence, box 17, file 106, no. 28, no date; Methodist Missionary Society, 12; Semple, *Lord's Dominion*, 82–6. French (*Parsons and Politics*, 134–5) states that probably the decisive factor in the union was the Wesleyan Committee's great interest in Native missions.
78 NA, Minutes of the Executive, R. Alder to Chairman of the Canada District, London, 23 Mar. 1835. The District Meeting's understanding of this agreement is outlined in NA, MMS, Synod Minutes, 1837.
79 Ibid., 1832.
80 Ibid., 1837.
81 Ibid., 1838, 1839. By refusing to take a salary, though he was married with a family, William Squire was able to pay the Missionary Society £70 during his three years in St Armand (1837–40). Jenkins, *Faithful Minister*, 171.
82 NA, MMS, Synod Minutes, 1841.
83 Ibid., 1843. The Lower Ireland chapel had been largely funded by a £100 donation from Thomas Stott of Quebec, formerly of Manchester, England. See VUA, UCA, Wesleyan Correspondence, box 28, file 194, no. 5, Thomas Campbell to Secretaries, Leeds, 15 Feb. 1844.
84 Thorne, 'Conversion of Englishmen,' 248–52; NA, MMS, Synod Minutes, 1849.
85 NA, MMS, Synod Minutes, 1852; Bacon, 'Wesleyan Methodist Church,' 11.
86 French, *Parsons and Politics*, 88; Semple, *Lord's Dominion*, 103–4, 107.

87 MDA, G.J. Mountain Correspondence, James Reid to G.J. Mountain, St Armand, 11 April 1823.
88 VUA, UCA, Wesleyan Correspondence, box 8, file 56, no. 25, Matthew Lang to J. Taylor, Shefford [date illegible]. Selly added that £300 had already been subscribed locally for a brick chapel in Melbourne Village, and he planned to build a second chapel in Kingsey with the help of £140 raised on the Montreal and Quebec circuits. See ibid., box 23, file 153, no. 18, John B. Selley to General Secretaries, Melbourne, 15 Apr. 1839.
89 Ibid., box 24, file 161, no. 3, E. Botterell to General Secretaries, Sherbrooke and Hatley Circuit, 10 Mar. 1840.
90 The chapel, which measured forty by fifty feet, was still lacking £100 for completion in February 1821. VUA, UCA, Wesleyan Minutes, 12 Feb. 1821. For an illustration and description, see Hamilton, *With Heart*, 221–2.
91 VUA, UCA, Wesleyan Minutes, 12 Feb. 1821.
92 Ibid., Wesleyan Correspondence, box 8, file, 56, no. 8, J.P. Stinson to Joseph Taylor, Shipton, 17 March [1824]; AO, Shefford Methodist Circuit Book, 22 Jan., 9 March 1833.
93 VUA, UCA, Wesleyan Correspondence, box 15, file 94, no. 28, James Booth to James Townley, Stanstead, 2 March 1831.
94 Hubbard, *Forests and Clearings*, 86. Booth claimed that the subscriptions were $4,000, but his successor reported that eighty-seven families had subscribed $2,354, and the total cost was $3,075.52. VUA, UCA, Wesleyan Correspondence, box 17, file 106, no. 9, William Squire to Robert Alder, Stanstead, 6 Dec. 1833; ETRC, UCA, Quebec/Sherbrooke Presbytery, Stanstead Trustee Board, Minute Book, 1833–61, 1–6, 9.
95 NA, MMS, Synod Minutes, 1842; VUA, UCA, Wesleyan Correspondence, box 27, file 186, no. 14, John B. Brownell to Dear Fathers and Brethern, Dunham, 18 April 1843. Persons subscribing $40 or more towards construction of the chapel had the right to a pew for themselves and their families as long as it stood. Rather than a pew auction, as in the Anglican and Catholic churches, there was a fixed schedule: $35 for thirty years, $30 for twenty-five years, $25 for eighteen years, $20 for twelve years, $15 for eight years, $10 for five years, and $5 for two years. Those who could not afford the $5 could pay a half-yearly rent, and all the seats in the gallery were free. Moore, *Historical Sketches*, 17–18.
96 Bennett, *Sacred Space*, 81–4.
97 Westfall, *Two Worlds*, 127.
98 See the churches depicted in Pomerleau, *Terre de Croyances*, 8, 17; and Hamilton, *With Heart*, 51–2, 57–8, 75.

99 Benes and Zimmerman, *New England Meeting House,* 1.
100 Westfall, *Two Worlds,* 141.

8 Revivals, Reversals, and Shifting Strategies

1 Muller and Duffy, 'Jedidiah Burchard,' 7.
2 Victoria University Archives (VUA), United Church Archives (UCA), Wesleyan Correspondence, box 8, file 56, no. 10, Richard Pope to J. Taylor, Stanstead, 18 April 1824. See Johnson, 'Development of the Love Feast,' esp. 78, 81; and for a useful description of the quarterly meeting in the United States, see Richey, 'From Quarterly to Camp Meeting,' 204–8.
3 Richey, 'From Quarterly to Camp Meeting,' 212; On camp meetings and protracted meetings in British North America, see Semple, *Lord's Dominion,* 128–36.
4 VUA, UCA, Wesleyan Correspondence, box 12, file 76, no. 18, James Knowlan to Rev. Morley, Stanstead, 24 Oct. 1828. Hubbard (*Forests and Clearings,* 86) claims that Knowlan's 'talents as a preacher or a controversialist were of the highest order.'
5 VUA, UCA, Wesleyan Correspondence, box 12, file 76, no. 3, Tho. Turner to Rev. Morley, Shefford, 2 Feb. 1828. While officially serving elsewhere, W.E. Shenstone continued to preside over Shefford's quarterly meetings in 1830 and early 1831, when other missionaries took over the duty on a rotating basis. AO, Shefford Methodist Circuit Book.
6 VUA, UCA, Wesleyan Correspondence, box 5, file 44, Henry Pope to Taylor, Shipton, 28 Nov. 1821.
7 Carroll, *Case,* 2: 487–8. Stinson, who also served Montreal and Kingston, was said to have 'played a prominent part in the evolution of Canadian Methodism.' Bacon, 'Wesleyan Methodist Church,' 11.
8 VUA, UCA, Wesleyan Correspondence, box 8, file, 56, no. 8, J.P. Stinson to Joseph Taylor, Shipton, 17 March [1824]; NA, MMS, Synod Minutes, 1825.
9 VUA, UCA, 78.130C, Wesleyan Minutes, 18 Feb. 1819, 7 Feb. 1820, 4 Feb. 1822. The Anglican minister for St Armand, James Reid, reported 570 Methodists in the parish in 1820. MDA, Parish Reports, Frelighsburg, Report for St Armand, 2 Oct. 1820.
10 VUA, UCA, Wesleyan Correspondence, box 6, file 48, no. 32, James Booth to Fathers and Brethren, Philipsburg, St Armands, 16 April 1822.
11 Ibid., box 12, file 76, no. 1, William Squire to Rev. Morley, St Armand, 4 Jan. 1828.
12 Quoted in Millman, 'Rev. Canon James Reid.'

330   Notes to pages 180–4

13 VUA, UCA, Wesleyan Correspondence, box 12, file 76, no. 1, William Squire to Rev. Morley, St Armand, 4 Jan. 1828.
14 Ibid., no. 21, William Squire to Rev. Morley, St Armand, 5 Dec. 1828.
15 ETRC, UCA, Dunham Methodist Minutes, 5 July 1829.
16 VUA, UCA, Wesleyan Correspondence, box 5, file 44, no. 26, John Hick to Taylor, 5 June 1821; box 6, file 48, no. 25, John Hick to Secretaries, Stanstead, 3 Oct. 1822.
17 Ibid., box 4, file 10, John DePutron to Rev. and Dear Sir, Shipton, 10 Apr. 1820; box 8, file 56, no. 10, Richard Pope to J. Taylor, Stanstead, 13 Apr. 1824.
18 Ibid., box 8, file 56, no. 19, Richard Pope to J. Taylor, Stanstead, 2 Oct. 1824. Three of the individuals in question were the merchants Marcus Child, Ichabod Smith, and Samuel Brooks. Stanstead Historical Society Archives (SHS), Ralph Merry Papers, 'A Memoir of Ralph Merry IV,' 28 June 1824.
19 VUA, UCA, Wesleyan Correspondence, box 8, file 56, no. 19, Richard Pope to J. Taylor, Stanstead, 2 Oct. 1824; no. 28, Richard Pope to George Morley, Stanstead [date illegible].
20 Carroll, *Case and His Cotemporaries*, 3: 48–50; VUA, UCA, *Methodist Magazine* (London), Oct. 1825, 709–10. In his report to the annual District Meeting in May, however, Pope reported a total of only 130 members, with another forty on trial. NA, MMS, Synod Minutes, 1825.
21 VUA, UCA, F.P. BX8350 M5, extract of a letter from Mr Pope, Que., 17 Aug. 1827, in *Missionary Notices Relating Principally to the Foreign Missions ... of the Methodist Conference, vol. 5, 1826–8* (London), 380; *Methodist Magazine*, Dec. 1827, 852.
22 VUA, UCA, Wesleyan Correspondence, box 11, file 70, no. 9, Tho. Turner to Rev. Mason, Barnston, 8 May 1827.
23 Ibid., box 12, file 76, no. 18, James Knowlan to Rev. Morley, Stanstead, 24 Oct. 1828.
24 For details of this case, see ibid., box 13, file 82, no. 25, James Knowlan to Rev. Morley, St Armand, 4 Oct. 1829; no. 26, James Booth to Rev. Morley, Stanstead, 5 Oct. 1829; no. 28, James Booth to Rev. Morley, Stanstead, 20 Oct. 1829; no. 34, James Knowlan to Rev. Morley [no address], 20 Nov. 1829; box 14, file 88, no. 15, James Knowlan to Rev. Morley, St Armand, 4 June 1830.
25 Two hundred and seven were recorded for Stanstead and Barnston the following spring, then seventy-seven in 1834, though the report added that there were an additional fifty who belonged to the society and regularly received the Lord's Supper, and would also 'meet in class if circumstances would permit.' NA, MMS, Synod Minutes, 1832, 1833, 1834.

26 Quoted in Jenkins, *Faithful Minister*, 131.
27 Eighty-seven families had subscribed $2,354 for this building, which was constructed of brick. The total cost of the building was $3,075.52. ETRC, UCA, Stanstead Trustee Board, Minute Book, 1833–61 (hereafter Stanstead Methodist Minute Book), 1–6, 9.
28 ETRC, UCA, Stanstead Methodist Minute Book, 1 Jan. 1835; VUA, UCA, Wesleyan Correspondence, box 17, file 106, no. 9, William Squire to Robert Alder, Stanstead, 6 Dec. 1833.
29 Quoted in Jenkins, *Faithful Minister*, 131–2.
30 VUA, UCA, Wesleyan Correspondence, box 17, file 106, no. 9, William Squire to Robert Alder, Stanstead, 6 Dec. 1833.
31 NA, MMS, Synod Minutes, 1834, 1835.
32 Carroll, *Case*, 3: 494–6; *Christian Guardian*, 29 April 1835, 98.
33 Jenkins, *Faithful Minister*, 90–1, Hubbard, *Forests and Clearings*, 157; Little, *State and Society*, 33.
34 VUA, UCA, Wesleyan Correspondence, box 19, file 121, no. 19, William Squire to Rev. Alder, Stanstead, 8 Dec. 1835.
35 NA, MG 17, C1 (reel 252), Minutes of the Executive Missionary Committee and Copies of Letters on Missionary Business Begun Sept. 2, 1814 (hereafter Minutes of the Executive), Robert Alder to Chairman of Canada District, London, 23 Mar. 1835.
36 VUA, UCA, Wesleyan Correspondence, box 22, file 145, no. 27, E. Botterell to General Secretaries, Lennoxville, 11 Oct. 1838; *Wesleyan* (Montreal), 1 Oct. 1840.
37 NA, MMS, Synod Minutes, 1835. This amount was clearly not all that was raised for the church in Shefford, for collections amounted to £43.14.6 in 1833–4. AO, Shefford Methodist Circuit Book, 22 March 1834.
38 NA, MMS, Synod Minutes, 1838. On the conservative shift of British Wesleyanism after the Napoleonic Wars, see Ward, 'Religion of the People,' 249–51, 255.
39 Carroll, *Case and His Cotemporaries*, 4: 178–9.
40 VUA, UCA, Wesleyan Correspondence, box 22, file 145, no. 2, William Squire to Rev. Alder, Philipsburg, 12 Jan. 1838.
41 Ibid., no 13, William Squire to R. Alder, St Armand, 3 May 1838.
42 Ibid.
43 Ibid., no. 2, William Squire to Rev. Alder, Philipsburg, 12 Jan. 1838; box 23, file 153, no. 13, William Squire to R. Alder, St Armand, 23 Feb. 1839.
44 Quoted in Jenkins, *Faithful Minister*, 137.
45 VUA, UCA, Wesleyan Correspondence, box 24, file 1616, no. 7, William Squire to R. Alder, Philipsburg, 8 May 1840.

46 NA, MMS, Synod Minutes, 1837.
47 VUA, UCA, Wesleyan Correspondence, box 21, file 137, no. 18, Thomas Turner to Rev. Alder, Stanstead, 30 Nov. 1837; box 22, file 145, no. 10, Thomas Turner to R. Alder, Stanstead, 23 Mar. 1838. On the planned raid, see Hubbard, *Forests and Clearings*, 12–16.
48 Turner later admitted that one of the men implicated was a Methodist. VUA, UCA, Wesleyan Correspondence, box 22, file 145, no. 32, Thomas Turner to Secretaries, Stanstead, 26 Nov. 1838.
49 Ibid., no. 31, Thomas Turner to Secretaries, Stanstead, 18 Nov. 1838.
50 Ibid., no. 32, Thomas Turner to Secretaries, Stanstead, 26 Nov. 1838.
51 ETRC, UCA, Stanstead Methodist Minute Book; On Child's exile, see Little, *Child Letters*, 17–18.
52 VUA, UCA, Wesleyan Correspondence, box 23, file 153, no. 9, Thomas Turner to Secretaries, Stanstead, 21 Jan. 1839; no. 7, Thomas Turner to R. Alder, Stanstead, 11 Nov. 1839.
53 Cooney, *Autobiography*, 117; NA, MMS, Synod Minutes, 1841.
54 NA, MMS, Synod Minutes, 1838.
55 VUA, UCA, Wesleyan Correspondence, box 23, file 153, no. 8, John Tomkins to Secretaries, Shefford, 16 Jan. 1839.
56 Ibid., no. 18, John B. Selley to General Secretaries, Melbourne, 15 Apr. 1839; box 22, file 145, no. 6, John Borland to R. Alder, New Ireland, 3 Mar. 1838.
57 ETRC, UCA, New Ireland Methodist Minutes, 1 Jan., 18 June 1838.
58 In 1843 the Eastern Townships had 1,898 of the 3,561 members reported for the Canada Eastern District, though Wesleyville, outside the region, submitted no statistics. There were 460 and 566 members in Quebec and Montreal, respectively. Of the 15,236 'to whom the Missionaries regularly preach, including the members and scholars,' there were 8,136 in the Eastern Townships. NA, MMS, Synod Minutes, 1843. For more data, see Tables A.1 and A.5.
59 NA, MMS, Synod Minutes, 1843, 1842, 1843.
60 Ibid., 1840, 1841, 1842.
61 NA, MMS, Synod Minutes, 1841; *Wesleyan* (Montreal), 15 April 1842.
62 NA, MMS, Synod Minutes, 1842; Missisquoi County Historical Society, *Annual Report*, 1908, 76.
63 NA, MMS, Sybod Minutes, 1844; *Wesleyan*, 4 March 1841.
64 VUA, UCA, Wesleyan Correspondence, box 26, file 178, no. 3, E. Botterell to General Secretaries, Melbourne, 20 Jan. 1842; *Wesleyan*, 9 March 1842.
65 NA, MMS, Synod Minutes, 1842.
66 VUA, UCA, Wesleyan Correspondence, box 24, file 161, no. 16, John Tomkins to R. Alder, Shefford, 2 Sept. 1840; box 26, file 178, nol 30, Thomas

Campbell to Secretaries, Shefford, 12 May 1842; NA, MMS, Synod Minutes, 1842.
67 VUA, UCA, Wesleyan Correspondence, box 26, file 178, no. 18, John Tomkins to Secretaries, Compton, 19 July 1842.
68 Ibid., box 27, file 186, no. 14, John B. Brownell to Dear Fathers and Brethern, Dunham, 18 Apr. 1843; NA, MS, Synod Minutes, 1843.
69 VUA, UCA, Wesleyan Correspondence, box 27, file 186, no. 14, John B. Brownell to Dear Fathers and Brethern, Dunham, 18 April 1843; Missisquoi County Historical Society, *Annual Report*, 1908, 76.
70 NA, MMS, Synod Minutes, 1843.
71 Ibid., 1844.
72 Ibid., 1847; Missisquoi County Historical Society, *Annual Report*, 1908, 76.
73 NA, MMS, Synod Minutes, 1843.
74 Ibid. On the expulsions of American clergy who had adopted Miller's teachings, see Knight, *Millennial Fever*, 147–51.
75 VUA, UCA, Wesleyan Correspondence, box 28, file 194, no. 21, R. Hutchinson to Dear Sir, Pike River, 19 Aug. 1844; W.M. Harvard to R. Hutchinson, Philipsburg, 26 Aug. 1844; box 32, file 226, no. 29, Richard Hutchinson to Secretaries, Waterloo, Shefford, 18 Oct. 1848; no. 30, Richard Hutchinson to District Meeting, Waterloo, 2 May 1848; box 34, file 243, no. 14, R. Hutchinson to Secretaries, Waterloo, 24 Sept. 1850; Fortin, 'L'Adventisme,' 89.
76 NA, MMS, Synod Minutes, 1843.
77 Ibid., 1844; Missisquoi County Historical Society, *Annual Report*, 1908, 76.
78 NA, MMS, Synod Minutes, 1847; ETRC, UCA, Dunham Methodist Minutes, 9 Jan. 1847. One cause for the decline in membership was that Clarenceville had been separated from the St Armand circuit in 1845.
79 NA, MMS, Synod Minutes, 1843.
80 VUA, UCA, Wesleyan Correspondence, box 26, file 178, no. 26, Robert Cooney to Secretaries, Stanstead, 9 Nov. 1842.
81 Ibid., box 28, file 186, no. 2, Robert Cooney to Secretaries, Stanstead, 20 Jan. 1843.
82 Ibid.
83 Ibid., box 27, file 186, no. 18, Ichabod Smith to W.M. Harvard, Stanstead, 24 March 1843 (6 April 1843 postscript).
84 NA, MS, Synod Minutes, 1844.
85 Ibid., 1847.
86 NA, MMS, Synod Minutes, 1842.
87 VUA, UCA, Wesleyan Correspondence, box 27, file 186, no. 16, E. Botterell to Rev. Alder, Melbourne, 18 April 1843; NA, MMS, Synod Minutes, 1843.
88 NA, MMS, Synod Minutes, 1844, 1847.

89 Ibid., 1843.
90 Ibid., 1844; AO, Shefford Methodist Circuit Book, 20 July 1844.
91 NA, MMS, Synod Minutes, 1847.
92 Ibid., 1843; VUA, UCA, Wesleyan Correspondence, box 27, file 186, no. 15, John Tomkins to Secretaries, Compton, 18 April 1843.
93 NA, MMS, Synod Minutes, 1843, 1844; VUA, UCA, Wesleyan Correspondence, box 27, file 186, no. 15, John Tomkins to Secretaries, Compton, 18 April 1843.
94 Journal of Benjamin Slight, vol. 2, 1 June, 28 June, 12 Dec. 1846.
95 Ibid., 18 June 1847.
96 NA, MMS, Synod Minutes, 1843; *British North American Wesleyan Methodist Magazine*, June 1843, 237–8. The 1842 membership lists identify fifteen men and two women as backsliders, with one class leader having been expelled.
97 ETRC, UCA, New Ireland Methodist Minutes, 18 March, 24 June 1844; NA, MMS, Synod Minutes, 1843, 1844.
98 Semple, *Lord's Dominion*, 140.
99 NA, MMS, Synod Minutes, 1847.
100 VUA, UCA, Wesleyan Minutes, 1848.
101 Brown, *Shooling in the Clearings*, 39, 41.
102 VUA, UCA, Wesleyan Correspondence, box 6, file 48, no. 19, Thomas Catterick to Rev. R. Watson, Shefford, 25 Mar. 1822; box 7, file 52, no. 7, Thomas Catterick to the Committee of the General Wesleyan Missionary Society, Shefford, 19 March 1823.
103 NA, MMS, Synod Minutes, 1837; VUA, UCA, Wesleyan Correspondence, box 21, file 137, no. 15, John Borland to Robert Alder, New Ireland, 7 July 1837; Cross, *Burned-Over District*, 136–7.
104 VUA, UCA, Wesleyan Correspondence, box 8, file 56, no. 25, Matthew Lang to J. Taylor, Shefford [date illegible].
105 NA, MMS, Synod Minutes, 1823.
106 VUA, UCA, Wesleyan Minutes, 13 May 1824; NA, MMS, Synod Minutes, 1825.
107 Ward, 'Religion of the People,' 247.
108 NA, MMS, Synod Minutes, 1840, 1835.
109 Ibid., 1837, 1840, 1841.
110 Ibid., 1841, 1842, 1843.
111 Ibid., 1844; 1849, 1852.
112 Ibid., 1841, 1842, 1843, 1844.
113 See Little, *State and Society*, 202–5.

114 NA, MMS, Synod Minutes, 1841, 1842. On the non-religious teaching role of the Sunday schools, see Greer, 'Sunday Schools,' 170–2.
115 Ibid., 1842. On the Anglican position in Upper Canada, see Greer, 'Sunday Schools,' 175–6.
116 Only a few members had moved away from the circuit. NA, MMS, Synod Minutes, 1849.
117 Ibid., 1852.
118 ETRC, UCA, Dunham Methodist Minutes, 30 March 1850.
119 NA, MMS, Synod Minutes, 1852.
120 Ibid., 1849. The number of Sunday schools dropped to one in 1852, but two more were said to be in planning.
121 Ibid., 1852; Vogt-Raguy, 'Le Québec, terre de mission,' 119.
122 AO, Shefford Methodist Circuit Book, 6 July 1850, 26 April 1851.
123 NA, MMS, Synod Minutes, 1852.
124 NA, MMS, Synod Minutes, 1849, 1852.
125 Journal of Benjamin Slight, vol. 2, 30 July 1849.
126 Ibid., 25 May, 21 March 1851.
127 NA, MMS, Synod Minutes, 1847, 1849.
128 Ibid., 1852; Journal of Benjamin Slight, vol. 2, 1852 entry. For a description of the original Methodist meeting place, see Little, 'Sherbrooke a Century and a Half Ago,' 51.
129 NA, MMS, Synod Minutes, 1849; ETRC, UCA, New Ireland Methodist Minutes, note by John Hutchinson, 24 Apr. 1848. The complainant was 'Brother Lambly,' who was obviously the Leeds local preacher, John R. Lambly, future deputy grand worthy patriarch of the Society of Temperance. Little, 'A Moral Engine,' 22–3.
130 Five were expelled, thirty-nine dropped for absenteeism, seventeen had moved elsewhere, and five had died, leaving 234 members and nine on trial. NA, MMS, Synod Minutes, 1849.
131 ETRC, UCA, New Ireland Methodist Minutes, 9 May 1850.
132 NA, MMS, Synod Minutes, 1852; ETRC, UCA, New Ireland Methodist Minutes, 12 July 1851, 20 March 1852.
133 Quoted in Jenkins, *Faithful Minister,* 153–4.
134 VUA, UCA, Wesleyan Correspondence, box 34, file 243, no. 16, John Borland to Rev. [?], Stanstead, 4 Nov. 1850.
135 Jenkins, *Faithful Minister,* 116, 128, 168. Squire had also stimulated a revival in Montreal during the cholera epidemic of 1832. Jenkins, *Faithful Minister,* 126–9.
136 Carroll, *Case,* 4: 489.
137 Semple, *Lord's Dominion,* 36. See also French, *Parsons and Politics,* 60–3.
138 Semple, *Lord's Dominion,* 35–6, 101–2.

336 Notes to pages 220-32

139 Carroll, *Case and His Cotemporaries,* 5: 22.
140 VUA, UCA, Wesleyan Correspondence, box 25, file 170, no. 5, Henry Lauton to General Secretaries, Stanstead, 29 March 1841.
141 Ibid.
142 Journal of Benjamin Slight, vol. 2, 14 April 1847.
143 Jenkins, *Faithful Minister,* 66; Cooney, *Autobiography,* 116-17.

9 Building a Colonial Church

1 Clark, *Church and Sect,* 109, 116.
2 Kesteman, Southam, and Saint-Pierre, *Histoire des Cantons de l'Est,* 186.
3 Doll, *Revolution, Religion, and National Identity,* 68-9.
4 QDA, Mountain Papers, vol. 74, 13, J. Mountain to Duke of Portland, Quebec, 7 July 1800 (draft); vol. 77, 63, J. Quebec to Sir, Quebec, 8 Mar. 1810 (draft).
5 Ibid., D9, G.J. Mountain to Rev. Anthony Hamilton, Quebec, 15 June 1821, ibid., Unbound Manuscripts, case 2, folder 10, Rev. G.J. Mountain Papers – original, 1818-1841 (hereafter G.J. Mountain Papers), G.J. Mountain to J. Reid, 29 July 1823, 24 July 1824. On the SPG missionary ideal, see, Grant, *Profusion of Spires,* 56.
6 D9, G.J. Mountain to Rev. Anthony Hamilton, Quebec, 15 June 1821.
7 Ibid., Quebec to Mr Hamilton, Belmont, 15 Aug. 1821.
8 SPG Papers (Reel A 204), box 34, folio 375, no. 86, S.S. Wood to Rev. Sir, Edinburgh, 9 Oct. 1827. The restrictive act was not repealed until 1967. Lambert, 'Reverend Samuel Simpson Wood,' 5-6.
9 QDA, D9, J. Quebec to Hamilton, Quebec, 19 March 1822.
10 NA, SPG Papers (Reel A 202), folio 368, no. 265, G. Montreal to SPG Secretary, Quebec, 26 July 1842.
11 Doll, *Revolution, Religion, and National Identity,* 29-31.
12 VUA, UCA. Wesleyan Correspondence, box 4, file 40, no. 9, John DePutron to Rev. and Dear Sir, Shipton, 18 May 1821.
13 ANQM, UCA, CEHMS, Danville Congregationalist Committee to C. Strong, 18 Jan. 1842; A.J. Parker to C. Strong, Danville, 21 Aug. 1842.
14 St Armand East Church Archives, vol. 1 (collection of loose documents in a bound volume), G.J. Mountain to James Reid, Que., 13 Jan. 1823; MDA, RG 1.5, G.J. Mountain, Archdeacon – Correspondence, James Reid to G.J. Mountain, St Armand, 11 April 1823.
15 The result was a protest by eight missionaries who felt that all the salaries should be equal. NA, SPG Papers (Reel A 206), box 36, folio 410, no. 69, Protest, 30 Oct. 1838.

16 The clerical poverty line in early nineteenth-century England is considered to be £150, and the typical income was £275 per annum. Walsh and Taylor, 'Introduction: the Church and Anglicanism,' 7.
17 QDA, D13, folder 94, Printed Circular to Clergy re Congregational Collections, 4 Jan. 1834. The foregoing summary of the financial arrangements is from Millman, *Life of Stewart,* 63, 114, 116–17, 121–2. For a useful summary of the clergy reserves issue from 1830 to 1837, see ibid., chapter 11. On public resistance to financial contributions in Upper Canada, see Fahey, *In His Name,* 16–18.
18 QDA, D16, folder 97, G.J. Mountain to A.M. Campbell, Quebec, 28 Aug. 1841. For further details, see Fahey, *In His Name,* 130–1, 217–23.
19 This was the case, for example, in Dunham, where £25 was pledged, 'considerable amounts of which it is not unlikely will have to be paid in produce on account of the want of money.' MDA, Rev. Caleb Cotton Papers, sleeve 1, C.C. Cotton to Archdeacon Mountain, Dunham, 1 July 1834.
20 The military chest had covered the bishop's salary of £2,600 a year, plus £400 house allowance and the salaries of a few of the clergy. Millman, *Life of Stewart,* 63.
21 QDA, D14, folder 95, Gosford to Lord Glenelg, Quebec, 19 May 1836. Fourteen Anglican rectories, including those of St Armand East and West, Dunham, and Charleston, were created by letters patent in Lower Canada, but in no case were rectories endowed from the clergy reserves or with land beyond that already in the parish's possession. Millman, *Life of Stewart,* 138–9; Millman *Short History of Dunham,* 15.
22 QDA, D14, folder 95, A.M. Campbell to Bishop of Quebec, Trafalgar Square, 6 Jan. 1836; D16, folder 97, G.J. Mountain to A.M. Campbell, Quebec, 24 March 1842; Millman, *Life of Stewart,* 120.
23 NA, SPG Papers (Reel A 201), box 31, folio 368, no. 213, G. Montreal to A.M. Campbell, Sherbrooke, 14 Feb. 1840.
24 Ibid., no. 236, G. Montreal to A.M. Campbell, Que., 28 Aug. 1841.
25 With parishes in the Eastern Townships, there were the Missisquoi District (whose boundaries conformed to those of the Missisquoi Municipal District), the Shefford District, the St Francis District, the Three Rivers District (which included Drummondville and Lower Durham), and the Megantic District (originally the South Quebec District, and including churches in the neighbouring seigneuries). See QDA, *Church Society Reports of the Diocese of Quebec, 1843–75* (Montreal: Lovell and Gibson), 1844, 15–16; 1846, 24. The 'General By-Laws' are reprinted in Reisner, *Measure of Faith,* 94.
26 QDA, St Francis District Association Minutes, 1843–1912, 23 Feb. 1843. On the theme of early synodical government, see Reisner, *Measure of Faith,* 78–9.

27 Ibid., St Francis District Association Minutes, 1843–1912, 12 Dec. 1843; Parish of St Armand East Archives, Missisquoi District Association Minutes, Parochial Subcommittee Meeting, 22 June 1843, 9.
28 Fahey, *In His Name*, 225.
29 In 1851 the district association still controlled only half the general funds raised within its boundaries. See bylaws adopted 28 May 1851.
30 QDA, *Church Society Reports*, 1844, 17–18.
31 Ibid., St Francis District Association Minutes, 1843–1912, 29 Jan. 1851. For the year ending in May 1852 subscriptions to the general fund increased to £94.0.4, while those for local purposes declined to £674.1.6. Minutes of 26 May 1852.
32 MDA, G.J. Mountain Papers, Joseph Scott to Bishop of Montreal, Cold Brook, Brome, 23 July 1845.
33 QDA, *Canadian Ecclesiastical Gazette*, 18 July 1850, 19.
34 Reisner, *Diary of a Country Clergyman*, 161; St Armand East Church Archives, Letterbook of Canon James Reid, 115–27; Missisquoi District Association Minutes, Parochial Subcommittee Meeting, 1 Jan. 1857.
35 In 1847 the SPG offered to double all contributions from other sources to Bishop's College up to a ceiling of £1,000, and in 1848 it sanctioned £300 a year from the clergy reserves fund. QDA, G2, vol. 108, SPG, 1844–61, 6, E. Hawkins to Bishop of Montreal; 31 Aug. 1845; 3 June 1846; 27, T.B. Murray to Bishop of Montreal, London, 17 July 1847; 36, E. Hawkins to Bishop of Montreal, London, 19 May 1848.
36 Ibid., 13; G5, vol. 111, Clergy Reserves, 1827–58, E. Hawkins to Bishop Mountain, London, 3 Dec. 1846; D19, folder 100, Bishop of Montreal to E. Hawkins, Grosse Isle, 5 Sept. 1846; Quebec 10 April 1848. The district associations were given the impression that the initiative came from the SPG. QDA, St Francis District Association, Minutes, 16 June 1847.
37 Quoted in Reisner, *Diary of a Country Clergyman*, 351n247.
38 Westfall, *Two Worlds*, 104–6.
39 George McLeod Ross, Jonathan Taylor, Richard Whitwell, and Christopher Jackson each received £150, while the two longest-serving ministers, Charles Cotton and James Reid, each received £100 from the SPG and £100 from the British government. QDA, D19, folder 100, Annual salary paid by SPG, Nov. 1846; G6, vol. 112, Clergy Reserves, 1825–54, Classification of missionaries, 1849; Reisner, *Diary of a Country Clergyman*, lxvii; Millman, *Short History of Dunham*, 16.
40 Reisner, *Diary of a Country Clergyman*, 137, 157–60, 166.
41 Quoted in Hawkins, *Annals of the Diocese of Quebec*, 286.
42 Ibid. On Chapman, see Drummond, *Grand Old Man of Dudswell*.

43 Bennett, *Sacred Space,* 74, 81.
44 NA, SPG Papers (Reel A 201), box 31, folio 368, no. 206, G. Montreal to A.M. Campbell, Quebec, 12 July 1839; no. 232, 28 May 1841; no. 297, G. Montreal to E. Hawkins, Quebec, 12 July 1843. In addition, R.N. Watts donated £20 and George Marler £15 to the Drummondville society. *A Journal of Visitation to a Part of the Diocese of Quebec by the Lord Bishop of Montreal in the Spring of 1843,* 3rd ed (London: Society for the Propagation of the Gospel, 1846) (hereafter *Visitation Journal 1843*), 63.
45 James Reid wrote in 1839 that there were very few British settlers in the parish, and 'they are either like Gallio [Galileo?], or sectaries.' MDA, Reid Papers, J. Reid to Bishop of Quebec, St Armand, 18 Feb. 1839.
46 [Charles Stewart], *Church of England in Canada,* 1–2. Copy found in QDA, G8, Travelling Missionaries.
47 QDA, vol. 106, Stuart, 'Episcopate of Jacob Mountain,' 45–8; Millman, *Life of Stewart,* 37; QDA, D8, 'Year 1820. Extract from S.P.G. Reports, Pages 101–36, The Hon. and Rev. Dr Stewart's Report submitted to the Board at the Meeting of the Society, December 15th, 1820'; D9, J. Quebec to Mr Hamilton, Belmont, 15 Aug. 1821; NA, SPG Papers (Reel A 203), box 33, folio 370, no. 9, 'The Church in Canada,' 17 July 1824. Stewart reported that the fund was nearly exhausted in November 1821. QDA, Mountain Papers, vol. 80, 128, C. Stewart to Archdeacon of Quebec, Hatley, 7 Nov. 1821. On its distribution, see vol. 81, 49.
48 QDA, D9, C. Stewart to Henry Goulburn, London, 27 April 1821; D9, folder 90, C. Stewart to Henry Goulburn, Orton near Peterbro,' 25 June 1821. Stewart sold 755 acres to the British American Land Company for £124 in 1835–6. Millman, *Life of Stewart,* 45n15. Stewart's plea for funds was essentially reprinted in 1823 but with an additional reference to the British immigrants who had been arriving in the Canadas since the end of the Napoleonic Wars. QDA, G8, *The Church in Canada* (London, 26 Aug. 1823), 1.
49 This fund produced gifts of up to £100 to forty-six churches, and loans to two others. Millman, *Life of Stewart,* 142.
50 QDA, D9, J. Quebec to Mr Hamilton, Belmont, 15 Aug. 1821.
51 NA, SPG Papers (Reel A 205), box 35, folio 388, no. 200, C. Jackson to My Lord, Hatley, 28 Feb. 1839.
52 Hawkins, *Annals of the Diocese of Quebec,* 41–3; Stuart, 'Episcopate of Jacob Mountain,' 14–17, 22–3, 26, 51–4. Kingston's original Anglican church, built in 1791–2, had a similar design though it was smaller. Varty, 'Building Identities,' 116–18.
53 A transcript of this article can be found in Brome County Historical Society, Frelighsburg Church file.

54 QDA, D Series, G.J. Mountain to A.M. Campbell, Quebec, 23 March 1843, 28-30; D17, folder 98, G.J. Mountain to E. Hawkins, Quebec, 26 June 1843, 3; *Visitation Journal 1843*, 33. The original St Paul's was fifty-five feet by thirty-nine feet. Hamilton, *With Heart*, 217.
55 QDA, B13, 58, St Armand West Report, [1838].
56 Measuring fifty feet by forty feet, the church could hold 390 people, with 290 in the pews and 100 in the gallery. NA, SPG Papers (Reel A199), box 29, folio 362, no. 68, C. Cotton to Rev. Sir, Dunham, 1 Feb. 1822; no. 79, C. Cotton to Rev. Sir, 1 Mar. 1834; no. 96, C. Cotton to Rev. Sir, Dunham, 28 Mar. 1842; QDA, B4, Dunham Report, 1833; QDA, D18, folder 99, Journal by the Bishop of Montreal to the Rev. E. Hawkins, 5148/46 (359), 32.
57 QDA, D8, 'Year 1820. Extract from S.P.G. Reports, Pages 101-36, The Hon. and Rev. Dr Stewart's Report submitted to the Board at the Meeting of the Society, December 15th, 1820'; Stuart, 'Episcopate,' 292.
58 *A History of Saint Peter's Parish*, 19.
59 QDA, B22, 3, C. Stewart to Archdeacon of Quebec, York, 8 May 1822. The deed specified that the donation was to the Protestant Episcopal Church, but it allowed the land to revert to the donor if the church was not built within five years. (Archives of St Peter's Church, Sherbrooke, Box 7, Legal file: 1833-87, donation of land by W.B. Felton). Felton had apparently promised in 1816 to build an Anglican church at his own expense, but in 1821 he applied for a grant from Charles Stewart's building fund. Hawkins, *Annals of the Diocese of Quebec*, 28.
60 QDA, B22, 5, C. Stewart to Archdeacon of Quebec, Lennoxville, 13 Feb. 1823; 6, Jason Wright to Edward Burrough, Esq., Sherbrooke, 13 Feb. 1824; 7, Petition of Jason Wright to Bishop Quebec, Ascot, 12 Feb. 1824.
61 Ibid., 8, C.F. LeFevre to Archdeacon Mountain, Sherbrooke, 26 Mar. 1824.
62 Ibid., 5, C. Stewart to Archdeacon of Quebec, Lennoxville, 13 Feb. 1823.
63 Ibid., QDA, Series D, G.J. Mountain to A.M. Campbell, Quebec, 23 March 1843, 50; Little, 'Journal,' 92 and 116 n40.
64 Westfall, *Two Worlds*, 130; Bennett, *Sacred Space*, 178, 129.
65 Quoted in Little, 'Journal,' 84. For a summary of Mountain's guidelines for the construction and furnishing of churches, see Vaudry, *Anglicans and the Atlantic World*, 56-9.
66 F.J.R., *Church at the Upper Mills*, 44-5; Lester, *A Church Provided*, 12-13. Lester mistakenly states that the church was built in 1828, which was what the contract stipulated, but Bishop Stewart did not consecrate the new church, known as St Anne's, until 1834. Little, 'Journal,' 85-7; QDA, D series, folder 94, Bishop Stewart's Visitation Report, Toronto, 30 Dec. 1834.
67 QDA, D17, folder 98, G.J. Mountain to E. Hawkins, Quebec, 26 June 1843, 4.

68 Hamilton, *With Heart,* 218–19. For an illustration, see Montgomery, *Missisquoi Bay.*
69 QDA, D18, folder 99, Journal by the Bishop of Montreal to the Rev. E. Hawkins, 5148/46 (359), 32. Thomas, *Contributions,* 142–4; MDA, Cotton Papers, C.C. Cotton to My Lord, Dunham, 26 June 1845 (typescript).
70 Archives of St Peter's Church, Sherbrooke, Box 7, Resolutions adopted at a public meeting of the Episcopal Congregation at Sherbrooke, 25 Nov. 1839; Legal file: 1833–87, Deed of sale, 26 Feb. 1844.
71 QDA, Series D, G.J. Mountain to A.M. Campbell, Quebec, 23 March 1843, 44, 47–51; *Visitation Journal 1843,* 56; *History of Saint Peter's,* 21.
72 NA, SPG Papers (Reel A 206), box 36, folio 412, no. 80, Charlotte Austin to [?], Lennoxville, 13 May 1840.
73 Ibid., no. 81, L. Doolittle to Bishop of Montreal, Lennoxville, 20 Jan. 1841; QDA, D18, folder 99, Journal by the Bishop of Montreal to the Rev. E. Hawkins, 5148/46 (359), 43; NA, SPG Papers (Reel A 206), box 36, folio 412,
74 The first organ, costing $450, was acquired in 1852. Preceding it was a bass-viol followed by a cello. *Parish Anecdotes,* 11–13.
75 NA, SPG Papers (Reel A 205), box 36, folio 404, no. 15, G.M. Ross to My Lord, Drummondville, 9 April 1839. For a brief account of the role played by Edmund Cox, see *Tread of the Pioneers,* 1: 165.
76 QDA, Series D, G.J. Mountain to A.M. Campbell, Quebec, 23 March 1843, 54; *Visitation Journal 1843,* 59–60.
77 QDA, Series D, Bishop of Montreal to E. Hawkins, Quebec, 2 March 1849; D18, folder 99, Journal by the Bishop of Montreal to the Rev. E. Hawkins, 5148/46 (359), 47–8.
78 NA, SPG Papers (Reel A 205), box 36, folio 404, no. 16, G.M. Ross to My Lord, Drummondville, 1 Oct. 1842; D18, folder 99, Journal by the Bishop of Montreal to the Rev. E. Hawkins, 5148/46 (359), 30–2. A photograph of this church can be found in Hamilton, *With Heart,* 270.
79 Moysey, 'George Slack,' 64.
80 QDA, D18, folder 99, Journal by the Bishop of Montreal to the Rev. E. Hawkins, 5148/46 (359), 34. Slack had not been sent to the Eastern Townships by the SPG, rather, he had taken up farming there as a retired naval officer, then become a deacon and an ordained minister. See Moysey, 'George Slack.'
81 QDA, D18, folder 99, Journal by the Bishop of Montreal to the Rev. E. Hawkins, 5148/46 (359), 38–9. On the question of church seating, see Bennett, *Sacred Space,* 193–4. Three years later the visiting SPG secretary, Ernest Hawkins, was somewhat less impressed, describing the Granby church as 'a very

tolerable one – wooden – in the usual style with a kind of sham gothic window & tower & spire.' Reisner, *Measure of Faith*, 109.
82 QDA, St Francis District Association Minutes, 1843–1912, 29 Jan. 1851. Chapman would design a number of Gothic-style Anglican churches in the region. Photographs of several can be seen in Pomerleau, *Terre de Croyances*.
83 MDA, Reid Papers, Sermon at dedication of All Saints Church, Dunham, 26 Sept. 1849.
84 QDA, G.J. Mountain Papers, G.J. Mountain to J. Reid, Quebec, 14 March 1829; Vaudry, *Anglicans and the Atlantic World*, 52.
85 MDA, Bishop Fulford, 'Private Journal,' vol. 1.
86 Finley, 'Stained Glass,' 87. C.P. Reid would, however, acquire a 'transparent painting' for the altar window of his Compton church in 1840. NA, SPG Papers (Reel A 200), box 29, folio 367, no. 103, C.P. Reid to Rev. Sir, Compton, 31 Dec. 1840.
87 Finley, 'Stained Glass,' 79. In stressing how distinctively Ontarian and Canadian this architectural style became, the otherwise excellent discussion in chapter 5 of Westfall's *Two Worlds* neglects its imperial aspect.
88 Clark, *Church and Sect*, 116.
89 The number of stations for each Anglican minister in the Eastern Townships ranged from two to ten in 1845. See Noël, *Competing for Souls*, Appendix 3, 240.
90 QDA, D14, folder 95, Bishop G.J. Mountain to A.M. Campbell, Quebec, 26 March 1836.
91 When one man asked for compensation for performing this service, Stewart replied that 'It was an indulgence, not an appointment, that was asked.' QDA, Reid Collection of Bishop Stewart Letters, vol. 1, 62, Stewart to Reid, Hatley, 25 Nov. 1819.
92 The SPG set aside £500 a year for this purpose. Millman, *Life of Stewart*, 101.
93 QDA, Unbound Manuscripts, case 2, folder 14, Catechists Reports; D Series, folder 93, C.J. Quebec to Archibald Hamilton, Quebec, 6 Aug. 1832.
94 NA, SPG Papers (Reel A 206), box 36, folio 410, no. 60, [?] to Venerable and Rev. Sir, Leeds, 1 March 1833.
95 NA, SPG Papers (Reel A 201), box 30, folio 368, no. 181, G. Montreal to A.M. Campbell, Quebec, 30 June 1838. There were four other catechists in Lower Canada at this time, and seven in Upper Canada. Ibid., no. 188, G. Montreal to A.M. Campbell, Quebec, 1 Dec. 1838.
96 QDA, B5, Frampton, 66, Jas. Alexander to Bishop Montreal and Quebec, 6 Sept. 1841; QDA, 69, Petition to Bishop of Montreal, by members of Church of England, and others, residing in Inverness Township, April 1842. Ward

clashed with the Tractarian Henry Roe over Christmas decorations in the church in 1852. (Vaudry, *Anglicans and the Atlantic World*, 126). Christ Church, near the Ireland–Inverness border, continues to be popularly known as Ward's Church.
97 QDA, B13, 60, Fred S. Neve to Bishop of Montreal, Philipsburg, 23 Oct. 1840; D Series, G.J. Mountain to A.M. Campbell, Quebec, 23 March 1843, 28–30; NA, SPG Papers (Reel A 202), box 31, folio 386, no. 4, G. Montreal to E. Hawkins, Quebec, 26 June 1843; *Visitation Journal 1843*, 33.
98 QDA, D16, folder 97, Bishop of Montreal to Campbell, Quebec, 28 May 1841; QDA, B9, 17, John Butler to Bishop of Montreal, Kingsey, 22 Jan. 1844; D18, folder 99, Journal by the Bishop of Montreal to the Rev. E. Hawkins, 5148/46 (359), 32.
99 Noël, *Competing for Souls*, 97–100. QDA, Church Society Reports, 1845, 18. On the travelling missionaries in Upper Canada, see Fahey, *In His Name*, 42–7.
100 Marston, 'George Jehoshaphat Mountain,' 34–5.
101 Quoted in Millman, *Jacob Mountain*, 198.
102 ETR, Nicolls Papers, Letters from G.J. Mountain, 1820–52, G.J.M. to Harriet Mountain, Charleston, 12 Feb. 1840.
103 Reisner, *Diary of a Country Clergyman*, 145.
104 Ibid., 104.

10 Messianism and Popular Response

1 Fahey, *In His Name*, xiv–xv, xvii.
2 Richard Vaudry makes the same point in *Anglicans and the Atlantic World* 11.
3 Westfall, *Two Worlds*, 90. For a fuller discussion of the imperialist theme, focusing on John Strachan, see Fahey, *In His Name*, chapter 5.
4 SPG Papers (Reel A 200), box 29, folio 367, no. 100, J. Reid to Bishop of Montreal, Frelighsburg, 17 June 1839; (Reel A 205), box 35, folio 388, no. 200, C. Jackson to My Lord, Hatley, 28 Feb. 1839.
5 Ibid. (Reel A 201), box 31, folio 368, no. 236, G. Montreal to A.M. Campbell, Quebec, 28 April 1841.
6 QDA, Series D, G.J. Mountain to A.M. Campbell, Quebec, 23 March 1843, 69.
7 Ibid., Mountain Papers, vol. 77, 63, J. Mountain to Dear Sir, Quebec, 8 March 1810.
8 QDA, Unbound Manuscripts, case 1, folder 8, G.J. Mountain 1759–1821, 'Sketch of the *Church of England in Canada* by the Ven. G.J. Mountain, 1821,' 17. For a summary of the Anglican position on church unification, see Hawkins, *Annals of the Diocese of Quebec*, 59–66.

9 QDA, Series D, G.J. Mountain to A.M. Campbell, Quebec, 23 March 1843, 68.
10 NA, SPG Papers (Reel A 206), box 36, folio 413, no. 87, to the Right Reverend Father in God, George by Divine Permission, Lord Bishop of Montreal, Brome, 15 Feb. 1841.
11 QDA, *Annual Report of the Quebec Diocesan Committee of the Society for Promoting Christian Knowledge,* 1824–5, 17–18.
12 Stewart, *Sermons,* 28. For a brief discussion of this publication, see Reisner, *Measure of Faith,* 56–60.
13 Stewart, *Sermons,* 17.
14 See Little, 'Fireside Kingdom.'
15 MDA, Cotton Papers, Sermon on 1 Corinth., 6 chap., 14 ver.; Headon, 'Influence of the Oxford Movement,' 99; MDA, Whitwell Papers, Sermons.
16 MDA, Reid Papers, J. Reid to Bishop of Quebec, St Armand, 18 Feb. 1839.
17 Reisner, *Diary of a Country Clergyman,* 62.
18 Quoted in Little, 'Journal of Archdeacon G.J. Mountain,' 114 n22, 87.
19 Quoted in Reisner, *Life of a Country Clergyman,* 311–12 n20.
20 MDA, G.J. Mountain Correspondence, James Reid to G.J. Mountain, St Armand, 30 June 1823.
21 QDA, Series D, folder 91, Bishop Quebec to A. Hamilton, Quebec, 14 April 1827.
22 QDA, B4, 44, Dunham Report, 23 Dec. 1827.
23 NA, SPG Papers (Reel A 199), box 29, folio 362, no. 74, C. Cotton to Rev. Sir, Dunham, 18 Feb. 1830; no. 82, C. Cotton to Rev. Sir, Dunham, 22 Feb. 1836.
24 Reisner, *Diary of a Country Clergyman,* 65–6.
25 QDA, D Series, G.J. Mountain to A.M. Campbell, Quebec, 23 March 1843, 33–4; *Visitation Journal 1843,* 37–8.
26 QDA, Series D, 1848, Bishop Montreal to E. Hawkins, Quebec, 21 Dec. 1848; Thomas, *Contributions,* 138, 142, 145.
27 The government allowed the parish, officially erected as Charleston in Stewart's honour in 1821, to deviate from the township boundaries. Instead, it included the first six ranges of Hatley, two ranges in Compton, and two ranges in Barnston because the church was more centrally located to these limits. QDA, G4, vol. 110, Clergy Reserves and Erection of Parishes, 1816–25, Extract of a Report made by a Committee of the whole Council date 28 May 1821, 12–13; J. Quebec to Col. Ready, Quebec, 17 Jan. 1821, 16; Col. Ready to Chief Justice, Quebec, 7 April 1821, 17.
28 Quoted in Hawkins, *Annals of the Diocese of Quebec,* 52–3; QDA, D91, Bishop of Quebec to Anthony Hamilton, 13 Dec. 1827.

29 QDA, B7, 1, C.J. Stewart to Bishop, Quebec, 19 Feb. 1818; 5, C. Stewart to Bishop of Quebec, Hatley, 24 July 1818.
30 Hawkins, *Annals of the Diocese of Quebec*, 108–12. Jacob Mountain had gone to England in December 1816 in order to resign from the episcopacy, but it was decided in the summer of 1818 that he would return to Quebec. Millman, *Life of a Stewart*, 38, 41–3; Stuart, 'Episcopate,' 226–7.
31 Quoted in Hawkins, *Annals of the Diocese of Quebec*, 53.
32 Clark, *Church and Sect*, 119.
33 QDA, *Church Society Reports*, 1851, 39–40. On the violence that coincided with the railway construction in the region, see Little, *State and Society*, 68–77.
34 *Canadian Ecclesiastical Gazette*, 10 April 1851.
35 QDA, B2, printed report of D. Robertson, Stanbridge, 1833.
36 Ibid., B4, 31, Drummondville Report, 1851.
37 Ibid., B4, 30, Drummondville Report, June 1833. My research does not support LaBrèque's statement that Ross 'particularly dreaded the influence of the Roman Catholics.' LaBrèque, 'George McLeod Ross,' 769.
38 QDA, B10, 54, Leeds Report, 16 March 1852; B5, Frampton, 65, Parish Report, Inverness and Upper Ireland, 1851.
39 Ibid., B11, Melbourne and Shipton Report [1838].
40 Quoted in Little, *Love Strong as Death*, 161. It was standard practice in England for non-communicants to leave the church after the ante-communion part of the service. Walsh and Taylor, 'Introduction,' 11.
41 QDA, B4, 31, Drummondville Report, 1851.
42 NA, SPG Papers (Reel A 205), box 35, folio 388, no. 197, C. Jackson to Rev. Sir, Charleston, 21 Jan. 1831.
43 MDA, G.J. Mountain Correspondence, J. Reid to G.J. Mountain, St Armand, 29 Nov. 1823; QDA, *Annual Report of the Quebec Diocesan Committee of the Society for Promoting Christian Knowledge*, 1824–5, 16; Brown, *Schooling in the Clearings*, 39–40.
44 NA, SPG Papers (Reel A 199), box 29, folio 362, no. 70, C. Cotton to Rev. Sir, Dunham, 1 Feb. 1824; no. 87, C. Cotton to Rev. Sir, Dunham, 22 July 1833; QDA, B4, 54, Dunham Report, 1833.
45 QDA, B2, John Kemp to My Lord, Bury, 20 June 1851; B10, 54, Leeds Report, 16 March 1852.
46 Ibid., B4, 31, Drummondville Report, 1851; B22, 39, Sherbrooke Report, 1851; 41, Mission of Lennoxville, 1851.
47 Ibid., B11, Melbourne and Shipton Report, 1833, 1838, 1851.
48 Ibid., B2, printed report of D. Robertson, Stanbridge, 1833.
49 Ibid., B23, Shefford Report, 1833, 1838; B5, Frampton, 65, Parish Report, Inverness and Upper Ireland, 1851.

50 QDA, Series D, G.J. Mountain to A.M. Campbell, Quebec, 23 March 1843, 42; *Visitation Journal 1843*, 47.
51 NA, SPG Papers (Reel A 199), box 29, folio 362, no. 66, C. Cotton to Rev. Sir, Dunham, 1 Feb. 1821; no. 74, C. Cotton to Rev. Sir, Dunham, 18 Feb. 1830; (Reel A 200), box 29, folio 367, no. 97, J. Reid to Rev. Sir, St Armand, 7 Dec. 1829.
52 Ibid. (Reel A 205), box 35, folio 388, no. 197, C. Jackson to Rev. Sir, Charleston, 21 Jan. 1831. 17 Jan. 1832. Brown would seem to be wrong, then, when she claims that there was no Anglican proselytizing in the Royal Institution schools. *Schooling in the Clearings*, 54.
53 Brown, *Schooling in the Clearings*, 57–62, 65–6; NA, SPG Papers (Reel A 200), box 29, folio 367, no. 97, J. Reid to Rev. Sir, St Armand, 7 Dec. 1829.
54 On George Mountain's view of baptism, see Vaudry, *Anglicans and the Atlantic World*, 108–10.
55 QDA, B1, 75, C. Stewart to Bishop Mountain, St Armand, 21 Nov. 1810; 80, Bishop Quebec to C. Stewart, Quebec, 6 Dec. [1810].
56 NA, SPG Papers (Reel A 204), box 34, folio, 375, no. 85, Samuel S. Wood to Rev. Sir, Drummondville, 18 Sept. 1826; (Reel A 205), box 35, folio 388, no. 197, C. Jackson to Rev. Sir, Charleston, 21 Jan. 1831; (Reel A 206), box 36, folio 415, no. 120, E. Cusack to Rev. C.B. Dalton, Cold Brook, Brome, 2 Jan. 1843.
57 QDA, B4, 54, Dunham Report, 1833; B2, printed report of D. Robertson, Stanbridge, 1833; B11, Melbourne and Shipton Report, 1833.
58 Ibid., B11, Melbourne and Shipton Report [1838]; B23, Shefford Report, 1833; 67, Shefford Report [1838].
59 Ibid., B7, 44, Hatley and Compton Report, 1833, 1838; B10, 54, Leeds Report, 16 March 1852; B11, 44, Melbourne and Shipton Report, 1851.
60 Ibid., B22, 41, Lennoxville Report, 1851.
61 Ibid., B1, 75, C. Stewart to Bishop Mountain, St Armand, 21 Nov. 1810; 80, Bishop of Quebec to C. Stewart, Quebec, 6 Dec. [1810].
62 Ibid., B1, 96, printed report for St Armand East, 15 Nov. 1827; D8, C. Stewart to Rev. Sir, 1 May 1811; C. Stewart to Dr Morice, 1 Nov. 1812.
63 Ibid., Series D, G.J. Mountain to A.M. Campbell, Quebec, 23 March 1843, 55; *Visitation Journal 1843*, 61; QDA, B11, 44, Melbourne and Shipton Report, 1851; B4, 31 Drummondville report, 1851.
64 Thomas, *Religion and the Decline of Magic*, 42–3, 68–9. See also Cressy, 'Purification, Thanksgiving,' 117–40. Cressy argues, in contrast to most scholars (112–14), that churching was not 'a cultural response to the fear of women,' or 'a man-made instrument for their control,' but 'an occasion of female social activity, in which the notion of "purification" was uncontentious, minimal or missing.'

65 QDA, D Series, G.J. Mountain to A.M. Campbell, Quebec, 23 March 1843, 28–30; D17, folder 98, G.J. Mountain to E. Hawkins, Quebec, 26 June 1843, 3; *Visitation Journal 1843*, 33; QDA, B11, 44, Melbourne and Shipton Report, 1851.

66 Ibid., B7, 42, Hatley and Compton Report, 1833; 44, Hatley and Compton Report, 1838; 49, Hatley and Stanstead Report, 1851; B22, 41, Mission of Lennoxville Report, 1851.

67 Ibid., Series D, G.J. Mountain to A.M. Campbell, Quebec, 23 March 1843, 46–7, 56–7; *Visitation Journal 1843*, 51–2, 61–2.

68 QDA, B10, 54, Leeds Report, 16 March 1852; B5, Frampton, 65, Parish Report, Inverness and Upper Ireland, 1851.

69 Ibid., B4, 5, Samuel S. Wood to Bishop, Drummondville, 13 Dec. 1819.

70 Ibid., D4, 25, Drummondville Report, 9 Aug. 1828; B4, 30, Drummondville Report, June 1833.

71 Ibid., 31, Drummondville Report, 1851.

72 Ibid., B11, Melbourne and Shipton Report, 1833; Stuart, 'Episcopate of Jacob Mountain,' 225–6.

73 NA, SPG Papers (Reel A 205), box 35, folio 388, no. 198, C. Jackson to Rev. Sir, Charleston, 17 Jan. 1832; QDA, B7, 42, Hatley and Compton Report, 1833; QDA, B7, 42, Hatley and Stanstead Report, 1833.

74 NA, SPG Papers (Reel A 200), box 29, folio 367, no. 103, C.P. Reid to Rev. Sir, Compton, 31 Dec. 1840; QDA, B7, 49, Hatley and Compton Report, 1851.

75 Millman, *Jacob Mountain*, 225–6; QDA, B5, 9, Eaton Report, 1833.

76 NA, SPG Papers (Reel A 199), box 29, folio 362, no. 82, C. Cotton to Rev. Sir, Dunham, 22 Feb. 1836; no. 88, 24 Feb. 1841; no. 91, 19 Feb. 1844.

77 QDA, B2, printed report of D. Robertson, Stanbridge, 1833; *Canadian Ecclesiastical Gazette*, 10 April 1851.

78 This was clearly considered a bold move, for in 1849 the bishop's son wrote of the principal of Bishop's College: 'I am afraid Nicolls will not escape the charge of Puseyism if he has permitted chanting the service.' Quoted in Vaudry, *Anglicans and the Atlantic World*, 6.

79 QDA, B2, John Kemp to My Lord, Bury, 20 June 1851; QDA, B11, 44, Melbourne and Shipton Report, 1851; B10, 54, Leeds Report, 16 March 1852.

80 QDA, *Church Society Reports*, 1850, 38–9; *Canadian Ecclesiastical Gazette*, 10 Apr. 1851.

81 Reisner, *Diary of a Country Clergyman*, 14.

82 MDA, Parish Reports, Frelighsburg, Report of St Armand, and addendum, 2 Oct. 1820; QDA, B4, 12, S.S. Wood to Archdeacon Mountain, Drummondville, 15 June 1822; Series D, G.J. Mountain to A.M. Campbell, Quebec, 23 March 1843, 45–6; B7, 44, Hatley and Compton Report, 1838; B11, 44, Melbourne and Shipton Report, 1851; B22, 41, 1851 Lennoxville Report.

83 Westfall, 'Constructing Public Religions,' 26–7.
84 Woolverton, *Colonial Anglicanism*, 27.
85 Quoted in Little, 'Journal of Archdeacon G.J. Mountain,' 99.
86 Gendron et al., *Histoire du Piémont*, 111. Clark (*Church and Sect*, 121) makes the same unsubstantiated assumption for the Canadas in general.
87 The questions can be found in QDA, B5, 65, Upper Ireland Report, 1851. Most clergy simply submitted the answers without the questions.
88 The practice continues, however, in some rural areas or England. Cressy, 'Purification,' 144.
89 Butler, *Awash in a Sea of Faith*, 128.
90 Ibid., 166; Vaudry, *Anglicans and the Atlantic World*, 45.
91 Stewart, *Sermons*, 9–10.
92 QDA, D12, folder 93, C.J. Quebec to Rev. L. Doolittle, Quebec, 24 May 1832; C.J. Quebec to J. Reid, Quebec, 8 May 1832. Reid was again reminded of the exclusivity of sanctified spaces in 1840. See G.J. Mountain Papers, G.J. Montreal to J. Reid, Coteau du Lac, 22 Jan. 1840.
93 Cressy, 'Purification,' 106.
94 NA, SPG Papers (Reel A 199), box 29, folio 362, no. 75, C. Cotton to Rev. Sir, Dunham, 12 July 1830.
95 Westfall, 'Constructing Public Religions,' 26; Clark, *Church and Sect*, 117–18; Grant, *Profusion of Spires*, 61–2. Two exceptional cases were Edmund Burke and Robert Balfe, successive incumbents in Stanbridge. See Reisner, *Measure of Faith*, 87–92.
96 Reisner, *Diary of a Country Clergyman*, 5
97 MDA, Reid Papers, J. Reid to Bishop of Quebec, St Armand, 18 Feb. 1839.
98 Nockles, 'Church Parties,' 351–5.
99 QDA, D17, folder 98, Extract from SPG quarterly papers, Jan. 1843, 14 Feb. 1842 entry, 65.
100 These are the topics discussed in Mountain's 1829 journal. See Little, 'Journal of Archdeacon G.J. Mountain,' 115 n33.
101 Walsh and Taylor, 'Introduction,' 14. For a useful discussion of the meaning of High Church, Low Church, and Evangelical Anglicanism, see Vaudry, *Anglicans and the Atlantic World*, 8–9.

Conclusion

1 *Quebec Gazette*, 2 Jan. 1812.
2 Noll, *History of Christianity*, 267.
3 Bayly, *Imperial Meridian*, 137.
4 Westfall, *Two Worlds*, 23. See also Fahey, *In His Name*, 123, 177–80.

5 Wise, 'God's Peculiar Peoples,' 59. Elsewhere, Wise recognized Bishop John Strachan's influence in forging what he and his disciples have called the 'conservative blueprint' of Upper Canadian society, but that influence is largely interpreted as being exerted through the Family Compact elite. Wise, 'Upper Canada and the Conservative Tradition.'
6 Doll, *Revolution, Religion and National Identity,* 262; French, 'Evangelical Creed,' 18; Moir, 'American Influences,' 440; Gauvreau, 'Protestantism Transformed,' 50.
7 See Houston and Smyth, *The Sash Canada Wore*; and Berger, *Sense of Power*.
8 Vaudry's *Anglicans and the Atlantic World* has recently given the Mountains their rightful place in this pantheon. A recent exception to this top-down approach, despite its institutional focus, is Semple, *Lord's Dominion*.
9 Westfall, *Two Worlds*, 120–2. See also Fahey, *In His Name*, 99–102.
10 Russell, 'Church of Scotland Clergy,' 91. Nearly half the 923 people belonging to the Church of Scotland in 1831 were in the two recently settled townships of Inverness and Leeds.
11 *Home and Foreign Missionary Record for the Free Church of Scotland*, Sept. 1846, 483. The Reformed Presbyterian Church would send a missionary to Inverness and Leeds in 1831, but lack of local financial support and his resistance to sending reports to his sponsoring society led to his dismissal in 1840. The initiative would not be renewed. See Hay, 'Reformed Presbyterians.'
12 In Upper Canada, where the Presbyterians were second only to the Anglicans by mid-century, there had been fifty-two Church of Scotland clergy as early as 1837. Russell, 'Church of Scotland Clergy,' 90. On religion in the Highland settlement of the Eastern Townships, see Little, *Crofters and Habitants*, chapter 7.
13 See, for example, Horowitz, 'Conservatism, Liberalism, and Socialism'; Bell, 'Loyalist Tradition in Canada'; Akenson, *Irish in Ontario*; and Noel, *Patrons, Clients, Brokers*.
14 See, for example, Errington, *The Lion, the Eagle*; and Romney, 'Re-Inventing Upper Canada.'
15 Eastern Townships Research Centre, Nicolls Papers, Letters from G.J. Mountain, 1820–52, G.J.M. to Harriet Mountain, Charleston, 12 Feb. 1840; Little, 'Mental World.'
16 The denominations in question were the Freewill Baptists, Universalists, and Wesleyan Methodists, with the Protestant Methodists joining shortly afterward. Stanstead Historical Society, BD-A-41.1, Minute Book of the Griffin Corner United [*sic*] Church, 1841-1927; Anniversary Service, Griffin Union Church, Sunday, June 26 [1932].

Bibliography

Manuscript Sources

Archives Nationales du Québec à Montréal, United Church Archives, Montreal-Ottawa Conference
Canada Education and Home Missionary Society Papers, 1833–45
Minute Book of the Presbytery of Quebec, 1841–74

Archives Nationales du Québec à Sherbrooke
Fonds Lyster, Rev. William Hamilton, Compton Church Record, Free Will Baptist Church (P1000, 1A13–6603A)

Archives of Ontario
Church Records Collection, Shefford Wesleyan Methodist Mission Circuit Book, 1821–56 (Ms 881, Reel 2)

Aurora College, Illinois
Jenks Memorial Collection, Millerites and Early Adventists, William Miller Correspondence, 1814–55

Bishop's University Library
Nicolls Papers, Letters from G.J. Mountain, 1820–52

Brome County Historical Society
Frelighsburg Church file

Compton County Historical Society
Records of the Congregational Church, Eaton, Canada East, Commencing 1835

Danville United Church Archives
Agreement made this 11th day of July 1839 between Rev. Ammi J. Parker on one part & Henry Barnard et al. on the other part
Rev. 17, verse 16 [?], Shipton, May 1830 [sermon by Ammi Parker]
Simeon Flint et al. to A.J. Parker, Shipton, 5 July 1834

Eastern Townships Research Centre (Bishop's University), Presbyterian Archives
Minutes of the Presbytery of Quebec of the Presbyterian Church of Canada in Connection with the Church of Scotland from 1831 to 1842 (PC 009/001/003)

Eastern Townships Research Centre, United Church Archives, Quebec-Sherbrooke Presbytery
Ammi Parker Papers
Danville Civil Registers, vol. 1, 1834–52
Danville Parish Records
Dunham Civil Registers (Methodist) and Quarterly Board Records, 1825–61
Durham Congregational Church Book, 1837–
Melbourne Congregational Church Book, 1837–83
Minutes, Quarterly Meetings, Methodist Mission, New Ireland, 1835–62
Plymouth United Church (Sherbrooke) fonds
Richmond and Melbourne Parish Records, Church History File
Stanstead Trustee Board, Minute Book, 1833–61
Trenholm Methodist Church fonds, Series: Church Board, Subseries: Board of Trustees, File: Minutes, 1845–1902

McCord Museum, Montreal
Hale Papers, Correspondence

McMaster University Divinity College, Canadian Baptist Archives
Abbott's Corner file
Barford Township Register of Births, Marriages, and Deaths, 1842–4
Barnston Baptist Church, parish records
Eaton Baptist Church (Sawyerville) file
Hatley Church Minute Book, 1799–1844
'Memoir of William Marsh'

Montreal Diocesan Archives
Bishop Fulford, 'Private Journal,' vol. 1
G.J. Mountain, Archdeacon – Correspondence (RG 1.5)

Jacob Mountain Papers (RG 1.3)
Parish Reports: Frelighsburg, St Armand West (Philipsburg), Waterloo (St Luke's)
Reverend [Charles] Caleb Cotton Papers
Reverend James Reid Papers, Correspondence
Reverend Richard Whitwell Papers

National Archives of Canada
Canada, Manuscript Census, 1831, 1852
Charles Caleb Cotton Fonds (MG24 J47)
Civil Secretary's Correspondence, Incoming, 1829 (RG4 A1)
Methodist Missionary Society, Synod Minutes, Lower Canada / Canada East, 1823–52 (MG17 C1)
Minutes of the Executive Missionary Committee and Copies of Letters on Missionary Business Begun Sept. 2, 1814 (MG17, C1 – reel 252)
Robert Hoyle Fonds (MG24 B141)
Society for the Propagation of the Faith Papers (reels A-199-206)

Quebec Diocesan Archives (Bishop's University)
Jacob Mountain Papers, 1800–21, vol.'s 74–80 (C3–9)
Reid Collection of Bishop Stewart Letters, 1807–36
St Francis District Association Minutes, 1843–1912
Diocesan Papers (B Series)
Copies of Letters and Documents, 1800–50 (D7-21)
SPG, 1800–61 [correspondence, mostly from London] (G1–2, vol.'s 107–8)
Clergy Reserves and Erection of Parishes, 1816–25 (G4, vol. 110)
Clergy Reserves, 1827–58 (G5, vol. 111)
Clergy Reserves, 1825–54 (G6, vol. 112)
Unbound Manuscripts, case 1, folder 3, Jacob Mountain Letters, 1802–25 (Private and Personal); folder 5, 1807–15, Stewart, Delivered at Trinity Church on Trinity Sunday, the 21st of May 1815, and St Paul's Church, Sept. the 10th; folder 8, G.J. Mountain 1759–1821, 'Sketch of the *Church of England in Canada* by the Ven. G.J. Mountain, 1821;' case 2, folder 10, Rev. G.J. Mountain Papers – original, 1818–1841; folder 14, Catechists' Reports

Saint Armand East Parish Archives (Frelighsburg)
Eighteen Sermons by Rev. James Reid
Letterbook of Canon James Reid
Missisquoi District Association Minutes
Volume 1 (collection of loose documents in a bound volume)

Saint Peter's Parish Archives (Sherbrooke)
Box 1, Pew Plans: 1844–82
Box 7, Legal file: 1833–87; Committees File, 8 April 1844

Société d'histoire de Sherbrooke
Sherbrooke Total Abstinence Society, Minute Book, 1845–7

Stanstead Historical Society
Minute Book of the Griffin Corner United [Union] Church (BD-A-41.1)
Ralph Merry Papers, 'A Memoir of Ralph Merry IV, 1786–1863' (typescript)

Victoria University Archives (Toronto), United Church of Canada Archives
Journal of Benjamin Slight (89.067c, vol. 2)
Methodist Episcopal Church, Journals of the New York Conference, 1800–39 (78.131C)
Methodist New Connexion Church Fonds, 1814–42, Correspondence (78.135c)
Methodist New Connexion Church. Foreign Colonial Missions Committee, Minutes of Meetings (BX8431, M5M)
Presbyterian Church of Canada (Free Church). Presbytery of Montreal. Minutes, vol. 1 (1844–53) (79.047c)
St Francis Association of Congregational and Presbyterian Ministers, 1836–66. Minutes
Wesleyan Methodist Church (Great Britain). Correspondence, reports, addresses concerning Canada, 1816–1836 (78.131C)
Wesleyan Methodist Church (Great Britain). Foreign Missions: America ... Correspondence, 1791–1825 (78.128c)
Wesleyan Missionary Society Minutes from Lower Canada and Canada East, vol. 1, 1817–27; vol. 2, 1828–48 (78.130C)

University of Vermont, Bailey-Howe Library
Stanstead Free Will Baptist Quarterly Meeting, First Record Book, 1828–1847
Stanstead Record Book, vol. 2

Printed Primary Sources

A Journal of Visitation to a Part of the Diocese of Quebec by the Lord Bishop of Montreal in the Spring of 1843 (3rd ed.). London: Society for the Propagation of the Gospel, 1846.
Annual Report of the Quebec Diocesan Committee of the Society for Promoting Christian Knowledge, 1824–5.

Braithwaite, Joseph Bevan. *Memoirs of Joseph John Gurney: With Selections from his Journal and Correspondence* (4th ed.), vol. 2. Philadelphia: Book Association of Friends, 1854.

Burroughs, Stephen. *Memoirs of Stephen Burroughs*, 2 vols. (Albany: B.D Packard, 1811).

Canada. *Census Reports*, 1830–1; 1851–2; 1870–1, vol. 4.

The Church in Canada. London, 26 Aug. 1823 [located in QDA, G8].

Church Society Reports of the Diocese of Quebec, 1843–75. Montreal: Lovell and Gibson.

Clark, Elmer T., J. Manning Potts, and Jacob S. Payton, eds. *The Journal and Letters of Francis Asbury*, vol. 3. London: Epworth Press; and Nashville: Abington Press, 1958.

Congregational Yearbook, 1859 (Bishop's University Library, Special Collections).

Cooney, Robert. *The Autobiography of a Wesleyan Methodist Missionary (Formerly a Roman Catholic)*. Montreal: E. Pickup, 1856.

Cox, F.A., and J. Hoby. *The Baptists in America. A Narrative of the Deputation from the Baptist Union in England to the United States and Canada*. London: T. Ward, 1836.

[Dow, Lorenzo]. *The Dealings of God, Man, and the Devil; As Exemplified in the Life, Experiences, and Travels of Lorenzo Dow*, vol. 1. Middletown, OH: Glasener and Marshall, 1849.

Hawkins, Ernest. *Annals of the Diocese of Quebec*. London: Society for Promoting Christian Knowledge, 1849.

Hubbard, E.G. *Memoir of Joseph Badger.* New York: C.S. Francis; Boston: Benjamin H. Greene 1854.

Jenkins, Rev. John. *The Faithful Minister: A Memorial of the Late William Squire*. Montreal: Wesleyan Book Depot, 1853.

Minutes of the annual conferences of the Methodist Episcopal Church, vol. 1 (New York: T. Mason and G. Lane, 1840). (Victoria University Library).

Missionary Notices Relating Principally to the Foreign Missions ... of the Methodist Conference, vol. 5, 1826–8 (London).

Reports of the American Home Missionary Society (New York), 1827–45.

'Thirty-eighth Annual Report of the New Hampshire Missionary Society, 1839.' Bishop's University Library, Special Collections.

[Mountain, G.J.]. *A Journal of Visitation to a Part of the Diocese of Quebec by the Lord Bishop of Montreal in the Spring of 1843*, 3rd. ed. London: Society for the Propagation of the Gospel, 1846.

Stewart, Charles. *A Short View of the Present State of the Easten Townships ... With Hints For Their Improvement.* Montreal, 1815; reprinted London: J. Hatchard, 1817.

356 Bibliography

- *Sermons on Family Prayer, With Extracts From Various Authors, and a Collection of Prayers.* Montreal: Nahum Mower, 1814.
- *The Church of England in Canada.* London, 24 June 1816.

Newspapers

Advent Herald (Boston), 1844–8.
British North American Wesleyan Methodist Magazine, 1841–7.
Canada Baptist Magazine and Missionary Reporter (Montreal), 1837–41.
Canadian Baptist, 1922.
Canadian Christian Examiner and Presbyterian Review (Niagara), 1837–40.
Canadian Church & Mission News, July-August 1888.
Canadian Ecclesiastical Gazette (Quebec), 1850–1.
*Christian Examiner and Presbyterian Review,*1837.
Christian Guardian, 1830–45.
Christian Messenger (Montreal), 1844–7.
Ecclesiastical and Missionary Record for the Presbyterian Church of Canada (Hamilton/Toronto), 1846–53.
Harbinger (Montreal), 1842–3.
Home and Foreign Missionary Record for the Church of Scotland (Edinburgh), 1838–43.
Home and Foreign Missionary Record for the Free Church of Scotland (Edinburgh), 1843–50.
Home Missionary (New York), 1828–45.
Methodist Magazine (London), 1820–40.
Methodist New Connexion Magazine (Manchester, England), 1838–46.
Quebec Gazette, 2 Jan. 1812.
Register (Montreal), 1843.
Report of the Canada Education and Home Missionary Society, 1834.
Scottish Congregational Magazine, New Series, vol. 6 (June 1846).
Signs of the Times (Boston), 1841–4.
Stanstead Journal, 1845–6.
Universalist Magazine (Boston), 1826–50.
Universalist Union, 1835–6.
Wesleyan (Montreal), 1840–3.

Published Secondary Sources

Acheson, T.W. 'Methodism and the Problem of Methodist Identity in Nineteenth-Century New Brunswick.' *The Contribution of Methodism to*

Atlantic Canada, edited by Charles H.H. Scobie and John Webster Grant. Montreal and Kingston: McGill-Queen's University Press, 1992.
– *Saint John: The Making of a Colonial Urban Community*. Toronto: University of Toronto Press, 1985.
Adelman, Jeremy, and Stephen Aron. 'From Borderlands to Borders: Empires, Nation-States, and the Peoples in Between in North American History.' *American Historical Review* 104 (1999): 814–41.
Akenson, Donald Harman. *The Irish in Ontario: A Study in Rural History*. Montreal and Kingston: McGill-Queen's University Press, 1984.
Atwood, Rev. A. *The Conquerors: Historical Sketches of the American Settlement of the Oregon Country Embracing Facts in the Life and Work of Rev. Jason Lee, the Pioneer and Founder of American Institutions on the Western Coast of North America.* Tacoma, WA: Jennings and Graham, 1907.
Bangs, Nathan. *A History of the Methodist Episcopal Church*, vol. 2. New York: Carlton and Porter, 1860.
Barkun, Michael. *Crucible of the Millenium: The Burned-Over District of New York in the 1840s.* Syracuse: Syracuse University Press, 1986.
Baskerville, Peter. 'Did Religion Matter? Religion and Wealth in Urban Canada at the Turn of the Twentieth Century: an Exploratory Study.' *Histoire sociale / Social History* 34 (2001): 61–96.
Bassett, T.D Seymour. 'Cabin Religion in Vermont, 1724–1791.' *Vermont History* 62 (1994): 69–87.
Baxter, Norman Allen. *History of the Freewill Baptists: A Study of New England Separatism.* Rochester, NY: American Baptist Historical Society, 1957.
Bayly, C.A. *Imperial Meridian: The British Empire and the World, 1780–1830.* London and New York: Longman, 1989.
Bell, D.G. *The Newlight Baptist Journals of James Manning and James Innes.* Hantsport, NS: Lancelot Press, 1984.
Bell, David V.J. 'The Loyalist Tradition in Canada.' *Journal of Canadian Studies* 5 (May 1970): 22–33.
Benes, Peter, and Philip D. Zimmerman. *New England Meeting House and Church, 1630–1850.* Boston: Boston University and the Currier Gallery for Art, 1979.
Bennett, Vicki. *Sacred Space and Structural Style: The Embodiment of Socio-Religious Ideology.* Ottawa: University of Ottawa Press, 1997.
Berger, Carl. *The Sense of Power: Studies in the Ideas of Canadian Imperialism, 1867–1914.* Toronto: University of Toronto Press, 1970.
Billington, Louis. '"Female Laborers in the Church": Women Preachers in the Northeastern United States, 1790–1840.' *Journal of American Studies* 19, no. 3 (1985): 369–94.
– 'The Millerite Adventists in Great Britain, 1840–1850.' *The Disappointed: Miller-*

ism and Millenarianism in the Nineteenth Century, edited by Ronald L. Numbers and Jonathan M. Butler. Bloomington: Indiana University Press, 1987.

– 'Northern New England Sectarianism in the Early Nineteenth Century.' *Bulletin of the John Rylands University Library of Manchester* 70 (Autumn 1988): 123–34.

Brown, Kathleen H. *Schooling in the Clearings: Stanstead, 1800–1850*. Stanstead: Stanstead Historical Society, 2001.

Buckner, P.A. 'The Borderlands Concept: A Critical Appraisal.' *The Northeastern Borderlands: Four Centuries of Interaction*, edited by Stephen J. Hornsby, Victor Konrad, and James J. Herlan. Orono and Fredericton: Canadian-American Center, University of Maine and Acadiensis Press, 1989.

Bull, Joshua. 'A Sketch of Farnham Monthly Meeting of Friends. Province of Quebec, Canada.' *Bulletin of the Friends Historical Association* 2 (1902): 113–18.

Butler, Jon. *Awash in a Sea of Faith: Christianizing the American People*. Cambridge, MA: Harvard University Press, 1990.

– 'The Future of American Religious History: Prospectus, Agenda, and Transatlantic *Problématique*.' *William and Mary Quarterly* 42 (1985): 167–83.

Carroll, John. *Case and His Cotemporaries*, vol. 1. Toronto: Samuel Rose, 1867; vol. 2–5, Toronto: Wesleyan Conference Office, 1869–77.

Centenary of the Consecration of St. George's Church, Lennoxville, Quebec. Lennoxville, 1948.

Channell, L.S. *History of Compton County*. Cookshire, QC: L.S. Channell, 1896.

Christie, Nancy. '"In These Times of Democratic Rage and Delusion": Popular Religion and the Challenge to the Established Order, 1760–1815.' *The Canadian Protestant Experience, 1760–1990*, edited by G.A. Rawlyk. Burlington, ON: Welch Publishing, 1990.

Clark, S.D. *Church and Sect in Canada*. Toronto: University of Toronto Press, 1948.

Clarke, Brian. *Piety and Nationalism: Lay Voluntary Associations and the Creation of an Irish-Catholic Community in Toronto, 1850–1895*. Montreal and Kingston: McGill-Queen's University Press, 1996.

Cleveland, Edward. *A Sketch of the Early Settlement and History of Shipton, Canada East*. Richmond: Richmond County Advocate, 1858.

Cook, T. 'John Beverley Robinson and the Conservative Blueprint for the Upper Canadian Community.' *Ontario History* 64, no. 2 (1972): 79–94.

Cooper, John Irwin. 'The Canada Education and Home Missionary Society.' *Canadian Historical Review* 26 (1945): 42–7.

Cressy, David. 'Purification, Thanksgiving and the Churching of Women in Post-Reformation England.' *Past and Present* 141 (1993): 117–40.

Crocker, Henry. *History of the Baptists of Vermont.* Bellows Falls, VT: P.H. Gobie Press, 1913.

Cross, Whitney. *The Burned-Over District: The Social and Intellectual History of Enthusiastic Religion in Western New York, 1800–1850.* Ithaca: Cornell University Press, 1982.

Daniell, Jere R. *Experiment in Republicanism: New Hampshire Politics and the American Revolution, 1741–1794.* Cambridge, MA: Harvard University Press, 1970.

Darroch, Gordon, and Lee Soltow. *Property and Inequality in Victorian Ontario: Structural Patterns and Cultural Communities in the 1871 Census.* Toronto: University of Toronto Press, 1994.

Day, Mrs C.M. *History of the Eastern Townships.* Montreal: John Lovell, 1869.

Dechêne, Louise. 'Observations sur l'agriculture du Bas-Canada au début du XIXe siècle.' *Évolution et éclatement du monde rurale,* edited by Joseph Goy and Jean-Pierre Wallot. Montreal: Les Presses de l'Université de Montréal, 1986.

Dessureault, Christian, and Christine Hudon. 'Conflits sociaux et élites locales au Bas-Canada; le clergé, les notables, la paysannerie et le contrôle de la fabrique.' *Canadian Historical Review* 80 (1999): 413–39.

Doan, Ruth. 'Millerism and Evangelical Culture.' *The Disappointed: Millerism and Millenarianism in the Nineteenth Century,* edited by Ronald L. Numbers and Jonathan M. Butler. Bloomington: Indiana University Press, 1987.

Doll, Peter M. *Revolution, Religion, and National Identity: Imperial Anglicanism in British North America, 1745–1795.* London: Associated Universities Press, 2000.

Dorland, Arthur Garratt. *A History of the Society of Friends (Quakers) in Canada.* Toronto: Macmillan, 1927.

Drummond, May Harvey. *The Grand Old Man of Dudswell. Being the Memors of the Rev. Thos, Shaw Chapman, M.A. Rector of St. Paul's Church, Marbleton.* Quebec: Telegraph Printing Co., 1916.

'Eaton Baptist Church, as prepared by L.W. French, church clerk, May 1905' (Canadian Baptist Archives).

Eddy, Earl B. 'The Congregational Tradition in Canada.' *The Churches and the Canadian Experience: A Faith and Order Study of the Christian Tradition,* edited by John Webster Grant. Toronto: Ryerson, 1963.

Epps, Bernard. *The Eastern Townships Adventure,* vol. 1. *A History to 1837.* Ayer's Cliff, QC: Pigwidgeon Press, 1992.

Errington, Jane. *The Lion, the Eagle, and Upper Canada: A Developing Colonial Ideology.* Montreal and Kingston: McGill-Queen's University Press, 1987.

Fahey, Curtis. *In His Name: The Anglican Experience in Upper Canada, 1791–1854.* Ottawa: Carleton University Press, 1991.

Febvre, Lucien. *The Problem of Unbelief in the Sixteenth Century: The Religion of Rabelais.* Cambridge, MA: Harvard University Press, 1982.

Findlay, G.G. and W.W. Holdsworth. *The History of the Wesleyan Methodist Missionary Society*, vol. 1. London: Epworth Press, 1921.

Finley, Greg. 'Stained Glass and Stone Tracery: The Gothic Revival and the Shaping of Canadian Sensibilities.' *British Journal of Canadian Studies* 5 (1990): 78–98.

Fitch, E.R. *The Baptists of Canada.* Toronto: Standard Publishing, 1911.

F.J.R. *The Church at the Upper Mills: The Anglicans of Stanbridge East, Stanbury and Pigeon Hill.* Bedford: A.T. Gould, 1929.

Fortin, Denis. '"The World Turned Upside Down": Millerism in the Eastern Townships, 1835–1845.' *Journal of Eastern Townships Studies* 11 (1997): 39–59.

French, Goldwin. *Parsons and Politics: The Role of the Wesleyan Methodists in Upper Canada and the Maritimes from 1780 to 1855.* Toronto: Ryerson Press, 1962.

– 'The Evangelical Creed.' *The Shield of Achilles: Aspects of Canada in the Victorian Age*, edited by W.L. Morton. Toronto: McClelland and Stewart, 1968.

Frye, Northrup. *The Bush Garden: Essays on the Canadian Imagination.* Toronto: Anansi, 1971.

Gauvreau, Michael. *The Evangelical Century: College and Creed in English Canada from the Great Revival to the Great Depression.* Montreal and Kingston: McGill-Queen's University Press, 1991.

– 'Protestantism Transformed: Personal Piety and the Evangelical Social Vision, 1815–1867.' *The Canadian Protestant Experience, 1760–1990*, edited by George Rawlyk. Burlington, ON: Welch Publishing, 1990.

Gendron, Mario et al. *Histoire du Piémont-des-Appalaches.* Sainte-Foy: Les Presses de l'Université Laval, 1999.

Gorman, George F. *Olivet Baptist Church Centenary, 1845–1945* (n.p., n.d.).

Grant, John Webster. *A Profusion of Spires: Religion in Nineteenth-Century Ontario.* Toronto: University of Toronto Press, 1988.

Greenlaw, Jane. 'Choix pratiques et choix des pratiques. Le non-conformisme protestant à Montréal (1825–1842).' *Revue d'histoire de l'Amérique française* 46 (1992): 91–114.

Greer, Allan. 'L'habitant, la paroisse rurale et la politique locale au XVIIIe siècle: Quelques cas dans la Vallée du Richelieu.' *Société Canadienne d'Histoire de l'Eglise Catholique, Sessions d'études* 47 (1980): 19–33.

– *The Patriots and the People: The Rebellion of 1837 in Rural Lower Canada.* Toronto: University of Toronto Press, 1993.

– 'The Sunday Schools of Upper Canada.' *Ontario History* 67 (1975): 169–84.

Ham, F. Gerald. 'The Prophet and the Mummyjums: Isaac Bullard and the Vermont Pilgrims of 1817.' *Wisconsin Magazine of History* 56 (1973): 290–9.

Hamilton, Phyliss. *With Heart and Hands and Voices: Histories of Protestant Churches of Brome, Missisquoi, Shefford and Surrounding Area.* Montreal: Price-Patterson, 1996.

Harris, R.C. 'The Canadian Archipelago and the Border Thesis.' *Association of American Geographers Annual Meeting and Abstracts.* Washington: Association of American Geographers, 1990.

Harrison, J.F.C. *The Second Coming: Popular Millenarianism, 1780–1850.* New Brunswick, NJ: Rutgers University Press, 1979.

Hatch, Nathan O. *The Democratization of American Christianity.* New Haven: Yale University Press, 1989.

– 'In Pursuit of Religious Freedom: Church, State, and People in the New Republic.' *The American Revolution: Its Character and Limits,* edited by Jack P. Greene. New York: New York University Press, 1987.

Hay, Eldon. 'The Reformed Presbyterians of Quebec.' *The Canadian Society of Presbyterian History* (1996): 10–33.

Hewett, Phillip. *Unitarians in Canada.* Toronto: Fitzhenry and Whiteside, 1978.

Hibbard, Lewis B., ed. *Exercises of the Centennial Anniversary of the Baptist Church, Abbott's Corner, P.Q., September 6, 1899.* Highland Park, IL.: Sheridan Road Newsletter, 1900.

Hill, Robert. *Voice of the Vanishing Minority: Robert Sellar and the Huntingdon Gleaner, 1863–1919.* Montreal and Kingston: McGill-Queen's University Press, 1998.

Horowitz, Gad. 'Conservatism, Liberalism, and Socialism in Canada: An Interpretation.' *Canadian Journal of Economics and Political Science* 32 (1966): 143–71.

Houston, Cecil, and William J. Smyth. *The Sash Canada Wore: A Historical Geography of the Orange Order in Canada.* Toronto: University of Toronto Press, 1980.

Hubbard, B.F. *Forests and Clearings: The History of Stanstead County, Province of Quebec.* Montreal: Lovell, 1874.

Hubert, Ollivier. 'Ritual Performance and Parish Sociability: French-Canadian Catholic Families at Mass from the Seventeenth to the Nineteenth Century.' *Households of Faith: Family, Gender, and Community in Canada, 1760–1969,* edited by Nancy Christie. Montreal and Kingston: McGill-Queen's University Press, 2002.

Hudon, Christine. *Prêtres et fidèles dans le diocèse de Saint-Hyacinthe, 1820–1875.* Sillery: Septentrion, 1996.

Ivison, Stuart, and Fred Rosser. *The Baptists in Upper and Lower Canada before 1820.* Toronto: University of Toronto Press, 1956.

Johnson, Richard O. 'The Development of the Love Feast in Early American Methodism.' *Methodist History* 19 (1981): 67–83.

Kennedy, Rev. J. *The Church of Arran From the Earliest Period to the Present Day.* Edinburgh: John Grant, 1912.
Kenny, Michael. *The Perfect Law of Liberty: Elias Smith and the Providential History of America.* Washington: Smithsonian Institution Press, 1994.
Kenyon, John. 'The Development of Congregationalism in Early Nineteenth-Century Ontario.' *Canadian Society of Church History Papers* (1978): 11–25.
Kesteman, Jean-Pierre. 'Au pays des "sectes." La difficile percée de l'anglicanisme dans le comté de Stanstead au XIXe siècle.' SCHEC, *Études d'histoire religieuse* 66 (2000): 9–28.
– *Histoire de Sherbrooke, Tome 1: De l'âge de l'eau à l'ère de la vapeur (1802–1866).* Sherbrooke: Éditions G.G.C., 2000.
Kesteman, Jean-Pierre, Peter Southam, and Diane Saint-Pierre. *Histoire des Cantons de l'Est.* Sainte-Foy: Les Presses de l'Université Laval, 1998.
Knight, George. *Millennial Fever and the End of the World: A Study of Millerite Adventism.* Boise, Idaho and Oshawa, ON: Pacific Press, 1993.
Konrad, Victor. 'Borderlines and Borderlands in the Geography of Canada–United States Relations.' *North America Without Borders? Integrating Canada, the United States, and Mexico,* edited by Stephen J. Randall, Herman Konrad, and Sheldon Silverman. Calgary: University of Calgary Press, 1992.
Labrèque, Marie-Paule. 'Les Églises dans les Cantons de l'Est (1800–1860).' Société d'histoire de l'Église Catholique, *Sessions d'Étude* (1974): 87–103.
– 'Gilbert Hyatt.' *Dictionary of Canadian Biography,* vol. 6.
– 'Jesse, Pennoyer.' *Dictionary of Canadian Biography,* vol. 6.
– 'George McLeod Ross.' *Dictionary of Canadian Biography,* vol. 8.
Lambert, James H. 'The Reverend Samuel Simpson Wood, BA, MA: A Forgotten Notable and the Early Anglican Church in Canada.' *Journal of the Canadian Church Historical Society* 16, no. 1 (1974): 2–27.
Lester, Norma Knowles. *A Church Provided: The Story of St. Anne's Anglican Church, Richmond, Quebec.* Acton Vale, QC: Gaétan Chevanelle, 1993.
Little, J.I. 'Agricultural Improvement and Highland Clearance: The Isle of Arran, 1828–29.' *Scottish Economic and Social History* 19 (1999): 132–54.
– 'British Toryism amidst "a horde of disaffected and disloyal squatters": The Rise and Fall of William Bowman Felton and Family in the Eastern Townships.' *Journal of Eastern Townships Studies* 1 (1992): 13–42.
– 'A Crime "Shrouded in Mystery": State, Church, and Community in the Kinnear's Mills Post Office Case, 1899–1905.' *Histoire sociale/Social History* 35 (2001): 1–34.
– *Crofters and Habitants: Settler Society, Economy, and Culture in a Quebec Township, 1848–1881.* Montreal and Kingston: McGill-Queen's University Press, 1991.

- *Ethno-Cultural Transition and Regional Identity in the Eastern Townships of Quebec.* Ottawa: Canadian Historical Association Booklet, 1989.
- William Bowman Felton.' *Dictionary of Canadian Biography*, vol. 7.
- 'The Fireside Kingdom: A Mid-Nineteenth-Century Anglican Perspective on Marriage and Parenthood.' *Households of Faith: Family, Gender, and Community in Canada, 1760–1969*, edited by Nancy Christie. Montreal and Kingston: McGill-Queen's University Press, 2002.
- 'From the Isle of Arran to Inverness Township: A Case Study of Highland Emigration and North American Settlement.' *Scottish Economic and Social History* 20 (2000): 3–30.
- 'The Journal of Archdeacon G.J. Mountain's Visitation of 1829, "Principally Thro' the Eastern Townships".' *Journal of Eastern Townships Studies* 16 (2000): 79–120.
- 'The Mental World of Ralph Merry: A Case Study of Popular Religion in the Lower Canadian/New England Borderland, 1798–1863.' *Canadian Historical Review* 83 (2002): 338–63.
- '"A Moral Engine of Such Incalculable Worth": The Temperance Movement in the Eastern Townships, 1830–52.' *Journal of Eastern Townships Studies* 11 (1997): 5–38.
- *Nationalism, Capitalism, and Colonization in Nineteenth-Century Quebec: The Upper St Francis District.* Montreal and Kingston: McGill-Queen's University Press, 1989.
- '"On the Borders of the Kingdom of the Beast": The Religious Ideas of a Nineteenth-Century Congregational Minister in the Eastern Townships.' *The Canadian Society of Presbyterian History Papers 1994 and the Douglas Walkington Memorial Lectures on Congregational History 1994*: 130–46.
- 'Perils in the Wilderness: Pioneer Tales from the Reverend Ammi Parker's "Memories of Life in Canada".' *Journal of Eastern Townships Studies* 5 (1994): 95–125.
- 'Revivalism Rejected: Protestantism in Sherbrooke During the First Half of the Nineteenth Century.' *Journal of Eastern Townships Studies* 21 (2002): 27–46.
- 'Serving "the North East Corner of Creation": The Community Role of a Rural Clergyman in the Eastern Townships of Quebec, 1829–1870.' *Histoire sociale/Social History* 30 (1997): 21–54.
- 'Sherbrooke a Century and a Half Ago: The Reminiscence of Mary Brooks Graves in 1901.' *Journal of Eastern Townships Studies* no. 17 (Fall 2000): 45–63.
- 'The Short Life of a Local Protest Movement: The Annexation Crisis of 1849–50 in the Eastern Townships.' *Journal of the Canadian Historical Association* NS no. 2 (1992): 45–67.

- *State and Society in Transition: The Politics of Institutional Reform in the Eastern Townships, 1838–1852.* Montrèal and Kingston: McGill-Queen's University Press, 1997.
- 'Watching the Frontier Disappear: English-Speaking Reaction to French-Canadian Colonization in the Eastern Townships, 1844–90,' *Journal of Canadian Studies* 15, no. 4 (1980–1): 93–111.
- , ed. *The Child Letters: Public and Private Life in a Canadian Merchant-Politician's Family, 1841–1845.* Montreal and Kingston: McGill-Queen's University Press, 1995.
- , ed. *Love Strong as Death: Lucy Peel's Canadian Journal, 1833–1836.* Waterloo: Wilfrid Laurier University Press, 2001.

Ludlum, David M. *Social Ferment in Vermont.* New York: AMS Press, 1966, reprint 1939.

MacDonald, Edith Fox. *Rebellion in the Mountains: The Story of Universalism and Unitarianism in Vermont.* Concord, NH: The New Hampshire Vermont District of the Unitarian Universalist Association, 1976.

McGuigan, G.F. 'Administration of Land Policy and the Growth of Corporate Economic Organization in Lower Canada, 1791–1809.' *Canadian Historical Association Report* 1963, 65–73.

McKillop, Dugald McKenzie. *Annals of Megantic.* Lynn, MA: D. McGillop, 1902.

McKinsey L., and V. Konrad. *Borderlands Reflections: The United States and Canada.* Orono: Canadian-American Center, University of Maine, 1989.

McNairn, Norman A. 'Mission to Canada.' *Methodist History* 13/4 (July 1975): 46–60.

Mair, Nathan H. *The Congregational Heritage in the United Church of Canada.* Archives of the Montreal and Ottawa Conference of the United Church of Canada, 1991.

Marini, Stephen. *Radical Sects of Revolutionary New England.* Cambridge, MA: Harvard University Press, 1982.

Marks, Lynne. 'Christian Harmony: Family, Neighbours, and Community in Upper Canadian Church Discipline Records.' *On the Case: Explorations in Social History,* edited by Franca Iacovetta and Wendy Mitchinson. Toronto: University of Toronto Press, 1998.
- 'Rattling, Tattling, and General Rumour: Gossip, Gender, and Church Regulation in Upper Canada.' *Canadian Historical Review* 81 (2000): 380–402.
- *Revivals and Roller Rinks: Religion, Leisure and Identity in Late Nineteenth-Century Small-Town Ontario.* Toronto: University of Toronto Press, 1996.

Millar, W.P.J. 'Thaddeus Osgood.' *Dictionary of Canadian Biography,* vol. 8.

- 'The Remarkable Rev. Thaddeus Osgood: A Study in the Evangelical Spirit in the Canadas.' *Histoire sociale/Social History* 10 (1977): 59–76.
Miller, Russell E. *The Larger Hope: The First Century of the Universalist Church in America, 1770–1870.* Boston: Unitarian Universalist Association, 1979.
Millman, Thomas R. *Jacob Mountain: First Lord Bishop of Quebec.* Toronto: University of Toronto Press, 1947.
- *The Life of the Right Reverend, the Honourable Charles James Stewart, D.D., Oxon., Second Anglican Bishop of Quebec.* London, ON: Huron College, 1953.
- 'Rev. Canon James Reid, D.D. Frelighsburg, 1815–1865.' *Montreal Churchman* 13 (undated article in Montreal Diocesan Archives, Reid Papers).
- *A Short History of the Parish of Dunham, Quebec.* Granby, QC: Granby Printng and Publishing, 1946.
Milner, Elizabeth Hearn. *Huntingville, 1815–1980: A Story of a Village in the Eastern Townships of Quebec.* Sherbrooke: René Prince, 1981.
'Miss M.A. Titemore Contributes More Notes, Historical and Reminiscent.' *Fourth Annual Report of the Missisquoi County Historical Society* 1909: 55.
Missisquoi County Historical Society, *Annual Report* 1908.
Moir, John S. 'American Influences on Canadian Protestant Churches Before Confederation.' *Church History* 36 (1967): 440–55.
- *Enduring Witness: A History of the Prebsyterian Church in Canada.* Toronto: Bryant Press, 1974.
Montgomery, George H. *Missisquoi Bay (Philipsburg, Que.).* Granby: Granby Printing and Publishing, 1950.
Moore, Ruby G. *Historical Sketches of the Churches in the Cowansville-Dunham Pastoral Charge.* n.p., 1962.
Moorhead, James H. 'Between Progress and Apocalypse: A Reassessment of Millennialism in American Religious Thought, 1800–1880.' *Journal of American History* 71 (1984): 524–42.
Moysey, Richard D. 'George Slack: A Pioneer Townships Clergyman.' *Journal of Eastern Townships Studies* no. 13 (1998–9): 59–73.
Mudge, James. *History of the New England Conference of the Methodist Episcopal Church, 1796–1810.* Boston: The Conference, 1910.
Muir, Elizabeth Gillan. *Petticoats in the Pulpit: The Story of Early Nineteenth-Century Methodist Women Preachers in Upper Canada.* Toronto: United Church Publishing House, 1991.
Muller, H.N. III. 'Trouble on the Border, 1838: A Neglected Incident from Vermont's Neglected History.' *Vermont History* 44 (1976): 97–102.
Muller, H.N., and John Duffy. 'Jedidiah Burchard and Vermont's "New Measure" Revivals; Social Adjustment and the Quest for Unity.' *Vermont History* 46 (1978): 5–20.

Murphy, Terrence. 'The English-Speaking Colonies to 1854.' *A Concise History of Christianity in Canada*, edited by Terrence Murphy and Roberto Perin. Toronto: Oxford University Press, 1996.
Murphy, Terrence, and Roberto Perin, eds., *A Concise History of Christianity in Canada*. Toronto: Oxford University Press, 1996.
Nelson, Wendie. '"Rage against the Dying of the Light": Interpreting the Guerre des Éteignoirs.' *Canadian Historical Review* 81 (2000): 551–81.
Nockles, Peter. 'Church Parties in the pre-Tractarian Church of England 1750–1833: the "Orthdox" – Some Problems of Definition and Identity.' *The Church of England c. 1689–c. 1833: From Toleration to Tractarianism*, edited by John Walsh, Colin Haydon, and Stephen Taylor. Cambridge: Cambridge University Press, 1993.
Noël, Françoise. *Competing for Souls: Missionary Activity and Settlement in the Eastern Townships, 1784–1851*. Département d'Histoire, Université de Sherbrooke, 1988.
Noel, S.J.R. *Patrons, Clients, Brokers: Ontario Society and Politics, 1791–1896*. Toronto: University of Toronto Press, 1990.
Noll, Mark A. *A History of Christianity in the United States and Canada*. Grand Rapids, MI: William B. Eardmans, 1992.
O'Connor, Daniel, et al. *Three Centuries of Mission: The United Society for the Propagation of the Gospel, 1701–2000*. London and New York: Continuum, 2000.
O'Leary, Stephen D. *Arguing the Apocalypse: A Theory of Millennial Rhetoric*. New York: Oxford University Press, 1994.
Ouellet, Fernand. *Histoire économique et sociale du Québec, 1760–1850*. Ottawa: Fides, 1966.
Parish Anecdotes: St. James' Church 1822–1845, St. George's Church 1845–1904. Lennoxville: 1967.
'Parker, Rev. A.J.' *Canadian Independent* (March 1894), 55–6.
Payne, Rodger. *The Self and the Sacred: Conversion and Autobiography in Early American Protestantism*. Knoxville: University of Tennessee Press, 1998.
Pitman, Walter G. *The Baptists and Public Affairs in the Province of Canada, 1840–1867*. New York: Arno Press, 1980.
Playter, George F. *The History of Methodism in Canada*. Toronto: Anson Green, 1862.
Plymouth Church: Past and Present: A Brief History of Plymouth United Church, Sherbrooke, Quebec. Sherbrooke, 1956.
Pomerleau, Julie, ed. *Terre de Croyances / Land of Churches*. Société d'Histoire et du Patrimoine du Haut-Saint-François [n.d.].
Potash, Paul Jeffrey. 'Welfare of the Regions Beyond.' *Vermont History* 46 (1978): 109–28.

Rawlyk, G.A. 'Introduction.' *Aspects of the Canadian Evangelical Experience.* Montreal and Kingston: McGill-Queen's University Press, 1997.
- *Ravished by the Spirit: Religious Revivals, Baptists, and Henry Alline.* Montreal and Kingston: McGill-Queen's University Press, 1984.
- 'Religion and Popular Culture.' *New Directions for the Study of Ontario's Past,* edited by David Gagan and Rosemary Gagan. Hamilton: McMaster University, 1988.
Rawlyk, G.A., and Gordon Stewart. 'Nova Scotia's Sense of Mission.' *Histoire sociale/Social History* 1 (1968): 5–17.
Reisner, M.E. *The Measure of Faith: Annals of the Diocese of Montreal, 1760–2000.* Toronto: Anglican Book Centre, 2002.
- *Strangers and Pilgrims: A History of the Anglican Diocese of Quebec, 1793–1993.* Toronto: Anglican Book Centre, 1995.
- , ed. *The Diary of a Country Clergyman, 1848–1851: James Reid.* Montreal and Kingston: McGill-Queen's University Press, 2000.
Richey, Russell E. 'From Quarterly to Camp Meeting: A Reconsideration of Early American Methodism.' *Methodist History* 23/1 (July 1985): 199–213.
Robertson, Hon. J.G. *Sketch of the Formation of the Congregational Church at Sherbrooke and Lennoxville.* Sherbrooke: W.A. Morehouse, 1890.
Robins, Roger. 'Vernacular American Landscape: Methodists, Camp Meetings and Social Responsibility.' *Religion and American Culture* 4 (1994): 165–91.
Romney, Paul. 'Re-Inventing Upper Canada: American Immigrants, Upper Canadian History, English Law, and the Alien Question.' *Patterns of the Past: Interpreting Ontario's History,* edited by Roger Hall et al. Toronto: Dundurn, 1988.
Roth, Randolph. *The Democratic Dilemma: Religion, Reform, and the Social Order in the Connecticut River Valley of Vermont, 1791–1850.* New York: Cambridge University Press, 1987.
Rousseau, Louis, and Frank W. Remiggi, eds. *Atlas Historique des Pratiques Religieuses: Le Sud-Ouest de Québec au XIXe Siècle.* Ottawa: Les Presses de l'Université d'Ottawa, 1998.
Rowe, David L. 'Millerites: A Shadow Portrait.' *The Disappointed: Millerism and Millenarianism in the Nineteenth Century,* edited by Ronald L. Numbers and Jonathan Butler. Bloomington and Indianapolis: Indiana University Press, 1987.
- *Thunder and Trumpets: Millerites and Dissenting Religion in Upstate New York, 1800–1850.* Chico, CA: Scholars Press, 1985.
Russell, Peter A. 'Church of Scotland Clergy in Upper Canada: Culture Shock and Conservatism on the Frontier.' *Ontario History* 73 (1981): 88–111.
Sandeen, Ernest R. 'Millenialism.' *The Rise of Adventism: Religion and Society in*

Mid-Nineteenth-Century America, edited by Edwin Scott Gaustad. New York: Harper and Row, 1974.

Sanderson, J.E. *The First Century of Methodism in Canada*, vol. 1, *1775–1839*. Toronto: William Briggs, 1908.

Schrauwers, Albert. *Awaiting the Millennium: The Children of Peace and the Village of Hope, 1812–1889*. Toronto: University of Toronto Press, 1993.

Schwartz, Hillel. 'The End of the Beginning: Millenarian Studies, 1969–1975.' *Religious Studies Review* 2 (July 1976): 1–15.

Scott, Donald. *From Office to Profession: The New England Ministry, 1750–1850*. Philadelphia: University of Pennsylvania Press, 1978.

Semple, Neil. *The Lord's Dominion: The History of Canadian Methodism*. Montreal and Kingston: McGill-Queen's University Press, 1996.

Shirley, Glenn, ed. *Buckskin Joe, being the unique and vivid memories of Edward Jonathan Hoyt, hunter-trapper, scout, soldier, showman, frontiersman, and friend of the Indians, 1840–1918*. Lincoln: University of Nebraska Press, 1966.

Shufelt, Harry B. *Nicholas Austin the Quaker and the Township of Bolton*. Knowlton, QC: Brome County Historical Society, 1971.

Stanley-Blackwell, Laurie. '"Tabernacles in the Wilderness": The Open-Air Communion Tradition in Nineteenth- and Twentieth-Century Cape Breton.' *The Contribution of Presbyterianism to the Maritime Provinces of Canada*, edited by Charles H.H. Scobie and G.A. Rawlyk. Montreal and Kingston: McGill-Queen's University Press, 1997.

Stewart, Rev. I.D. *The History of the Freewill Baptists*, vol. 1, *1780 to 1830*. Dover: Freewill Baptist Printing, 1862.

Stilgoe, John R. *Common Landscape of America, 1580 to 1845*. New Haven: Yale University Press, 1982.

Sweet, Leonard. 'Nineteenth-Century Evangelicalism.' *Encyclopedia of the American Religious Experience: Studies of Traditions and Movements*, vol. 2, edited by Charles H. Lippey and Peter W. Williams. New York: Charles Scribner's Sons, 1988.

Sweet, William Warren. *Religion in the Development of American Culture, 1765–1840*. Gloucester, MA: Peter Smith, 1963.

Sylvain, Phillipe and Nive Voisine. *Histoire du catholicisme québécois*, vol. 2, *Les XVI–IIe et XIXe siècles: tome 2, Réveil et consolidation (1840–1898)*. Montreal: Boréal, 1991.

Terry, D.W. 'Sawyerville Baptist Church, 100 Year Anniversary (1822–1922).' *Canadian Baptist* (28 Dec. 1922).

Thomas, C. *Contributions to the History of the Eastern Townships*. Montreal: John Lovell, 1866.

Thomas, Keith. *Religion and the Decline of Magic*. London: Penguin Books, 1971.

Thompson, Zadoch. *History of Vermont, Natural, Civil and Statistical.* Burlington, VT: Chauncey Goodrich, 1842.

Thorne, Susan. '"The Conversion of Englishmen and of the World Inseparable": Missionary Imperialism and the Language of Class in Early Industrial Britain.' *Tensions of Empire: Colonial Cultures in a Bourgeois World,* edited by Frederick Cooper and Ann Laura Stoler. Berkeley: University of California Press, 1997.

The Tread of the Pioneers, Annals of Richmond County and Vicinity, vol. 1. Richmond, QC: Richmond County Historical Society, 1966.

Thibault, Charlotte. *Samuel Brooks, entrepreneur et homme politique de Sherbrooke, 1793–1849.* Sherbrooke: Département d'Histoire, Université de Sherbrooke, 1985.

Tucker, W. Bowman. 'A Brief History of Philipsburg Methodist Church.' Missisquoi County Historical Society, *Annual Report* (1908), 55–7.

Vallières, Marc. 'Joseph Gibb, Robertson.' *Dictionary of Canadian Biography,* vol. 12.

Van Die, Marguerite. 'The Marks of a Genuine Revival: Religion, Social Change, Gender and Community in Mid-Victorian Brantford Ontario.' *Canadian Historical Review* 79 (1998): 524–63.

Vansittart, Jane, ed. *Lifelines: The Stacey Letters, 1836–1858.* London: Peter Davies, 1976.

Varty, Carman Nielson. 'Building Identities: St. George's Anglican Churches, Kingston, Upper Canada, 1792–1826.' Canadian Society of Church History, *Historical Papers 1998,* 113–28.

Vaudry, Richard W. *Anglicans and the Atlantic World: High Churchmen, Evangelicals and the Quebec Connection.* Montreal and Kingston: McGill-Queen's University Press, 2003.

Veilleux, Christine. 'John Fletcher,' *Dictionary of Canadian Biography,* vol. 7.

Vogt-Raguy, Dominique. 'Le Québec, terre de mission: Le début du prosélytisme protestant francophone (1834–1840).' *Études Canadiennes / Canadian Studies* 21, no. 1 (1986): 115–25.

Walsh, John, and Stephen Taylor. 'Introduction: The Church and Anglicanism in the "Long" Eighteenth Century.' *The Church of England c. 1689–c. 1833: From Toleration to Tractarianism,* edited by John Walsh, Colin Haydon, and Stephen Taylor. Cambridge: Cambridge University Press, 1993.

Ward, Reginald W. 'The Religion of the People and the Problem of Control, 1790–1830.' *Popular Belief and Practice,* edited by G.J. Cuming and Derek Baker. Cambridge: Cambridge University Press, 1972.

Westfall, William. 'Constructing Public Religions at Private Sites: The Anglican Church in the Shadow of Disestablishment.' *Religion and Public Life in Canada:*

Historical and Comparative Perspectives, edited by Marguerite Van Die. Toronto: University of Toronto Press, 2001.
– *Two Worlds: The Protestant Culture of Nineteenth Century Ontario*. Kingston and Montreal: McGill-Queen's University Press, 1989.
Widdis, Randy William. 'Borders, Borderlands and Canadian Identity: A Canadian Perspective.' *International Journal of Canadian Studies* 15 (Spring 1997): 49–66.
Wise, S.F. 'God's Peculiar Peoples.' *Shield of Achilles: Aspects of Canada in the Victorian Age*, edited by W.L. Morton. Toronto: McClelland and Stewart, 1968.
– 'Upper Canada and the Conservative Tradition.' *Profiles of a Province: Studies in the History of Ontario*. Toronto: Ontario Historical Society, 1967.
Wood, Rev. John. *Memory of Henry Wilkes, D.D., L.L.D., His Life and Times*. Montreal: F.E. Grafton and Sons, 1887.
Woolverton, John Frederick. *Colonial Anglicanism in America*. Detroit: Wayne State University Press, 1984.
Wright, Stephen. *History of the Shaftsbury Baptist Association from 1781 to 1853*. Troy, N.Y.: A.G. Johnson, 1853.
Zielinski, S.A. *The Story of the Farnham Meeting, A Quaker Meeting in Allen's Corner, East Farnham Township, Brome County, Province of Quebec, Canada, 1820–1902*. Fulford, QC: Self-published, 1961.

Unpublished Secondary Sources

Bacon, Rev. D.A. 'Wesleyan Methodist Church (Great Britain). Foreign Missions: America. The British Dominions in North America. Correspondence, 1791–1825' (United Church Archives, Victoria University).
Burnside, Albert. 'The Canadian Wesleyan Methodist New Connexion Church, 1841–1874,' 1967 (United Church Archives, Victoria University).
'Eaton Baptist Church, as prepared by L.W. French, church clerk, May 1905' (Canadian Baptist Archives, Sawyerville file).
Eddy, Earl B. 'The Beginnings of Congregationalism in the Early Canadas.' ThD dissertation, Emmanuel College, University of Toronto, 1957.
Fortin, Denis. 'John Porter and the Danville Advent Christian Church,' typescript.
– 'L'Adventisme dans les Cantons de l'Est du Québec: Implantation et Institutionalisation au XIXe Siècle.' PhD dissertation, Laval University, 1996.
Headon, Christopher F. 'The Influence of the Oxford Movement upon the Church of England in Eastern and Central Canada, 1840–1900.' PhD dissertation, McGill University, 1974.

'Historical Sketch by J.H. Hunter, Sherbrooke, 29 March 1935' (Canadian Baptist Archives, Inverness file).

[Hunter, J.H.] '1933. Baptist Church. Barnston, Que., 100th Anniversary' (Canadian Baptist Archives, Barnston file).

Marston, Monica. 'George Jehoshaphat Mountain: Aspects of His Life and Work.' MA thesis, Bishop's University, 1971.

Methodist Episcopal Church, Journals of the New York Conference.

Mussio, Louise A. 'Communities Apart: Dissenting Traditions in Nineteenth-Century Central Canada.' PhD dissertation, McMaster University, 2000.

Sarah Lorimer to Dr J.G. Brown, Beebe, 26 May 1921 (Canadian Baptist Archives, Beebe file).

Stuart, H.C. 'Episcopate of Jacob Mountain, 1793–1825' (typescript) (Quebec Diocesan Archives, vol. 106).

'Titus Mooney Merriman, 1822–1903' (Canadian Baptist Archives, Canadian Baptist Historical Collection, Biographical file no. 815593).

Ward, Donal. 'Religious Enthusiasm in Vermont, 1761–1847.' PhD dissertation, University of Notre Dame, 1980.

Webb, Todd. '"With the Tenderness of a Feather Dipt in Oil": Encounters between British and American Methodists in Lower and Upper Canada, 1815–1828,' presented to the annual meeting of the Canadian Historical Association, May 2000.

Index

Abbott's Corner, 175
Adams, Zenas, 28
Addison Association (Congregationalist), 64
Addoms, John T., 38, 39
Addyman, John, 119, 123–4
Adelman, Jeremy, xii
Adrion, Edwin, 132
Advent Conference in Eastern Canada, 140
Advent Herald, 130, 137–9, 141. *See also Signs of the Times*
Adventism. *See* Second Advent Church
Albany Conference (Adventist), 139
Alburg, Vermont, 190
Alder, Robert, 170, 327n76
Alexander, James Lynne, 247, 248
Alline, Henry, 30
American Anti-Slavery Society, 68
American attitudes towards Canada, 56–7, 61, 62
American Bible Society, 68
American Home Missionary Society, 55, 57, 59, 60, 63, 68, 70, 73, 74, 85, 88
American Sunday School Union, 68
American Temperance Society, 68
Andover Theological Seminary, 74, 86
Anglican Church: baptism, 265–7; burials, 272–3; and Canadian identity, 280–1; chanting, 271–2, 274, 347n78; church construction, 237–46; churching, 268–9, 274, 346n64; doctrine of usefulness, 275–6; economic variables, 20, 22, 24; exclusivism, question of, 274–6, 281; godparenting, 267–8; High Church principles, 228, 233, 242, 271, 273–4, 277, 281; hymn singing, 269–71; institutional and material support, 231–7; meaning of adherence to, 260–2, 273, 276; membership, 227, 240, 248, 258, 261–2, 276; messianism, 252–6, 259–60, 277; missionary recruitment, 228–31, 259; missionary salaries, 232–3, 236; organizational structure, 246–50; pew rental issue, 240, 242, 244, 246; prayer, 254–5, 269–72; pre-1815, 41–50; sermons, 255–6; subscription lists, 238–9; travelling missionaries, 249, 259. *See also* church

374 Index

design; salaries, clergy; Sunday schools; temperance; War of 1812
Annexation movement, 10, 251, 284, 285
Annual Conference, Methodist, 154
Aron, Stephen, xii
Asbury, Bishop, 37
Ascot, 18, 28, 29, 118
Ascot Monthly Meeting (Freewill Baptist), 98–100, 106
Ashgrove District (Methodist), 37
assessments, church, 93, 97–8, 100, 101, 108, 113, 236
Austin, Nicholas, 41

Badger, Joseph, 25–31, 35, 37, 39, 40, 65, 109–10, 121
Badger, Milton, 88
Badger, Peaslee, 27, 28
Baker, Joseph, 119, 314n33
Baldwin, J., 312n28
Balfe, Robert, 348n95
Ballou, Eli, 118
Ballou, Hosea, 39
Bangs, Nathan, 237
baptism, ritual of, 67, 69, 187, 265–7, 279
Baptist Canadian Missionary Society, 94
Baptist Church, 16–17, 20, 22, 187, 206, 222: close-communion stand, 93, 192; polity, 16, 90; pre-1815, 32–5. *See also* Freewill Baptists; temperance; War of 1812
Barford, 94
Barkun, Michael, 9, 128
Barnston, 18, 34, 125, 132, 140, 183; Baptists in, 92–3, 98, 100, 101, 105
Bates, Joseph, 141
Bathurst, Lord, 239

Bayly, C.A., 280
Bedford, 261
Beebe Plain, 94
Benes, Peter, 176
Bennett, Vicki, 175–6, 237, 241
Berlin, Vermont, 31
Billington, Louis, 97
Bishop's College, 235, 253, 255, 338n35
Blanchard, David, 26, 37–8
Blunt, Rebecca, 154, 323n20
Bolton, 18, 41, 98, 119, 123–6, 130, 131, 139, 155
Boody, Joseph, 35
Booth, James, 14, 166–7, 173, 175, 179, 184
border raids. *See* Rebellions of 1837–8
borderlands concept, x-xi, xiii
Borland, John, 160, 161, 194, 196, 204, 208, 211, 213, 214, 218
Botterell, Edmund, 136, 162–3, 187, 196, 203, 208, 211
Bourn, Roswell, 300n39
Bowen, G.F., 233
British Colonist, 117, 129
Brock, James, 203
Brome, 15, 20, 22, 33, 118, 119, 120, 123, 155, 234, 266
Brompton, 155
Brown's Hill, 64
Brownell, John, 124, 125, 156, 175, 195, 198–9, 211–12
Buckley, H., 320n46
Buckner, Phillip, xiii
Bull, Gideon, 41
Bullard, Isaac, 109–11
Burchard, Jedidiah, 67, 187
burial customs, 182, 272–3, 275, 279
Burke, Edmund, 348n95
Burrage, Henry, 269, 270, 272

Burwell, Adam Hood, 116–17
Bury, 102, 234, 271
Butler, John, 248, 267–8
Butler, Jonathan, 36, 119, 274

Caldwell, Luther, 132, 133, 138
Caldwell's Manor, 33, 34, 155
Calvinist Baptist Church. *See* Regular Baptist Church
Camden Society, 241
camp meetings, 66, 122, 131, 134, 140, 178, 187, 201, 207. *See also* revivals
Campbell, Thomas, 172, 197, 206, 215
Canada Baptist College, 95
Canada District (Wesleyan Methodist), 154, 157, 158, 164, 165, 167, 172, 173, 188, 198, 200
Canada Education and Home Missionary Society, 57, 64, 65, 67, 68, 70, 74, 75, 79, 82, 83, 85
Canada Western District (Methodist), 164, 173
Canadian identity, ix, x, 6, 280–5
Canadian Wesleyan Methodist New Connection Church, 125
Carroll, John, 37, 38, 149, 152, 153, 160, 178, 219
Carry, John, 260–4, 269
catechism: Anglican, 212, 264–5; Methodist, 212
catechists, Anglican, 247–8
Catterick, Thomas, 152, 155, 165, 208
Caughey Revivals, 207
cemeteries. *See* burial customs
census, construction of, 15–17
Champlain District (Methodist Episcopal), 37

Champlain District (Protestant Methodist), 123
Chapin, H.B., 60, 80–4
Chapman, Thomas, 237, 244–5, 342n82
Charleston. *See* Hatley
Child, Marcus, 192
Christian Advent Church, 126
Christian Brethren, 18, 120–1, 127
Christian Connection, 18
Christian Palladium, 121
Christie, Gabriel, 42
Church of England. *See* Anglican Church
Church of Scotland, 17, 21
Church Society (Anglican), 233–8 *passim*
church design: 284; Danville Congregational, 71–2; Drummondville Anglican, 241; Dudswell Anglican, 245; Dunham Anglican (All Saints), 240, 242; Dunham Methodist, 174; Eaton Anglican, 240; Eaton Corner Congregational, 88; Farnham Quaker, 113; Granby Anglican, 244, 341n81; Ham Anglican, 245; Hatley Anglican, 240; Hatley Methodist, 176; Frelighsburg Anglican (Holy Trinity), 239–40; Huntingville Universalist, 120; Kingsey Anglican, 243–4; Knowlton Methodist, 176; Lennoxville Anglican, 241, 243; Melbourne Congregational, 88; Milton Anglican, 244; Philipsburgh Methodist, 174; Richmond Anglican, 241; St Armand Baptist, 92; St Armand West Anglican (St Paul's), 240, 242; Sherbrooke Anglican, 240, 242; Stanbridge East Anglican, 241;

Stanbridge Ridge Baptist, 92; Sutton Flat Anglican, 244
church-sect dichotomy, xiii-xiv
churching. *See* Anglican Church
civil disabilities, 68–9, 100, 118, 156–7, 161, 266, 272, 279, 280, 324n30
Clarenceville, 196
Clark, Colonel, 49
Clark, Harvey, 33, 92
Clark, S.D., xiv, 227, 246, 249, 260, 276
class leaders, Methodist, 161, 163, 201
class meetings, Methodist, 222
clergy reserves, 232, 235, 281
clergy, secular role of, 76, 275–6
Cleveland, Edward, 6
Cleveland, F.P., 72
climate, regional, 143–4, 167
Coaticook, 102, 105, 106
Colby, Moses French, 60
Colonial Missionary Society, 88–9
Colonial Missions Committee (New Connection Methodist), 125
community, sense of, 19, 76–7, 221–2, 273, 275, 283. *See also* localism; voluntarism
Compton, 15, 18, 27, 35, 37–8, 40, 118, 135–6, 239, 270
Compton and Hatley Methodist Circuit, 154, 162, 193, 197, 205, 211, 215, 222, 323n22
Compton Monthly Meeting (Freewill Baptist), 95–107 *passim*
Congregational Church, 174, 192; American-British factionalism in, 57, 78–88 *passim*; economic variables, 17, 21, 24; fund-raising, 72–3; pre-1815, 31–2; recruitment of clergy, 72–4. *See also* Millerism;
Rebellions of 1837–8; salaries, clergy; temperance
Congregational Missionary Society, 89
Congregational Union of Lower Canada, 83
Cooney, Robert, 193, 197, 222–3; and Millerism, 132, 135, 201–3, 221
Cotton, Charles Caleb, 42–6, 119, 120, 248, 256–8, 261, 263, 265, 266, 268, 271, 275–6
counterfeiting, 56–7
Cox, F.A., 90
Creek Church, 108
Crofts, H.O., 124, 125
Crooker, Susan, 92–3
crop failures. *See* economic conditions
Cross, Whitney, 118, 208
Cummings, Jonathan, 141
Curry, W.F., 73, 74, 81
Curtis, O.T., 65, 66
Cusack, Edward, 266
Cushing, Elmer, 28

Danville, 56, 65–77 *passim*, 232; Millerism in, 143
Danville, Vermont, Calvinist Baptist Convention, 90–2, 310n1
Darroch, Gordon, 22
Dartmouth, 86
deacons: Anglican, 247, 248, 267–8; Congregationalist, 66
Dennet, Joseph, 37–8
DePutron, John, 151, 152, 154, 164–5, 167, 182, 209
Derby, Vermont, 58, 59, 61, 63, 94, 191
Dickerson, Silas, 61
Doan, Ruth, 142

Doll, Peter, 228, 280–1
Doolittle, Lucius, 242, 243, 262, 264, 269, 275
Dorey, Gifford, 216–18
Dorland, Arthur Garratt, 113
Doty, John, 41–2
Douglas, John, 216
Dow, Lorenzo, 36–7
Drummondville, 155, 238, 241, 261, 262, 264, 266, 268–70, 272
Dudley, Levi, 141
Dudswell, 234, 237; Freewill Baptists, 102, 105, 106
Duke of Portland, 228
Dunbar, Samuel, 39, 301n51
Dunham, 15, 17, 33, 119, 124, 174; Anglican parish of, 16, 240, 242, 245, 248–9, 257–8, 261, 266, 268, 271; Methodist Circuit, 16, 37, 38–9, 137, 150–2, 154, 156, 175, 179, 195, 198–9, 211–12, 214
Dunham Flat, 140, 199, 214
Dunn, Thomas, 42
Durham, 75, 98, 102
Durham, Lord, 114, 189

Eastern District (New Connection Methodist), 126
Eastern Townships: physical characteristics of, 55; early settlement, 3–5; political culture, 9–10, 277; population, 5
Eaton, 15, 17, 18, 23–4, 75, 93, 102, 105–6, 234, 271, 272
Eaton Corner, 88
economic conditions, 19–24, 71, 85, 88, 101, 102, 143–4, 167, 172, 185, 187, 191, 202, 217–19, 233, 285
Eddy, Earl B., 69
Edwards, Jonathan, 128

Elders' conference, Freewill Baptist, 97
Embury, Samuel, 151, 322n7
emigration, 102, 215, 218
Emory, John, 167
English settlers, 18, 82
epidemics, 63, 144, 182
Episcopal Methodists, pre-1815, 36–9
erysipelas, 321n67. *See also* epidemics
Essex, Vermont circuit (Methodist), 36
Evans, Henry, 248–9
exhorters, Methodist, 161, 177, 194

Fahey, Curtis, 234, 252
Fairbanks, Joseph, 300n40
Fairfield Association (Baptist), 34
Faithful Watchman, 133
Falloon, D.D., 264, 267–9, 271
Farewell, William, 40
Farnham, 15, 41, 120, 155
Farnham Meeting (Quaker), assessments, 113; factionalism/discipline, 114–15; membership, 18, 115; polity, 111–14
Faulkner, William, 168
Felton, John, 233
Felton, William Bowman, 240
Ferrisburg, Vermont, Monthly Meeting (Quaker), 112–15
Finley, Greg, 246
Finney, Charles, 66
Fitch, E.R., 32
Flanders, Christopher, 35
Flanders, R.A., 215, 216–17
Fleming, Charles B., 137, 262, 264–6, 268, 270
Fletcher, John, 69, 233
Folsom, Moses, 107, 313n52
Fortin, Denis, 142–3

Index

Four Corners, 78
Four Days' Meetings, 122. *See also* camp meetings
Fox, George, 41
Fox, Nathaniel B., 85–6
Freewill Baptists, 16–17, 21–2, 192, 197, 202, 266; covenant, 95, 96, 103; polity/regulations, 96–108 *passim*. *See also* Millerism
Freligh brothers, 48
Frelighsburg, 47–8, 239, 244, 250–1, 271, 272
French Canadians, 12, 20, 131, 179, 191, 194, 212, 214
French, Goldwin, 173, 281
Frontier Sentinel, 186
frontier thesis, 229, 281
Frost Village, 82, 84, 134, 138
Frye, Northrup, ix
Fulford, Bishop, 246

Galusha, William, 91
Gates, I.R., 140
Gauvreau, Michael, 281
Genessee Conference, 149, 170
George III, 47
Georgeville, 33, 64, 93, 94, 98, 130
Gibb, David, 86
Gibb, Joseph, 59, 64
Gillies, Archibald, 93
Gilson, John, 29, 39
Gleed, John, 78–80
Gosford, Lord, 233
Granby, 3, 155; Anglican parish of, 236, 244; Congregational Church, 77–86
Grant, John Webster, 41, 276
Great Awakenings, 7, 32, 65, 227
Great Disappointment, 283–4. *See* Millerism

Griffin's Corner union church, 14–15, 284
Gurney, John Joseph, 114, 115

Hale, Edward, 233, 242
Hale, Jeffrey, 242
Half-Way Covenant, 69
Hall, R.V., 60–4, 132, 134–5, 144, 282
Hall, Simeon, 141
Ham, 237
Hampshire Central Association, 59, 60, 80
Harper's New Monthly Magazine, 240
Harris, Cole, ix
Harrison, J.F.C., 144
Harvey, W., 247
Hatley, 18, 27, 33, 35, 122; Anglican parish of, 14, 129, 234, 240, 258–9, 262–6, 269, 270, 272, 344n27; Baptists, 92, 98, 100, 102, 105, 107–8; Methodist Circuit; Millerism in, 130, 131, 134, 138, 139. *See also* Compton and Hatley Methodist Circuit
Haynes, F., 125
Head of the Bay (Fitch Bay), 98, 106
Head, Colonel, 84
Hedding, Elijah, 300n38
Hellmuth, Isaac, 264, 271
Henshaw, John, 46–7
Heriot, G.F., 238
Hibbard, Jedediah, 33–4
Hibbard, Lewis, 136
Hibbard, Robert, 37, 301n49
Hick, Daniel, 165
Hick, John, 65, 66, 181
Hicks, Edward, 114
Highgate, Vermont, 179
Himes, Joshua, 129, 133, 138–40
Hitchcock, Barnabas, 159–60, 214

Hoag, Joseph, 113
Hobart, James, 31
Hoby, J., 90
Home and Foreign Record of the Free Church of Scotland, 282
Hubbard, Austin Osgood, 59–60
Hubbard, B.F., 35, 94
Hubbard, E.G., 26
Hulburt, William, 311n27
Huntington, Christopher, 40
Huntingville, 120
Hutchinson, John, 161
Hutchinson, Richard, 133, 138–40, 143, 195–6, 199–200
Hyatt, Gilbert, 29

Ide, John, 92, 312n28
Ingalls, Edmund S., 160–1, 203, 204, 212, 214
Inverness (and Ireland), 17, 77, 94, 248, 262, 264, 269, 349n11
Ireland. *See* Inverness; Lower Ireland; New Ireland Circuit; Upper Ireland
Irish settlers/workers, 12, 18, 20, 24, 163, 216, 260, 282
Ivison, Stuart, 34

Jackson, Christopher, 122, 253, 262–6, 269, 270
Johnson, Reverend, 129
Johnston, J., 79
Jones, James, 256
Jones, William, 98–9

Kemp, John, 263, 271
Kenny, Michael, 9
Kesteman, Jean-Pierre, 13, 227
Kilborn, Captain, 192
Kilborn, David, 37
Kilham, Alexander, 123, 124

Kimball, Leonard, 138
Kingsey, 29, 234, 277
Kingston, Upper Canada, 58, 184, 339n52
Knowlan, James, 157, 168–71, 178, 184, 329n4
Knowles, David, 113
Knowles, Drusilla, 113
Knowles, Samuel, 113
Knowles, Sarah, 113
Knowlton, 118

Ladies' Home Missionary Society: in Danville, 68
Ladies' Sewing Circle: of Montreal, 70, 72; of Stanstead, 62, 63
Lake Memphremagog, 33, 36, 41, 64
Lambly, John R., 335n129
Lancashire, Henry, 86
Lang, Matthew, 174, 199
Lansingburgh, New York, 130
Lauton, Henry, 220–1
lay readers, Anglican, 247
Lebourveau, C.S., 118
Lee, Daniel, 186
Lee, Elias, 186
Lee, Jason, 159, 186
Leeds, 94, 261, 267, 269, 271
Leeds Circuit. *See* New Ireland Methodist Circuit
LeFevre, Clement Fall, 116–17, 240–1
Lennoxville, 240–1, 262, 264, 267, 269, 271, 272
Lindsay, Robert, 236–7
Litch, Josiah, 106, 131, 140–3
localism, 234, 284. *See also* community
Lock, William S., 186
Lonsdell, Richard, 277

Lothrop, Howard, 104
love feasts, Methodist, 158, 177, 181, 183, 217, 221–2
Lower Ireland, 161, 172
Loyalists, 32, 36, 42, 50, 282
Ludlum, David M., 7
Lyndon, Vermont, 120

Magog, 33, 64, 124, 130, 131, 139, 271–2
Maine, 9, 32, 34
Mallory, Caleb P., 120
Marini, Stephen, 7, 9, 32, 40, 96
Maritime colonies, Methodism in, 153, 156, 173, 177, 219
Marks, Lynne, 99
Marsh, Joseph, 121
Marsh, William, 33, 38
martial law, 192
Massachusetts, 32
Massachusetts Baptist Missionary Society, 34
Massachusetts Society (Congregational), 73
Massawippi, 102, 105
McCord, Judge, 235
McDonald, Malcolm, 215
McKendrie, William, 152
Meeting for Worship, Quaker, 111
Megantic County, 21
Melbourne, 3, 18, 23–4, 60, 75, 88, 136, 137, 139, 144
Melbourne and Shipton, Anglican parish of, 234, 256, 262, 264, 266–71 *passim*
Melbourne Methodist Circuit, 150, 154–5, 160, 162–5, 168, 174, 178–9, 184, 193–4, 196, 203–4, 208–11, 215–16
Merriman, Titus, 93–4

Merry, J., 138
Merry, Ralph, 124, 130, 141, 284
Methodist Church, 20; chapels, 173–6, 223; church discipline, 221–3; circuit system, 155–6, 158–64, 220–1, 223, 246; and imperialism, 281; institutional and material support, 164–73, 186; internal divisions, 149–54, 164, 188, 207, 221, 284; local missionary societies, 186; local preachers, 158, 159, 161, 163–4, 194, 206, 220–1; membership numbers, 149, 151, 152, 155, 160–1, 170, 181, 184–5, 186, 192, 193, 195–6, 205, 207, 213–18 *passim*; and politics, 156–7; role of women, 154; union question, 158, 164, 170–1, 173, 186. *See also* Methodist Episcopal Church; Millerism; New Connection Methodists; Rebellions of 1837–8; revivals; salaries, clergy; Sunday Schools; temperance; War of 1812
Methodist Episcopal Church, 36–9, 149–54, 202, 220–1
middle ground concept, xii-xiii
Miles, Richard, 83, 85
millennialism, varieties of, 128
Miller, William, 18, 93, 94, 129–31, 139, 140, 142
Millerism: challenge to British religious hegemony, 24, 283; impact on Christian Brethren, 121; impact on Congregational Church, 62–3, 64, 89; impact on Freewill Baptist Church, 104–6; impact on Methodists, 124–6, 132–3, 194–207, 213, 214, 219; impact on Regular Baptist Church, 93, 95; and insanity, 132–3, 136; opposition to, 138–9, 254;

theories about its popularity, 141–5. *See also* Second Advent Church
Milton, 155
Missisquoi, 37
Missisquoi Bay, 167
Missisquoi District Association / Church Society (Anglican), 234–7
Mitchell, Edward, 93, 94–5, 312n28
Moffat, George, 118
Moir, John S., 281
Montgomery, Hugh, 200–1
Monthly Meeting, Freewill Baptist, 97–9; Quaker, 112
Montreal, 62, 64, 70, 76, 133, 158, 186, 207
Montreal Baptist Association, 92
Montreal Theological College, 86
Montreal Transcript, 13, 132, 134
Mormons, 56, 127, 283–4
Morning Star, 103, 104
Morris, William, 233
Moulton, Abial, 97
Moulton, Avery, 27, 29, 35, 96
Mountain, George J., 11, 14, 72, 118–19, 134, 237, 253, 254, 258, 259, 264, 267–74 *passim*, 277, 284; and catechists, 246–9; and church design, 240–6 *passim*; and clergy recruitment, 229–30; diocesan tours, 7–8, 241, 249–50, 256; and support for clergy, 232–3, 236
Mountain, Jacob, 45, 47–9, 228–32, 239, 249–50, 253, 259, 265–7
Mountain, Mary, 47
Murray, John, 39
music in church, 48–9, 72

Neve, Fred S., 248
New Connection Methodists, 16, 24, 100, 123–6, 161, 218
New England, 7, 9, 30, 31, 35, 153
New England Conference (Methodist), 36, 37
New Hampshire, 32, 34, 73–4, 76, 227, 297n20
New Hampshire Conference (Methodist), 187
New Hampshire General Association (Congregationalist), 75
New Hampshire Yearly Meeting (Freewill Baptist), 98
New Ireland Methodist Circuit, 154, 160–1, 172, 194, 198, 206–7, 208, 212, 216–18
New Lights, 7, 14
New York, 118, 296n14
New York Conference (Methodist), 37, 39
Newport, Vermont, 98
Nichols, Moses, 29
Nickle, Colonel, 250
Nicols, Jasper, 255–6
Noll, Mark, 279
Northern Association (Universalist), 40

O'Leary, Stephen, 142
Ontario, 22. *See also* Upper Canada
Orange Lodge, 281
Osgood, Thaddeus, 58, 208
Ottawa Baptist Association, 92
Ottawa/Montreal Baptist Association, 95
Outlet, the. *See* Magog
Oxford University, 230

Parker, Ammi, 56, 59, 64–77 *passim*, 87, 100, 232
Parker, Eveline, 65, 66
Peel, Lucy, 262

Pennoyer, Jesse, 29
Perkins, Barnabas, 34
Perry, Nathaniel, 96
Pettes, Drusilla, 46
Phelp's Settlement, 191
Philipsburg, 47, 49, 188–9, 190, 240, 248
Pigeon Hill, 196
Pike River, 167, 191
Pilgrim sect, 56, 109–11
Pitman, Walter G., 90
Playter, George, 37
political culture, 280–3
Pomroy, Benjamin, 60
Pope, Henry, 116, 155–6, 165, 178
Pope, Richard, 150, 158, 165, 177–8, 181–3
Porter, John, 139, 141, 143
postmillennialism, 68, 128
Potton, 94, 123, 125, 126, 130
premillennialism, 128–9, 284. *See also* Millerism
Preparative Meeting, Quaker, 111–12
Presbyterians, 17, 21, 23, 31, 32, 72, 86, 282
presiding elders, Methodist, 158, 323n15
Protestant Methodists, 16, 24, 124, 162, 197, 201–2, 220; polity/doctrine, 122–3
protracted meetings. *See* revivals
providential mission, 64
Putnam, Benjamin, 35

Quakers, 40–1. *See also* Farnham Meeting
Quarterly Meeting: Freewill Baptist, 95–8; Methodist, 154
Quebec, 58

Quebec Methodist Circuit, 160, 207

Rain, John, 102, 203–4, 209, 211
Randall, Benjamin: his 1792 covenant, 95, 96, 99
Rawlyk, George, ix
Rebellions of 1837–8, 10, 282–3; and the Anglican Church, 250, 255; and the Congregational Church, 57–8, 60–2, 82, 84, 85, 282; and the Freewill Baptist Church, 102; and Millerism, 130–1, 143, 145; and the Quakers, 114; and the Universalists, 119; and the Wesleyan Methodist Church, 161, 186, 188–94, 203
Red School, 78
Redfern, Joseph, 217
Reed, Fitch, 150–1
Reformed Presbyterian Church, 349n11
Reid, Charles P., 270, 342n86
Reid, James, 8, 47, 91, 122, 173–4, 180, 232, 235–7, 245, 250–1, 253, 255–8, 263, 265, 272, 275, 276
Relly, James, 39
revivals: Congregational, 65–6, 86; Freewill Baptist, 95; Methodist Episcopal, 151; New Connection Methodist, 125; new measures, 66, 187; Protestant Methodist, 122; Regular Baptist, 93, 94; Wesleyan Methodist, 175, 177–88, 190, 195–9, 206, 214
Richey, Matthew, 205
Richey, Russell, 178
Richmond Association (Baptist), 34
Richmond, town of, 241, 272
Ritchie, William, 60
Robertson, David, 261, 264, 266, 271
Robertson, James, 59

Robinson. *See* Bury
Roe, Henry, 342n96
Roman Catholics, 12, 19, 21–4, 133
Ross, George McLeod, 243–4, 261, 262, 268–70
Ross, William, 38
Rosser, Fred, 34
Roth, Randolph, 7, 99, 144
Rowe, David L., 108, 137, 144
Royal Institution of Learning, 173, 240, 265
Ryan, Henry, 149
Ryder, S.B., 312n28
Ryerson, Egerton, 158, 281

Sabbath observance, 87
Sabbath Schools. *See* Sunday Schools
Sabin, Benjamin, 149
Sabin, Lewis, 60
salaries, clergy: Anglican, 232, 233, 235–7, 259; Congregational, 70–1, 73, 75, 78–9, 81, 85, 86; Methodist, 153, 164–73
Salmon, George, 264, 273
schools, day, 76, 85–6, 173–4, 265, 275. *See also* Royal Institution of Learning
Schoolscraft, 208
Scots settlers, 17, 18, 21, 23, 59, 81–4, 282
Scott, Joseph, 234–5, 258
Scott, William, 214
Second Advent Church, 18, 138–41, 283; social analysis of members, 144–5. *See also* Millerism
Selley, John, 174, 193
Semple, Neil, 36, 154, 219–20
Sewell, Judge, 156
Shaker sect, 127, 283
Shay's Rebellion, 297n20

Shefford, 15, 18, 20, 22, 118, 121, 139, 264; Congregational church, 77–86; Methodist Circuit, 154, 155, 159, 165, 174, 177–8, 188, 193, 197, 204–6, 208–10, 214–15
Sheldon, Vermont, 49
Shenstone, W.E., 201, 329n5
Sherbrooke, 61, 63, 69, 75, 133; Anglican parish of, 155, 233, 234, 240, 242, 262, 264, 271, 272; Methodist Circuit, 154, 162, 174, 216
Sherman, Charles, 80
Shipman, I.H., 138, 139
Shipton, 17, 28–9, 118, 144, 155, 174, 279; Congregationalism, 64–77. *See also* Melbourne and Shipton
Short, Robert Quircke, 42
Signs of the Times, 131, 133. *See also* *Advent Herald*
Simpson, Samuel Hoare, 262, 264
Skinner, H.B., 132, 133, 136–7
Slack, George, 236, 244, 341n80
Slight, Benjamin, 163, 206, 215, 216, 220, 222
Smith, Ashur, 301n46
Smith, Elias, 120
Smith, Homer, 91
Smith, Ichabod, 192
Smith, Robinson, 35
Smith, Roswell, 34
smuggling, 38
Society for Propagating the Gospel to the Destitute Settlers and Indians in Lower Canada, 249
Society for the Promotion of Christian Knowledge, 228, 242, 248, 254
Society for the Propagation of the Gospel, 32, 41, 42, 49, 228–38 *passim*, 240, 242, 244, 247, 251–3, 259, 280, 283

384 Index

Society of Friends. *See* Quakers
Socinianism, 205
Soltow, Lee, 22
South Ridge, 78, 85
Spafford, Dudley, 95
Spalding, Martha, 97
Spiritualizers, 140
Squire, William, 123, 155, 158–63 *passim*, 173, 179–81, 184–5, 187, 189–91, 209, 218, 219, 222, 223, 323n25, 327n81
St Alban's, Vermont, 59
St Armand, 15, 20, 122, 128, 136
St Armand Anglican Church, 16, 42–5, 47–50, 267, 268. *See also* Reid, James
St Armand Methodist Circuit, 16, 137, 150, 154, 155, 161–2, 166–7, 173–4, 179–81, 188–93, 195–6, 199–201, 208, 214
St Armand Regular Baptist Church, 34, 91–2
St Francis Association (Anglican), 233–4
St Francis Methodist Circuit, 37, 39, 149–50, 152
St Francis Ministerial Association, 75–6, 87, 89
St Francis Quarterly Meeting (Freewill Baptist), 104–5. *See also* Freewill Baptists
St Johns, 49
St Lawrence and Atlantic Railway, 216, 260
Stanbridge Mills, 132, 208
Stanbridge, 15, 16, 20, 174, 179, 190, 241, 261, 264, 266, 271
Stanstead, 35, 58–64, 118, 119, 123, 125, 234
Stanstead Journal, 13, 140

Stanstead Methodist Circuit, 37, 39, 149, 151, 152, 154, 159, 165, 175, 181–7, 197, 201–3, 208–9, 212, 221–2
Stanstead Plain; during the Rebellions, 191–2; Millerism in, 130–9 *passim*; Union Chapel, 14, 58, 59, 131, 132, 175; Wesleyan Methodist chapel, 185, 186
Stanstead Quarterly Meeting (Freewill Baptist): assessments, 97–104 *passim*, 108; formation, 96–7, 98; itinerancy, 100, 101–2; membership, 102, 104, 106; moral/social reform, 101, 103, 104. *See also* Freewill Baptists
Stevens, Norman, 105
Stewart, Charles James, 46–50, 116–17, 181, 232, 238, 241, 247, 249, 254–5, 257, 258–60, 265, 267, 271, 272, 275
Stewart, I.D., 35
Stinson, Joseph, 174, 178–9, 329n7
Storrs, R.S., 55–7, 73
Stott, Thomas, 327n83
Strachan, John, 281, 349n5
Stukely, 120–1, 125
Sunday School Union Society of Canada, 208, 263
Sunday Schools: and Anglican Church, 212, 247, 251, 263–5, 275; in Bury, 263; in Compton and Hatley, 162, 163; in Drummondville, 264; in Dunham, 199, 263; in Granby and Shefford, 78, 82, 84; in Leeds, 263–4; in Lennoxville, 264; in Sherbrooke, 264; in Shipton, 65, 264; in St Armand, 263; in Stanstead, 58–64 *passim*; and New Connection Methodism, 125; and

Wesleyan Methodism, 208–18 *passim*
Sutton, 16, 17, 33, 45–6, 91, 123, 126, 244

Talbert, Samuel, 100
Taplin, John, 31
taxation, church. *See* voluntarist principle
Taylor, Jonathan, 32, 271
Taylor, Joseph, 165
Taylor, Stephen, 277
temperance, 142, 284; and the Anglicans, 275–6; and the Baptists, 101, 103, 104; and the Congregationalists, 57, 67–8, 76, 82–7 *passim*; and the Methodists, 157–8, 189, 190, 217
Thomas, Keith, 268
Thompson, Alexander, 123
Thompson, E.P., 144
Thompson, Zadoch, 110
Titemore, Miss S.A., 128
Tomkins, John, 121, 135–6, 157, 193, 197, 205, 213, 214
Topping and Bosworth report, 94
Townley, Adam, 188
Tractarianism. *See* Anglican Church: High Church principles
Troy, Vermont, 94
Tunstall, John Marmaduke, 42
Turner, Frederick Jackson, 9
Turner, Thomas, 119, 120–1, 123–4, 155, 183–4, 191–2
Tylor, Amos, 100, 106–7

union chapels, 174–5, 284. *See also* Stanstead Plain Union Chapel
Unitarianism, 94
Universalist Magazine, 118
Universalists, 39–40, 131, 192; church design, 120; economic variables, 21–2, 24; hostility towards, 94, 100, 118–19, 191; itinerant preachers, 118; membership, 17–18, 120; polity, 115–16. *See also* LeFevre, Clement Fall
Upper Canada, 12, 16, 33, 153, 157, 164, 167, 170, 171, 186, 234, 239, 282
Upper Ireland, 161, 238, 262, 264

Vannest, Peter, 37
Vaudry, Richard, 246
Vermont, 7–9, 16, 33–6, 72–3, 153, 177, 184, 187, 189, 227, 284, 296nn11, 12; University of, 66–7
Vermont Baptist State Convention, 91, 94
Vermont Domestic Missionary Society, 64
Vermont General Association (Congregationalist), 75
Vermont State Convention (Universalist), 117, 118
Vermont Yearly Meeting (Freewill Baptist), 105, 106, 313n54
vestry, Anglican, 232, 272
Voice of Elijah, 133, 139
voluntarist ethos, x, 9, 10, 76, 236. *See also* assessments

Walsh, John, 277
Walton, J.S., 61
War of 1812, 65, 279–80, 282; and Anglicans, 49–50; and Baptists, 28–9, 34, 90, 91, 95; and Congregationalists, 32; and Methodists, 29, 33, 149, 150
Ward, James, 118, 119

Ward, Robert G., 248, 342n96
Ware, A.S., 118
Warner, William, 105–6
watch-night, Methodist, 183, 194
Waterloo, 78, 82, 84, 119, 120; Millerism in, 134, 138–41, 143
Watson, Jacob L., 118, 315n39
Weber's theory, 19–20, 24
Wesley, John, 36, 154, 177
Wesleyan Methodist Church. *See* Methodism
Wesleyan Missionary Society, 157, 159, 162, 164–72 *passim*, 180, 187, 214, 215, 219–20, 223, 280, 283
Wesleyan, 187–8
West, Paul Vining, 126
Westbury, 28, 98, 100, 102
Westfall, William, 6, 236, 241, 273, 276, 281
Wheelock, Vermont, Quarterly Meeting (Freewill Baptist), 96, 106
White, Ellen and James, 321n58
Whitwell, Richard, 256, 273

Wilberforce, William, 46
Wilbur, John, 115
Wilkes, Henry, 3
Williams, Richard, 150, 151
Winchester, Elhanan, 39, 40
Winchester Profession of Faith, 40
Winchester's *Lectures on the Prophecies*, 129
Wise, S.F., 280
women and religion, 47, 62, 63, 65, 67, 68, 85, 93, 97, 103, 108, 113, 154, 206, 239, 268–9
Wood, Samuel Simpson, 230–1, 266, 269, 272
Woodstock, Vermont, 110
Woodstock Association (Baptist), 33–4
Woolverton, John, 273
Wright, Jason, 240

Zielinski, S.A., 112
Zimmerman, Philip, 176
Zion's Herald, 186